Cracking the

AP® PSYCHOLOGY EXAM

2020 Edition

The Staff of The Princeton Review

PrincetonReview.com

Penguin
Random
House

The Princeton Review
110 East 42nd St, 7th Floor
New York, NY 10017

E-mail: editorialsupport@review.com

Published in the United States by Penguin Random House LLC,
New York, and in Canada by Random House of Canada,
a division of Penguin Random House Ltd., Toronto.

ISBN: 978-0-525-56833-9
eBook ISBN: 978-0-525-56871-1
ISSN: 1546-9093

The material in this book is up-to-date at the time of publication.
However, changes may have been instituted by the testing body in
the test after this book was published.

If there are any important late-breaking developments, changes,
or corrections to the materials in this book, we will post that
information online in the Student Tools. Register your book and
check your Student Tools to see if there are any updates posted
there.

Editors: Sarah Litt, Meave Shelton
Production Editors: Kathy G. Carter, Jim Melloan
Production Artist: John Stecyk
Content Contributors: Anne Goldberg-Baldwin, Anthony Krupp

Printed in the United States of America.

10 9 8 7 6 5 4 3 2

2020 Edition

Editorial
Rob Franek, Editor-in-Chief
David Soto, Director of Content Development
Stephen Koch, Student Survey Manager
Deborah Weber, Director of Production
Gabriel Berlin, Production Design Manager
Selena Coppock, Managing Editor
Aaron Riccio, Senior Editor
Meave Shelton, Senior Editor
Chris Chimera, Editor
Eleanor Green, Editor
Orion McBean, Editor
Brian Saladino, Editor
Patricia Murphy, Editorial Assistant

Penguin Random House Publishing Team
Tom Russell, VP, Publisher
Alison Stoltzfus, Publishing Director
Amanda Yee, Associate Managing Editor
Ellen Reed, Production Manager
Suzanne Lee, Designer

Acknowledgments

The Princeton Review would like to give special thanks to Anne Goldberg-Baldwin and Anthony Krupp for their valuable contributions to the latest edition of this book.

Contents

Get More (Free) Content
at PrincetonReview.com/cracking

As easy as 1·2·3

1 Go to PrincetonReview.com/cracking and enter the following ISBN for your book:

9780525568339

2 Answer a few simple questions to set up an exclusive Princeton Review account. *(If you already have one, you can just log in.)*

3 Enjoy access to your **FREE** content!

Once you've registered, you can...

- Get our take on any recent or pending updates to the AP Psychology Exam

- Take a full-length practice SAT and/or ACT

- Get valuable advice about the college application process, including tips for writing a great essay and where to apply for financial aid

- If you're still choosing between colleges, use our searchable rankings of *The Best 385 Colleges* to find out more information about your dream school.

- Access comprehensive study guides and a variety of printable resources, including: Key Terms lists, score conversion tables for the Practice Tests, and bubble sheets

- Check to see if there have been any corrections or updates to this edition

Need to report a potential **content** issue?

Contact **EditorialSupport@review.com** and include:

- full title of the book
- ISBN
- page number

Need to report a **technical** issue?

Contact **TPRStudentTech@review.com** and provide:

- your full name
- email address used to register the book
- full book title and ISBN
- Operating system (Mac/PC) and browser (Firefox, Safari, etc.)

Look For These Icons Throughout The Book

 ONLINE ARTICLES

 PROVEN TECHNIQUES

 APPLIED STRATEGIES

Part I
Using This Book
to Improve Your
AP Score

PREVIEW: YOUR KNOWLEDGE, YOUR EXPECTATIONS

Your route to a high score on the AP Psychology Exam depends a lot on how you plan to use this book. To help you determine your approach, respond to the following questions.

1. Rate your level of confidence about your knowledge of the content tested by the AP Psychology Exam:

    A. Very confident—I know it all

    B. I'm pretty confident, but there are topics for which I could use help

    C. Not confident—I need quite a bit of support

    D. I'm not sure

2. Circle your goal score for the AP Psychology Exam:

    5   4   3   2   1   I'm not sure yet

3. What do you expect to learn from this book? Circle all that apply to you.

    A. A general overview of the test and what to expect

    B. Strategies for how to approach the test

    C. The content tested by this exam

    D. I'm not sure yet

YOUR GUIDE TO USING THIS BOOK

This book is organized to provide as much—or as little—support as you need, so you can use this book in whatever way will be most helpful to improving your score on the AP Psychology Exam.

*   The remainder of **Part I** will provide guidance on how to use this book and help you determine your strengths and weaknesses.

*   **Part II** of this book contains Practice Test 1, its answers and explanations, and a scoring guide. (Bubble sheets can be found in the very back of the book for easy tear-out.) We strongly recommend that you take this test before going any further, in order to realistically determine:

    o   your starting point right now
    o   which question types you're ready for and which you might need to practice
    o   which content topics you are familiar with and which you will want to carefully review

Once you have nailed down your strengths and weaknesses with regard to this exam, you can focus your test preparation, build a study plan, and be efficient with your time.

- **Part III** of this book will:
  - o provide information about the structure, scoring, and content of the AP Psychology Exam
  - o help you to make a study plan
  - o point you toward additional resources

- **Part IV** of this book will explore various strategies, including the following:
  - o how to attack multiple-choice questions
  - o how to write effective essays
  - o how to manage your time to maximize the number of points available to you

- **Part V** of this book covers the content you need for the AP Psychology Exam.

- **Part VI** of this book contains Practice Test 2, its answers and explanations, and a scoring guide. If you skipped Practice Test 1, we recommend that you do both (with at least a day or two between them) so that you can compare your progress between the two. Additionally, this will help to identify any external issues: if you answer a certain type of question wrong both times, you probably need to review it. If you answered it incorrectly only once, you may have run out of time or been distracted by something. In either case, comparing the two exams will allow you to focus on the factors that caused the discrepancy in scores and to be as prepared as possible on the day of the test.

You may choose to use some parts of this book over others, or you may work through the entire book. Your approach will depend on your needs and how much time you have. Let's now look at how to make this determination.

HOW TO BEGIN

1. **Take a Test**

   Before you can decide how to use this book, you need to take a practice test. Doing so will give you insight into your strengths and weaknesses, and the test will also help you make an effective study plan. If you're feeling test-phobic, remind yourself that a practice test is a tool for diagnosing yourself—it's not how well you do that matters but how you use information gleaned from your performance to guide your preparation.

Score Conversion Sheets

After each practice test in this book, you'll find conversion sheets that can help you approximate what you would get if it was an actual AP exam. Don't be alarmed if it's lower than you expected; use your score on the first practice test to help you better improve on the second practice test!

So, before you read further, take Practice Test 1 starting on page 11 of this book. Be sure to do so in one sitting, following the instructions that appear before the test.

2. **Check Your Answers**

Using the answer key on page 28, count the number of multiple-choice questions you answered correctly and how many you missed. Don't worry about the explanations for now, and don't worry about why you missed questions. We'll get to that soon.

3. **Reflect on the Test**

After you take your first test, respond to the following questions:

- How much time did you spend on the multiple-choice questions?

- How much time did you spend on each essay?

- How many multiple-choice questions did you miss?

- Do you feel you had the knowledge to address the subject matter of the essays?

- Do you feel you wrote well-organized, thoughtful essays?

On the following pages, circle the content areas that were most challenging for you, and draw a line through the ones in which you felt confident/did well.

Foundations (10–14%)

History

- behavior and mind
- René Descartes and dualism
- John Locke and empiricism (tabula rasa)
- Thomas Hobbes and behaviorism
- Charles Darwin and evolutionary theory
- Wilhelm Wundt, Edward Titchener, structuralism, and introspection
- William James and functionalism
- Dorothea Dix, Mary Whiton Calkins, Margaret Floy Washburn

Approaches

- biological
- behavioral genetics
- behavioral
- cognitive
- humanistic
- psychodynamic/psychoanalytic
- sociocultural
- evolutionary

Domains

- biological
- social
- clinical
- cognitive
- counseling
- developmental
- educational
- experimental
- industrial-organizational
- personality
- psychometric
- positive

Methods

- study types
  - experimental
  - correlational
  - survey
  - naturalistic observation
  - case study
  - longitudinal
  - cross-sectional
- variables
  - independent
  - dependent
  - confounding
- operational definitions
- control vs. experimental group
- random assignment and random selection
- causation and correlation
- inductive reasoning
- internal and external validity
- inter-rater reliability
- descriptive and inferential statistics
- naturalistic observation
- ethics

Biological Bases of Behavior (8–10%)

- heredity and environment
- effect of endocrine system on behavior
- responsibilities of the pituitary gland, pineal gland, and hypothalamus
- dopamine associated with pleasure
- serotonin associated with sleep
- norepinephrine associated with alertness
- brain lobes
- brain lateralization
- neuroplasticity
- Michael Gazzaniga
- consciousness
- circadian rhythms
- sleep/dream cycles
- current and historical uses of hypnosis
- three categories of psychoactive drugs
- drug dependence, addiction, withdrawal, and tolerance

Sensation and Perception (6–8%)

General

- priming
- transduction
- absolute vs. difference threshold
- sensory adaptation

Visual
- order of transmission of visual information
- visual cliff studies
- perceptual constancy
- shape constancy

Auditory
- order of transmission of auditory information

Chemical and body senses
- taste and smell
- touch and pain
- vestibular and kinesthetic

Learning (7–9%)

Classical conditioning
- stimulus and conditioning
- discrimination, stimulus

Operant conditioning
- reinforcement and reinforcement schedules
- learned helplessness and expectation relationship

Observational/vicarious learning
- Albert Bandura, Bobo Doll Experiment

Other forms of learning
- latent learning
- insight learning
- social and emotional learning

Cognitive Psychology (13–17%)

Memory
- encoding
- storing
- retrieval and retrieval strategies
  - method of loci as visual memory aid
  - maintenance rehearsal
  - serial position curve and recall
- forgetting and distortion
- biological bases of memory

Problem solving: barriers and strategies
- representativeness heuristic
- availability heuristic
- halo effect
- functional fixedness

Intelligence and testing
- abstract vs. verbal measures of measuring intelligence
- speed of processing
- meaning of scores on a normal curve
- use of testing practices, reliability, and validity

Language
- brain areas devoted to language
- language acquisition

Developmental Psychology (7–9%)
- physical: pre-natal to neonatal
- social
  - Mary Ainsworth
  - Albert Bandura
  - Diana Baumrind
  - Sigmund Freud
  - Harry Harlow
  - Konrad Lorenz
- cognitive
  - Jean Piaget
  - Lev Vygotsky
- adolescent, adulthood, and aging
  - Erik Erikson
- moral
  - Lawrence Kohlberg
  - Carol Gilligan
- gender and sexual orientation

Motivation, Emotion, and Personality (11–15%)

Motivation
- drive-reduction theory and homeostasis
- arousal theories
- Maslow's hierarchy of needs
- incentive theories

Emotion
- James-Lange theory of emotion
- Cannon-Bard theory of emotion
- Schachter-Singer theory of emotion
- Paul Ekman and universal emotions

Stress
- Hans Selye
- general adaptation theory

Personality
- researching and measuring personality
  - case studies
  - surveys
  - personality inventories
  - projective tests
- approaches
  - behavioral
  - social cognitive
  - psychoanalytic
  - humanistic
  - trait
- issues
  - cultural context (individualist vs. collectivist societies)

Clinical Psychology (12–16%)
General perspectives and issues
- DSM-5 and major diagnostic categories
- confidentiality, legal defense
- labels

Categories of Disorders
- neurodevelopmental and neurocognitive
- schizophrenic spectrum
- bipolar, depressive, anxiety, and OCD
- trauma- and stressor-related
- dissociative and somatic symptom
- feeding and eating, substance and addictive
- personality disorders

Treatment
- Major orientations of psychotherapy
  - behavioral
  - cognitive
  - humanistic
  - psychodynamic

Social Psychology (8–10%)
- attribution theory (fundamental attribution error, self-serving bias, etc.)
- the impact of others on behavior (bystander effect, deindividuation, social facilitation, group polarization, etc.)
- individuals' responses to expectations of others (groupthink, obedience, conformity)
- attitudes and how they can change (attitude vs. behavior, cognitive dissonance, persuasion)
- differential treatment of groups (ethnocentrism, bias, prejudice, in/out-groups)
- gender, race, ethnicity and person perception (self-perception / perception of others)
- attraction, altruism, and aggression
- important figures in social psychology
  - Solomon Asch
  - Philip Zimbardo
  - Stanley Milgram
  - Leon Festinger

Please refer to the College Board website for the most up-to-date and in-depth breakdown of subjects.

4. **Read Part III of This Book and Complete the Self-Evaluation**
   Part III will provide information on how the test is structured and scored. It will also list areas of content that are tested.

   As you read Part III, reevaluate your answers to the questions on page 4. At the end of Part III, you will revisit and refine the questions you answer on page 4. You will then be able to make a study plan, based on your needs and time available, that will allow you to use this book most effectively.

5. **Engage with Parts IV and V as Needed**

   Notice the word *engage*. You'll get more out of this book if you use it intentionally than if you read it passively, hoping for an improved score through osmosis. Strategy chapters in Part IV will help you think about your approach to the question types on this exam. This part opens with a reminder to think about how you approach questions now and then closes with a reflection section asking you to think about how/whether you will change your approach in the future.

   Content chapters in Part V are designed to provide a review of the content tested on the AP Psychology Exam, including the level of detail you need to know and how the content is tested. You will have the opportunity to assess your mastery of the content of each chapter through test-appropriate questions and a reflection section.

6. **Take Practice Test 2 and Assess Your Performance**

   Once you feel you have developed the strategies you need and gained the knowledge you lacked, you should take Practice Test 2, which starts on page 335 of this book. You should do so in one sitting, following the instructions at the beginning of the test.

   When you are done, check your answers to the multiple-choice sections. See if a teacher will read your essays and provide feedback.

   Once you have taken the test, reflect on what areas you still need to work on, and revisit the chapters in this book that address those deficiencies. Through this type of reflection and engagement, you will continue to improve.

7. **Keep Working**

   As we'll discuss in Part III, there are other resources available to you, including a wealth of information on the section of the College Board's AP website called AP Students. You can continue to explore areas that can stand to improve and engage in those areas right up to the day of the test.

Part II
Practice Test 1

Practice Test 1

AP® Psychology Exam

SECTION I: Multiple-Choice Questions

DO NOT OPEN THIS BOOKLET UNTIL YOU ARE TOLD TO DO SO.

Instructions

Section I of this exam contains 100 multiple-choice questions. Fill in only the ovals for numbers 1 through 100 on your answer sheet.

Indicate all of your answers to the multiple-choice questions on the answer sheet. No credit will be given for anything written in this exam booklet, but you may use the booklet for notes or scratch work. After you have decided which of the suggested answers is best, completely fill in the corresponding oval on the answer sheet. Give only one answer to each question. If you change an answer, be sure that the previous mark is erased completely. Here is a sample question and answer.

Sample Question   Sample Answer

Omaha is a

(A) state
(B) city
(C) country
(D) continent
(E) village

Use your time effectively, working as quickly as you can without losing accuracy. Do not spend too much time on any one question. Go on to other questions and come back to the ones you have not answered if you have time. It is not expected that everyone will know the answers to all of the multiple-choice questions.

About Guessing

Many candidates wonder whether or not to guess the answers to questions about which they are not certain. Multiple-choice scores are based on the number of questions answered correctly. Points are not deducted for incorrect answers, and no points are awarded for unanswered questions. Because points are not deducted for incorrect answers, you are encouraged to answer all multiple-choice questions. On any questions you do not know the answer to, you should eliminate as many choices as you can, and then select the best answer among the remaining choices.

At a Glance

Total Time
1 hour and 10 minutes
Number of Questions
100
Percent of Total Score
66.6%
Writing Instrument
Pencil required

This page intentionally left blank.

GO ON TO THE NEXT PAGE.

PSYCHOLOGY
Section I
Time—1 hour and 10 minutes
100 Questions

Directions: Each of the questions or incomplete statements below is followed by five answer choices. Select the one that is best in each case and then completely fill in the corresponding oval on the answer sheet.

1. When she was in elementary school, Matilda became quite good at playing the recorder. She is a teenager now and has not picked up a recorder in many years. When she tries to resume playing the instrument, she finds it very difficult to locate the correct finger positions. This is an example of

   (A) constructive memory
   (B) retroactive interference
   (C) pruning of neural networks
   (D) proactive interference
   (E) source monitoring errors

2. Pruning refers to

   (A) loss of hippocampus activity due to Alzheimer's disease
   (B) reduced sensory organ stimulation in response to an unchanging stimulus
   (C) activation of the ventromedial hypothalamus when someone is full
   (D) cutting back of unused neural networks during adolescence
   (E) heightened metabolism due to malfunction of the thyroid

3. Which of the following types of scientists were the first to contend that an individual's ways of thinking are shaped primarily by cultural values and ideas?

   (A) Structuralists
   (B) Ethologists
   (C) Sociobiologists
   (D) Behaviorists
   (E) Anthropologists

4. Which of the following is the best example of an attribute that is culturally based rather than primarily psychologically based?

   (A) Caring for one's children
   (B) Arriving on time for work
   (C) Having the desire to reproduce
   (D) Seeking food and water
   (E) Smiling

5. Every time you buy ice cream from the Yellow Brick Road ice cream parlor, you get your over-the-rainbow card stamped. Once you purchase ten items, you get your next item free. The Yellow Brick Road ice cream parlor has you on which of the following reinforcement schedules?

   (A) Variable-ratio
   (B) Variable-interval
   (C) Fixed-ratio
   (D) Fixed-interval
   (E) Continuous

6. Which of the following neurotransmitters is most explicitly associated with the experience of pleasure?

   (A) GABA
   (B) Acetylcholine
   (C) Serotonin
   (D) Dopamine
   (E) Adrenaline

7. As he was passing out math tests to his class, the teacher mentioned that, traditionally, females had done worse on this test than males. When he looked at the results of this test, not only had the females done worse than males, they had done worse than their performance on recent assessments. The teacher may have contributed to these results by way of

   (A) cross-section bias
   (B) availability heuristic
   (C) stereotype boost
   (D) stereotype threat
   (E) representativeness heuristic

GO ON TO THE NEXT PAGE.

8. An educational psychologist is administering a basic skills exam to second-graders of two different schools in order to compare the students' performance. The researcher administers the exam to the students of the Antrim School on a Wednesday morning and then administers the same exam in exactly the same fashion on that same Wednesday afternoon to the second-graders of the Barton School. Which of the following best identifies a confounding variable in the psychologist's research?

   (A) The psychologist is comparing two different schools.
   (B) The psychologist is comparing the same grade in each school.
   (C) The psychologist is testing the students in the two schools at two different times.
   (D) The psychologist is testing the students in the two schools on the same day.
   (E) The psychologist is administering a basic skills exam.

9. The primary research method used by developmental psychologists is

   (A) case study
   (B) cross-sectional research
   (C) naturalistic observation
   (D) experimentation
   (E) correlational research

10. Narcotics work because they are chemically very similar to

    (A) endorphins
    (B) hormones
    (C) secretions
    (D) GABA
    (E) acetylcholine

11. Research indicates that a test participant exposed to a list of positive words and then asked to recall the words from that list a week later will be more likely to remember those words if he

    (A) is tested by a researcher who deliberately exhibits a positive attitude
    (B) is in a positive mood when initially exposed to the words
    (C) considers himself a "positive" person, regardless of his mood during the experience
    (D) considers the initial testing experience positive
    (E) perceives the list of words as positive, regardless of the true meaning of the words

12. The minimum amount of physical energy needed for a person to notice a stimulus is called a(n)

    (A) JND
    (B) difference threshold
    (C) absolute threshold
    (D) median difference
    (E) hit threshold

13. As a result of a blasting cap accident, Phineas Gage had a metal rod pass through his head, damaging his frontal lobes. Which of the following was NOT a problem he experienced in the aftermath of this accident?

    (A) He could not adequately regulate his emotions.
    (B) He could no longer adequately supervise workers on his railroad gang.
    (C) He could not plan activities as expected of a railroad foreman.
    (D) He could not remember anything about the circumstances of the accident.
    (E) He had occasions when he could not control his anger.

14. A person who sustains major injuries that involve the destruction of the medulla oblongata will

    (A) be paralyzed
    (B) fall into a coma
    (C) suffer severe speech impairment
    (D) experience total loss of vision
    (E) die

15. In a crisis, the adrenal glands of the body secrete "emergency" hormones, while the body prepares for fight or flight, directed by

    (A) the central nervous system
    (B) the somatic nervous system
    (C) the sensorimotor nervous system
    (D) the sympathetic nervous system
    (E) the parasympathetic nervous system

16. In the Harlow study of emotional attachment, infant monkeys were placed in a cage and given both a "wire" mother and a "cloth" mother. Researchers then moved a bottle of milk from one mother to the other while introducing various stimuli to see if the monkeys would form an attachment to either of the "mothers." In this experiment, the independent variable is

    (A) with which "mother" the bottle of milk is placed
    (B) the "wire" mother versus the "cloth" mother
    (C) the preference of the infants for the source of milk
    (D) the preference of the infants for the "wire" mother
    (E) the preference of the infants for the "cloth" mother

GO ON TO THE NEXT PAGE.

17. As an experiment, a group of newborn kittens was allowed to see through only one eye at a time. Each day, one of the eyes would be covered, switching between the two eyes on subsequent days. Which of the following best describes the visual limitations experienced by these cats as adults?

    (A) They were unable to make use of interposition depth perception.
    (B) They were unable to maintain perceptual constancy.
    (C) They were unable to distinguish left from right monocular cues.
    (D) They were unable to use binocular cues for depth perception.
    (E) They were unable to extinguish their visual blind spot.

Questions 18-19 refer to the situation described below.

A researcher wished to study the impact of classical music on memory in children. She, therefore, randomly selected two groups of children. One group was asked to read and later to recall lists of words while soft classical music played in the background. The second group was asked to read and recall lists of words with no background music playing.

18. The control group in this experiment is the group that

    (A) the researcher expected to demonstrate greater memory
    (B) demonstrated greater memory through recalling more words
    (C) demonstrated lesser memory through recalling fewer words
    (D) read the lists of words while classical music played in the background
    (E) read the lists of words with no background music playing

19. The dependent variable in this experiment is the

    (A) number of words recalled by the children
    (B) amount of time each child needs to recall the words
    (C) amount of music each child can recall
    (D) classical music playing in the background
    (E) lack of classical music playing in the background

20. Students diagnosed with attention deficit hyperactivity disorder (ADHD) are four to nine times more likely to be

    (A) females than males
    (B) males than females
    (C) children than adults
    (D) Caucasian children than African American children
    (E) urban area children than rural area children

21. Which of the following best summarizes the psychoanalytic perspective's view of behavior?

    (A) Behavior is motivated by inner, unconscious forces.
    (B) Behavior is a response to external reward and punishment.
    (C) Behavior is a product of genetic programming and evolution.
    (D) Behavior is a compilation of the ways in which people think and interact.
    (E) Behavior is each person's striving to reach his or her full potential.

22. Which of the following is the best example of a categorical variable?

    (A) Intelligence
    (B) Disposition
    (C) Optimism
    (D) Gender
    (E) Personality

23. Donia was soaked by an unexpected cloudburst while walking to her car from the office. The fact that she failed to realize that the newspaper she was carrying would have made a great makeshift umbrella is an example of

    (A) confirmation bias
    (B) limited visualization
    (C) functional fixedness
    (D) conceptual constriction
    (E) negative variation

24. While driving to school, Elise hears about a concert ticket giveaway on the radio. She has to be the seventh caller to win. While pulling over so that she can call in, she repeats the number to herself several times. Elise was using which of the following to remember the phone number?

    (A) Iconic memory
    (B) Elaborative rehearsal
    (C) Chunking
    (D) Maintenance rehearsal
    (E) Retrieval

25. A participant in a single-trial free-recall task is presented with a list of words, one at a time, in the following order: house, flower, dog, table, license, water, computer, salad. In accord with the serial position curve, which of the following words is the participant most likely to forget?

    (A) House
    (B) Computer
    (C) Flower
    (D) Salad
    (E) License

GO ON TO THE NEXT PAGE.

26. The smallest units of meaning in a language are

    (A) phonemes
    (B) phenotypes
    (C) semantics
    (D) morphemes
    (E) syntactical rules

27. Which of the following psychological disorders is characterized by an abnormally elevated or expansive mood?

    (A) Depression
    (B) Schizophrenia
    (C) Euphoria
    (D) Dysthymia
    (E) Mania

28. During periods of darkness, the pineal gland in the middle of the brain produces which of the following hormones that is essential to sleep regulation?

    (A) Estrogen
    (B) Adrenaline
    (C) Testosterone
    (D) Melatonin
    (E) Dopamine

29. Jacob cries uncontrollably every time his mother takes him down the candy aisle in the supermarket and refuses to let him buy anything. Eventually, Jacob's mother gives in and lets him choose one candy item to buy if he stops crying. Jacob's crying behavior is _____ by his mother.

    (A) punished
    (B) associated
    (C) reinforced
    (D) extinguished
    (E) shaped

30. Which of the following scientists was among the first to study the relationship between reinforcement and learning?

    (A) Sigmund Freud
    (B) B. F. Skinner
    (C) Carl Rogers
    (D) Mary Ainsworth
    (E) Charles Darwin

31. Jonathan's IQ score is in the 97th percentile. Of the following, which score is most likely his?

    (A) 85
    (B) 100
    (C) 130
    (D) 150
    (E) 170

32. Which one of the following best states Ivan Pavlov's accidental discovery?

    (A) While experimenting with rats, Pavlov discovered that if he repeatedly placed pellets of food in one side of a "T-maze," the rats would automatically run to that side of the maze.
    (B) While experimenting with dogs, Pavlov discovered that once his dogs became accustomed to seeing and hearing the attendant who brought them food at mealtime, they would salivate in response to the sight and sound of the attendant.
    (C) While experimenting with cats, Pavlov discovered that if he placed a hungry cat inside a box and food outside the box, the cat could "learn" to press a lever to open the door of the box.
    (D) While experimenting with pigeons, Pavlov discovered that if he placed a pigeon in a box, he could condition it to recognize that if it pecked at a particular key, it would receive a food pellet.
    (E) While experimenting with dogs, Pavlov discovered that if he fed the dogs the same type of food each day, the dogs would salivate whenever they ate that type of food.

33. Grounding a child for two weeks after the child has misbehaved is an example of

    (A) avoidant attachment
    (B) negative punishment
    (C) compliance learning
    (D) negative reinforcement
    (E) attentional neglect

GO ON TO THE NEXT PAGE.

34. Which of the following best summarizes why people tend to stay in a slightly elevated state of arousal after a crisis has occurred?

    (A) Their neurons remain in a state of graded potentiality even after they have fired.
    (B) Their neurons continue to keep the body in an alert state.
    (C) Their adrenal glands continue to secrete epinephrine even after the crisis is over.
    (D) Their parasympathetic nervous system remains in a state of fight or flight.
    (E) Their bloodstream continues to contain elevated levels of adrenaline.

35. Which of the following subsystems of the autonomic nervous system help the body return to "business-as-usual" after an emergency?

    (A) Somatic nervous system
    (B) Peripheral nervous system
    (C) Sympathetic nervous system
    (D) Parasympathetic nervous system
    (E) Central nervous system

36. Tina is a very good student: Her grades are high, she is involved in extracurricular activities, and she typically excels at anything she tries. Therefore, when she caused an accident her second day of driver's ed., her instructor was shocked. The instructor's disbelief is most probably a result of

    (A) modeling
    (B) accommodation
    (C) a halo effect
    (D) convergence
    (E) behavioral dissonance

37. The organ in the auditory process where transducing takes place is the

    (A) tympanic membrane
    (B) malleus
    (C) cochlea
    (D) pinna
    (E) stapes

38. You enter a bakery and are delighted by the aroma. After a short time, however, you no longer notice the odors because of sensory

    (A) perception
    (B) adaptation
    (C) transduction
    (D) detection
    (E) attrition

39. Carlotta is a well-adjusted, socially competent adolescent. Which of the following most likely represents her family's parenting style?

    (A) Minimal supervision
    (B) Permissive
    (C) Authoritarian
    (D) Authoritative
    (E) Indulgent

40. The semicircular canals of the inner ear are important for helping a person to maintain

    (A) tone quality
    (B) melatonin
    (C) balance
    (D) olfaction
    (E) transduction

41. The ability to perceive your front door as a rectangle even when it is open, displaying a different retinal image, is known as

    (A) color constancy
    (B) closure
    (C) shape constancy
    (D) size constancy
    (E) sensory adaptation

42. Stimulation of norepinephrine receptors appears to produce

    (A) euphoria
    (B) increased motor activity
    (C) alertness
    (D) anxiety
    (E) hypertension

43. Research using the visual cliff suggests that human infants

    (A) would go "over the cliff" if their mothers called them
    (B) had learned by experience in crawling to perceive depth
    (C) were not able to use any visual depth cues
    (D) use monocular but not binocular cues for vision
    (E) have innate depth perception at birth

GO ON TO THE NEXT PAGE.

44. All of the following are conditions sanctioned by the APA regarding the use of deception in a study EXCEPT

    (A) the research is of great importance and cannot be conducted without the use of deception
    (B) participants are expected to find the procedures reasonable upon being informed of them
    (C) participants must be allowed to withdraw from the experiment at any time
    (D) the research must be conducted as a double-blind study
    (E) experimenters must debrief the participants after the study is concluded

45. The examination of the connection between mental states and physical states is referred to as

    (A) *tabula rasa*
    (B) the mind-body problem
    (C) nature vs. nurture
    (D) parallel processing
    (E) correlational conditioning

46. Which of the following best summarizes a view of classical behaviorism?

    (A) Behavior is under the control of external stimuli that either reinforce or punish actions, thereby affecting the likelihood of the occurrence of these behaviors.
    (B) Behavior can be controlled by introspection.
    (C) Behavior is the result of competing motives that result from mental events that occur outside of one's awareness.
    (D) Behavior is influenced by internal drives and motivation.
    (E) Although behavior can be influenced by environmental factors, most actions and reactions occur as a result of genetic inference.

47. To which perspective are the roles of knowledge, information processing, and their interactions most central?

    (A) Psychoanalytic
    (B) Cognitive
    (C) Behaviorist
    (D) Evolutionary
    (E) Biopsychological

48. The study of cognitive, behavioral, and social changes across the life span are most directly studied by which of the following?

    (A) Psychometricians
    (B) Occupational psychologists
    (C) Developmental psychologists
    (D) Social psychologists
    (E) Cognitive behaviorists

49. One's ability to make inferences about the behavior of a population from the behavior of a sample of that population is referred to as

    (A) reliability
    (B) external validity
    (C) internal validity
    (D) inter-rater reliability
    (E) correlational statistical inference

50. A study designed to investigate the friendship patterns of abused children was conducted by filming the interactions of the children and later having three raters view the footage and rate each child's pattern of behavior on a conflictual-behavior scale with values ranging from "constant conflict" to "minimal conflict." Which of the following kinds of reliability is most critical to this study, given the methodology used to measure the variables?

    (A) Coefficient-alpha reliability
    (B) Alternate-forms reliability
    (C) Inter-rater reliability
    (D) Test-retest reliability
    (E) Correlational statistical reliability

51. Hunger and eating are primarily regulated by the

    (A) somatosensory cortex
    (B) hypothalamus
    (C) medulla oblongata
    (D) occipital lobes
    (E) amygdala

52. The method of loci is a memory aid that employs which of the following?

    (A) Semantic encoding
    (B) Visual imagery
    (C) Auditory cues
    (D) Echoic memory
    (E) Read, recite, review

GO ON TO THE NEXT PAGE.

53. Which of the following are most directly designed to help determine whether the findings of a study reflect a truly replicable phenomenon rather than the outcomes of chance processes?

   (A) Inferential statistics
   (B) Descriptive statistics
   (C) Standard deviation
   (D) Extraneous variables
   (E) Correlation coefficients

54. REM sleep is often referred to as a "paradox" because

   (A) as people age and sleep less, they actually spend more time in REM
   (B) people's eyes are moving, but they are generally unable to dream
   (C) people's metabolism slows down, much like animal hibernation
   (D) people dream and are aroused, but they generally are paralyzed
   (E) people are most active mentally while in the deepest sleep

55. The gland sometimes referred to as the "master gland," which regulates much of the action of the other endocrine glands, is called the

   (A) thyroid gland
   (B) pancreas
   (C) pituitary gland
   (D) adrenal gland
   (E) lymph system

56. The tendency of young children learning language to overuse the rules of syntax is referred to as

   (A) overconfidence
   (B) confirmation bias
   (C) overgeneralization
   (D) overjustification
   (E) the two-factor theory

57. To demonstrate causation, a researcher must

   (A) manipulate the way a participant responds to some aspect of a situation
   (B) operationalize dependent and independent variables
   (C) develop a hypothesis that predicts the relationship between variables
   (D) show that the manipulation of one variable invariably leads to predicted changes in another
   (E) demonstrate a positive rather than a negative correlation between variables

58. Learned helplessness is an example of the power of

   (A) expectation
   (B) positive reinforcement
   (C) negative reinforcement
   (D) classical conditioning
   (E) prepared learning

59. Jose is talkative and likes to engage in pretend play. When offered two identical balls of putty, he insists on having the one that has been rolled out into a long snake instead of the one that remains in the shape of a ball. He is probably in which of Piaget's stages of cognitive development?

   (A) Sensorimotor
   (B) Preoperational
   (C) Conservation
   (D) Conventional
   (E) Formal operations

60. Georgia works in the local hospital because she wishes to help others, while Kathy works in the hospital strictly to make money. Their individual motivations demonstrate the difference between

   (A) primary and secondary drives
   (B) positive and negative loci of control
   (C) sympathetic and autonomic motivation
   (D) instinctive and derived drives
   (E) intrinsic and extrinsic motivation

61. People who struggle with depression often have trouble sleeping in part because of

   (A) elevated endorphin levels
   (B) decreased GABA levels
   (C) depleted epinephrine levels
   (D) increased dopamine levels
   (E) low serotonin levels

62. Vivian is watching her college's football team play on television. Suddenly, she spots her friend Rudy among the spectators. Rudy is usually mild-mannered and obedient. However, Vivian sees him screaming at the other team's mascot during the game; then, she sees him join several others in rushing onto the field at the end of the game and tearing down the goalposts. This is an example of

   (A) deindividuation
   (B) group polarization
   (C) groupthink
   (D) social facilitation
   (E) mere exposure effect

GO ON TO THE NEXT PAGE.

63. Through reinforcement, pigeons are taught to peck at paintings by a particular artist. The fact that pigeons do not peck at the paintings of other artists represents

    (A) modeling response
    (B) reflexive response
    (C) distinctive stimulus
    (D) stimulus generalization
    (E) stimulus discrimination

64. While browsing in a bookstore, Vhamala is drawn to a particular book title. After a moment, she realizes that this book is one that a friend had been talking about at lunch the other day. The fact that Vhamala remembers that the book was mentioned at a recent lunch is an example of which of the following types of memory?

    (A) Phonemic
    (B) Systemic
    (C) Semantic
    (D) Structural
    (E) Episodic

65. The process of converting physical energy from the environment into neural impulses is known as

    (A) sensation
    (B) priming
    (C) transduction
    (D) encoding
    (E) detection

66. An experiment that presents participants with a stimulus and then, at a later interval, presents them with incomplete perceptual information related to the initial stimulus to see if they recognize the incomplete information more quickly is most likely studying the effects of

    (A) retroactivity
    (B) mnemonic devices
    (C) declarative memory
    (D) iconic memory
    (E) priming

67. Alfred Binet was primarily concerned with

    (A) discussing the role of genetics in levels of intelligence
    (B) measuring intelligence levels in children
    (C) measuring personality in children
    (D) measuring personality in adults
    (E) showing how adult personality can be modified

68. Hunter, a high school senior, excels at music, art, reading, problem-solving, and soccer. Which of these strengths most clearly demonstrates his fluid intelligence?

    (A) Music
    (B) Art
    (C) Reading
    (D) Problem-solving
    (E) Soccer

69. In psychoanalytic theory, which of the following statements most accurately explains the purpose of repression?

    (A) It allows individuals to indirectly express their anger toward others.
    (B) It encourages clients to shift difficult feelings about loved ones onto their therapists.
    (C) It is a means of dealing with thoughts that are very anxiety-provoking.
    (D) It allows individuals to explain away acts to avoid uncomfortable feelings.
    (E) It is an unconscious model that allows people to describe the way things work.

70. If genetic factors play an important role in the development of intelligence as measured by an IQ test, then which of the following statements is most likely to be true?

    (A) The IQ scores of parents and their offspring will be more nearly alike than the IQ scores of fraternal twins reared together.
    (B) The IQ scores of fraternal twins reared together will be more nearly alike than the IQ scores of identical twins reared together.
    (C) The IQ scores of fraternal twins reared together will be more nearly alike than the IQ scores of identical twins reared apart.
    (D) The IQ scores of fraternal twins will be equivalent in similarity to the IQ scores of identical twins.
    (E) The IQ scores of identical twins reared apart will be more nearly alike than the IQ scores of fraternal twins reared together.

71. Negative symptoms of schizophrenia include which of the following?

    (A) Visual hallucinations
    (B) Auditory hallucinations
    (C) Blunted emotional responses
    (D) Delusions
    (E) Excessive motor activity

GO ON TO THE NEXT PAGE.

72. Three students are going in to take the SAT. Felice is not sure that she wants to go to college, is lackadaisical about the test, and is half asleep as she enters the test center. Skip is very concerned about the test; he sees his score as determining his entire future and he can be seen pacing nervously as he prepares to enter the test center. Armando takes the test seriously, but he knows that he will have additional chances to take it and that there are other factors that affect college admission. He has a mild case of nerves as he enters the test center. When Armando outperforms Felice and Skip, this supports which of the following?

    (A) Cannon Bard theory
    (B) Piaget's Formal Operations stage
    (C) Yerkes-Dodson law
    (D) Selye's General Adaptation Syndrome
    (E) Gardner's Multiple Intelligences

73. Jim and Tim are identical (monozygotic) twins that were reared together. Scott and Michael are fraternal (dizygotic) twins that were reared together. Given the results of heritability studies of intelligence, which of the following outcomes are most likely to emerge?

    (A) Jim and Tim will have very similar IQs.
    (B) Scott and Michael will have very similar IQs.
    (C) Both pairs will have very similar IQs.
    (D) Neither pair will have similar IQs.
    (E) Jim and Michael will have similar IQs.

74. For which of the following would drive-reduction theories not provide a reasonable explanation?

    (A) In the middle of his five-mile race, Jerome grabs water from the water station to quench his thirst.
    (B) Ernest gobbles a few cookies on his way to class because he did not have time for lunch.
    (C) Tish decides to skip lunch because she is still full from eating a very large breakfast.
    (D) Cameron drives ten minutes out of her way to a fast-food place because she is hungry and has only two dollars.
    (E) Kezia is very full after eating dinner but decides to order the strawberry cheesecake anyway.

75. Abraham Maslow proposed the idea that some motives are more imperative to survival than others. Which of the following approaches expresses this?

    (A) Homeostatic regulation
    (B) Goal-setting
    (C) Expectancy-value
    (D) Cognitive dissonance
    (E) Hierarchy of needs

76. Which of the following is an example of a person who suffers from anterograde amnesia?

    (A) A six-year-old child who can't remember events related to her second birthday party
    (B) A twenty-year-old woman who can't remember the details of a traumatic event that occurred six months ago
    (C) A thirty-six-year-old man who experiences damage to his hippocampus and can't transfer information into his long-term memory
    (D) A fifteen-year-old boy who fell off his bicycle without his helmet and can't remember the events right before his accident
    (E) A forty-year-old woman who is recounting a story but can't remember where she first heard the story

77. Which of the following responses was most likely acquired through classical conditioning?

    (A) The anxiety reaction of a woman who is driving on the highway for the first time after being involved in a major accident on that highway
    (B) The frightened cry of a baby who is disoriented upon waking up from a nap
    (C) The uncontrollable blinking of a contact lens wearer who has just gotten something in his eye
    (D) The startled cry of a child who has just been awakened in the middle of the night by a loud clap of thunder
    (E) The salivation of a laboratory rat who has begun to eat the treat that awaited her at the end of a T-maze

78. Which of the following would be most useful in understanding a neighbor's interpretation of a certain family's recent crisis as being due to extreme financial distress?

    (A) Reinforcement theory
    (B) Classical behaviorism
    (C) Attribution theory
    (D) Hierarchy of needs
    (E) Cognitive dissonance

79. Children develop internal representational systems that allow them to describe people, events, and feelings verbally during which of Piaget's stages of cognitive development?

    (A) Sensorimotor
    (B) Preoperational
    (C) Symbolic
    (D) Concrete operational
    (E) Formal operational

GO ON TO THE NEXT PAGE.

80. According to Kohlberg, at the third (postconventional) level of moral development, individuals

    (A) follow rules in order to obtain reward
    (B) follow rules in order to avoid punishment
    (C) define what is right by what they have learned from others, especially authority figures
    (D) justify their moral action based on the need to maintain law and order
    (E) self-define principles that may or may not match the dominant morals of the times

81. Which of the following represents the correct order of auditory transmission from the time the sound is first heard to when it is processed in the brain?

    (A) Oval window→ cochlea→ tympanic membrane→ auditory nerve→ auditory canal
    (B) Auditory canal→ auditory nerve→ cochlea→ tympanic membrane→ ossicles
    (C) Tympanic membrane→ oval window→ cochlea→ auditory nerve→ auditory canal
    (D) Auditory canal→ ossicles→ oval window→ cochlea→ auditory nerve
    (E) Cochlea→ ossicles→ oval window→ auditory canal→ auditory nerve

82. A tribe has been found that has no past tense in its language. Researchers also found that the members of this tribe spend less time thinking about the past than other people. This finding is consistent with which theory?

    (A) The Behaviorist model for language development
    (B) Chomsky's Language Acquisition Device
    (C) Selye's General Adaptation Syndrome
    (D) Schachter's two-factor theory
    (E) Whorf's linguistic relativity

83. Heidi and Claus are in their 60s. They recently retired from their jobs and are planning to spend their time traveling and seeing their grandchildren. They enjoy looking back on their lives and counting their blessings. They are in Erikson's stage of

    (A) intimacy versus isolation
    (B) initiative versus guilt
    (C) integrity versus despair
    (D) autonomy versus shame
    (E) generativity versus stagnation

84. Which of the following clinicians most likely follows Carl Rogers's approach to psychotherapy?

    (A) Dr. Jones, who emphasizes the need for modification of undesirable behaviors in his patients
    (B) Terence Springer, who counsels individuals to find their inner spirituality and develop their relationship with a supreme being
    (C) Cathy Cooper, who is an empathic counselor who encourages clients through unconditional support to find their own path to better health and growth
    (D) Utrese Leed, who creates a framework for her patients that defines ideal psychological growth and development, and who supports their efforts toward professional achievement
    (E) Ute Shrom, who takes a physiological approach to recovery through strenuous physical challenges that break down and subsequently build up one's character

85. An obese individual with a breathing-related sleep disorder most likely suffers from which of the following?

    (A) Narcolepsy
    (B) Hypersomnia
    (C) Insomnia
    (D) Sleep apnea
    (E) Hypnotic susceptibility

86. Certain cross-cultural studies have suggested that six facial expressions are recognized by people of virtually every culture. Which of the following correctly lists these expressions?

    (A) Happiness, sadness, anger, loathing, lust, and surprise
    (B) Happiness, sadness, indifference, fright, surprise, and dislike
    (C) Happiness, sadness, desire, repulsion, fear, and surprise
    (D) Happiness, sadness, fight, flight, indifference, and anger
    (E) Happiness, sadness, fear, anger, surprise, and disgust

87. Which of the following is primarily a chemical sense?

    (A) Touch
    (B) Vision
    (C) Taste
    (D) Hearing
    (E) Kinesthesis

GO ON TO THE NEXT PAGE.

88. Anorexia nervosa is a life-threatening illness that can lead to permanent physiological changes (such as brittle bones) and even death. Which of the following individuals would be the most likely to develop this illness?

    (A) Maria, a 16-year-old Caucasian female, who is an A student and talented musician, but who feels that her life is out of control
    (B) Leticia, a 15-year-old African American female, who is an A student and exceptional athlete, plus an avid reader
    (C) Rosa, a 26-year-old Hispanic female, who has just received her law degree, is struggling with debt from school, and having difficulty finding employment
    (D) Virginia, a 14-year-old Caucasian female, who is a C student, is sexually promiscuous, and is experimenting with drugs
    (E) Jaeling, a 29-year-old Asian American female, who is a stay-at-home mother of two and has a very tight budget to maintain

89. Individuals in which of the following occupations will be potentially LEAST likely to be susceptible to health problems as a result of disrupted circadian rhythms?

    (A) Shift nurse
    (B) Police officer
    (C) Flight attendant
    (D) Medical resident
    (E) College professor

90. When Cordelia was a child, she was abused and she has been angry about it ever since. She is now a choreographer. When she creates dance routines for theatrical productions, critics and audiences often praise her realistic portrayals of anger and aggression. This would fit under the Freudian defense mechanism of

    (A) projection
    (B) reaction formation
    (C) repression
    (D) denial
    (E) sublimation

91. While visiting a museum, you study a statue by walking around it and examining it from many different places in the room. The retinal images of the statue change, but you do not perceive these changes because of

    (A) convergence
    (B) motion parallax
    (C) perceptual constancy
    (D) interpositioning
    (E) perceptual acuity

92. REM sleep is considered to be paradoxical sleep because

    (A) brain patterns change from alpha waves to delta waves over the course of a night's sleep
    (B) people can always act out the content of their dreams
    (C) people will try to increase REM sleep if deprived of REM sleep for a period of time
    (D) sleep cycles may change with age
    (E) the mind is very active, but the body is in a state of paralysis

93. Carmella has experienced a stroke. She now needs to use a communication board because her speech is difficult to understand. Carmella has probably sustained damage to her

    (A) Wernicke's area
    (B) hippocampus
    (C) amygdala
    (D) Broca's area
    (E) medulla oblongata

94. Probabilistic reasoning from specific observations to general propositions is known as

    (A) deductive reasoning
    (B) inductive reasoning
    (C) intuitive reasoning
    (D) statistical reasoning
    (E) observational reasoning

95. Claudio lives in an area with a few college students and several retirement communities. He is trying to start a computer consulting business that will make home visits to deal with customers' technology problems. He does all of his marketing for the business in a hip coffeehouse and on a dating website because he assumes that the elderly are relatively uninterested in technology. His business is not doing well. What obstacle to effective problem-solving may be interfering with his success?

    (A) Availability heuristic
    (B) Representativeness heuristic
    (C) Functional fixedness
    (D) Optimism bias
    (E) Confirmation bias

GO ON TO THE NEXT PAGE.

96. Which of the following accurately states the order of the transmission of visual information?

    (A) Optic nerve; ganglion cells; bipolar cells; rods and cones
    (B) Bipolar cells; ganglion cells; fovea; optic nerve
    (C) Rods and cones; retina; optic nerve; ganglion cells
    (D) Bipolar cells; rods and cones; fovea; optic disk
    (E) Rods and cones; bipolar cells; ganglion cells; optic nerve

97. Which of the following best summarizes Carl Rogers's view of personality?

    (A) Personality traits such as inhibition, extroversion, and conscientiousness are constant over time.
    (B) People's personality traits are overwhelmingly positive and goal-directed.
    (C) Personality is mainly formed by behavioral expectations.
    (D) Individual personalities vary based on differences in traits, emotions, and thought processes.
    (E) Situational variables are more important in determining the way a person will act than are broad personality dispositions.

98. Research has shown a possible connection between the neurotransmitter acetylcholine and which of the following mental disorders?

    (A) Parkinson's disease
    (B) Alzheimer's disease
    (C) Schizophrenia
    (D) Mania
    (E) Depression

99. Which of the following best explains why babies have poor vision for the first few weeks of life?

    (A) The nodes of Ranvier have not yet formed.
    (B) The neural connections to the primary visual cortex are not fully connected.
    (C) The axons are covered in tight coats of lipids, which impede neural firing.
    (D) The synaptic cleft of the neuron is filled with an aqueous humor.
    (E) The glial cells are absent at birth.

100. Scientists have long sought a physical manifestation of learning and memory in the brain. Perhaps the closest they have come is in identifying strengthened synaptic connections. This is referred to as

    (A) long-term potentiation (LTP)
    (B) tip-of-the-tongue phenomenon
    (C) cortical conditioning
    (D) myelinization
    (E) reuptake

END OF SECTION I

IF YOU FINISH BEFORE TIME IS CALLED, YOU MAY CHECK YOUR WORK ON THIS SECTION. DO NOT GO ON TO SECTION II UNTIL YOU ARE TOLD TO DO SO.

PSYCHOLOGY
Section II
Time—50 minutes

Percent of total score—33$\frac{1}{3}$

Directions: You have 50 minutes to answer BOTH of the following questions. It is not enough to answer a question by merely listing facts. You should present a cogent argument based on your critical analysis of the question posed, using appropriate psychological terminology.

1. Kai is the field-goal kicker for his high school's football team and he has been invited to a college evaluation clinic where coaches will watch him perform along with other kickers looking for scholarship opportunities. Two things that have made Kai a good kicker are great self-confidence and careful preparation for whatever conditions he will face in a game. However, he has concerns about this clinic because of three things:

   - Only his teammates who snap and hold the ball will be on the field with him. All of the evaluators will be in the press box and he will not see them.
   - The field is an artificial surface and he has never played or practiced on such a field.
   - Several days ago, he sustained an eye injury and he will be wearing a patch over his left eye. He has been unable to practice since this accident.

   Explain how each of the following factors could influence Kai's performance at the clinic:

   - The "Big Five" trait of Openness to Experience
   - Convergence (depth perception)
   - Cognitive dissonance
   - Social facilitation
   - Sympathetic nervous system
   - Non-declarative memory
   - Self-efficacy

2. Many people are concerned with the seeming inability of the prison system to rehabilitate criminals.

   A. Based on your knowledge of learning, argue against the traditional prison system by explaining how each of the following could be used in a rehabilitation program:

   - Operant conditioning
   - Positive and negative reinforcement
   - Shaping

   B. Choose ONE of the above methods of learning and then explain how it could be used to reform a convicted thief.

STOP

END OF EXAM

Practice Test 1:
Answers and
Explanations

ANSWER KEY

1. C	26. D	51. B	76. C
2. D	27. E	52. B	77. A
3. E	28. D	53. A	78. C
4. B	29. C	54. D	79. B
5. C	30. B	55. C	80. E
6. D	31. C	56. C	81. D
7. D	32. B	57. D	82. E
8. C	33. B	58. A	83. C
9. B	34. E	59. B	84. C
10. A	35. D	60. E	85. D
11. B	36. C	61. E	86. E
12. C	37. C	62. A	87. C
13. D	38. B	63. E	88. A
14. E	39. D	64. E	89. E
15. D	40. C	65. C	90. E
16. A	41. C	66. E	91. C
17. D	42. C	67. B	92. E
18. E	43. B	68. D	93. D
19. A	44. D	69. C	94. B
20. B	45. B	70. E	95. B
21. A	46. A	71. C	96. E
22. D	47. B	72. C	97. B
23. C	48. C	73. A	98. B
24. D	49. B	74. E	99. B
25. E	50. C	75. E	100. A

MULTIPLE-CHOICE SECTION: ANSWERS AND EXPLANATIONS

Note: The explanations in this section make use of the smart-tester strategies introduced in Part IV. Please refer to pages 57–63 first in order to make the most of this section.

1. **C** *Understand the Question/Key Words:* Why is Matilda struggling to play an instrument that she has not played for many years? *Predict the Answer:* Think about what type of memory phenomenon is at play here, and note Matilda's age. Teenagers strengthen neural connections for activities in which they continue to engage, but these connections weaken with disuse ("pruning"). There is no indication of learning another instrument or anything else that would "interfere" with her prior knowledge, so (B) and (D) do not apply. She has not altered her memory, so (A) is out. This is not a situation in which she recalls information, but cannot recall from what source she received it, so (E) does not apply.

2. **D** Choice (D) is the correct definition. Choice (A) is what Alzheimer's does. Choice (B) is sensory adaptation. Choice (C) is satiety. Choice (E) is hyperthyroidism.

3. **E** *Understand the Question/Key Words:* Which kind of scientist emphasizes the importance of culture? *Predict the Answer:* Culture should mean *anthropology* to you. If not, get reviewing, and use POE. Are structuralists, (A), the kind of scientists that emphasize culture? Even if you don't remember what structuralists are, the name does not imply culture. If you are completely unfamiliar with (B), leave it and move on. Choice (C), sociobiologists, may throw you, but (D), behaviorists, should be one you can easily eliminate. When you plug in (E), anthropologists, it should jog your memory. Remember, this is only the third question on the exam and the questions often start off easier then get increasingly difficult (more on that later), so keep it simple, and go for the easier choice.

4. **B** *Understand the Question/Key Words:* Culturally based versus psychologically based? *Predict the Answer*: Look for something that is not considered "innate." Is (A), caring for one's children, cultural? It seems that most cultures do it in some form, but if you are unsure, leave it. Choice (B), arriving on time for work, is not something that is done in every culture, so this looks good. Choices (C), having the desire to reproduce, and (D), seeking food and water, are primary drives present in all cultures, and (E), smiling, has also been found as a universal facial expression. (B) is clearly something that occurs only in time-oriented cultures.

5. **C** *Understand the Question/Key Words:* Which of the following means "reward after specific number of purchases"? *Predict the Answer*: Fixed-ratio. If you don't remember, anything like "fixed number" will get you to your answer using POE. Get rid of (A), variable-ratio, and (B), variable-interval, because they are variable, and (E), continuous, because you are not being continuously rewarded. Choice (C), fixed-ratio, refers to a ratio or number, whereas (D), fixed-interval, refers to *interval* or *time*.

6. **D** *Understand the Question/Key Words:* Circle *neurotransmitters* and *pleasure*. *Predict the Answer*: Dopamine. If you don't remember, use POE to get rid of the ones you do recognize. Is (A), GABA, associated with pleasure? No, so cross it off. Is (B), acetylcholine, associated with pleasure? No, it has something to do with memory. Choice (C), serotonin, may throw you off, so leave it if you are unsure. Choice (E), adrenaline, is not a neurotransmitter, so cross it off.

7. **D** *Understand the Question/Key Words:* What in the teacher's behavior may have caused the girls to perform so badly? *Predict the Answer:* This is an example of a stereotype (that girls are bad at math) and it's not a positive thing, so it cannot be a boost. Telling a group of people that it is expected to underperform other groups on a task may produce a self-fulfilling prophecy. Choice (C) is the opposite: telling the group that it is expected to do particularly well. Choices (B) and (E) are obstacles to effective problem-solving because they cause people to ignore base rates.

8. **C** *Understand the Question/Key Words:* What in this study is making the psychologist's research impossible to accurately interpret? *Predict the Answer:* She gives the test in the morning at one school and in the afternoon at another. If you missed this point, use your definition of confounding variable to evaluate each answer choice. Is (A), the fact that the research is done at two *different schools*, a potential problem with the study? No, that is part of what she is comparing. Is (B), the fact that she is comparing the *same grade*, a potential problem? Definitely not. Is (C), the fact that the students are tested at *different times*, a potential problem? Bingo. Is (D), the fact that she is testing the students *on the same day*, a potential problem? No. Is (E), the fact that she is administering a *basic skills exam*, a potential problem? No.

9. **B** *Understand the Question/Key Words:* Developmental psychologists do what kind of research? *Predict the Answer:* Cross-sectional research. If you don't know this, review Chapter 6. Use POE to eliminate the rest of the choices.

10. **A** *Understand the Question/Key Words:* How do narcotics work? *Predict the Answer:* They imitate endorphins. If you are not sure exactly how they work but know they imitate a chemical substance in the brain, use POE. Do narcotics imitate (A), endorphins? Endorphins are chemicals in the brain that have to do with pleasure, so this could be it. Do narcotics imitate (B), hormones? This is less likely because hormones are secreted throughout the body and for a wide variety of purposes. Cross it off. Do narcotics imitate (C), secretions? What secretions? Too broad, so cross it off. Do narcotics imitate (D), GABA? This is a specific neurotransmitter—too specific to be the thing that all narcotics imitate. Cross it off. Choice (E), acetylcholine, can also be eliminated on these grounds. The answer must be (A).

11. **B** *Understand the Question/Key Words:* Someone will be more likely to recall a list of positive words if... *Predict the Answer:* S/he was in a positive frame of mind while hearing the words. Use POE: does (A), the *researcher* exhibiting a positive mood, mean the same thing as the participant being in a positive frame of mind? No, so cross it off. Does (B), the *participant* being in a positive mood, mean the same thing as the participant being in a positive frame of mind? Yup. Does (C), the participant considering himself a positive person *regardless of his mood during the experience*, mean the same thing as the participant being in a positive frame of mind during the experience? No. Does (D), the participant considering the *initial testing experience* positive, mean the same thing as the participant having a positive frame of mind during the experience? Careful—it doesn't mean the same thing. Cross it off. Does (E), the participant *perceiving the list of words as positive* regardless of the true meaning of the words, mean the same thing as the participant being in a positive frame of mind during the experience? No, plus you know that the words are positive. Cross it off. Your answer must be (B).

12. **C** *Understand the Question/Key Words:* Circle *minimum amount of physical energy. Predict the Answer:* Absolute threshold. If you don't remember, use POE. Would (A), JND (just noticeable difference), be the amount of energy needed to notice a stimulus? No, the JND involves noticing the difference between two stimuli. Cross it off. The same is true of (B), difference threshold. Choices (D), median difference, and (E), hit threshold, are both made-up terms, and sound like it.

13. **D** The frontal lobes are involved with decision-making, planning, and emotional regulation, so (A), (B), (C), and (E) are all problems that Gage had. The frontal lobes are not a specific repository of memories.

14. **E** *Understand the Question/Key Words:* Circle *medulla oblongata*. The medulla oblongata is critical for basic life functions, such as respiration. *Predict the Answer:* If the medulla oblongata is destroyed, it's all over. If you don't remember, you can probably still get rid of a few choices with POE. Choices (C) and (D) involve speech and vision, which are clearly tied to other areas of the brain. Be sure to review the major components of the brain if you missed this item.

15. **D** *Understand the Question/Key Words:* Which system prepares the body for fight or flight? *Predict the Answer:* Sympathetic nervous system. If you have trouble remembering if it's the sympathetic, (D), or parasympathetic, (E), try this mnemonic: the sympathetic nervous system is *sympathetic* to your problems, so it responds. POE should have gotten rid of (A), the central nervous system, (B), the somatic nervous system, and (C), the sensorimotor nervous system, even if you couldn't remember whether it was (D) or (E).

16. **A** *Understand the Question/Key Words:* Which aspect of this study is the independent variable? *Predict the Answer:* The placement of the bottle of milk. The milk is being moved back and forth to see if the monkeys attach to the food or to the mothers. In other words, the milk is being manipulated to see what response will occur—it is therefore the independent variable. If you don't remember, POE your way to the answer using your common sense. In (B), why would the independent variable be the wire mother versus the cloth mother? Choices (D) and (E) are essentially the same answer, so they can't be right, and (C), (D), and (E) all talk about preferences, meaning responses, meaning dependent variables. Choice (A) has to be it.

17. **D** *Understand the Question/Key Words:* Cats that were allowed to see through only one eye at a time will have what kind of vision problems? *Predict the Answer:* Using both eyes together. Which answer choice means using both eyes together? Binocular vision. Choice (D) is the only answer that mentions binocular cues. Choice (A), interposition depth perception, would be hard to evaluate in a cat, as would be (B), perceptual constancy. Be careful of (C)—just because it mentions left and right doesn't mean it contains the full answer; it is still talking about monocular cues. Choice (E) would again be hard to evaluate because it involves perception.

18. **E** *Understand the Question/Key Words:* Circle the words *control group*, and then go to the experiment and label the control group. *Predict the Answer:* Because the study is about the effects of music on memory, the second group, which had no music, is the control group. Use POE to get rid of the other choices.

19. **A** *Understand the Question/Key Words*: Circle *dependent variable*; then go find it. *Predict the Answer*: The dependent variable is the thing being tested, so the number of words recalled is the dependent variable. Use POE to get rid of the other choices.

20. **B** *Understand the Question/Key Words:* Who is most often diagnosed with ADHD? *Predict the Answer*: Boys. This is something you should know. Don't get sucked in by overly detailed answers such as (D) or (E).

21. **A** *Understand the Question/Key Words*: Circle *psychoanalytic*. *Predict the Answer*: Psychoanalytic = Freud = unconscious forces. Use POE: Does (A), unconscious forces, mean unconscious forces? Yup. Does (B), response to external reward and punishment, mean unconscious forces? No. Does (C), product of genetic programming, mean unconscious forces? No. Does (D), compilation of the ways in which people think and interact, mean unconscious forces? Not really, so cross it off. Does (E), each person's striving to reach full potential, mean unconscious forces? Not necessarily. The answer must be (A).

22. **D** *Understand the Question/Key Words:* Circle *categorical*. Categorical versus continuous. *Predict the Answer*: Something that is an either/or versus an ongoing kind of trait. Use POE. Is (A), intelligence, an either/or? No, it is more of an ongoing trait. Cross it off. Is (B), disposition, an either/or? No. Is (C), optimism, an either/or? Careful, it is not true that you must be either optimistic or pessimistic. It is more of a continuum. Cross it off. Is (D), gender, an either/or? Yes, in most cases you are either male or female. Is (E), personality, an either/or? No.

23. **C** *Understand the Question/Key Words:* The fact that she didn't see alternative uses for the paper is known as... *Predict the Answer*: Functional fixedness. Choices (B), (D), and (E) are made up, and (A), confirmation bias, refers to something else.

24. **D** *Understand the Question/Key Words:* What was Elise doing to remember the number? *Predict the Answer*: Rehearsing it over and over. Use POE. Because you know she is rehearsing, you can get rid of (A), (C), and (E). Does it seem like a rehearsal that is elaborative or based on maintenance? Your answer must be (D), maintenance rehearsal.

25. **E** *Understand the Question/Key Words:* The serial position curve has something to do with the position of the words in regard to recall. Which of the words would the person be most likely to forget, given the position of the word in the list? *Predict the Answer*: The serial position phenomenon actually says people tend to forget items in the middle of a list, so the answer must be (E), license, because it is in the center of the list.

26. **D** *Understand the Question/Key Words:* Circle *smallest unit*. *Predict the Answer*: Morphemes. If you don't remember, use POE to get rid of (B), phenotypes, and (E), syntactical rules.

27. **E**   *Understand the Question/Key Words:* Circle *abnormally elevated or expansive mood.* Which disorder involves extreme happiness or "bigness"? *Predict the Answer:* Mania. If you don't remember, use POE. Does (A), depression, manifest itself in extreme happiness? No. Does (B), schizophrenia, manifest itself in extreme happiness? Extreme happiness is not a defining characteristic of schizophrenia. Does (C), euphoria, manifest itself in extreme happiness? Yes, but is it a disorder? Be careful—this response is a trap. Does (D), dysthymia, manifest itself in extreme happiness? If you don't know, leave it. Does (E), mania, manifest itself in extreme happiness? Yes. Your answer is (E).

28. **D**   *Understand the Question/Key Words:* Which hormone is essential for sleep regulation? *Predict the Answer:* Melatonin. If you don't remember, use POE. Is (A), estrogen, essential for sleep regulation? No. Cross it off. Is (B), adrenaline, essential for sleep regulation? No. Is (C), testosterone, essential for sleep regulation? No. Is (D), melatonin, essential for sleep regulation? If you don't remember, leave it. Is (E), dopamine, essential for sleep regulation? No, and it's not a hormone. The answer has to be (D).

29. **C**   *Understand the Question/Key Words:* How does Jacob's mother influence his behavior? *Predict the Answer:* She gives in to his demands, thereby reinforcing his behavior. The other terms (associated, extinguished, shaped) are all relevant to learning theory, but not relevant to answering this question.

30. **B**   *Understand the Question/Key Words:* Circle the words *reinforcement* and *learning.* Both of these terms mean you want to modify behavior. *Predict the Answer:* B. F. Skinner is the only behaviorist in this list. If you don't remember his name, use POE to get rid of the ones you know are not behaviorists: (A), Freud, (C), Rogers, (D), Ainsworth, and (E), Darwin.

31. **C**   *Understand the Question/Key Words:* Circle *97th percentile.* Which of the choices is a pretty high, but not the highest, IQ score? *Predict the Answer:* 130s. If you don't know, use your common sense and POE. Choices (A), 85, and (B), 100, are definitely too low. Choice (C), 130, is considered very high but not extreme. Choices (D), 150, and (E), 170, are rare, more like the 99th percentile.

32. **B**   *Understand the Question/Key Words:* Circle *Pavlov.* What was Pavlov's big discovery? *Predict the Answer:* While experimenting with dogs, he discovered that they would salivate at the sight and sound of the person bringing their food, even before eating their food. This fact led Pavlov to discover classical conditioning. Because you know he experimented with dogs, get rid of (A), (C), and (D). Choice (B) is the answer closest to yours.

33. **B**   *Understand the Question/Key Words:* Which concept relates to grounding someone for misbehaving? *Predict the Answer:* It's a form of punishment. Choices (A) and (E) are irrelevant to learning theory, and (C) is made up. Only (B) and (D) are concepts of learning theory, and only (B) fits the prediction. Choice (B) is the correct answer.

34. **E**   *Understand the Question/Key Words:* Why do people stay aroused after an emergency? *Predict the Answer*: Adrenaline is still in their blood. Use POE. Cross off both (A) and (B) because they deal with neurons. Choice (A) is also a false statement—neurons do not remain graded after they fire. Watch out for (C): adrenal glands do secrete epinephrine but they would not continue to do so after the crisis has passed. This is the trap answer. Be sure to read each choice completely. Choice (D) is false because it is the sympathetic system that puts the body in a state of fight or flight. Choice (E) is the closest to your answer.

35. **D**   *Understand the Question/Key Words:* Which system returns the body to normal after an emergency? *Predict the Answer*: Parasympathetic nervous system. Choices (B), peripheral nervous system, and (E), central nervous system, are not part of the autonomic system. Remember our mnemonic for distinguishing between (C) and (D): the *sympathetic* nervous system is *sympathetic* to your stress, so it responds.

36. **C**   *Understand the Question/Key Words:* Tina's teacher is shocked at her bad driving because… *Predict the Answer*: Tina is always good—halo effect. If you don't remember the term, use POE. Does (A), modeling, mean always being perceived as good? No, cross it off. Does (B), accommodation, mean always being perceived as good? No. Does (C), halo effect, mean always being perceived as good? Sounds like it. Does (D), convergence, mean always being perceived as good? No. Does (E), behavioral dissonance, mean always being perceived as good? No. The answer must be (C).

37. **C**   This is where wave energy is transformed into a nerve impulse, so the correct answer is (C).

38. **B**   *Understand the Question/Key Words:* Why don't you notice the bakery smells after a while? *Predict the Answer*: Adaptation. You get used to the smell, and your senses don't pay attention to it as much because it is constant and not a critical piece of information. Use POE to get rid of (A), (C), and (D) because they wouldn't explain why you would no longer notice the aroma. Choice (E) is not a real psychological term.

39. **D**   *Understand the Question/Key Words:* If Carlotta is so well-adjusted, what's her family's parenting style? *Predict the Answer*: Authoritative. This parenting style generally seems to be the most effective. The parents set rules and expectations, but they are not completely domineering. Even if you don't remember the term, you know the style is structured but not overbearing. Use POE to get rid of (A), (B), and (E). Watch out for (C)—it is the trap. Authoritarian parents are domineering, which can be unhealthy for children.

40. **C**   *Understand the Question/Key Words:* Circle *semicircular canals*. What do they do? *Predict the Answer*: Help a person maintain his/her balance. If you don't remember, use POE. Could the semicircular canals of the inner ear help maintain (A), tone quality? Maybe. Leave and check the others. Could the semicircular canals of the inner ear help maintain (B), melatonin? No, melatonin involves sleep regulation. Cross it off. Could the semicircular canals of the inner ear help maintain (C), balance? Hopefully this answer reminds you of the connection between the ear and balance. Could the semicircular canals of the inner ear help maintain (D), olfaction? No, olfaction is smell. Could the semicircular canals of the inner ear help maintain (E), transduction? Although transduction occurs in the inner ear, that is not the purpose of the semicircular canals.

41. **C**   *Understand the Question/Key Words:* Why does the shape seem the same even though sensory information changes? *Predict the Answer*: You have to account for experience and expectation of constancy. Because we're talking about the door being rectangular, it is (C), shape constancy, and not (A), color constancy, or (D), size constancy.

42. **C**   *Understand the Question/Key Words:* Circle *norepinephrine receptors*. What happens when they are stimulated? *Predict the Answer*: A person experiences increased alertness. Does (A), euphoria, mean increased alertness? No. Cross it off. Does (B), increased motor activity, mean increased alertness? No. Does (C), alertness, mean increased alertness? Yup. Does (D), anxiety, mean increased alertness? Not exactly. Does (E), hypertension, mean increased alertness? No.

43. **B**   *Understand the Question/Key Words:* Circle *visual cliff*. This is a study in which infants are subjected to an optical illusion of a drop. *Predict the Answer*: The infants won't crawl into the area that looks like a drop. You need to read all the choices and compare them, if you don't remember visual-cliff studies. POE should get rid of (C) and (D) as very unlikely. Choice (B) is the most probable.

44. **D**   *Understand the Question/Key Words:* Which of the answers is NOT one of the conditions of the APA (American Psychological Association) regarding deception? Be careful—four of the five answer choices here are "right," while only one is "wrong." *Predict the Answer*: A study must be very important, unable to be done without deception, not objectionable to the participant, and it must both allow a participant to stop at any time and inform the participant at the end of the study. Cross off any answer that matches these. The one remaining is your answer.

45. **B**   *Understand the Question/Key Words:* What is the mind versus body problem called? *Predict the Answer*: Mind-body problem. Don't make it harder than it is. This is only a medium question.

46. **A**   *Understand the Question/Key Words:* Circle *behaviorism*. *Predict the Answer*: Behaviorists believe that behavior is the result of learning and consequences. Find an answer that exemplifies this tenet, and use POE. "Introspection" makes (B) wrong. Choice (C) is psychodynamic, (D) is almost the opposite, and (E) is way off.

47. **B**   *Understand the Question/Key Words:* Circle *knowledge* and *information processing*. Who cares about how knowledge and information processing interact? *Predict the Answer*: Cognitive psychologists. Use your knowledge to get rid of the other four choices.

48. **C** *Understand the Question/Key Words:* Who studies psychological development through the *life span*? *Predict the Answer*: Developmental psychologists. If you don't remember, use what you know to POE. Do (A), psychometricians, study people throughout the life span? No. Cross it off. Do occupational psychologists, (B), study people throughout the life span? No, they study occupations. Do developmental psychologists, (C), study people throughout the life span? Yes, as people develop. Do social psychologists, (D), study people throughout the life span? Not necessarily. Do cognitive behaviorists, (E), study people throughout the life span? No.

49. **B** *Understand the Question/Key Words:* If a relationship shown in a sample can be generalized so as to apply to the population from which it was taken, you can say the relationship is... *Predict the Answer*: Generalizable. Use your work to POE the other choices. Reliability, (A), refers to whether a test produces consistent results, not whether the results themselves are valid, so you can eliminate this choice, as well as (D). Validity, on the other hand, deals with those conclusions. External validity, (B), specifically refers to whether results can be generalized to deal with situations outside the sample or test conditions. Internal validity, (C), looks only at whether a casual relationship can be drawn between the tested variables, and can be eliminated, along with (E), which is looking for correlation, not behavior.

50. **C** *Understand the Question/Key Words:* What makes this study valid? The methodology used involves researchers evaluating various behavior patterns of children. Therefore, the evaluators need to do an unbiased, accurate job. *Predict the Answer*: Inter-rater reliability. Use POE if you don't remember the term. Choices (A) and (B) are made-up terms. Does (C), inter-rater reliability, address the accuracy of the evaluators? Yes. Does (D), test-retest reliability, address the accuracy of the evaluators? No. Does (E), correlational statistical reliability, address the accuracy of the evaluators? No.

51. **B** *Understand the Question/Key Words*: What area of the brain regulates hunger and eating? *Predict the Answer*: Hypothalamus. If you don't remember, use POE. Does (A), the somatosensory cortex, regulate hunger and eating? Probably not—it is a cortex and somehow involves "sensory" stuff, and hunger is a primary drive. Cross this off. Does (C), the medulla oblongata, regulate hunger and eating? Probably not, because you know it is a part of vital organ functioning. Do the occipital lobes, (D), regulate hunger and eating? No, they involve vision. Does (E), the amygdala, regulate hunger and eating? No, it is involved in emotions. The answer must be (B).

52. **B** *Understand the Question/Key Words:* How does the method of loci memory aid work? *Predict the Answer*: Loci is plural for locus, which means place. With this aid, you associate new material with places you're familiar with, like places in your house. So you have to imagine these spaces, or visualize them. Use POE. Does (A), semantic encoding, mean visualization? No. Cross it off. Does (B), visual imagery, mean visualization? Yes. Does (C), auditory cues, mean visualization? No. Does (D), echoic memory, mean visualization? No, it also means auditory (think echo). Does (E), read, recite, review, mean visualization? No.

53. **A** *Understand the Question/Key Words:* Which helps determine if the findings of a study mean something or if they were a fluke? *Predict the Answer*: Inferential statistics. If you don't remember, use POE to evaluate the answer choices. Could (A), inferential statistics, help determine if the

findings of a study mean something? They help to infer stuff, so probably. Keep it, and read the others. Could (B), descriptive statistics, help determine if the findings of a study mean something? They only describe, so probably not. Cross it off. Could (C), standard deviation, help determine if the findings of a study mean something? Cross it off. Same goes for (D), extraneous variables. Could (E), correlation coefficients, help determine if the findings of a study mean something? No, so the answer must be (A).

54. **D**   During REM there is great mental and physiological arousal, but very little muscular activity. There is still about 25% REM when people age, but it is a percentage of less sleep overall, so less REM occurs and you can cross off (A). REM is when most dreaming occurs, so cross off (B). People's heart rate, blood pressure, etc., increase during REM, so cross off (C). REM is a light sleep phenomenon, so cross off (E).

55. **C**   *Understand the Question/Key Words:* Which gland is called the master gland? *Predict the Answer:* Pituitary gland. If you don't remember, use POE to get rid of (B) and (E) because they are not glands. You also know that (D), adrenal gland, isn't responsible for much more than adrenaline, so cross it off, too.

56. **C**   *Understand the Question/Key Words:* What types of mistakes do all children make when learning language? *Predict the Answer:* They learn to use the rules of grammar, but they apply them too generally. Use POE. It must be (C), overgeneralization.

57. **D**   *Understand the Question/Key Words:* What does a researcher have to do to show that one thing causes another? *Predict the Answer:* Show that manipulating one variable consistently leads to changes in another variable. Use POE to find the answer that is closest to yours. Choice (A) is unethical, and (B) and (C) would do nothing to show causation. Regarding (E), remember that correlation does not mean causation!

58. **A**   *Understand the Question/Key Words:* Circle *learned helplessness*. This means being helpless because you believe you are helpless. *Predict the Answer:* It's a result of expectation. If you don't remember the term *expectation*, use POE. Could (A), expectation, lead to being helpless simply because you believe you are helpless? Yes—your expectations determine your ability. Could (B), positive reinforcement, lead to being helpless simply because you believe you are helpless? This doesn't make sense, and neither does (C), negative reinforcement. Could (D), classical conditioning, lead to being helpless simply because you believe you are helpless? No—there is no classical conditioning involved. Could (E), prepared learning, lead to being helpless simply because you believe you are? This doesn't make sense. The answer must be (A).

59. **B**   Jose demonstrates characteristics of the Preoperational stage, including the fact that he has yet to learn principles of conservation of matter. Choice (C) is not a stage in Piaget's theory. Choice (A) involves infants and toddlers who are just learning to walk and talk. Choice (D) is the stage during which children learn principles of conservation. Choice (E) is the stage when children become capable of abstract and higher-level thinking.

60. **E** *Understand the Question/Key Words:* Georgia is motivated by internal issues or emotions, while Kathy is motivated by money. How are these motivations different? *Predict the Answer*: Georgia is motivated intrinsically; that is, she is rewarded by the work itself. Kathy is motivated extrinsically; that is, by an external reward—money. If you don't remember the terms, use POE. Choice (A), primary and secondary drives, doesn't make sense, so cross it off. Choice (B), positive and negative loci of control, also doesn't address the internal versus external motivations. Choice (C), sympathetic and autonomic motivation, are made-up terms, and (D), instinctive and derived drives, refer to basic drives, not social motivations.

61. **E** *Understand the Question/Key Words:* Circle *depression*. What chemicals in the brain are involved in depression? *Predict the Answer*: Depression should make you think "serotonin." If it doesn't, use POE to get rid of a few choices. Get rid of (A) and (D) due to elevated levels (not likely with depression). Review disorders and their relationship to chemicals in the brain.

62. **A** Deindividuation applies to situations of high arousal and low perceived personal identification, when individuals might succumb to mob mentality. Choice (B) involves group members becoming more extreme in their preexisting views as time goes on. Choice (C) occurs in a group that prizes consensus over free exchange of competing views. Choice (D) involves performing better when other people are around. Choice (E) involves people forming more positive views of something simply because they have encountered it repeatedly.

63. **E** *Understand the Question/Key Words:* Why do the pigeons not peck at other artists' paintings? *Predict the Answer*: Stimulus discrimination. They peck at the one they have learned and can distinguish from the others. With this information, use POE to cross off (A), modeling response, (B), reflexive response, and (D), stimulus generalization, because it is the opposite idea.

64. **E** *Understand the Question/Key Words:* She recalls the book by also recalling the lunch. What type of memory is she calling up? *Predict the Answer*: Episodic memory. She relates the memory to a recent episode. Use POE to get rid of the other four choices.

65. **C** *Understand the Question/Key Words:* Converting physical energy into neural impulses is called… *Predict the Answer*: Transduction. If you don't remember, use POE. Choice (A), sensation, is out because it involves only detection of energy, not conversion. The same is true of (E), detection. You can also eliminate (D), encoding, because it is not involved in energy conversion.

66. **E** *Understand the Question/Key Words:* A person is shown something. Later, she is shown incomplete information related to the first thing she was shown. The experimenter watches to see if she recognizes the incomplete information more quickly than usual. In other words, does the fact that she saw related stimuli make identifying the second set easier? *Predict the Answer*: The researcher is studying the effects of priming. If you don't remember the term, use POE. Cross off (B) because no mnemonic devices are used. Choice (C), declarative memory, is out because it deals with retrieved and "declared" information. Choice (D), iconic memory, is out because we don't know if these are visual images or other types of information.

67. **B** *Understand the Question/Key Words:* What did Binet study? *Predict the Answer*: Binet = intelligence. He studied intellectual potential in children. Knowing he studied intelligence and not personality will help you cross off (C) through (E). Then take a smart guess. You know he developed some kind of test, and most intelligence testing is done on children. Choice (B) is your smart guess.

68. **D** *Understand the Question/Key Words:* Circle *fluid intelligence*. Fluid, as in real-time, flexible information-processing intelligence, versus crystallized intelligence, as in acquired factual knowledge. Which of the subjects involves real-time, flexible intelligence? *Predict the Answer*: Problem-solving. All the others require primarily crystallized intelligence.

69. **C** *Understand the Question/Key Words:* Circle *repression*. Repression means keeping stressful thoughts out of conscious awareness. *Predict the Answer*: Repression is a defense mechanism that keeps anxiety-producing information out of conscious awareness for our protection. Use POE to find the answer that is closest to yours. Choice (A) is the definition of passive aggression, (B) is transference, and (D) is rationalization. Choice (E) doesn't make any sense—people can't describe what is unconscious.

70. **E** *Understand the Question/Key Words:* Which answer shows that genetics, as opposed to environment, has a direct effect on intelligence? *Predict the Answer*: Find an answer that shows genes/biology as more important than environment. Use POE. Choices (B) and (C) say the opposite. Choice (D) also would not support genetics. In (A), fraternal twins are more genetically similar than parents and their offspring, so this answer does not support genetics. The answer must be (E).

71. **C** *Understand the Question/Key Words:* Circle *negative symptoms*. Remember that "negative" means the absence of something. *Predict the Answer*: Lack of normal emotional responses. If you don't remember, POE will get rid of all the other choices because each describes the presence, not the absence, of something.

72. **C** The Yerkes-Dodson law posits that, for most people, most of the time, in most activities, a moderate level of arousal is best. Choice (A) is about sequencing of emotion and physiological arousal. Choice (B) is about when children become capable of abstract thinking. Choice (D) is about how people tolerate stress. Choice (E) is about different types of intelligence.

73. **A** *Understand the Question/Key Words:* Circle *heritability*. In other words, inherited. Another question about genetics over environment. *Predict the Answer*: The monozygotic (identical) twins will be more similar than the dizygotic (fraternal) twins. If you don't know the terms, POE and common sense will get rid of (D) and (E).

74. **E** *Understand the Question/Key Words:* Circle *drive-reduction theories*. *Predict the Answer*: Cross off all the answers that show a response that reduces a drive. The remaining choice will be the answer. In (A), Jerome is thirsty and quenches his thirst, thus satisfying his drive. Cross off this response. In (B), Ernest didn't eat lunch, implying hunger, so he eats cookies, trying to reduce his hunger drive. Cross it off. In (C), Tish is not hungry, so she doesn't eat. Although this is not drive *reduction*, it is not against natural drives. Leave it, and see if there is a better choice. In (D), Cameron is hungry

and needs food, so she goes out of her way to get it. This is drive reduction, so cross it off. In (E), Kezia orders more food even though she is very full. This desire goes against drive reduction, so this is your answer.

75. **E** *Understand the Question/Key Words*: Circle *Maslow* and *motives*. *Predict the Answer*: Maslow theorized that needs are arranged hierarchically, from physiological needs to self-actualization needs. Use POE. Does (A), homeostatic regulation, have to do with hierarchy? No. Cross it off. Does (B), goal-setting, have to do with hierarchy? No. Does (C), expectancy-value, or (D), cognitive dissonance, have to do with hierarchy? No. Choice (E), hierarchy of needs, is it.

76. **C** *Understand the Question/Key Words*: Circle *anterograde amnesia*. *Predict the Answer*: Look for an example of someone who can't form new memories. Get rid of (B) and (D) because they are clearly "after" memories. Choice (A) involves infantile amnesia, and (E) is an example of source amnesia.

77. **A** *Understand the Question/Key Words*: Circle *classical conditioning*. *Predict the Answer*: Find a choice that demonstrates a conditioned response to a stimulus. Choices (B), (C), and (D) are not conditioned responses. Beware of (E); it's a trap because it uses rats, but notice that the rats salivate only after they begin to eat. Choice (A) demonstrates a conditioned fear response after experiencing an accident on the highway.

78. **C** *Understand the Question/Key Words*: Which will help you understand how a person or persons interpret the behavior of others? *Predict the Answer*: Attribution theory. Attribution theory addresses how one person or group attributes certain things to another person or group in order to understand the other person's or group's actions or behaviors. If you don't remember this, use POE. Could (A), reinforcement theory, help explain how one group interprets the actions of another? Reinforcement has nothing to do with how groups interrelate. Cross it off. Could (B), classical behaviorism, help explain how one group interprets the actions of another? No. Could (C), attribution theory, help explain how one group interprets the actions of another? How they attribute things to others? Could be. Leave it. Could (D), hierarchy of needs, help explain how one group interprets the actions of another? No. Could (E), cognitive dissonance, help explain how one group interprets the actions of another? No. Your answer must be (C).

79. **B** *Understand the Question/Key Words*: During which of Piaget's stages of development do children develop symbolic and verbal representations? *Predict the Answer*: Preoperational. If you don't remember, think about the age at which this behavior occurs. You may recall the order of the stages and their approximate ages: sensorimotor, ages zero to two; preoperational, ages two to seven; concrete operational, ages seven to twelve; formal operational, ages twelve and up. The development of language and symbolic thinking occurs between the ages of two and seven. Use POE to get rid of (A) because *sensorimotor* definitely does not imply symbolic thought and (C) because *symbolic* is not one of Piaget's stages.

80. **E** *Understand the Question/Key Words:* Circle *Kohlberg* and *third (postconventional) level. Predict the Answer:* As "postconventional" implies, this stage of morality centers on carefully weighed principles that may or may not be conventional—they are determined by the individual. You may remember that Kohlberg posited only three stages, and this third one is the most advanced, so look for an answer that encompasses the most advanced form of moral thinking. Choices (A) and (B) illustrate the first or preconventional stage of development. Choices (C) and (D) represent the second or conventional stage of development.

81. **D** *Understand the Question/Key Words:* Circle *order of auditory transmission. Predict the Answer:* Use POE to assess the correct order based on what you know about this process.

82. **E** This is Whorf's theory: Thinking doesn't just affect language—the language used affects thinking. The Behaviorist theory of language development is that children produce language that is reinforced. Chomsky's theory is that people have an innate capacity for learning language rules, especially grammar. Selye's theory involves stress. Schachter's theory involves emotion.

83. **C** According to Erikson, when looking back on their lives, elderly individuals hope to find that they have gained wisdom. Choice (A) applies to young adults, (B) to children in the three-to-six age range, (D) to children in the one-to-three range, and (E) to middle-aged adults.

84. **C** *Understand the Question/Key Words:* Circle *Carl Rogers.* How did he approach psychotherapy? *Predict the Answer:* Rogers believed in empathy and unconditional support that would promote self-discovery. If you don't remember, you know that Rogers is a big name in psychology, so get rid of the clearly un-psychological answer choices—(B) and (E)—and (D), due to the "professional achievement" goal.

85. **D** *Understand the Question/Key Words:* Circle *breathing-related sleep disorder. Predict the Answer:* Apnea. Your clue is "breathing-related." If you don't remember, you can still cross off (B), (C), and (E) because they are not breathing-related.

86. **E** *Understand the Question/Key Words:* What facial expressions are found in all cultures? *Predict the Answer:* List the ones you can think of: happiness, sadness, anger, fear, surprise. Then use POE. You can also use POE to get rid of lists that have inappropriate choices: (A) is out because of "lust," (C) is out because of "desire," and (D) is out because of both "fight" and "flight." "Indifference" is the problem with (B).

87. **C** *Understand the Question/Key Words:* Circle *chemical sense. Predict the Answer:* Find something that is a result of chemical interaction. Even if you don't remember that taste is a chemical sense, use POE to get rid of the answers that are definitely physical properties: (A), (B), (D), and (E) are all physical or mechanical processes.

88. **A**   *Understand the Question/Key Words:* Who is most likely to become anorexic? *Predict the Answer*: List what you know about the typical anorexic: white female, teenager, usually good student, need for control. Then use POE. Because she is more likely to be Caucasian, get rid of (B), (C), and (E). Choice (D) is your trap answer—anorexia tends to afflict young women who seem confident and successful.

89. **E**   *Understand the Question/Key Words:* Circle *circadian rhythms* and *LEAST*. Circadian rhythms involve sleep patterns. Four of the choices will show people who may work odd or night hours. *Predict the Answer*: Choose the profession that is a normal "day" job. That eliminates (A) through (D).

90. **E**   Cordelia has harnessed what might otherwise be socially unacceptable impulses and turned them into something positive. She has not imagined these impulses in other people, (A), treated someone the opposite of how she truly feels about him/her, (B), fully buried her traumatic experiences, (C), or denied those experiences, (D).

91. **C**   *Understand the Question/Key Words:* Why don't you notice the changes in the statue as you view it from different places? Why does the image remain constant? *Predict the Answer*: Perceptual constancy. If you don't remember the term, use POE and your common sense. Choice (E) is definitely out. Could (A), convergence, mean that the image remains constant? "Convergence" means coming together, so not really. Cross it off. The same is true of (D), interpositioning. You may not be sure about (B), motion parallax, but (C), perceptual constancy, makes the most sense because the image remains constant.

92. **E**   *Understand the Question/Key Words:* Circle *paradoxical sleep*. *Predict the Answer*: A paradox is a statement that seems self-contradictory but is actually true. Choices (A), (B), (C), and (D) are properties of sleep, but no paradox is noted.

93. **D**   Broca's area is responsible for the production of fluent speech. Choice (A) is about speech, but it is about comprehension and meaning rather than fluency. Choice (B) is responsible for consolidating memory in the brain. Choice (C) is the "fear center" in the brain. Choice (E) controls basic processes like breathing and swallowing.

94. **B**   *Understand the Question/Key Words:* Inferring from an observation to a generalization is what kind of reasoning? *Predict the Answer*: Inductive reasoning. If you don't remember, use POE where you can. Be careful on (A); deductive reasoning is something that can be clearly deduced, not inferred or probabilistic. Choice (D), statistical reasoning, is also out. Choices (C) and (E) are not the correct psychological terms.

95. **B** Claudio has created a prototypical, or stereotypical, elderly person who is not interested in technology and this may conflict with the actual number of elderly individuals who are interested in his services. Choice (A) is also an obstacle, but it involves Claudio having more information about one group than others. Choice (C) is an obstacle, but involves being unable to see novel uses for familiar objects. Choice (D) is an attribution bias that causes people to view their own prospects too favorably. Choice (E) is an obstacle that involves seeking only evidence to support one's predetermined views or ignoring evidence that conflicts with those views.

96. **E** *Understand the Question/Key Words:* What's the route visual information takes? *Predict the Answer*: Retina, bipolar cells, ganglion cells, and optic nerve. If you don't remember, you probably know that transduction starts in the retina, so rods and cones are first. Cross off (A), (B), and (D). Rods and cones are in the retina, so that takes care of (C).

97. **B** *Understand the Question/Key Words:* Circle *Rogers* and *view of personality*. What did Rogers say about personality? *Predict the Answer*: Rogers believed in the goodness of the individual. If you are not sure, use POE. Cross off (A) because it is extreme and untrue (is that always the case?), and (C) is a behavioral explanation of personality. Choices (D) and (E) were not statements of Rogers.

98. **B** *Understand the Question/Key Words:* Circle *acetylcholine*. It's related to what disease? *Predict the Answer*: Alzheimer's. If you don't remember, you may remember that dopamine is somehow tied to Parkinson's, so you can cross off (A). If you have reviewed disorders enough, you will also know that it is not tied to (C), (D), or (E), so the answer must be (B).

99. **B** *Understand the Question/Key Words:* Why do babies lack clear vision shortly after birth? *Predict the Answer*: Not all neural connections are in place at birth. If you don't know, use POE to get rid of what you can. Choice (D) is way off (aqueous humor is in the eye). Glial cells do not deflect messages so (E) is out, and myelination is a tight coat of lipids, so watch out for (C).

100. **A** Choice (A) is the correct definition. None of the other choices applies. This is one of those questions for which only straight memorization will help you.

FREE-RESPONSE SECTION: ANSWERS AND EXPLANATIONS

1.   Essay number one is worth seven points. Points are given based on a student's ability to touch on certain theories and reference specific AP Psychology phenomena. Each essay is unique, but here is our run-down of what a student should definitely address in his or her Free Response Essay for this question:

- The "Big Five" trait of Openness to Experience: if Kai ranks high in this trait, he will enjoy the opportunity to perform in a new environment and do well; if he ranks low, he would prefer his usual environment and this might negatively affect his performance.

- Convergence (depth perception): Kai may have difficulty judging depth in the mid-distance; for example, following the snap to the holder, or seeing where the holder places the ball. But remember that he should be okay judging depth to the goalposts, because that is too far for convergence to be a factor.

- Cognitive dissonance: he believes in the importance of careful preparation, yet he was unable to practice. This discordance will cause him tension and this might negatively affect his performance. He could cope by changing his attitude; for example, he could rationalize that his excitement will overcome the lack of preparation.

- Social facilitation: since this is a simple, well-practiced skill, having other people around could enhance his performance. Not having others around will deprive him of this benefit. But the other side of that coin is that his knowing that the evaluators are around, even if he cannot see them, will still enhance his performance.

- Sympathetic nervous system: this arousal mechanism activates the fight-or-flight response. If he is nervous, this could negatively affect his performance. But you may wish to take this answer a step further and admit that his success as a kicker in the past has demonstrated that he is able to control this response in stressful situations, so he should do well in this situation.

- Non-declarative memory: kicking a football is a procedural memory that is relatively resistant to decay. Also worth noting is the fact that "muscle memory" should remain intact in a stressful situation.

- Self-efficacy: he believes that he is a capable kicker and this belief makes it more likely that he will succeed in a stressful situation.

2. Essay number two is worth seven points. Two points are awarded for defining classical conditioning and giving an example, plus explaining how it could be used to improve a prisoner's behavior. Two points are awarded for defining positive and negative reinforcement and giving an example of each, plus explaining how they could be used to improve a prisoner's behavior. Two points are awarded for defining shaping and giving an example, plus explaining how it could be used to improve a prisoner's behavior. One point is given for applying one of the learning techniques to modify a thief's behavior.

This is what our student chose to do for her essay. She scored a seven out of seven on this essay. Use this as a sample of a high-scoring essay.

Sample Essay

Although the concept sounds fine, prisons just don't seem to work. Instead of rehabilitating prisoners, they create a separate culture in which crime and criminal thinking are the norm. Instead of putting convicted criminals into a system that is destined to fail, a rehabilitation setting could be created using operant conditioning. Operant conditioning is the conditioning of behavior through the association of a desired behavior with some type of reward. For example, with animals, if a scientist wanted to teach a pigeon to peck only at selected artistic works, he could condition the pigeon to do so by rewarding him when he pecked at those works and punishing him when he pecked at others. The same thing could be done with criminals. To get a criminal to not want to commit a crime again, a psychologist could condition an aversive response into the criminal whenever he saw— and eventually whenever he thought of— the crime.

Another option would be to use positive and negative reinforcement to shape a criminal's behavior. Positive reinforcement, giving a reward to someone for doing the right thing, could be used to provide criminals with needed or desired items for X period of time of good behavior. Similarly, negative reinforcement is the removal of something bad as a reward for good behavior. Therefore, a criminal, who would most likely start out under serious restrictions, would be granted more and more freedom the longer he demonstrated the desired behavior.

Finally, shaping is a great way to mold someone's behavior. Shaping involves first praising actions that are remotely close to what you want to achieve, and then later praising actions only as they get closer and closer to the desired behavior. For example, at the beginning of the process, if a criminal does anything right, he is praised or rewarded. Then, after he begins to consistently demonstrate good behaviors, he is only praised or rewarded when he sustains that good behavior for longer and longer periods of time.

Shaping could be used to modify a thief's behavior so that he will never steal again. In the beginning, the thief is praised simply for using his own things. After he begins to consistently use his own things, the psychologist could begin to put him into more tempting situations, and then praise him when he doesn't take anything. Once the thief overcomes a low-level temptation— like the lunch room— he could be taken to a K-Mart, then a Macy's, then a jewelry store. Each time, he would be praised at first for lasting without taking anything for five minutes, then ten, and so on. Once the K-Mart didn't seem tempting anymore, he could be brought to the next level and again shaped into the right kind of behavior. This could not be accomplished in a prison setting because he would never be allowed out into the real world, so he would never overcome his temptations.

HOW TO SCORE PRACTICE TEST 1

Section I: Multiple Choice

$$\underline{\hspace{3cm}} \times 1.0000 = \underline{\hspace{3cm}}$$

Number Correct   Weighted
(out of 100)   Section I Score
(Do not round)

Section II: Free Response

Question 1: $\underline{\hspace{2cm}}$ $\times\ 2.7777 =$ $\underline{\hspace{2cm}}$
                (out of 7)   (Do not round)

Question 2: $\underline{\hspace{2cm}}$ $\times\ 3.5714 =$ $\underline{\hspace{2cm}}$
                (out of 7)   (Do not round)

AP Score Conversion Chart Psychology	
Composite Score Range	AP Score
107–150	5
90–106	4
73–89	3
56–72	2
0–55	1

Sum $=$ $\underline{\hspace{3cm}}$
                         Weighted
                      Section II Score
                      (Do not round)

Composite Score

$$\underline{\hspace{3cm}} + \underline{\hspace{3cm}} = \underline{\hspace{3cm}}$$

Weighted   Weighted   Composite Score
Section I Score   Section II Score   (Round to nearest
                                        whole number)

Part III
About the
AP Psychology
Exam

THE STRUCTURE OF THE AP PSYCHOLOGY EXAM

The AP Psychology Exam is divided into two sections with the following time allotments:

→ Section I—Multiple-Choice

100 questions . . . . 70 minutes

→ Section II—Free-Response

2 essay questions . . . . 50 minutes

Section I

Section I of the AP Psychology Exam contains 100 multiple-choice questions. You have 70 minutes to complete the section, and your Section I score counts for approximately two-thirds of your overall AP Psychology grade.

If you did a double-take when you saw that you are given only 70 minutes to do 100 questions, take a deep breath. Although having less than a minute per question poses a definite challenge, knowing certain techniques, which we will discuss in more detail in Part IV, will make this severe time constraint seem much less daunting.

Section II

Section II of the AP Psychology Exam consists of two free-response questions (aka essays). They each count for the same percentage of your grade, and you must answer both. Section II counts for approximately one-third of your AP Psychology grade. You have 50 minutes to complete BOTH essays—again, take a deep breath. Part IV will teach you strategies so that you can be a smart essay-writer. Plus, you will have several opportunities to practice writing essays before exam day. Use your tools and your practice tests to master this portion of the exam. When the time comes, you will have all the tools you need to create high-scoring essays in a limited period of time.

HOW THE AP PSYCHOLOGY EXAM IS SCORED

Your Section I score counts for approximately two-thirds of your overall AP Psychology Exam grade: 66 2/3 percent, to be exact. Why the unusual division? Only the College Board knows, and it's not saying. Regardless, you can still score well on this section with the techniques covered in this book. Similarly, Section II accounts for 33 1/3 percent of your total score. With this breakdown, you can think of the exam as totaling 150 points, with Section I accounting for 100 points and Section II accounting for the remaining 50 points.

How Much Is Each Section Worth?

Each of the two essays in Section II is worth 25 of the total 150 points, and each asks you to provide between 6 to 10 pieces of information. Based on data released by the College Board, most essays ask for 7 to 8 pieces of information. On average, each piece of information is usually worth a little bit more than 2 points.

Even with all this information, we don't know exactly how many points are needed to score a 5, but we know exactly how well students have performed in the past. The May 2019 score distribution is provided in the following table.

Score (Meaning)	Percentage of test-takers receiving this score	Equivalent grade in a first-year college course	Credit granted for this score?
5 (extremely qualified)	20.2%	A	Most schools (contact admissions department to verify)
4 (well qualified)	25.4%	A–, B+, B	Most schools (contact admissions department to verify)
3 (qualified)	18.8%	B–, C+, C	Some do, but some don't (contact admissions department to verify)
2 (possibly qualified)	13.7%	C–	Very few do (contact admissions department to verify)
1 (no recommendation)	22%	D	No

OVERVIEW OF CONTENT TOPICS

The multiple-choice questions in Section I cover the 14 main areas of psychology taught in most AP courses. The College Board gives a range for the number of questions devoted to each topic. For example, 8–10 percent of Section I will be devoted to social psychology. Except for history, approaches, and states of consciousness, the distribution remains fairly evenly spread out.

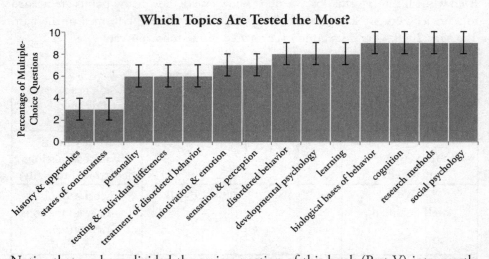

Which Topics Are Tested the Most?

Notice that we have divided the review portion of this book (Part V) into exactly those chapters for your convenience. Again, by focusing strictly on psychology as it's tested by the AP Exam, we'll teach you what you need to know to make the grade.

HOW AP EXAMS ARE USED

Different colleges use AP Exam scores in different ways, so it is important that you go to a particular college's website to determine how it uses those scores. The following three items represent the main ways in which AP Exam scores can be used.

- **College Credit.** Some colleges will give you college credit if you score well on an AP Exam. These credits count toward your graduation requirements, meaning that you can take fewer courses while in college. Given the cost of college, this could be quite a benefit, indeed.

- **Satisfy Requirements.** Some colleges will allow you to "place out" of certain requirements if you do well on an AP Exam, even if they do not give you actual college credits. For example, you might not need to take an introductory-level course, or perhaps you might not need to take a class in a certain discipline at all.

- **Admissions Plus.** Even if your AP Exam will not result in college credit or even allow you to place out of certain courses, most colleges will respect your decision to push yourself by taking an AP course or even an AP Exam outside of a course. A high score on an AP Exam shows mastery of more difficult content than is taught in many high school courses, and colleges may take that into account during the admissions process.

OTHER RESOURCES

There are many resources available to help you improve your score on the AP Psychology Exam, not the least of which are your **teachers**. If you are taking an AP class, you may be able to get extra attention from your teacher, such as obtaining feedback on your essays.

Another wonderful resource is AP Students, the official site of the AP Exams. The scope of the information at this site is quite broad and includes the following:

- Two free full-length practice tests from 1994 and 1999
- Free Response Question prompts from previous years
- Essay scoring guidelines
- Sample essay responses
- AP score distributions by year
- AP fee information, including fee reductions

The AP Students home page address is <u>apstudent.collegeboard.org/home</u>.

The AP Psychology Course home page address is <u>https://apstudents.collegeboard.org/courses/ap-psychology</u>.

Finally, The Princeton Review offers tutoring for the AP Psychology Exam. Our expert instructors can help you refine your strategic approach and add to your content knowledge. For more information, call 1-800-2REVIEW.

Note that the method for scoring multiple-choice sections changed after the May 2011 AP Psychology Exam, so when browsing older tests, make sure you also download the corrections from AP Students and that you compare the content to the course description.

Changes to the AP Psychology Course and Exam

The College Board recently announced that the course and exam have undergone revision beginning with the 2019–2020 academic year and the 2020 exam administration.

While this book was updated to align with the most recent information from the College Board as of Summer 2019, we recommend that you check your online Student Tools for any late-breaking news. See pages viii–ix for details.

You can also visit the College Board's AP Central page for this course: https://apcentral.collegeboard.org/courses/ap-psychology

Don't Forget!

Register your book online to access your AP Psychology Study Guide by following the directions on the "Get More (Free) Content" page!

DESIGNING YOUR STUDY PLAN

In Part I you identified some areas of potential improvement. Let's now delve further into your performance on Practice Test 1, with the goal of developing a study plan appropriate to your needs and time commitment.

Read the answers and explanations associated with the multiple-choice questions (starting at page 29). After you have done so, respond to the following questions:

- Review the content topics on pages 5–7 and, next to each one, indicate your rank of the topic as follows: "1" means "I need a lot of work on this," "2" means "I need to beef up my knowledge," and "3" means "I know this topic well."

- How many days/weeks/months away is your AP Psychology Exam?

- What time of day is your best, most focused study time?

- How much time per day/week/month will you devote to preparing for your AP Psychology Exam?

- When will you do this preparation? (Be as specific as possible: Mondays and Wednesdays from 3:00 to 4:00 P.M., for example.)

- Based on the answers above, will you focus on strategy (Part IV), content (Part V), or both?

- What are your overall goals in using this book?

Based on your answers to these questions, you should now have a better understanding of how to study for the exam. Use your answers to build a study plan that meets your specific needs based on the amount of time you have until test day. It is important to tailor your study plan to your schedule and topics you need to further review.

Part IV
Test-Taking Strategies for the AP Psychology Exam

PREVIEW

Review your responses to the questions on page 4 of Part I and then respond to the following questions:

- How many multiple-choice questions did you miss even though you knew the answer?

- On how many multiple-choice questions did you guess blindly?

- How many multiple-choice questions did you miss after eliminating some answers and guessing based on the remaining answers?

- Did you create an outline before you wrote each essay?

- Did you find any of the essays easier/harder than the others—and, if so, why?

HOW TO USE THE CHAPTERS IN THIS PART

Before you read the following chapters, think about what you are doing now. As you read and engage in the directed practice, be sure to consider the ways you can change your approach. At the end of Part III, you will have the opportunity to reflect on how you will change your approach.

Chapter 1
How to Approach
Multiple-Choice
Questions

OVERVIEW OF THE MULTIPLE-CHOICE SECTION

As we discussed in Part II, Section I of the AP Psychology Exam contains 100 multiple-choice questions that cover 14 main areas of psychology. You have 70 minutes to complete this section, and it counts for roughly two-thirds of your overall score. This time limit gives you less than one minute to answer each question. You might ask: "How can I possibly do well on this test when I have only about 42 seconds to answer each question?"

The answer: You do *not* need to work through all of the questions to do well on Section I of the AP Psychology Exam. In fact, smart testers often do not try to attempt every question and risk careless errors. Instead, smart testers choose which questions to tackle and which questions to simply guess on. "How do I choose?", you ask. To answer that question, let's take a closer look at the way the test is set up.

Order of Difficulty

If you have taken tests like the SAT, you may have noticed that each time you begin a multiple-choice section, you find the questions manageable or even easy. But after a while, the test seems to become more difficult. Finally, near the end of the test, you may feel overwhelmed, as though you don't know any of the answers. Lots of students attribute this phenomenon to time pressure or exhaustion. But there's something else going on.

Many multiple-choice tests, including the AP Psychology Exam, have test questions arranged in a rough order of difficulty. In other words, the first part of the test contains mostly easy questions, the middle of the test contains questions of medium difficulty, and the last third of the exam contains primarily difficult questions. Now, why would a testing company set up a test in order of difficulty? Think about it: the company is trying to assess the psychology knowledge of thousands of students. If they placed all the hard questions at the beginning of the test or stuck them in intermittently, lots of students with pretty good, but not great, psychology knowledge would get stuck on the early questions and never get to the questions they could answer. They would lose time, have trouble building momentum, and generally get bogged down. The results would show two groups—a high-scoring group (the students who know almost all of the material and can answer almost all of the questions) and a low-scoring group (everyone else)—as opposed to a nice bell curve (where most students score somewhere around the middle).

Easy Ones First, Please

When a test is arranged in order of difficulty, everyone starts out answering easy questions. As students work through the test, they will hit a point at which they begin to have trouble. Companies that write standardized tests assert that this stumbling point shows where a student's knowledge of a subject pretty much ends. Although this is open to debate, arranging a test in order of difficulty does create a more nearly fair test for everyone.

So What?

How does all this information help you? If the easiest questions are at the beginning of the exam, followed by questions of medium difficulty, and then the tough stuff, what is the point of rushing through the first questions to get to the questions you can't answer? Easy questions are worth just as much as difficult questions. Therefore, to score well on Section I, you need to slow down and get as many of the easy and medium questions right as you can.

How to Score Your Personal Best on Section I

- Get all easy questions right

- Get most medium questions right

- Do the right thing on hard questions*

*See "Do The Right Thing" later in this chapter.

In Chapter 3, we'll discuss in more depth how to pace yourself to maximize your score. Now, we'll introduce you to some specific multiple-choice strategies.

SMART-TESTER STRATEGIES

Your own knowledge of psychology will be the key to doing well, but certain strategies will help you stretch your psych knowledge and crack the trickier questions. Once you've mastered some of the smart-tester strategies, we'll talk about how you can develop your personal approach to Section I.

Smart-Tester Strategy #1:
Understand the Question/Key Words

How often have you zipped through a question and picked the obvious answer, only to find that you misread the question? The most important thing you can do to increase your score on Section I is to make sure you understand what you are being asked.

After you read a question, take a second to make sure you understand it. Put the question in your own words, or circle the key words in the question. Taking this first step will eliminate the possibility of your answering the wrong thing. Try the following example:

1. A person's refusal to accept an accurate diagnosis of a spouse's mental illness demonstrates the use of which of the following defense mechanisms?

How would you ask this question in your own words?

When someone doesn't want to accept really bad news, they are in...

Now the answer should be obvious: *denial.* By stating this question in everyday language, the answer pops out at you. Try another example:

19. The failure of bystanders to respond to a stranger's cries for help is sometimes explained as an instance of

How would you ask the question?

Why don't people do anything when someone is yelling "help"?

In the case of question 19, you may not know the answer off the top of your head, but clarifying the question makes you better prepared to deal with the answer choices.

Let's look at one more:

22. The dependent variable in the experiment above is

In this case, you don't need to put the question into your own words. However, you want to make sure you look for the right thing when you hit the answer choices. Therefore, circle the key words *dependent variable* before you head to the answer choices.

Understand the Question/Key Words

For each of the following questions, circle the key words in the question. Then, if appropriate, jot down in your own words exactly what is being asked. Answers are on page 304.

Answers are on page 304.

3. Angie is a scientist who is interested in the physical basis of psychological phenomena such as motivation, emotion, and stress. She is called a(n)

10. One of the primary tools of the school of structuralism was

18. Binocular cues provide important cues for depth perception because

35. Constance is presented with a list of words. When asked to recall the words, she remembers only the words from the beginning and the end of the list. This phenomenon demonstrates which of the following types of effect?

47. The recognition-by-components theory asserts that we categorize objects by breaking them down into their component parts and then

56. Veronica is competing in a regional gymnastics competition. As she waits for her turn on the mat, she ignores the sounds of the crowd and instead mentally reviews her routine. Veronica is managing an anxiety-producing situation by employing

Question Numbering
Whenever you start a question, check out the question number. It will tell you approximately how hard the question is (easy: 1–33ish; medium: 34–66ish; difficult: 67ish–100). We've numbered all the questions in this book to reflect their approximate difficulty.

70.   Which of the following was true of Stanley Milgram's studies of obedience?

88.   In their discussions of the process of development, the advocates of the importance of nurture in the nature-nurture controversy emphasize which of the following?

Smart-Tester Strategy #2: Predict the Answer

Once you've translated the question, you go to the answer choices, right? *Stop right there…* Do you really think it's that easy? Of course not, or everyone would get all the questions right. You need to do a little work before you get mired down in the answer choices.

Beware of the Answer Choices

Answer choices are not our friends. In fact, think about what it takes for a test writer to develop five answer choices for each question. First, she needs to write the correct answer, making sure it is accurate but not too obvious. Then, she has to put in at least one or two close second choices. Finally, she needs to fill in the remaining choices and move on to the next question.

When taking a standardized test, most students read the question and then read each answer choice. What they fail to realize is that the answer choices are riddled with tricks, traps, and distractors designed to bump them off course.

Enter: The Smart Tester

Unlike your less savvy compatriots, you are a smart tester. You know that if you have an idea of the answer before you read the answer choices, you won't be tempted to pick something that is way off base. You also know that, because four of the five choices you read are wrong, it's best to assume that an answer is wrong until proven right.

After you translate the question into your own words, answer it *in your own words.* Now, that may mean actually knowing the exact answer (as in the case of *denial*), or it may mean putting yourself in the right ballpark before looking at the answer choices. Sometimes, it's actually helpful to cover the answer choices to make your best prediction of what the answer should be. Then look at the choices and see which comes closest to your original thought. Let's look at one of the questions from your last drill:

3.   Angie is a scientist who is interested in the physical basis of psychological phenomena such as motivation, emotion, and stress. She is called a(n)

Question Types
Although many of the questions on Section I ask you for factual information, about 30 percent of the questions are application questions—questions that ask you to use your knowledge of psychology to address a given situation. Application questions are no problem as long as you understand the question first. Just be sure to *Understand the Question/ Key Words!*

First, how would you ask this question in your own words? Okay, now maybe you know the answer to this question, and maybe you don't. No problem. You can still answer the question before you look at the answer choices. If you can't spit out Angie's correct title immediately, answer the question by saying:

Angie is called a person who is into the physical basis of psychology.

With your answer in mind, look at each answer choice.

      (A)   psychologist
      (B)   anthropologist
      (C)   physical therapist
      (D)   paleontologist
      (E)   biopsychologist

Now, use your answer to find the credited response:

(A) Is a *psychologist* a person who's into the physical basis of psychology? No, this person is into more than just the physical basis.

(B) Is an *anthropologist* a person who's into the physical basis of psychology? No, an anthropologist is into cultures.

(C) Is a *physical therapist* a person who's into the physical basis of psychology? No, this person is not into the psychology part.

(D) Is a *paleontologist* a person who's into the physical basis of psychology? No idea what this person is.

(E) Is a *biopsychologist* a person who's into the physical basis of psychology? Yes.

Your answer? Choice (E), *biopsychologist*. By predicting the answer to the question before reading the answer choices, you were able to avoid getting tripped up in the first three answer choices. Plus, you realized the answer had to be (E), *biopsychologist*, without necessarily knowing anything about (D), *paleontologist* (a paleontologist studies fossils, by the way).

Smart-Tester Strategy #3: Process of Elimination (POE)

You have just learned your next big strategy: Process of Elimination (POE for short). Every time you answer a question, you will use POE, which means eliminating wrong answer choices and then choosing from what you have left. Why does it make sense to always answer questions this way? Because four of the five answer choices you read for each question are wrong. In other words, most of the answers you read on the test are wrong. Sometimes, it is much easier to identify two or three wrong answers on each question than it is to concentrate on finding the one right answer each time. By getting rid of two or three wrong answer choices on each question, you have substantially increased your accuracy and your guessing power.

Let's try another example:

> 97. Which of the following is an example of
>   metacognition?

Understand the Question/Key Words: Circle *metacognition*, and then define it:

Understanding cognitive (thought) processes.

Predict the Answer:

Find an example of people understanding how they think and learn.

Now, use POE to get rid of wrong answers:

> (A) Recognizing the faces of new in-laws after seeing
>   them only in pictures
> (B) Memorizing 100 words from the dictionary
> (C) Understanding the role of various parts of the
>   brain in perception
> (D) Accurately completing the logic in a deductive
>   reasoning problem
> (E) Knowing the effectiveness of different strategies
>   for learning statistical formulas

(A) Is *recognizing the faces* of people the same as understanding how one thinks and learns? No. Cross off this answer choice. Every time you decide an answer is not the one you want, cross it off.

(B) Is *memorizing* something the same as understanding how one thinks and learns? No. Cross it off.

(C) Is *understanding the role of various parts of the brain in perception* the same as understanding how one thinks and learns? Not sure? Keep it and read the rest.

(D) Is *accurately completing* a logic problem the same as understanding how one thinks and learns? No. Cross it off.

(E) Is *knowing the effectiveness of different strategies for learning* the same as understanding how one thinks and learns? Sounds pretty close.

By using POE, you were able to easily narrow your choices down to (C) or (E). Once you have it down to two, compare your choices. Which one is closer to the answer you came up with? In this case, the answer is (E). *Understanding the role of various parts of the brain in perception* is still only knowledge of fact, not of mental processes. Notice the word *understanding* was used in (C), and not by coincidence. By using POE, you were able to escape the trap and answer the question correctly. Did you notice that this was question number 97? (Remember, questions are arranged from least to most difficult, making highest-numbered questions the hardest.) Only about 20 percent of test-takers would answer this question correctly.

Meta What?

Okay, so POE is a great strategy, but what if you don't know what the key term in a question actually means? You have two choices: If this is a very hard question, which it was, you can simply skip it and come back to it if you have time. However, don't underestimate your knowledge. You may not be able to cough up the dictionary definition of metacognition, but you can pull the word apart. If you have spent more than a week in AP Psych class, you know that cognition has something to do with thinking. Then recall how you have heard the prefix *meta* used. How about metaphysics? So there's physics and metaphysics, and there's thinking (cognition) and meta-thinking (metacognition). It's probably some higher level of thinking. Although this rough definition may not get you to the exact answer, it will help you cross off some answer choices that will, in turn, help you make an educated guess.

Smart-Tester Strategy Review

Strategy #1: Understand the Question/Key Words: Read the question, and put it into your own words. Circle any key words or phrases that might point you in the right direction.

Strategy #2: Predict the Answer: Come up with your own answer to the question (exact or ballpark).

Strategy #3: Process of Elimination (POE): Cross off each answer that is not close to yours. Pick the best match.

More on POE

Now let's say you read a question and don't know the answer. All is not lost. You can use your brain, the information in the question, and POE to get to the answer (or at least to a fifty-fifty chance of guessing the right answer). Look at the following example:

74. Which of the following best supports the assertion that intelligence is at least in part inherited?

(A) Pairs of fraternal twins have a greater correlation of IQ score than do other pairs of siblings.

(B) Pairs of twins reared together have a greater correlation of IQ score than do pairs of twins reared apart.

(C) Pairs of identical twins have a greater correlation of IQ score than do pairs of fraternal twins.

(D) Adopted children and their adoptive parents have a correlation of IQ score that is greater than zero.

(E) Adopted children and their adoptive parents have a greater correlation of IQ score than do the same children and their biological parents.

Did you read the answer choices for question 74 before you answered on your own? Don't forget, wrong answers are designed to confuse, not to assist. Be sure to follow your smart strategy and *not* look at the answer choices too soon. First, let's do smart strategies for question 74.

Understand the Question/Key Words: Circle the words *intelligence* and *inherited*. Then restate the question:

> Which of the answers says genetics affects smarts?

Predict the Answer: If you answered, I don't know, no problem. Simply use what you do know and POE.

Use POE for each answer choice:

(A) Does the fact that *pairs of fraternal twins have a greater correlation of IQ score than do other pairs of siblings* indicate that genetics affects smarts? Careful—are fraternal twins any different genetically from other sibling pairs? If you are unsure, leave this choice and go on.

(B) Does the fact that *pairs of twins reared together have a greater correlation of IQ score than do pairs of twins reared apart* indicate that genetics affects smarts? No, it indicates the opposite because it implies that the nongenetic factors are more significant. Cross it off.

(C) Does the fact that *pairs of identical twins have a greater correlation of IQ score than do pairs of fraternal twins* indicate that genetics affects smarts? Yes. Identical twins come from one egg, while fraternal twins come from two, making fraternal twins genetically less similar. Keep this answer choice and read on.

(D) Does the fact that *adopted children and their adoptive parents have a correlation of IQ score that is greater than zero* indicate that genetics affects smarts? No, it indicates the opposite—nurture over nature. Cross this choice off.

(E) Does the fact that *adopted children and their adoptive parents have a greater correlation of IQ score than do the same children and their biological parents* indicate that genetics affects smarts? No, it also indicates nurture over nature. Cross it off.

You've at least narrowed it down to two choices without even really knowing the answer—that's pretty cool. Now look at the two choices you have not crossed off. Choice (C) very clearly shows genetics affects smarts, while (A) may or may not. What's your best guess? You got it: (C).

Even if you're left with two very hard answer choices to choose between, just choose one and move on. Don't sweat it; **there's no penalty for guessing**. And you can't score another point without moving on to another question!

There's no penalty for guessing, so don't leave anything blank! Maybe you don't spend time on every question, but take an educated guess on those you work on, and choose the same letter for all those you have no idea on or don't have time for. By using the same letter when guessing randomly (what we call your Letter of the Day, or LOTD), you will most likely guarantee yourself a couple extra points!

Your Personal Pace

It is imperative that you choose a pace that is efficient and effective for *you*. It doesn't matter if your best friend can complete the entire section in 30 minutes. You need to work at a pace that will allow you to do as many questions as you can while maintaining accuracy. Set your own personal pace and you will do your personal best.

HOW LONG IS 70 MINUTES?

Right about now you are probably thinking, "Nice idea, and I'll probably finish about 10 questions in 70 minutes following this strategy." Even though you don't need to work through every question on the test to do well, you do need to work efficiently and effectively.

As you know, rushing through the test and getting easy questions wrong is a bad idea. But how slow is too slow? After all, this is a timed test, and you do need to complete a significant number of the questions to do well.

Work Efficiently and Effectively

The best way for you to determine your own personal pace is to work efficiently (don't dawdle) and effectively (get right what you do answer). In other words, although you don't want to rush through and make careless errors, you don't want to spend all day on one question. Work at a pace that allows you to get questions right without dragging your heels. If you find yourself lingering for too long over a question, make a decision and move on. However, if you are doing some good, effective work on a question and have narrowed it down to two choices, don't lose the point because you "need to get to the next question."

Let's take a closer look at the order of difficulty to help you with this idea of working efficiently and effectively.

Question Difficulty, Redux

Easy Questions

- Tend to come early in the test

- *Always* ask about something you know

Even if you're on Question 3, if you don't know anything about the subject of the question, it won't be easy for you. Conversely, a question on the last third of the test may be tricky, but if you know the topic well, it won't be that hard for you.

How can you score your personal best? Use your smart strategies efficiently and effectively.

Easy Questions Drill

On easy questions, you will be able to accomplish these steps rapidly. Most short, easy questions will take very little time from start to finish. Try this drill, working quickly but carefully. Before you begin, jot down your start time. Once you have finished, note your end time and check your answers for accuracy. Remember, the goal is to be efficient (work rapidly) and effective (work accurately). Let's dive in and test drive those smart-tester strategies.

Start Time: _____

1. Sigmund Freud is thought of as the originator of which of the following perspectives of psychology?

   (A) Biological
   (B) Psychoanalytic
   (C) Behavioral
   (D) Humanistic
   (E) Cognitive

2. A person who is attempting to overcome a heroin addiction is experiencing hallucinations, tremors, and other side effects. These painful experiences associated with the termination of an addiction are known as

   (A) denial
   (B) transduction
   (C) withdrawal
   (D) transference
   (E) psychosis

3. After several trials during which a dog is given a specific type of food each time a light is lit, there is evidence of conditioning if the dog salivates when

   (A) the food is presented and the light is not lit
   (B) the light is lit and the food is not present
   (C) the food and the light occur simultaneously
   (D) a different kind of food is presented
   (E) a tone is sounded when the food is presented

4. The basic unit of the nervous system is called the

   (A) soma
   (B) axon
   (C) cell
   (D) neuron
   (E) synapse

5. Which of the following methods of research is central to the behaviorist perspective?

   (A) Inferential statistics
   (B) Naturalistic observation
   (C) Surveying
   (D) Case study
   (E) Experimentation

End Time: _____

Right: _____

Turn to page 304–305 to check your answers. How did you do? Remember, if you finished in two minutes but missed even one question, you were working too fast. Don't throw away points on the easy questions.

By the Way…

The more psychology you have under your belt, the easier this test will be. The strategies you are learning here are designed to make the most of the psychology knowledge you possess—to keep you from missing answers to questions that you should be getting right. The strategies will also help you stretch your knowledge so you can answer questions about topics you only sort-of know. However, although they will help you make smart guesses, the strategies won't make a question on a completely unfamiliar topic easy.

Medium Questions Drill

You will spend most of your test time on the medium questions. These are the questions that you will know, or sort-of know, but will need to answer very carefully so you don't lose points to tricks and traps. Try the next five questions as you did on the previous drill, working more slowly but still efficiently and effectively, that is, using the strategies that we've been discussing throughout this chapter.

Start Time: _____

33. The primary drives of hunger and thirst are, for the most part, regulated by which of the following?

   (A) The medulla oblongata
   (B) The thalamus
   (C) The hypothalamus
   (D) The kidneys
   (E) The adrenal glands

34. Imposing order on individual details in order to view them as part of a whole is a basic principle of which of the following types of psychologists?

   (A) Behaviorist
   (B) Psychodynamic
   (C) Humanistic
   (D) Gestalt
   (E) Cognitive socialist

35. To determine the number of students in the school who own personal computers, a school bookstore decides to survey the members of the introductory computer science class. A problem with this study is that

(A) the survey may not elicit the information the store is looking for
(B) the store is not surveying a representative sample of students
(C) the survey is being constructed without a hypothesis
(D) it is unclear as to whether the bookstore will be able to establish causation
(E) the survey is being given during school hours

36. When an individual looks through the window in the morning, the two regions of the cortex that are stimulated are

(A) the temporal lobes and the occipital lobes
(B) the parietal lobes and the frontal lobes
(C) the frontal lobes and the temporal lobes
(D) the temporal lobes and the parietal lobes
(E) the occipital lobes and the parietal lobes

37. Which of the following statements is true of behaviorism?

(A) It holds that most behaviors are the result of unconscious motives that come into conflict.
(B) It focuses on the development of the cognitive self in regard to behavior.
(C) It holds that development is largely a product of learning.
(D) It emphasizes the role of nature over the impact of nurture.
(E) It was developed to replace the cognitive and humanistic perspectives.

End Time: _____

Right: _____

Turn to pages 305–306 to check how you did this time. If you missed a question, no big deal. (All the questions in the above two drills are about topics covered in the first two psych-review chapters of this book, so you'll have a chance to review them if you had trouble.) If you missed more than one question and were finished in less than five minutes, you were working too fast. Slow your pace, and pick up your accuracy.

Long Questions

You may have noticed on the medium drill that some questions have much longer answer choices than others. In the earlier sections of the test, you will have a *long-answer* question about every seven or so questions. Near the later part of the test, a long-answer question will occur more frequently. Throwing in questions with long answer choices is one of the ways a test writer can make a question more difficult and more time-consuming.

To Skip or Not to Skip

Should You Ever Leave a Question Blank?

Maybe you skip it for later, but make sure to bubble in a response through POE and common sense, or your Letter of the Day if you are completely lost.

Imagine yourself taking Section I. You're cruising along through the easy section, feelin' fine. Suddenly, you hit a speed bump. Question 10, a question that should be easy, seems much harder than you would expect. Keep in mind that no order of difficulty is perfect for each individual, especially on an exam that is testing each individual's knowledge of a particular subject. Chances are this particular question is either a misplaced difficult question, or it's about a topic you don't happen to know very well. In any case, does it make sense for you to spend several minutes on question 10 when there are 90 questions to go, many of which will be easier for you than this one? Of course not. Remember, this is your test—you should take it in the order that is best for you. If you have time, circle it and come back. If you have no idea, bubble in your Letter of the Day and move on!

Are We There Yet?—The Toughest Third

How about those tough questions? Should you just skip all of them? Of course not. You should work efficiently and effectively through the easy and medium portions of the test, making sure that you've gotten as many points as you can from those sections. With your remaining time, you should work your way smartly through the most challenging questions.

Once you pass question 70, you can be pretty sure that you have entered the most difficult third of the test. Even without looking at the question number, you can often tell when you've hit the difficult third because, suddenly, every question requires a lot more brainpower than before. How can you get the most points out of this portion of the test?

Do the Right Thing. As we've mentioned, a question is difficult not only if it appears in the tough section of the test, but also if it is about a topic with which you are unfamiliar. Conversely, if you know a particular topic well, a question about it that happens to appear in the difficult portion of the test need not be difficult. Therefore, once you pass question 70, *Do the Right Thing!* This means, you should read each question first to see if you are familiar with the topic. If you are, go for it. If it sounds like Greek, skip it (draw a box around it so you can come back to it). If you are familiar with the topic of a question, proceed as usual but with caution. Remember, this question was placed late in the test because it is somehow more difficult than the rest. Be sure to use your smart-tester strategies: Understand the Question/Key Words, Predict the Answer, and POE. If you get it down to two choices and don't know which one is correct, make a smart guess and move on. You have a fifty-fifty chance of guessing correctly, so you are a lot better off than when you started.

Smart Guessing = Common Sense. Sometimes you will be familiar with the topic of a question, but not enough to answer the question. In addition to using your usual strategy, you can also use your common sense, and the information you do have, to use POE and then take a smart guess. Look at the following example:

87. Which of the following most accurately lists the stages of Hans Selye's general adaptation syndrome?

    (A) Shock, anger, self-control
    (B) Appraisal, stress response, coping
    (C) Alarm, resistance, exhaustion
    (D) Anxiety, fighting, adapting
    (E) Attack, flight, defense

Now, let's assume you have no idea what Hans Selye's general adaptation syndrome is. You can still follow the smart strategy, and use your common sense to get close to the answer.

Understand the Question/Key Words: Circle *general adaptation syndrome*. Think about what that term might mean:

It has something to do with adapting, and it's a syndrome, which often means something negative.

Predict the Answer: Stages of adaptation that seem to characterize a kind of syndrome.

Use POE:

(A) Are *shock, anger,* and *self-control* stages of adaptation that characterize a kind of syndrome? No, a syndrome would not end up in self-control. Cross it off.

(B) Are *appraisal, stress response,* and *coping* stages of adaptation that characterize a kind of syndrome? No, they seem much more normal and positive. Cross it off.

(C) Are *alarm, resistance,* and *exhaustion* stages of adaptation that characterize a kind of syndrome? This is the most feasible choice so far. Keep it and read on.

(D) Are *anxiety, fighting,* and *adapting* stages of adaptation that characterize a kind of syndrome? Again, a syndrome would not have a last stage of adapting. Cross it off. Don't let the word *adapting* in this choice throw you off.

(E) Are *attack, flight,* and *defense* stages of adaptation that characterize a kind of syndrome? This one also has negative attributes that could constitute a syndrome.

You are left with (C) and (E). Take a guess, and remember that you have narrowed your choices down to a fifty-fifty shot on a question about which you had no clue. The correct answer, by the way, is (C). Given that the name of the syndrome is the "general adaptation syndrome" and not the "best way to cause a fight" syndrome, (C) is your smarter guess.

Here's another example of how your common sense can help you eliminate wrong answers:

(A)   Personal conscience is innate, and all human beings develop it at the same rate.

(B)   By adulthood, all people judge moral issues in terms of self-chosen principles.

Hey, wait a minute. Where's the question? We've given you these two answer choices to demonstrate how common sense can play an important role in getting rid of wrong answer choices. Let's evaluate these two answer choices. Choice (A) says that *personal conscience is innate, and all human beings develop it at the same rate*. Does that sound accurate? Even without knowing the question, it is hard to imagine that any psychologist would suggest that all human beings develop personal conscience at the same rate. You know this answer cannot be the answer to the question simply by using common sense. Cross it off.

How about (B): *By adulthood, all people judge moral issues in terms of self-chosen principles*. Again, is this statement true? Even if a lot of people judge moral issues in terms of self-chosen principles, it is rare that all people ever do anything the same way. The extreme language of this answer choice can help you determine that it is wrong. Without even knowing the question, you are able to eliminate two answer choices by using your common sense.

Be Selective. In dealing with hard questions, remember that you don't need to work through them all. You choose the difficult questions you want to do and in what order you want to do them. For example, after question 70, you may wish to concentrate on all the short-answer questions because the long-answer questions are more time-consuming and difficult. Place a box around each question you skip so that you can go back to them, and make sure to be careful when bubbling in your answer sheet. If there are particular questions you want to attempt, mark them with a star.

CREATE YOUR PERSONAL PACING STRATEGY

Finally, you will score your best on Section I of the AP Psychology Exam by developing your own optimal strategy. Use the tools we have given you; practice them to make them second nature (the strategy drills in Chapter 4 will help you fine-tune your skills). Once you are comfortable with your question strategy, do some timed work to help determine your personal pacing strategy. As you strengthen your test-taking skills, try to finish more and more of Section I. Determine what working *efficiently and effectively* means for you. And remember, you have an essay portion that will contribute to your final grade, as well. Emphasize your strengths to get the best grade you can. Oh yeah, and you'd better review some psychology, too!

Chapter 2
How to Approach
Free-Response
Questions

OVERVIEW OF THE FREE-RESPONSE SECTION

Section II: free response. It has a nice ring to it, doesn't it? That word *free* gives it a melodic sound. Well, don't be fooled. On the AP Psychology Exam, "free response" is simply a euphemism for *timed essays*. Let's review the facts about Section II.

- You are required to answer two essays.

- There is no choice—two essays are presented, and you must do both.

- Each essay is worth $16\frac{2}{3}$ percent of your score, or 25 out of the 150 points on the exam.

- Each essay has a specified number of pieces of information you need to provide, usually between 6 and 10.

How Do They Score Them?

Before the graders begin reading essays, they are given a "checklist" of points they should look for. The AP Psych bigwigs determine exactly how many points each essay is worth by doing a count. Keep in mind that the readers are locked into that scale—they will not give you an extra point for unrelated information or anything else.

Sound Familiar?

Often, when a student realizes he needs to write an essay under timed conditions, panic sets in. As he begins to read the question, his heart races, and he has difficulty concentrating on what the question is asking. He knows he should outline something, but he is afraid he will run out of time, so he just jumps in and starts writing. Midway through paragraph one, feeling a little light-headed, he realizes that he doesn't really understand the question. He glances back at the question but, worried that he's losing precious minutes, decides he needs to forge ahead.

Partway through paragraph two (yes, he did remember to use paragraphs), he realizes that he has skipped a big point he needs to make. Should he cross off what he has written, or do the verbal backpedal until he can work it in? "How much time is left, anyway?" he asks himself. And on it goes.

Relax: All of us at one time or another have felt our sympathetic nervous system kick into gear at the mention of a timed essay. How can you effectively write not one but two essays in a limited period of time? By being a smart tester, of course.

SMART-TESTER ESSAY WRITING

Compare the smart tester's approach to our panicked tester from above. The smart tester knows that she can't write an effective essay without understanding the question. She spends her first 1–2 minutes "working the question over," pulling it apart to make sure she knows exactly what she is being asked to do. Next, she sets up a chart and spends 3–5 minutes outlining the points she will make. She then counts up her points and sketches out the layout of the essay.

In that first 7–10 minutes, the smart tester has done the bulk of the work for her essay without actually writing a word of it. She can then spend the next 15 minutes writing the essay, whose framework she has already created; no skipped points, no major cross-outs. She may even be able to put in some impressive vocabulary. Spending time planning the essay actually gives you more time for writing the essay.

Be the Smart Tester

Because you have read this far in the book, you must be a smart tester. We're now going to teach you all the secrets of writing a great essay (or two, for that matter) without activating your adrenal glands. To become the smart essay writer, you first need to know what the readers—the people who will grade your essays—are looking for.

What's in an Essay

There are lots of different ways to write a quality essay. However, you have a more specific goal in mind when it comes to the AP Psychology essays—you want to get points. Therefore, you need to know what the graders want so that you can write an essay that will earn a good score. Let's start by taking a peek at what they say they want from a good essay.

According to the College Board's published materials on the AP Psychology free-response questions, you are expected to do the following:

- Describe an overarching framework.

- Be specific in both your references to and discussion of psychological principles or problems.

- Cite evidence and examples to illustrate your explanations.

- Clearly state the intent of your evidence (to support or contrast a claim).

- State your points clearly and directly.

"Huh?" you ask. Let's simplify. To get a good score on an AP Psych essay, you should do the following in order to make it easy for the grader to award points to you:

- Get right to the point—a sentence or two is enough of an introduction.

- Use psychology terms and proper names of theories, theorists, and so on.

- Define all terms.

- Support everything with an example or study, preferably from your course work (*not* an example from your own personal life).

- Clearly state the purpose of the example or study (support or contrast).

- Be clear, concise, and direct.

- Underline all key terms.

What Not to Do

In addition, there are a few no-nos that the College Board implies or states outright.

- Do *not* restate the question in your essay.

- Do *not* suggest anything that can be misconstrued as unethical.

- Do *not* write everything you know on the topic; stay focused on the question.

- Do *not* spend a lot of time writing your introduction and conclusion.

- Do *not* begin writing until you have a clue about what you are going to write.

Beginning to get the picture? Although this may seem like a tall order, let us ease your mind a bit: each of your essays will receive approximately five minutes of the reader's time. What? All that work for a lousy five minutes? Yup. Check out how AP essays are scored.

The Reading

After the AP Exams are given, the College Board and ETS get together a slew of high school teachers and college professors and stick them in a room for six days to do nothing but read essays. ETS and the Board fondly refer to this process as the Reading (always capitalized). During the Reading, the readers are typically required to read hundreds of essays.

The readers first create a rubric by which to grade the essays. Most essays require between 6 and 10 pieces of information. Each essay is then read, and a point is given for each required component covered accurately and completely. The points are then added together; most recently, each essay was worth 7 points. Here's an example. A particular essay question has 10 required pieces of information, of which you wrote accurately and completely about 7. In this case, 2.5 is the multiplier because there were 10 points available ($2.5 \times 10 = 25$). Because you supplied 7 pieces of information correctly and accurately, 7 is multiplied by 2.5, giving you 17.5 out of a possible 25. Note that there are no deductions—just points given for discussing the information correctly and completely. Your essay may be read and scored by a number of readers. For the most recent essay questions, you can read the individual rubrics and required information at collegeboard.org.

Talkin' About Good News

This is all good news for you because it means that you can put together a high-scoring essay without panicking about time constraints and exact wording. Let's work through the smart-tester strategies for writing a high-scoring essay, and then finish up with some pointers for adding the polish.

Smart-Tester Strategy #1: Work It

Imagine you are in the boxing ring of the AP Psychology Championship. You have already sustained 70 minutes of multiple-choice sparring, and now you have to take on two more big questions in 50 minutes to come out the winner. When the proctor says "go," you come out of your corner ready to take on that essay question. You're not hanging back, passively reading the question, hoping to understand it. If you took that approach, you'd get pummeled, and so would your score. Instead, you get in there and work it over; you pull it apart, examine each piece, and determine what the important stuff is.

Work It

The first step is reading the entire question. Then, start taking it apart piece by piece.

1. Although popular in American culture, the efficiency of the "time-out" method in modifying children's behavior is under much debate.

Now you should "work over" the above statement. Circle the trigger words—words that indicate transitions and changes in the direction of the sentence—and then underline the critical terms. Make notes as needed to ensure that you understand the point of the sentence.

Here's what we did:

1. (Although) popular in American culture, the efficiency of the "time-out" method in modifying children's behavior is under much debate.

Popular here, but does it work?

Smart-Tester Strategy #2: Chart It

Most Section II essay questions begin with a statement like the one we just saw and then go on to ask you to do some detailed stuff. Often, the essays have two parts (A and B) that you have to write about. Look at one part at a time:

A. Basing your answer on psychological knowledge, discuss both the pros and cons of the time-out in regard to each of the following:

Attachment

Cognitive Development

Adult Relationships

Let's work Part A together. The first phrase emphasizes the importance of using what you have learned, not just what you feel about the subject. This is the AP Psychology Exam, after all. Next, the statement says to discuss both the pros and cons of time-out in regard to the three topics. Before you go any further, draw a chart next to the list of three topics. At the top of one column, write "pro," and at the top of the other, write "con." You know you have to do at least two things for each of the topics: address the pros of each in regard to the time-out and then the cons. The chart will help you keep track of what you are doing.

Next, look at each topic to make sure that you can 1) define it and 2) illustrate it. Before you can list the pros and cons for any of the three topics, you will need to clarify what each is and give an appropriate example. You may wish to add a column to your chart in front of the other two that reminds you to define and illustrate each term.

This is what Part A should look like now:

A. ~~Basing your answer on psychological knowledge~~, discuss both the (pros) and (cons) of the <u>time-out in regard to each of the following</u>:

	def/illus	pro	con
Attachment			
Cognitive Development			
Adult Relationships			

So far, so good. Now let's look at Part B:

B. Explain how the following methods of teaching behavior could be used <u>instead of the time-out</u>:

Shaping

Positive Reinforcement

Once again, mark the critical stuff—what are you being asked to do? Define each method, and illustrate how each could be used in place of time-out. Draw a chart with two columns: "define" (you should always define the term even if the question doesn't ask you to) and "use instead" (illustrate how this method will be used in place of the time-out). Here's how the chart should look:

But Wait, There's More

You're well on your way to a great essay, but there are a few more things you need to do. And don't worry about this taking a long time; it won't after a little practice. Let's put everything together and look at what we have:

1. (Although) popular in American culture, the efficiency of the "time-out" method in modifying children's behavior is under much debate.

Popular here, but does it work?

    A. ~~Basing your answer on psychological knowledge,~~ discuss both the (pros) and (cons) of the time-out in regard to each of the following:

	def/illus	pro	con
Attachment			
Cognitive Development			
Adult Relationships			

    B. Explain how the following methods of teaching behavior could be used instead of the time-out:

	define	use instead
Shaping		
Positive Reinforcement		

Before you write your essay, fill in your charts. Blank charts are not going to make your life easier. If you jot just a few notes under each column, you will be able to better organize your thoughts before you begin writing. Let's do the first part of A together:

    For the "Attachment" part of A, write the following in your first column:

    Bond with parents, ex. geese, separation anxiety

You will define attachment in your essay as critical bonding with primary caregivers (parents). The first column shows that you plan to emphasize the critical nature of this attachment by explaining imprinting—the tendency of young animals, such as goslings, to attach to the first moving object they see (presumably their mother). Next, you will underscore the importance of human attachment with an explanation and illustration of separation anxiety.

But What If?

What if you are unfamiliar with the topics the essay is addressing? Unfortunately, there's no way to fabricate your way to a good essay. You need to get working on those review chapters. The stuff you need to know to answer this question can be found in Chapter 13: Developmental Psychology.

What are the pros and cons of time-out in regard to attachment? Jot notes in your pros column such as:

> Not many, authority figure, should attach after time-out

These notes indicate that the time-out is not a benefit to attachment. However, it does establish the parent as the authority figure and can be done without significant damage to attachment if loving attachment is pursued at the conclusion of the time-out.

> How about cons?

> Mistrust of parent, separation anxiety

The time-out may in fact lead to problems associated with attachment, such as mistrust of the parent's care and affection or problems associated with separation anxiety. By taking the time to jot down your thoughts, you ensure that your essay is well on its way to being written—and written well, for that matter. Continue this process for the points of Part A and Part B.

Smart-Tester Strategies #1 and #2

Let's review. Smart-Tester Strategy #1: Work It—work the question over so that you know exactly what you are being asked. While you are working over the question, you will also begin to do Smart-Tester Strategy #2: Chart It—draw your charts and, if you feel comfortable, fill them in at the same time (why add another step?). You may wish to give the question a quick read-through before you begin, but you don't need to artificially separate working the question from writing your outline. This entire process should take you between five and seven minutes.

Smart-Tester Strategy #3: Count It

Remember, we said that your essay is scored on a scale ranging from 0 to usually between 6 and 10. You can actually estimate what that number is and use that information to make sure that you don't lose any points. Once you have finished the Work It and Chart It steps, take a minute to number all the possible points that you could earn. A point is given for each of the main things you are asked to do in a given essay. Flip back to the time-out essay question and number each part that you would consider "point-worthy." Then count up. We'll wait here.

Finished? What did you get? If you counted 13 points, that's right. Here's how we got it:

> If you write your essay well, you will get 3 points for each of the three categories in Part A (attachment, cognitive development, and adult relationships)—1 point will be awarded for defining each term, 1 point will be awarded for illustrating a con argument, and 1 point for having a pro argument. Therefore, Part A is worth 9 points.

Part B is worth 4 points—1 point for each of the two topics that you address: 1 point awarded for the definition of each term and 1 point for each explanation of how they can be used instead of time-out. Part B is typically awarded fewer points than Part A.

Why should you care about how many points an essay is worth? Because you don't want to miss a major component and, consequently, lose points. You also will use this information to complete the last smart-tester strategy before you start to write the essay.

Smart-Tester Strategy #4: Sketch It

Sketch out your essay in the one minute or so before you begin to write. Insert your "points" so that you know exactly how the whole thing is organized. Then use your sketch as your checklist while you write your essay.

First, draw a box to represent a paragraph. In the box, write the word *open* so that you don't forget your opening line and then insert the first points you will make:

Open
1   define and illustrate attachment
2   pros and cons re: time-out and attach.

Each time you think you need a new paragraph, draw a new box and insert your points.

3   define and illustrate cognitive dev.
4   pros and cons re: time-out and cogn. dev.

5   define and illustrate adult relationships
6   pros and cons re: time-out and adult relat.

7   define shaping—use instead of time-out
8   define pos. reinforcement—use instead of time-out
Closing

But What If?

What if you don't know one of the terms in the question? Remember, you will get no points for supplying no information, so do your best to analyze (pull apart) the possible meaning of the word and then make up an answer.

Smart-Tester Strategy #5: Write It

Now that you have a sketch, your essay will practically write itself. You just need to piece it together in a clear, concise manner. As you write, check off each point on your sketch as you complete it. That way you'll be sure not to skip anything. Keep in mind that the readers will not grade your charts or outlines. The essay must be written in paragraph form. Be sure to write in complete sentences. Don't use symbols or bulleted lists to define or give examples. If you are running out of time, continue writing pertinent information. Your essay should take about 10 to 15 minutes to write. Then it's on to the second essay!

The Opening

Did you think we'd desert you without first guiding you through the actual writing? Never! Let's review how to get a good score according to the College Board.

Essay-Writing Guidelines

- Write an introductory sentence that is *not* a repeat of the question.

- Use psychology terms and proper names of theories, theorists, and other important concepts.

- Define and underline all key terms.

- Support everything with an example or study, preferably from your course work (*not* an example from your own personal life).

- Clearly state the purpose of the example or study (support or contrast).

- Be clear, concise, and direct.

First, write an opening. Your opening sentence needs to introduce what you are going to say and to incorporate what the question says *without* simply rewriting the question. Restating the question is a big pet peeve of the College Board. Let's try an opening sentence for the "time-out" essay:

> In the United States, the "time-out" has become an acceptable means of dealing with inappropriate behavior of children, but it may have both positive and negative effects on the development of our youth.

Pretty good, huh? It says what it needs to, introduces your point, and tells the reader that you are going to look at both sides of the issue. From here, jump right into your discussion of attachment.

Choose Your Words Wisely

The more appropriate psychological terms you use, the better the point-value of your essay. In the "time-out" essay, a point-getter is to use the term *separation anxiety*, relating to attachment issues. Even though the readers are scanning your essay pretty quickly, they have been trained to look for appropriate psychological terms. When they see one, they will slow down (possibly even smile a little) to read more carefully. But remember this, you cannot earn points if you do not define, illustrate, or give an example of the psychological term.

Examples, Examples, Examples

All the College Board literature clearly states that the graders like, and often expect, to see students' points supported by appropriate examples. When inserting examples, remember the following:

1. Don't use examples from your personal life.

2. Make sure they are relevant to your point and make a clear reference to the question being asked.

3. Flag your examples with the words "for example."

A good example is something that you learned in your course, from your own reading, or from this book. A bad example is, "my little brother hates it when Mom puts him in time-out." Enough said.

Before you give the example, make it clear whether it is supporting your point or contesting your point. This procedure ties in perfectly with the third point about examples: always flag your examples with an introductory phrase. Again, the readers are reading your essay quickly. They will pause if they see an example and will be impressed by examples that are clearly delineated. If your example supports a point you just made, flag it with "for example." If it contrasts the point, insert a sentence that introduces it:

> Most will agree that the time-out is clearly an improvement over corporal punishment. However, attachment dysfunction can have far-reaching effects. For example...

Note that the word *however* introduces the change in direction of the paragraph. Putting your example after that sentence makes it clear that your example is in contrast to a previous point.

Closing

Once you have included all the points you need to make, write a final closing sentence that summarizes your overriding theme:

> Thus, while the time-out may have some benefits, the potential emotional scars it can leave behind should not be underestimated.

You tell 'em!

Plain, Good Writing

Finally, don't add in a lot of fluff. The AP Psych essay questions are pretty meaty. Your job is to write an essay that has no additives or fillers. At the same time, it's important that your essay be complete. Don't skip over points. Your reader is counting up the 8, or 9, or 10 points you are to make. If you miss one, you lose a point. That also goes for running out of time. There is no reason to run out of time on an essay, and if you do, it will hurt your score. To avoid this problem, use the plan below.

Essay Smart-Tester Strategies	Total Time 7–10 minutes
#1 Work It	1–2 minutes
#2 Chart It	3–5 minutes
#3 Count It	1 minute
#4 Sketch It	1–2 minutes

Essay Smart-Tester Strategies	Total Time 10–15 minutes
# 5 Write It	Keep track of your own time. Finish the essay before time is called.

Follow this same timetable for both essays. When you hit the 25-minute mark, you better hustle on to the second essay. If you are still working on essay number one, finish up as quickly as possible and move on.

Finishing Touches

There are just a few more things to make sure you get all the points you can. First, when you've finished an essay, double-check that you have addressed all the points you originally counted. Second, as you move from one thought to another, use trigger words and transitional phrases. For example:

Another important area to examine when considering the possible repercussions of the "time-out" is the cognitive development of children.

As compared with:

Cognitive development of children comes in stages.

Although there is nothing inherently wrong with the second sentence, the first sentence creates better flow and more overall cohesion to your essay.

Also, use the highest level of vocabulary that is comfortable for you. In other words, don't use too much slang, but don't write in a way that will sound awkward or forced. Do your best to use the most concise terminology possible. Misused words stick out like sore thumbs. Err on the side of caution.

TIME!

Don't rely on your proctor to keep the time accurately or to remember to give you the 25-minute warning. If, for some reason, your proctor is a flake, you won't be able to use that excuse to explain why your essay is only half done. Wear a watch, and keep your own time.

Lookin' Good

Lastly, remember that first impressions count. In the case of your essays, the better they look, the more positive a reader is likely to regard them at the outset. Readers can't help but feel better about an essay that is legible and long enough to appear complete. Make sure you indent the paragraphs and neatly cross out mistakes (if you need to).

Put It All Together

Now that you have the knowledge to be a smart essay writer, put your skills to the test on the following question. When you are finished, check your work against ours (pages 306–307). You can find many more sample prompts from real tests to practice on at apstudent.collegeboard.org/apcourse/ap-psychology/exam-practice. Good luck and good writing!

2. More and more, stress is being cited as a major contributor to both physiological and psychological problems.

    A. Define how stress can have both physiological and psychological consequences in light of each of the following scenarios:

        Daily hassles

        Significant life events

        Catastrophes

    B. What tactics can individuals employ to better cope with stress? Choose two methods that would effectively reduce the individual's stress level.

Chapter 3
Using Time
Effectively to
Maximize Points

BECOMING A BETTER TEST-TAKER

Very few students stop to think about how to improve their test-taking skills. Most assume that if they study hard, they will test well, and if they do not study, they will do poorly. Most students continue to believe this even after experience teaches them otherwise. Have you ever studied really hard for an exam and then blown it on test day? Have you ever aced an exam for which you thought you weren't well prepared? Most students have had one, if not both, of these experiences. The lesson should be clear: factors other than your level of preparation influence your final test score. This chapter will provide you with some insights that will help you perform better on the AP Psychology Exam and on other exams, as well.

PACING AND TIMING

Remember, when guessing randomly, choose a letter that you will use consistently, your Letter of the Day (LOTD). If you choose the same letter, odds are that one in five random guesses will be correct. If you guess entirely randomly, you may get them all right, or you may get none right.

A big part of scoring well on an exam is working at a consistent pace. The worst mistake made by inexperienced or unsavvy test-takers is that they come to a question that stumps them, and rather than just skip it, they panic and stall. Time stands still when you're working on a question you cannot answer, and it is not unusual for students to waste five minutes on a single question (especially a question involving a graph or the word EXCEPT) because they are too stubborn to cut their losses. It is important to be aware of how much time you have spent on a given question and on the section you are working. There are several ways to improve your pacing and timing for the test.

- **Know your average pace.** While you prepare for your test, try to gauge how long you take on 5, 10, or 20 questions. Knowing how long you spend on average per question will help you identify the number of questions you can answer effectively and how best to pace yourself for the test.

- **Have a watch or clock nearby.** You are permitted to have a watch or clock nearby to help you keep track of time. It is important to remember, however, that constantly checking the clock is in itself a waste of time and can be distracting. Devise a plan. Try checking the clock after every 15 or 30 questions to see if you are keeping the correct pace or whether you need to speed up. This will ensure that you're cognizant of the time but will not permit you to fall into the trap of dwelling on it.

- **Know when to move on.** Because all questions are scored equally, investing appreciable amounts of time on a single question is inefficient and can potentially deprive you of the chance to answer easier questions later on. If you are able to eliminate answer choices, do so, but don't worry about picking a random answer (try picking your Letter of the Day!) and moving on if you cannot find the correct answer. Remember, tests are like marathons; you do best when you work through them at a steady pace. You can always come back to a question you don't know. When you do, very often you will find that your previous mental block is gone, and you will wonder why the question perplexed you the first time around (as you gleefully move on to the next question). Even if you still don't know the answer, you will not have wasted valuable time you could have spent on easier questions.

- **Be selective.** You don't have to do any of the questions in a given section in order. If you are stumped by an essay or multiple-choice question, skip it or choose a different one. In the section below, you will see that you may not have to answer every question correctly to achieve your desired score. Select the questions or essays that you can answer, and work on them first. This will make you more efficient and give you the greatest chance of getting the most questions correct.

- **Use Process of Elimination on multiple-choice questions.** Many times, one or more answer choices can be eliminated. Every answer choice that can be eliminated increases the odds that you will answer the question correctly. Review the strategies in Chapter 1 to find these incorrect answer choices and increase your odds of getting the question correct.

Remember, when all the questions on a test are of equal value, no one question is that important, and your overall goal for pacing is to get the most questions correct. Finally, you should set a realistic goal for your final score. In the next section, we will break down how to achieve your desired score and ways of pacing yourself to do so.

GETTING THE SCORE YOU WANT

Depending on the score you need, it may be in your best interest not to try to work through every question. Check with the schools to which you are applying. Do you need a 3 to earn credit for the test? If you get a raw score of 68 (out of 100) on the multiple-choice section and do as well on the essays, you will get a 3.

AP Exams in all subjects no longer include a "guessing penalty" of a quarter of a point for every incorrect answer. Instead, students are assessed only on the total number of correct answers. A lot of AP materials, even those you receive in your AP class, may not include this information. It is really important to remember that if you are running out of time, you should fill in all the bubbles before the time for the multiple-choice section is up, using your LOTD. Even if you don't plan to spend a lot of time on every question and even if you have no idea what the correct answer is, it is to your advantage to fill something in.

The elimination of the guessing penalty in 2011 impacted the way tests were scored, so the College Board provided updated scoring information for their official AP Psychology released exams. Based on this data, 110 points are needed for a score of 5, 92 points for a 4, 72 points for a 3, and 61 points for a 2, on average. Because the College Board has not recently released its grading statistics, the following is an approximation of how to pace yourself on the multiple-choice section:

If you want to get a:	Work on this many:
2	60
3	70
4	80
5	90

Below is a table to give you an idea of how many questions you must get right and how you must do on the essays to get the score you need. Realize that these numbers are approximations and will vary from year to year depending upon test performance. From the data, it becomes readily apparent that you must attempt and perform well on the essays to have a chance to score a 4 or 5. As you take practice tests, you can use this information to evaluate how best to get the score you want and what areas of the exam are hindering your progress. You can approximately calculate your own score on the Practice Tests in this book using the worksheets on pages 46 and 370. There are multiple ways to achieve your desired score. It is important to remember that guessing is no longer penalized and that you must put in the energy and effort on the essays to perform well.

How the Average AP Score is Acquired		
AP Score Average Breakdown	Multiple-Choice Correct (out of 100)	Essay Score (out of two 7-point essays)
5	85	8
	80	10
4	75	6
	70	8
3	65	4
	60	5
2	55	2
	50	4

TEST ANXIETY

Everybody experiences anxiety before and during an exam. To a certain extent, test anxiety can be helpful. Some people find that they perform more quickly and efficiently under stress. If you have ever pulled an all-nighter to write a paper and ended up doing good work, you know the feeling.

However, *too much* stress is definitely a bad thing. Hyperventilating during the test, for example, almost always leads to a lower score. If you find that you stress out during exams, here are a few preemptive actions you can take.

- **Take a reality check.** Evaluate your situation before the test begins. If you have studied hard, remind yourself that you are well prepared. Remember that many others taking the test are not as well prepared, and (in your classes, at least) you are being graded against them, so you have an advantage. If you didn't study, accept the fact that you will probably not ace the test. Make sure you get to every question you know something about. Don't stress out or fixate on how much you don't know. Your job is to score as high as you can by maximizing the benefits of what you do know. In either scenario, it is best to think of a test as if it were a game. How can you get the most points in the time allotted to you? Always answer questions you can answer easily and quickly before you answer those that will take more time.

- **Try to relax.** Slow, deep breathing works for almost everyone. Close your eyes, take a few slow, deep breaths, and concentrate on nothing but your inhalation and exhalation for a few seconds. This is a basic form of meditation, and it should help you to clear your mind of stress and, as a result, concentrate better on the test. If you have ever taken yoga classes, you probably know some other good relaxation techniques. Use them when you can (obviously, anything that requires leaving your seat and, say, assuming a handstand position won't be allowed by any but the most free-spirited proctors). Additionally, chewing gum may help relax you, and studies have suggested that chewing gum before (but not during) an exam may increase your score.

- **Eliminate as many surprises as you can.** Make sure you know where the test will be given, when it starts, what type of questions are going to be asked, and how long the test will take. You don't want to be worrying about any of these things on test day or, even worse, after the test has already begun.

The best way to avoid stress is to study both the test material and the test itself. Congratulations! By buying or reading this book, you are taking a major step toward a stress-free AP Psychology Exam.

Chapter 4
Strategy Drills

USING THE DRILLS IN THIS CHAPTER

The drills in this chapter are designed to help you hone your test-taking skills before you begin your psychology review. Use these drills to practice the various smart-tester strategies you have learned.

DRILL 1: UNDERSTAND THE QUESTION/KEY WORDS

Before you can answer a question, you need to know what it is asking. To avoid careless errors, put the question into your own words before you try to answer it. On some questions, you may find it useful to circle the key word(s) in the question. Use the following drill questions to practice Smart-Tester Strategy #1: Understand the Question/Key Words. The answers are on page 307.

7. Which of the following best summarizes the differences between the psychoanalytic and the behaviorist perspectives?

22. Louis is suffering from severe headaches and occasional moments of disorientation or even mental paralysis. His doctors are interested in examining his brain for lesions. Which of the following technologies would prove most useful in examining various regions of Louis's brain?

39. The somatosensory cortex is the primary area of the

58. In the processing of visual information, a fully integrated image does not appear until the information has reached which of the following regions of the brain?

78. If a participant does not report a stimulus when no stimulus is present in a signal-detection experimental trial, it is known as a

89. The lower the p-value of a study, the

DRILL 2: PREDICT THE ANSWER

Before you even think about looking at the answer choices, you need to have an idea of what the answer to the question might be; otherwise, you will be adrift in a sea of confusion, tricks, and traps. Use the following questions to practice both Understand the Question/Key Words and Predict the Answer. Speaking of answers, see pages 307–308 to check your work on these questions.

5. Thomas knows how to roast meat, cook vegetables, and prepare salad. In order for him to learn to prepare a meal for 20 people, Thomas will most likely employ which of the following learning techniques?

What does the question ask?

What's your answer?

    22.   The endocrine system is a collection of glands that

What does the question ask?

What's your answer?

    35.   What was Wilhelm Wundt's contribution to the field of psychology?

What does the question ask?

What's your answer?

    45.   Which of the following best explains why regeneration is essential for taste receptors?

What does the question ask?

What's your answer?

    72.   Which of the following technologies is most useful in the study of brain waves?

What does the question ask?

What's your answer?

DRILL 3: USING ALL THREE

Now, practice the first two smart-tester strategies (Understand the Question/Key Words and Predict the Answer) and then find the "credited response" from the choices given. If you're having trouble, use POE to get your answers into the right ballpark. Once you've crossed off what you can, take a smart guess! Answers are on pages 308–309.

    15.   Of the following variables, which typically requires a measurement that is more complex?

Understand the Question/Key Words.

Predict the Answer.

    (A) Categorical
    (B) Continuous
    (C) Extraneous
    (D) Independent
    (E) Dependent

35. Which of the following most accurately states the role of the iris?

Understand the Question/Key Words.

Predict the Answer.

(A) To provide adaptive trait distinctions (eye color) within a species
(B) To dilate or constrict the pupil in order to regulate the amount of light that enters the eye
(C) To refract light that enters the eye, projecting it onto the retina
(D) To house the aqueous humor and supply the eye with oxygen and nutrients
(E) To transduce visual sensations into visual perceptions of color

42. The nature-nurture controversy concerns

Understand the Question/Key Words.

Predict the Answer.

(A) the question of determinism versus free will
(B) the degree to which the kinesthetic prowess of an individual overrides other aspects of intelligence
(C) the degree to which inborn processes versus environmental factors determine behavior
(D) the natural tendency of humans to nurture their young
(E) the role of unconscious processes as a determinant of behavior

66. Prior to the fall of the Berlin wall, East Berlin schools de-emphasized the individuality of the student. As a result, many of the children from those schools tend to have a(n)

Understand the Question/Key Words.

Predict the Answer.

(A) optimistic explanatory style
(B) pessimistic explanatory style
(C) internal locus of control
(D) external locus of control
(E) indiscriminant set of expectancies

85.   A prototypic example of a category is called a(n)

Understand the Question/Key Words.

Predict the Answer.

(A)   expectancy
(B)   defining feature
(C)   concept
(D)   phenotype
(E)   exemplar

DRILL 4: ESSAY DRILL

Before you can write a smart essay, you need to Work Over the Question, then Chart It, Count It, and Sketch It. Practice your smart essay steps on the following essay question. You don't need to write the full essay now, but if you feel like taking it all the way, go "write" ahead! Before you do, be sure to compare your smart steps with ours on pages 309–310.

1.   One of the major approaches to learning is classical conditioning.

A.   Explain the process of classical conditioning, defining and illustrating all necessary terms. Show how classical conditioning could be used to

(1) Condition a monkey to "appreciate" the works of only certain artists

(2) Teach a group of students a mathematical concept

B.   Explain how both extinction and spontaneous recovery transpire. Use one of the above examples to illustrate.

DRILL 5: POE

You are going to read an awful lot of wrong answer choices while working on Section I of the AP Psychology Exam. And, believe it or not, a lot of those choices are not only wrong, but also just plain silly. Using your knowledge of psychology, plus the information in the question itself, examine each of the following sets of answer choices to determine which is the best answer to the question. Remember, if it's silly, extreme, or fallacious, it cannot be the answer to any question. Check your POE smarts on page 311 when you're finished.

4.   Blah, Blah, Blah?
(A)   Obese people have fewer but larger fat cells than average-weight people.
(B)   Obese people have many more fat cells than average-weight people.

27. Connectionist approaches blah, blah

    (A) are carried out by individual segments of the
         brain
    (B) occur simultaneously through the action of
         multiple networks

47. Blah, blah, chunking?

    (A) Christina remembers two new phone numbers by
         recognizing that each has a familiar exchange
         and that the second half of each represents a
         familiar date in history.
    (B) Chelsea learns her times tables by methodically
         practicing one set each night and then
         reviewing with flashcards.

85. Blah, blah, person-centered psychotherapy blah

    (A) suppresses negative feelings that arise within the
         client
    (B) uses a didactic approach to teach the client to
         correct maladaptive behavior
    (C) accepts the client unconditionally so that his or
         her desire for healing will grow

92. Blah, blah, blah, blah, blah

    (A) repressing the client's deviant feelings
    (B) slowly altering the contingencies of
         reinforcement for the client
    (C) removing the underlying causes of a client's
         problems for the client

REFLECT

Think about what you've learned in Part III, and respond to the following
questions:

- How will you change your approach to multiple-choice questions?

- What is your multiple-choice guessing strategy? On which part of the test
  should you be most willing to guess?

- What will you do before you begin writing an essay?

- How will you change your approach to the essays, now that you know that
  graders are usually looking for 7 or 8 pieces of information on which to
  judge your essay?

- Will you seek further help, outside of this book (such as a teacher, Princeton
  Review tutor, or AP Students), on how to approach multiple-choice questions,
  the essay, or a pacing strategy?

Part V
Content Review for the AP Psychology Exam

HOW TO USE THE CHAPTERS IN THIS PART

You may need to come back to the following content chapters more than once. Your goal is to obtain mastery of the content you are missing, and a single read of a chapter may not be sufficient. At the end of each chapter, you will have an opportunity to reflect on whether you truly have mastered the content of that chapter. Bear in mind that this is NOT a comprehensive review; we strongly urge you to study your textbook and class notes, as well. If there is a topic that you don't fully understand or is not covered here, be sure to go through your textbook and ask your teacher about it well before test day.

Chapter 5
Foundations:
History

LOGIC, PHILOSOPHY, AND HISTORY OF SCIENCE

Psychology is the study of behavior and the mind. **Behavior**, a natural process subject to natural laws, refers to the observable actions of a person or an animal. The **mind** refers to the sensations, memories, motives, emotions, thoughts, and other subjective phenomena particular to an individual or animal that are not readily observed.

Psychology is a science because it uses systematic observation and the collection of data to try to answer questions about the mind, behavior, and their interactions. Psychology seeks to describe, predict, and explain behavior and the mental processes underlying behavior. As we discuss the history of psychology, we will encounter many theories that embody sets of assumptions and beliefs about the mind and behavior. In psychology, as in science in general, people tend to accept one theory and proceed under the assumptions of that theory. Psychologists accept the prevailing theory until sufficient data inconsistent with the theory is collected. At this point, what was the prevailing theory is replaced by another theory. Many theories are simply elaborations or revisions of previous ones. As you read over the history of psychology, pay attention to how theories relate to and influence one another.

The ancient Greeks were among the first to speculate on the nature of the mind. Socrates considered the philosophical issues of beauty, justice, and human rights. Socrates's student, Plato, argued that humans possess innate knowledge that is not obtainable simply by observing the physical world. Aristotle, a student of Plato, believed that we derive truth from the physical world. Aristotle's application of logic and systematic observation of the world laid the basis for the scientific method.

The questions raised by the early Greeks pertain to the concept of **dualism**. Dualism divides the world and all things in it into two parts: body and spirit. Dualism is a theme that recurs often in psychology. The distinction between body and spirit mirrors the current debate around the difference between the **brain** (that is, the command center of the central nervous system) and the mind (that is, the sensations, memories, emotions, thoughts, and other subjective experiences of a particular individual).

After the heyday of the Greek philosophers, there was a long period of time during which relatively little systematic investigation of psychological issues was conducted. This dearth of investigation was due, in part, to religious beliefs that said that the "spirit" portion of human nature could not be studied scientifically. These same prevailing theological views indicated that studying the natural world was only useful for what it demonstrated about God. These views changed with the advent of the scientific revolution (c. 1600–1700) when great discoveries were being made in biology, astronomy, and other sciences. These discoveries, along with corresponding movements in philosophy and art, made it clear that human nature was subject to scientific inquiry.

René Descartes (1596–1650) conducted some of the most important speculations on human nature. He believed that the physical world is not under divine influence but rather follows a set of observable laws or rules. The world and all of the creatures in it are like machines, in that they behave in observable, predictable ways. Descartes believed that humans were the exception to this rule because they possess minds. The mind, according to Descartes, is not observable and is not subject to natural laws. Descartes hypothesized that the mind and body interact, and the mind controls the body while the body provides the mind with sensory input for it to decipher. Descartes believed that this interaction occurs in the **pineal gland**, which is located deep within the brain at the top of the brain stem. Finally, Descartes realized that some body movements, which he named reflexes, are not controlled by the mind. A **reflex** is an immediate, unconscious reaction to an environmental event, such as pulling your hand away from a flame.

John Locke (1632–1704) extended Descartes's application of natural laws to all things, believing that even the mind is under the control of such laws. Locke's school of thought is known as **empiricism**—the acquisition of truth through observations and experiences. In his book, *Essay Concerning Human Understanding,* Locke proposed that humans are born knowing nothing; Locke used the term **tabula rasa** (Latin for "blank slate") to describe the mind of an infant. Almost all knowledge we have must be learned; almost nothing is innate. Locke felt that all knowledge must derive from experience. He emphasized nurture over nature as the greater influence on development.

Thomas Hobbes (1588–1679) believed that the idea of a soul or spirit, or even of a mind, is meaningless. Hobbes's philosophy is known as **materialism**, which is the belief that the only things that exist are matter and energy. What we experience as consciousness is simply a by-product of the machinery of the brain. Whereas Locke emphasized nurture over nature, Hobbes stressed the role played by nature. Hobbes's philosophy of materialism greatly influenced **behaviorism**, which will be discussed later.

The 19th century was a time of great discovery in biology and medicine. These discoveries influenced the science of psychology to varying extents; however, one new theory revolutionized science—the theory of natural selection. **Charles Darwin** (1809–1882) published *On the Origin of Species* in 1859. In this book, Darwin proposed a theory of **natural selection**, which said that all creatures have evolved into their present state over long periods of time. This evolution occurs because there exists naturally occurring variation among individuals in a species, and the individuals that are best adapted to the environment are more likely to survive to reproduce—and are likely to produce more successful offspring. Their offspring, in turn, will probably have some of the traits that made their predecessors more likely to survive. Over time, this process selects physical and behavioral characteristics that promote survival in a particular environment. **Evolutionary theory** set the stage for psychology by providing a way to explain differences between species and justifying the use of animals as a means to study the roots of human behavior.

Darwin in a Nutshell
Behavior evolves just like physiology: both function to help individuals survive.

Many credit **Wilhelm Wundt** (1832–1920) as the founder of the science of psychology. In 1879 in Leipzig, Germany, Wundt opened a laboratory to study consciousness. Wundt was trained in physiology and hoped to apply the methods that he used to study the body to the study of the mind. **Edward Titchener** (1867–1927) was a student in Wundt's laboratory and was one of the first to bring the science of psychology to the United States. Titchener sought to identify the smallest possible elements of the mind, theorizing that understanding all of the parts would lead to the understanding of the greater structure of the mind. This theory is known as **structuralism**, and it means looking for patterns in thought, which are illuminated through interviews with a subject describing his or her conscious experience. This interview process is known as **introspection**. For example, Wundt would manipulate a stimulus in front of a subject, ask him or her to describe the conscious experience, and then he would work to identify commonalities among participants' conscious descriptions.

William James (1842–1910) was an American psychologist who opposed the structuralist approach. Instead, he argued that what is important is the function of the mind, such as how to solve a complex problem. James, who was heavily influenced by Darwin, believed that the important thing to understand is how the mind fulfills its purpose. This function-oriented approach is appropriately called **functionalism**.

A number of major historical figures in psychology are discussed in the following chapters, as their work informs the units of study in AP Psychology. But other figures also play an important role in the history of psychology, due to both their individual accomplishments as well as the light they shed on the gender biases that affected their careers in particular and the field as a whole.

Dorothea Dix was crucial in advocating for the rights of mentally ill poor people, and she was instrumental in founding the first public mental hospital in the United States. **Mary Whiton Calkins** was the first female graduate student in psychology, although she was denied a PhD because of her gender. (She outscored all of the male students in her qualifying exams.) **Margaret Floy Washburn** was not only the first female PhD in psychology, she also served as the second female president of the American Psychological Association (APA), an organization formed in 1892. (**G. Stanley Hall** was its first president.) Although Washburn's thesis was the first foreign study published by Wilhelm Wundt, she was not allowed to join the official organization of experimental psychologists because of her gender.

Today, about two-thirds of doctorates in psychology are held by women, and about half of the presidents of the Association for Psychological Science have been women.

APPROACHES

The theories discussed above laid the groundwork for modern psychology as a science. This next section will deal with eight of the most prominent approaches to modern psychology. The roots of these approaches are in the theoretical perspectives we discussed above.

Approach 1: Biological

Biological psychology is the field of psychology that seeks to understand the interactions between anatomy and physiology (particularly, the physiology of the nervous system) and behavior. This approach is practiced by directly applying biological experimentation to psychological problems, for example, in determining which portion of the brain is involved in a particular behavioral process. To accomplish this, researchers might use CAT scans, MRIs, EEGs, or PET scans.

Approach 2: Behavioral Genetics

Behavioral genetics is the field of psychology that emphasizes that particular behaviors are attributed to specific, genetically based psychological characteristics. This perspective takes into account biological predispositions as well as the extent of influence that the environment had on the manifestation of that trait. For example, a person studying behavioral genetics might investigate to what extent risk-taking behavior in adolescents is attributable to genetics.

Approach 3: Behavioral

Behaviorism posits that psychology is the study of observable behavior. The mind or mental events are unimportant to the behaviorists, as they cannot be observed. **Classical conditioning**, first identified by Ivan Pavlov (1849–1936), was one of the behaviorists' most important early findings. Classical conditioning is defined as a basic form of learning in which a behavior comes to be elicited by a formerly neutral stimulus. **John Watson** (1878–1958) and his assistant Rosalie Rayner applied classical conditioning to humans in the famed Little Albert experiment. **B. F. Skinner** (1904–1990) was a behaviorist, who through the development of his Skinner Box, described operant conditioning in which a subject learns to associate a behavioral response with an environmental outcome. Although behaviorism is no longer the prevailing approach, many behavioral principles are still used in **behavior modification**—a set of techniques in which psychological problems are considered to be the product of learned habits, which can be unlearned by the application of behavioral methods.

Approach 4: Cognitive

Cognitive psychology is an approach rooted in the idea that to understand people's behavior, we must first understand how they construe their environment—in other words, how they think. This approach combines both the structuralist approach of looking at the subcomponents of thought and the functionalist approach of understanding the purpose of thought. Cognitive psychologists use a variety of methods, including reaction-time tasks, computer models, and participants' self reports, to better understand thought. The cognitive approach largely replaced the behavioral approach as the predominant psychological method used in the United States. It remains popular today, and this approach has influenced and blended with others.

Approach 5: Humanistic

The **humanistic approach** is rooted in the philosophical tradition of studying the roles of consciousness, free will, and awareness of the human condition. This is a holistic study of personality that developed in response to a general dissatisfaction with behaviorism's inattention to the mind and its function. Humanistic psychologists emphasize personal values and goals and how they influence behavior, rather than attempting to divide personality into smaller components. **Abraham Maslow** (1908–1970) proposed the idea of self-actualization, the need for individuals to reach their full potential in a creative way. Attaining **self-actualization** means accepting yourself and your nature, while knowing your limits and strengths. **Carl Rogers** (1902–1987) stressed the role of **unconditional positive regard** in interactions and the need for positive self-concept as critical factors in attaining self-actualization.

Approach 6: Psychoanalytic/Psychodynamic

While laboratory psychology was passing through its various theories, a very different approach to psychology was forming. **Sigmund Freud** (1856–1939) developed a theory of human behavior known as **psychoanalytic theory**. Freud was concerned with individuals and their mental problems. Freud drew a distinction between the **conscious mind**—a mental state of awareness that we have ready access to—and the **unconscious mind**—those mental processes that we do not normally have access to but are yet influenced by in some way. The interaction of the forces of the conscious and unconscious mind shapes behavior. Psychoanalytic theory stresses the importance of childhood experiences and a child's relationship with his or her parents to the development of personality. The focus of the psychoanalytic approach is on the resolution of unconscious conflicts through uncovering information that has been **repressed**, or buried in the unconscious. **Carl Jung** later expanded on the psychoanalytic theory with his concept of the **collective unconscious**, a part of the individual's unconscious which derives memory and knowledge from an ancestral memory, common to the human experience.

Approach 7: Sociocultural

Those subscribing to the **sociocultural approach** believe that the environment a person lives in has a great deal to do with how the person behaves and how others perceive that behavior. According to this approach, cultural values vary from society to society and must be taken into account when trying to understand, predict, or control behavior.

Approach 8: Evolutionary

Similar to the behavioral-genetics approach, the **evolutionary approach** focuses on the theories of Darwin. Behavior can best be explained in terms of how adaptive that behavior is to our survival. For example, fear is an adaptive evolutionary response; without fear, our survival would be jeopardized.

The distinctions among the different approaches in psychology are absolutely one of the most essential ideas for you to understand for the AP Psychology Exam. Let's use the common example of risk-taking in adolescence and explore that using each of the eight different approaches.

Approach	Question	Cause of Behavior	Methods
Biological	How is the physiology of high risk-takers different from that of non-risk-takers?	Physiology	Brain scans
Behavioral genetics	Which genes contribute to the development of risk-taking?	Genes	Genetic analysis
Behavioral	How does rewarding or punishing a risk-taker affect his or her behavior?	Learning and reflexes	Behavior modification
Cognitive	How do risk-takers think and solve problems?	Thoughts	Computer models of memory networks
Humanistic	How does the adolescent's self-esteem encourage or discourage risk-taking behavior?	Self-concept	Talk therapy
Psychoanalytic/ Psychodynamic	How might a child's early experiences affect risk-taking in adolescence?	Unconscious mind	Dream analysis, talk therapy
Sociocultural	How might an adolescent's culture lead to risk-taking?	Cultural environment	Cross-cultural studies
Evolutionary	Is risk-taking an evolutionary adaptive trait?	Natural selection	Species comparison

DOMAINS

Broad areas of psychological research are also known as domains. A question that asks about the effect of drugs on behavior refers to the **biological domain**. But a question that deals with relationships between drug users and their families belongs to the **social domain**. And a question that considers treatment options for someone addicted to drugs deals with the **clinical domain**.

Other domains include: **cognitive** (What thoughts might someone entertain to justify their drug use?), **counseling** (How might a school counselor talk to a student about drugs?), **developmental** (At what ages might someone be more susceptible to peer pressure?), and **educational** (How effective are school-based programs?).

Yet other domains include: **experimental** (dealing with experiments, as discussed immediately below), **industrial-organizational** (dealing with workplaces), **personality** (dealing with—you guessed it!—personality), **psychometric** (dealing with how to measure things in psychology), and the **positive domain** (which focuses on positive aspects and strengths of human behavior).

KEY TERMS

History

psychology
behavior
mind
dualism
brain
René Descartes
pineal gland
reflex
John Locke
empiricism
tabula rasa
materialism
Thomas Hobbes
behaviorism
Charles Darwin
On the Origin of Species
natural selection
evolutionary theory
Wilhelm Wundt
Edward Titchener
structuralism
introspection
William James
functionalism
Dorothea Dix
Mary Whiton Calkins
Margaret Floy Washburn
G. Stanley Hall

Approaches

biological psychology
behavioral genetics
behaviorism
classical conditioning
John Watson
B.F. Skinner
behavior modification
cognitive psychology
humanistic approach
Abraham Maslow
self-actualization
Carl Rogers
unconditional positive regard
Sigmund Freud
psychoanalytic theory
conscious mind
unconscious mind
repressed
Carl Jung
collective unconscious
sociocultural approach
evolutionary approach

Domains

biological
social
clinical
cognitive
counseling
developmental
educational
experimental
industrial-organizational
personality
psychometric
positive

Chapter 5 Drill

See Chapter 19 for answers and explanations.

1. A cognitive psychologist would likely be most interested in

   (A) concentration of neural transmitters in the spinal cord
   (B) unconditional positive regard in the therapeutic setting
   (C) token economies in prisons
   (D) perceptual speed on word-association tests
   (E) development of fine motor skills in toddlers

2. The concept of *tabula rasa*, or "blank slate" (the idea that human beings come into the world knowing nothing, and thereafter acquire all of their knowledge through experience) is most closely associated with

   (A) David Hume
   (B) Charles Darwin
   (C) John Locke
   (D) Sigmund Freud
   (E) Erich Fromm

3. The concept of dualism refers to the division of all things in the world into

   (A) thought and action
   (B) body and spirit
   (C) structural and functional
   (D) theoretical and practical
   (E) dependent and independent

4. The humanistic approach to psychology emphasizes the importance of

   (A) childhood experiences
   (B) biological predispositions
   (C) maladaptive thoughts
   (D) free will and conscious awareness
   (E) cultural experiences

5. Psychologists who emphasize the importance of repressed memories and childhood experiences subscribe to which of the following perspectives?

   (A) Cognitive
   (B) Behavioral
   (C) Psychodynamic
   (D) Social cultural
   (E) Medical/biological

6. Psychologists who believe behaviors are learned most likely ascribe to the philosophy of

   (A) Abraham Maslow
   (B) B.F. Skinner
   (C) Carl Rogers
   (D) Sigmund Freud
   (E) Wilhelm Wundt

7. According to the psychoanalytic perspective, a person who does not remember a painful event experiences which defense mechanism?

   (A) Denial
   (B) Self-actualization
   (C) Projection
   (D) Consciousness
   (E) Repression

8. Carl Rogers is most closely associated with which psychological approach?

   (A) Unconditional positive regard
   (B) Cognitive psychology
   (C) Humanistic
   (D) Sociocultural
   (E) Behaviorism

9. According to Abraham Maslow's hierarchy of needs, the most basic of human needs is

   (A) self-actualization
   (B) esteem
   (C) belonging
   (D) safety
   (E) physiological

10. Many people credit the discovery of psychology as its own field of study to

   (A) Wilhelm Wundt
   (B) John Locke
   (C) John Watson
   (D) Sigmund Freud
   (E) René Descartes

REFLECT

Respond to the following questions:

- Which topics in this chapter do you hope to see on the multiple-choice section or essay?

- Which topics in this chapter do you hope not to see on the multiple-choice section or essay?

- Regarding any psychologists mentioned, can you pair the psychologists with their contributions to the field? Did they contribute significant experiments, theories, or both?

- Regarding any theories mentioned, can you distinguish between differing theories well enough to recognize them on the multiple-choice section? Can you distinguish them well enough to write a fluent essay on them?

- Regarding any figures given, if you were given a labeled figure from within this chapter, would you be able to give the significance of each part of the figure?

- Can you define the key terms at the end of the chapter?

- Which parts of the chapter will you review?

- Will you seek further help, outside of this book (such as a teacher, Princeton Review tutor, or AP Students), on any of the content in this chapter—and, if so, on what content?

Chapter 6
Foundations:
Methods and
Approaches

EXPERIMENTAL, CORRELATIONAL, AND CLINICAL RESEARCH

Three major types of research in psychology include: experimental, correlational, and clinical. An **experiment** is an investigation seeking to understand relations of cause and effect. The experimenter changes a variable (cause) and measures how it, in turn, changes another variable (effect). At the same time, the investigator tries to hold all other variables constant so she can attribute any changes to the manipulation. The manipulated variable is called the **independent variable**. The **dependent variable** is what is measured. For example, an experiment is designed to determine whether watching violence on television causes aggression in its viewers. Two groups of children are randomly placed either in front of violent or nonviolent television programs for one hour. This would be considered the independent variable because it can be manipulated by the experimenter. Afterward, a large doll may be placed in front of each child for one hour while the experimenter records the number of times that child hits, kicks, or punches the doll. This would be considered the dependent variable because it is the variable that remains constant and is being measured.

Also Remember…

Other terms to remember include the following: the group receiving or reacting to the independent variable is the **experimental group;** the **control group** does not receive the independent variable but should be kept identical in all other respects. Using two groups allows for a comparison to be made and causation to be determined.

In order to draw conclusions about the result of the controlled experiment, it is important that certain other conditions are met. The researcher identifies a specific **population,** or group of interest, to be studied. Because the population may be too large to study effectively, a **representative sample** of the population may be drawn. **Representativeness** is the degree to which a sample reflects the diverse characteristics of the population that is being studied. **Random sampling** is a way of ensuring maximum representativeness. Once sampling has been addressed, subjects are **randomly assigned** into both the experimental and control groups. Random assignment is done to ensure that each group has minimal differences.

Sampling Bias

A classic example of unintentional sampling bias occurred during the 1948 U.S. Presidential Election: a survey was conducted by randomly calling households and asking them whom they intended to vote for, Harry Truman or Thomas Dewey. Based on this phone survey, Dewey was projected to win. The results of the election proved otherwise, as Truman was re-elected. What could have possibly gone wrong? In 1948, having a telephone was not such a common thing, and households that had them were generally wealthier. As a result, the "random" selection of telephone numbers was not a representative sample because many people (a large proportion of whom voted for Truman) did not have telephone numbers. For the purposes of the test, you should be able to identify the following types of sampling biases:

- The **bias of selection** from a specific real area occurs when people are selected in a physical space. For example, if you wanted to survey college students on whether or not they like their football team, you could stand on the quad and survey the first 100 people that walk by. However, this is not completely random because people who don't have class at that time are unlikely to be represented.

- **Self-selection** bias occurs when the people being studied have some control over whether or not to participate. A participant's decision to participate may affect the results. For example, an Internet survey might elicit responses only from people who are highly opinionated and motivated to complete the survey.

- **Pre-screening or advertising bias** occurs often in medical research; how volunteers are screened or where advertising is placed might skew the sample. For example, if a researcher wanted to prove that a certain treatment helps people to stop smoking, the mere act of advertising for people who "want to quit smoking" might provide only a sample of people who are already highly motivated to quit and might have done so without the treatment.

- **Healthy user bias** occurs when the study population tends to be in better shape than the general population. As with the bias of selection from a specific real area, this is an instance in which those subjects might not, in turn, accurately represent their neighborhoods—even though the gym might have a diverse population.

To avoid inadvertently influencing the results, as in the previous examples, researchers use a **single-** or **double-blind design**. Single-blind design means that the subjects do not know whether they are in the control or experimental group. In a double-blind design, neither the subjects nor the researcher knows who is in the two groups. Double-blind studies are designed so that the experimenter does not inadvertently change the responses of the subject, such as by using a different tone of voice with members of the control group than with the experimental group. Obviously, a third party has the appropriate records so that the data can be analyzed later. In some double-blind experiments, the control group is given a **placebo**, a seemingly therapeutic object or procedure, which causes the control group to believe they are in the experimental group but actually contains none of the tested material.

Correlational research involves assessing the degree of association between two or more variables or characteristics of interest that occur naturally. It is important to note that, in this type of design, researchers do not directly manipulate variables but rather observe naturally occurring differences. If the characteristics under consideration are related, they are correlated. It is important to note that *correlation does not prove causation;* correlation simply shows the strength of the relationship among variables. For example, poor school performance may be correlated with lack of sleep. However, we do not know if lack of sleep caused the poor performance, or if the poor school performance caused the lack of sleep, or if some other unidentified factor influenced them both. If an unknown factor is playing a role, it is known as a **confounding variable**, a third variable, or an extraneous variable. One way to gather information for correlational studies is through surveys. Using either questionnaires or interviews, one can accumulate a tremendous amount of data and study relationships among variables. Such techniques are often used to assess voter characteristics, teen alcohol and drug use, and criminal behavior. For example, survey studies might examine the relationship between socioeconomic status and educational levels. Correlational studies can be preferred to experiments because they are less expensive, not as time consuming, and easier to conduct. In addition, some relationships cannot be ethically studied in experiments. For example, you may want to study how child abuse affects self-efficacy in adulthood. But no one will allow you to randomly assign half of your baby participants to the child abuse condition.

> ### Types of Research
> Two specific types of research that can be set up as correlational or experimental designs are **longitudinal studies** and **cross-sectional studies**. Longitudinal studies happen over long periods of time with the same subjects (e.g., studying the long-term effects of diet and exercise on heart disease), and cross-sectional studies are designed to test a wide array of subjects from different backgrounds to increase generalizability.

Clinical research often takes the form of case studies. **Case studies** are intensive psychological studies of a single individual. These studies are conducted under the assumption that an in-depth understanding of single cases will allow for general conclusions about other similar cases. Case studies have also been used to investigate the circumstances of the life of notable figures in history. Frequently, multiple case studies on similar cases are combined to draw inferences about these issues. Researchers must be careful, though, because case studies, like correlational ones, cannot lead to conclusions regarding causality. Sigmund Freud and Carl Rogers used numerous case studies to draw their conclusions about psychology. The danger of assessing the outcome of case studies is that the individual studied may be atypical of the larger population. This is why researchers try to ensure that their studies are **generalizable**—that is, applicable to similar circumstances because of the predictable outcomes of repeated tests.

Experimental Design

Two important features of studies are the **conceptual definition** and the **operational definition**. Whereas the conceptual definition is the theory or issue being studied, the operational definition refers to the way in which that theory or issue will be directly observed or measured in the study. For example, in a study on the effects of adolescent substance abuse, the way in which taking drugs affects adolescent behavior is the conceptual definition, while the number of recorded days the student is absent from school due to excessive use of substances is the operational definition.

Operational definitions have to be internally and externally valid. **Internal validity** is the certainty with which the results of an experiment can be attributed to the manipulation of the independent variable rather than to some other, confounding variable. **External validity** is the extent to which the findings of a study can be generalized to other contexts in the "real world." It is also important that the study have **reliability**, which is whether or not the same results appear if the experiment is repeated under similar conditions.

OTHER TYPES OF RESEARCH

In addition to organizing experiments inside of a lab, researchers can observe behavior outside of the lab; **such naturalistic observation** has enriched our knowledge of psychology. Much knowledge has derived from studying groups of people over years or even decades; this is called **longitudinal** research. Finally, one can also study different age groups at one point in time; this is called **cross-sectional** research.

STATISTICS

Psychologists and other scientists collect data. This data is then subjected to statistical analysis. Statistical methods can be divided into descriptive and inferential statistics. **Descriptive statistics** summarize data, whereas **inferential statistics** allow researchers to test hypotheses about data and determine how confident they can be in their inferences about the data.

Descriptive

Descriptive statistics do just what their name implies—they describe data. They do not allow for conclusions to be made about anything other than the particular set of numbers they describe. Commonly used descriptive statistics are the mean, the mode, and the median. These descriptive statistics are measures of **central tendency**—that is, they characterize the typical value in a set of data.

MMM MM!
The Mean, Mode, and Median Measure the Middle!

The **mean** is the arithmetic average of a set of numbers. The **mode** is the most frequently occurring value in the data set. The **median** is the number that falls exactly in the middle of a distribution of numbers. These statistics can be represented by a **normal curve.** In a perfectly normal distribution, the mean, median, and mode are identical.

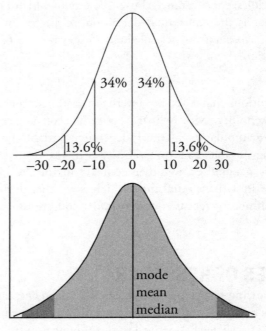

Perfect Normal Curve

Q: What is standard deviation?

Answer on page 117.

The graph of the normal distribution depends on two factors—the mean and the standard deviation. The mean of the distribution determines the location of the center of the graph, and the standard deviation determines the height and width of the graph. When the standard deviation is large, the curve is short and wide; when the standard deviation is small, the curve is tall and narrow. All normal distributions look like a symmetric, bell-shaped curve, as shown above.

In a typical distribution of numbers, about 68 percent of all scores are within one standard deviation above or below the mean, and about 95 percent of all scores are within two standard deviations above or below the mean. So, for example, IQ is typically said to have a mean of 100 and a standard deviation of 15, so a person with a score of 115 is one standard deviation above the mean.

Be aware that math questions about normal distributions can appear on the test. Because skewed distributions do not all share the same mathematical properties, questions about percentages and these distributions are often trick questions.

The curve on the left is shorter and wider than the curve on the right, because the curve on the left has a bigger standard deviation.

In skewed distributions, the median is a better indicator of central tendency than the mean. A **positive skew** means that most values are on the lower end, but there are some exceptionally large values. This creates a "tail" or skew toward the positive end. A **negative skew** means the opposite: most values are on the higher end, but there are some exceptionally small values. This creates a "tail" or skew toward the negative end.

| Positive Skew | Negative Skew |

A: Standard deviation measures the average distribution of numbers around the mean.

Although the mean, the mode, and the median give approximations of the central tendency of a group of numbers, they do not tell us much about the variability in that set of numbers. **Variability** refers to how much the numbers in the set differ from one another. The **standard deviation** measures a function of the average dispersion of numbers around the mean and is a commonly used measure of variability. Therefore, we can have a set of numbers that has a mean of 100. If most of those numbers are close to 100, say, ranging from 95 to 105, then the standard deviation will be small. However, if the mean of 100 comes from a set of numbers ranging from 50 to 150, then the standard deviation will be large.

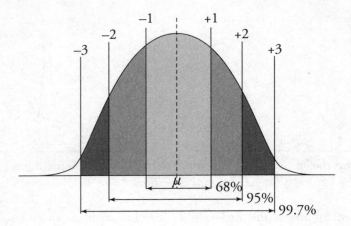

It's unlikely that there will be any questions that actually exercise your math skills, but you should be able to read and interpret a graph and understand what the standard deviation represents in a study. For example, suppose that 1,000 subjects participate in a study on reaction time and that the reaction times of the subjects are normally distributed with a mean of 1.3 seconds and a standard deviation of 0.2 seconds. In this particular instance, participants with a reaction time between 1.1 and 1.5 seconds would represent the normal distribution and one standard deviation above and below, which as we've established is generally around 68 percent of the population. Therefore, roughly 680 of 1,000 people would have this reaction time. Meanwhile, a reaction time of over 1.9 seconds would be extremely rare—more than three standard deviations above the mean. It's likely that only 0.3 percent of the data would fall into that category, or about 3 of the 1,000 subjects.

Another common descriptive statistic is the **percentile**. This statistic is used frequently when reporting scores on standardized tests. Percentiles express the standing of one score relative to all other scores in a set of data. For example, if your SAT score is in the 85th percentile, then you scored higher than 85 percent of the other test-takers.

When looking at correlational data, as described above, we need statistical techniques to describe how the attributes we are studying relate to one another. The **correlation coefficient** is a statistic that will give us such information. The correlation coefficient is a numerical value that indicates the degree and direction of the relationship between two variables. Correlation coefficients range from +1.00 to −1.00. The sign (+ or −) indicates the direction of the correlation, and the number (0 to + or −1.00) indicates the strength of the relationship. The **Pearson correlation coefficient** is a descriptive statistic that describes the linear relationship between two attributes. Pearson correlations can be positive, zero, or negative and are typically measured on a scale ranging from 1 to 0 to −1. A correlation of 1 indicates a perfect positive correlation. This means that as attribute X increases, attribute Y always increases proportionally. A correlation of −1 is a perfect negative correlation: as the value of attribute X increases, the value of attribute Y always decreases proportionally. A correlation of 0 indicates that the attributes are not related.

Positive Correlation (As years of education increase, income increases.)

Negative Correlation (As absences for math lessons increase, math score decreases.)

To use another example, take the following study, which assessed 200 male children from ages 1 to 12. A standardized questionnaire was given to the parents of the children and used to check their "agreeableness" on a scale from 0 to 5. Additionally, psychologists took standard measures of the behavioral problems exhibited by the children. After the incidents were totaled for each subject, the psychologists found a correlation between child agreeableness and later behavioral problems of −0.6.

You don't need any math here either, but you do have to understand that this is an inverse correlation between the scores: as the child's agreeableness increases, their behavioral problems decrease. Don't forget, however, what we stressed earlier in this chapter: *correlation does not imply causation.*

Correlation and Causation

A famous example of correlation and causation can be taken from an observation once made about New York City, in that the murder rate is directly correlated to the sale of ice cream (as ice cream sales increase, so do the number of murders). Does this mean that buying ice cream is definitively the cause of the increase in murders? Of course not! When two variables are correlated (especially two variables that are as complex as the measures of human behavior studied in the example above), there are always a number of other factors that could be influencing either correlated variable. In the ice cream/murder example, one such potential confounding variable might be temperature; as the temperature rises, more crimes are committed, but people also tend to eat more cold foods, like ice cream.

Inferential

Inferential statistics are used to determine our level of confidence in claiming that a given set of results would be extremely unlikely to occur if the result were only up to chance. When experiments are conducted, they are typically conducted using a small group of people. However, psychologists typically want to be able to **generalize** the results of the experiment to a larger group of people, perhaps even to all people. The small group of people in the experiment constitutes the **sample**, and the large group to whom the psychologist is trying to generalize is called the **population**. It is important that the sample reflects the characteristics of the population as a whole. If it does, then the sample is referred to as being **representative**.

Sample size refers to the number of observations or individuals measured. Simply enough, if an experiment involves 100 people, the sample size is 100. The sample size is typically denoted by N (the total number of subjects in the sample being studied) or n (the total number of subjects in a subgroup of the sample being studied). While larger sample sizes always confer increased accuracy, the sample size used in a study is typically determined based on convenience, expense, and the need to have sufficient statistical power (the likelihood that your sample includes a sufficient number of subjects to conclude that the hypothesis being evaluated is true within an acceptable margin of error). Larger sample sizes are always better—the larger the sample size, the more likely it is that the inferences about the broader population are correct.

Q: What is a null hypothesis?

Answer on page 122.

Inferential statistics are tools for hypothesis testing. The **null hypothesis** states that a treatment had no effect in an experiment. The **alternative hypothesis** is that the treatment did have an effect. Inferential statistics allow us the possibility of rejecting the null hypothesis with a known level of confidence—that is, of saying that our data would be extremely unlikely to have occurred were the null hypothesis true. Tests such as these are statistically significant because they enable us to examine whether effects are likely to be a result of treatment or are likely to be simply the normal variations that occur among samples from the same population. If a result is found to be statistically significant, then that result may be generalized with some level of confidence to the population.

Alpha is the accepted probability that the result of an experiment can be attributed to chance rather than the manipulation of the independent variable. Given that there is always the possibility that an experiment's outcome can happen by chance, no matter how improbable, psychologists usually set alpha at 0.05, which means that an experiment's results will be considered statistically significant if the probability of the results happening by chance is less than 5 percent.

Q: What is a Type I error? What is a Type II error?

Answer on page 122.

Two primary types of errors can occur when testing a hypothesis. A **Type I error** refers to the conclusion that a difference exists when, in fact, this difference does not exist. A **Type II error** refers to the conclusion that there is no difference when, in fact, there is a difference. Psychologists pay particularly close attention to Type I errors because they want to be conservative in their inferences: they do not want to conclude that a difference exists if, in fact, it does not. A good analogy for Type I and Type II errors is that a Type I error is a "false positive," and a Type II error is a "false negative." The probability of making a Type I error is called the **p-value**. A p-value indicates that the results are statistically significant (not due only to chance). If $p = 0.05$, we have only a 5 percent chance of making a Type I error. In other words, a difference as extreme as what was obtained would be found only 5 percent of the time if the null hypothesis were correct.

		Reality	
		The null is True	The null is False
Your Statistical Decision	Fail to reject the null	Correct decision	**Type II error**
	Reject the null	**Type I error**	Correct decision

Statistical Decision-Making: The Four Possible Outcomes

ETHICS IN RESEARCH

Occasionally, psychological experiments involve deception, which may be used if informing participants of the nature of the experiment might bias results. This deception is typically small, but in rare instances it can be extreme. For example, in the 1970s, **Stanley Milgram** conducted obedience experiments in which he convinced participants that they were administering painful electric shocks to other participants, when, in fact, no shocks were given. The shocked "participants" were in fact **confederates**; that is, they were aware of the true nature of the experiment but pretended to be participants. Those giving the shocks were the real participants. Many people felt that this study was unethical because the participants were not aware of the nature of the study and could have believed that they had done serious harm to other people. Since this time, ethical standards have been set forth by the American Psychological Association (APA) to ensure the proper treatment of animal and human subjects. Institutional Review Boards (IRBs) assess the research plans before the research is approved to ensure that it meets all ethical standards. Additionally, participants must give **informed consent**; in other words, they agree to participate in the study only after they have been told what their participation entails. Participants are also allowed to leave the experimental situation if they become uncomfortable about their participation. After the experiment is concluded, participants must receive a **debriefing,** in which they are told the exact purpose of their participation in the research and of any deception that may have been used in the process of experimentation.

Painless Experiments

Pain, both physiological and psychological, is also an issue in experiments. In the past, shock was an acceptable technique with human participants. However, physical pain is infrequently used in experiments today. Psychological stress is also minimized.

Confidentiality is another area of concern for psychology. Many experiments involve collecting sensitive information about participants that the participants might not want to be revealed. For this reason, most psychological data is collected anonymously, with the participant's name not attached to the collected data. If such anonymity is not possible, it is the researcher's ethical obligation to ensure that names and sensitive information about participants are not revealed.

Animal rights within psychological experiments are a topic of controversy. According to animal-rights activists, animals often endure both physiological and psychological stress in experiments. Often, the animals are euthanized at the end of the research. Psychologists counter that many lifesaving drugs could not be tested were it not for tests with animals. Moreover, animal models afford a level of experimental control that is not attainable with human participants. Of course, no ethical researcher wants to cause unnecessary pain or discomfort to any subject—animal or human.

A: A null hypothesis assumes that the manipulation of the independent variable will have no effect on the results of an experiment.

A: A Type I error concludes that there is a difference when there isn't one (a false positive). A Type II error concludes that there is no difference when there is one (a false negative).

KEY TERMS

Experimental, Correlational, and Clinical Research

experiment
independent variable
dependent variable
experimental group
control group
population
representative sample
representativeness
random sampling
randomly assigned
bias of selection
self-selection bias
pre-screening/advertising
   bias
healthy user bias
single-blind design
double-blind design
placebo
correlational research
confounding (3rd) variable
longitudinal studies
cross-sectional studies
naturalistic observation
clinical research
case studies
generalizable
conceptual definition
operational definition
internal validity
external validity
reliability

Statistics

descriptive statistics
inferential statistics
central tendency
mean
mode
median

normal curve
negative skew
positive skew
variability
standard deviation
percentile
correlation coefficient
Pearson correlation
   coefficient
positive correlation
negative correlation
inferential statistics
generalize
sample
population
representative
sample size
null hypothesis
alternative hypothesis
alpha
Type I error
Type II error
p-value

Ethics in Research

Stanley Milgram
informed consent
confederate
debriefing
confidentiality

Chapter 6 Drill

See Chapter 19 for answers and explanations.

1. In a double-blind experimental design, which of the following would be true?

   (A) The experimental subjects know whether they are in an experimental group or in a control group, but the researchers do not.
   (B) The researchers know whether particular subjects have been assigned to an experimental group or a control group, but the experimental subjects do not.
   (C) Both the researchers and the experimental subjects know whether the latter have been assigned to an experimental group or a control group.
   (D) Neither the researchers nor the experimental subjects know whether the latter have been assigned to an experimental group or a control group.
   (E) The observers are unable to see the responses or behaviors of the experimental group during the course of the experimental manipulation.

2. In a normal distribution of scores, approximately what percentage of all scores will occur within one standard deviation from the mean?

   (A) 34
   (B) 68
   (C) 95
   (D) 97.5
   (E) 100

3. A Type II error involves

   (A) concluding a difference between groups exists after the experimental manipulation when, in fact, a difference does not exist
   (B) concluding a difference between groups does not exist after the experimental manipulation when, in fact, a difference does exist
   (C) concluding a score is two standard deviations above the mean when, in fact, it is two standard deviations below the mean
   (D) concluding a score is two standard deviations below the mean when, in fact, it is two standard deviations above the mean
   (E) rejecting the null hypothesis when, in fact, it should have been accepted

4. Which of the following would NOT be considered essential for a proposed research design to meet the requirements for ethicality?

   (A) Research subjects must consent to participate in the project, and a full description of what their participation consists of must be spelled out before they are asked to give consent.
   (B) Participants must be allowed to withdraw from the project at any time.
   (C) Both the subjects and the researchers must know which of the subjects will be part of the experimental group.
   (D) If deception is involved, a full debriefing of the subjects must occur soon after the completion of the project.
   (E) In keeping with protecting the privacy and confidentiality of the subjects, data should be obtained as anonymously as possible.

5. The correlation between two observed variables is −0.84. From this, it can be concluded that

   (A) as one variable increases, the other is likely to increase, showing a direct relationship
   (B) as one variable increases, the other is likely to decrease, showing an inverse relationship
   (C) the two variables are unrelated
   (D) one variable causes the other variable to occur
   (E) one variable causes the other variable not to occur

6. A study seeks to find the effects of video games on violent behavior. The researcher creates an experimental design in which 100 random participants play violent video games and another 100 play nonviolent video games for one hour. The researcher then records and observes the behavior of the subjects. The behavior of the subjects is known as the

   (A) control variable
   (B) independent variable
   (C) dependent variable
   (D) confounding variable
   (E) categorical variable

7. Which of the following is NOT a categorical variable?

   (A) Gender
   (B) School attended
   (C) Hair color
   (D) Height
   (E) Breed of dog

8. A study that analyzes the effects of heart disease in different regions of the country and socioeconomic statuses is called a

   (A) longitudinal study
   (B) experimental design
   (C) double-blind study
   (D) cross-sectional design
   (E) case study

9. A researcher seeks to study the effects of a weight-loss supplement and decides to place an advertisement on busses and subways in New York City to attract subjects. All could happen with this type of subject selection EXCEPT

   (A) pre-screening bias
   (B) self-selection bias
   (C) selection bias
   (D) healthy user bias
   (E) representative bias

10. When graphing the distribution of a study, the researcher notices that a disproportionate amount of subjects scored low on their test, shifting the peak of the bell curve she was expecting. This is called a

   (A) positive skew
   (B) negative skew
   (C) normal curve
   (D) positive correlation
   (E) negative correlation

REFLECT
Respond to the following questions:

- Which topics in this chapter do you hope to see on the multiple-choice section or essay?

- Which topics in this chapter do you hope not to see on the multiple-choice section or essay?

- Regarding any psychologists mentioned, can you pair the psychologists with their contributions to the field? Did they contribute significant experiments, theories, or both?

- Regarding any theories mentioned, can you distinguish between differing theories well enough to recognize them on the multiple-choice section? Can you distinguish them well enough to write a fluent essay on them?

- Regarding any figures given, if you were given a labeled figure from within this chapter, would you be able to give the significance of each part of the figure?

- Can you define the key terms at the end of the chapter?

- Which parts of the chapter will you review?

- Will you seek further help, outside of this book (such as a teacher, Princeton Review tutor, or AP Students), on any of the content in this chapter—and, if so, on what content?

Chapter 7
Biological Bases:
The Brain and
Nervous System

INTRODUCTION TO BIOLOGY AND BEHAVIOR

Physiological psychology is the study of behavior as influenced by biology. It draws its techniques and research methods from biology and medicine to examine psychological phenomena.

PHYSIOLOGICAL TECHNIQUES

Many different techniques are used to examine the interrelationship between the brain and behavior. An **EEG** (electroencephalogram) measures subtle changes in brain electrical activity through electrodes placed on the head. This data can be filtered mathematically to yield evoked potentials, which allow for localization of functions in the brain. This technique has allowed psychologists to get an electrical picture of brain activity during various cognitive states or tasks.

Computerized axial tomography scans, better known as **CAT scans**, generate cross-sectional images of the brain using a series of X-ray pictures taken from different angles. **MRI** (magnetic resonance imaging) uses extremely powerful electromagnets and radio waves to get 3-D structural information from the brain. These techniques capture only "snapshots" of the brain. They do not allow observation of the brain in action over time. Functional MRI (**fMRI**) and **PET scans** (positron emission tomography) are techniques that allow scientists to view the brain as it is working. Functional MRI provides such viewing by rapid sequencing of MRI images. PET scans provide images via diffusion of radioactive glucose in the brain. Glucose is the primary "fuel" of brain cells; the more glucose being used in a given brain area, the more that area is in active use. This procedure allows psychologists to observe what brain areas are at work during various tasks and psychological events.

FUNCTIONAL ORGANIZATION OF THE NERVOUS SYSTEM

The **nervous system** can be divided into two distinct subsystems: the **central nervous system** (CNS)—comprising the brain and the spinal cord—and the **peripheral nervous system** (PNS)—comprising all other nerves in the body.

The brain is located in the skull and is the central processing center for thoughts, motivations, and emotions. The brain, as well as the rest of the nervous system, is made up of **neurons**, or nerve cells. The neurons form a network that extends to the spinal cord, which is encased in the protective bones of the spine, or the vertebrae. Both the brain and the spinal cord are bathed in a protective liquid called cerebrospinal fluid. In the spinal cord, the neurons are bundled into strands of interconnected neurons known as nerves. The nerves of the spine are responsible for conveying information to and from the brain and the PNS. Nerves sending information to the brain are sensory (or **afferent**) neurons; those conveying information from the brain are motor (or **efferent**) neurons. Although

Test Tip

A memory tip for *afferent* and *efferent* is that afferent connections are arriving to the brain and efferent are exiting the brain.

most movements are controlled by the brain, a certain small subset of movements are controlled by direct transmission from afferent to efferent cells at the level of the spinal cord. These responses, known as **reflexes**, are quick and involuntary responses to environmental stimuli. The path of a reflex arc goes from sensory neurons to motor neurons.

The PNS comprises all of the nerve cells in the body with the exception of those in the CNS (the brain and spinal cord). The PNS can be subdivided into the **somatic nervous system** and the **autonomic nervous system**. The somatic nervous system is responsible for voluntary movement of large skeletal muscles. The autonomic nervous system controls the nonskeletal or smooth muscles, such as those of the heart and digestive tract. These muscles are typically not under voluntary control. (Think autonomic = automatic.) The autonomic nervous system can be further divided into the sympathetic and parasympathetic nervous systems.

The **sympathetic nervous system** is associated with processes that burn energy. This is the system responsible for the heightened state of physiological arousal known as the **fight-or-flight reaction**—an increase in heart rate and respiration, accompanied by a decrease in digestion and salivation. The **parasympathetic nervous system** is the complementary opposite system responsible for conserving energy. When the sympathetic system is aroused in a fight, for example, digestion ceases, blood transfers to skeletal muscle, and heart rate increases. When the fight ends, however, the parasympathetic system becomes active, sending blood to the stomach for digestion, slowing the heart rate, and conserving energy. This returns the body to homeostasis.

> **Mnemonic Tip!**
> The *sympathetic* system is *sympathetic* to you while you deal with a problem. The *parasympathetic* system helps you come down afterwards, like a *parachute*.

NEUROANATOMY

The brain is divided into three distinct regions that have evolved over time. These are the **hindbrain**, **midbrain**, and the **forebrain** (limbic system and cerebral cortex).

The Hindbrain

- The oldest part of the brain to develop in evolutionary terms
- Composed of the cerebellum, medulla oblongata, reticular activating system (RAS), and pons
- **Cerebellum**—controls muscle tone and balance
- **Medulla oblongata**—controls involuntary actions, such as breathing, digestion, heart rate, and swallowing (basic life functions)
- **Reticular activating system (RAS)**—controls arousal (wakefulness and alertness). This is also known as reticular formation.
- **Pons**—Latin for "bridge," the pons is a way station, passing neural information from one brain region to another. The pons is also implicated in REM sleep.

The Midbrain

- Major components of the midbrain are **tectum** and **tegmentum**

- These two act as the brain's roof (tectum) and floor (tegmentum).

- The tectum and tegmentum govern visual and auditory reflexes, such as orienting to a sight or sound.

The Forebrain

Q: What parts of the brain are housed in the forebrain?

Answer on page 132.

- Contains the **limbic system**, or emotional center of the brain

- Composed of the thalamus, hippocampus, amygdala, and hypothalamus

- **Thalamus**—relays sensory information; receives and directs sensory information from visual and auditory systems

- **Hippocampus**—involved in processing and integrating memories. Damage to the hippocampus does not eliminate existing memories because memories are stored in the neocortex, but rather it prevents the formation of new memories. This condition is known as **anterograde amnesia**.

- **Amygdala**—implicated in the expression of anger and frustration

- **Hypothalamus**—controls the temperature and water balance of the body; controls hunger and sex drives; orchestrates the activation of the sympathetic nervous system and the endocrine system; and it can be divided into the **lateral hypothalamus** and **ventromedial hypothalamus**, the combination of which regulates eating behaviors and body weight. The lateral hypothalamus is the "on switch" for eating, while the ventromedial hypothalamus is the "off switch." A lesion to the ventromedial part would cause obesity and even death from overeating, while a lesion to the lateral part would lead to a decreased hunger drive and even self-starvation.

- Also contains the **cerebral cortex**, or the wrinkled outer layer of the brain

- The cortex is involved in higher cognitive functions such as thinking, planning, language use, and fine motor control.

- This area receives sensory input (**sensory cortex**) and sends out motor information (**motor cortex**).

- The cortex covers two symmetrical-looking sides of the brain known as the **left and right cerebral hemispheres**. These hemispheres are joined together by a band of connective nerve fibers called the **corpus callosum**.

- The left hemisphere is typically specialized for language processing, as first noticed by **Paul Broca**, who observed that brain damage to the left hemisphere in stroke patients resulted in **expressive aphasia**, or loss of the ability to speak. This area of the brain is known as **Broca's area**. Another researcher, **Carl Wernicke**, discovered an area in the left temporal lobe that, when damaged in stroke patients, resulted in **receptive aphasia**, or the inability to comprehend speech. This is called **Wernicke's Area**.

- Others have noted that the right hemisphere processes certain kinds of visual and spatial information. **Roger Sperry** demonstrated that the two hemispheres of the brain can operate independently of each other. He did this by performing experiments on **split-brain patients** who had their corpus callosums severed to control their epileptic seizures. Split brain patients can describe objects without deficit if presented in the right visual field (processed on the left, more verbal side of the brain), but they have great difficulty drawing the image; whereas, if the image is presented in the left visual field (and processed in the more visual right side of the brain), the person can draw or choose the object but cannot explain it verbally. This is called **contralateral processing**.

Mnemonic Tip!

Ventromedial lesion => Give me **V**ery much food!

Lateral lesion => Give me **L**ess food!.

Cortex Components

- The cortex can be divided into four distinct lobes: the frontal, the parietal, the temporal, and the occipital.
  - The **frontal lobe** is responsible for higher-level thought and reasoning. That includes working memory, paying attention, solving problems, making plans, forming judgments, and performing movements.
  - The **parietal lobe** handles somatosensory information and is the home of the primary somatosensory cortex. This area receives information about temperature, pressure, texture, and pain.
  - The **temporal lobe** handles auditory input and is critical for processing speech and appreciating music.
  - Finally, the **occipital lobe** processes visual input. This information crosses the **optic chiasm**.

- Much of the cerebral cortex is composed of **association areas**, which are responsible for associating information in the sensory and motor cortices (this is the plural of cortex!). Damage to these association areas can lead to a variety of dysfunctions, including **apraxia**, the inability to organize movement; **agnosia**, a difficulty processing sensory input; **alexia**, the inability to read; and **agraphia**, the inability to write.

A: The forebrain is home to the hippocampus, amygdala, and hypothalamus.

NEURAL TRANSMISSION

Much of our discussion has involved the idea of information or stimulation being passed along nerves. **Nerves** are bundles of **neurons**, the basic unit of the nervous system. Neurons are cells with a clearly defined, nucleated cell body, or **soma**. Branching out from the soma are **dendrites**, which receive input from other neurons through receptors on their surface. The **axon** is a long, tubelike structure that responds to input from the dendrites and soma. The axon transmits a neural message down its length and then passes its information on to other cells. Some neurons have a fatty coating known as a **myelin sheath** surrounding the axon. Myelin serves as insulation for the electrical impulses carried down the axon and also speeds up the rate at which electrical information travels down the axon. The better insulated the myelin sheath, the faster and more efficient the sending of action potentials. The myelin looks like beads on a string; the small gaps between the "beads" are known as the **nodes of Ranvier**. These nodes help speed up neural transmission. The axons end in **terminal buttons**, knobs on the branched end of the axon. The terminal buttons come very close to the cell body and dendrites of other neurons, but they do not touch. The gap between them is known as a **synapse**. The terminal buttons release **neurotransmitters**, chemical messengers, across the synapse, where they bind with receptors on subsequent dendrites.

Neuronal communication occurs both within and between cells. Communication within cells is electrochemical. An electric potential across the plasma membrane of approximately –70 millivolts (mV), known as the **resting membrane potential**, exists, in which the interior of the cell is negatively charged with respect to the exterior of the cell. Two primary membrane proteins are required to establish the resting membrane potential: the Na^+/K^+ ATPase and the potassium leak channels. The Na^+/K^+ ATPase pumps three sodium ions out of the cell and two potassium ions into the cell. The result is a sodium gradient with high sodium concentration outside of the cell and a potassium gradient with high potassium concentration inside the cell. **Leak channels** are channels that are open all the time and that simply allow ions to "leak" across the membrane according to their gradient. Potassium leak channels allow potassium, but no other ions, to flow down its gradient out of the cell. The combined loss of many positive ions through Na^+/K^+ ATPases and the potassium leak channels leaves the interior of the cell with a net negative charge, approximately 70 mV more negative than the exterior of the cell; this difference is the resting membrane potential. Note that there are very few sodium leak channels in the membrane (the ratio of K^+ leak channels to Na^+ leak channels is about 100:1), so the cell membrane is virtually impermeable to sodium.

The resting membrane potential establishes a negative charge along the interior of axons (along with the rest of the neuronal interior). Thus, the cells can be described as polarized: negative on the inside and positive on the outside. An **action potential**, also referred to as a **nerve impulse**, is a disturbance in this membrane potential. It can be thought of as a wave of depolarization of the plasma membrane that travels along an axon. Depolarization is a change in the membrane potential from the resting membrane potential to a less negative, or even positive, potential. The change in membrane potential during passage of an action potential is caused by movement of ions into and out of the neuron through ion channels, leading to the eventual release of the neurotransmitter. After depolarization, repolarization returns the membrane potential to normal.

Action potentials are "all or none," meaning that they are either generated or not, with nothing in between. They are always of a fixed strength, never weaker or stronger. After a neuron fires, it passes through an absolute refractory phase, during which no amount of stimulation can cause the neuron to fire again. The absolute refractory phase is followed by the relative refractory phase, in which the neuron needs much more stimulation than usual to fire again.

Communication between cells happens via neurotransmitters, which bind to receptors on the dendrites of the adjacent neurons. **Excitatory** neurotransmitters serve to excite the cell or cause the neuron to fire. **Inhibitory** neurotransmitters inhibit (or stop) cell firing. After a neurotransmitter is released and has conducted the impulse to the next cell or cells, it is either broken down by **enzymes** or is absorbed back into the cell that released it in a process called **reuptake**. A helpful metaphor for the process of cell communication is thinking of neurotransmitters as keys that open the locks on the postsynaptic cell.

The following are a few key neurotransmitters:

- **Acetylcholine**, which affects memory function, as well as muscle contraction, particularly in the heart

- **Serotonin**, which is related to arousal, sleep, pain sensitivity, and mood and hunger regulation

- **Dopamine**, which is associated with movement, attention, and reward; dopamine imbalances may play a role in Parkinson's disease and in schizophrenia

- **GABA**, or *gamma*-Aminobutyric acid, which is an inhibitory neurotransmitter

- **Glutamate**, which is an excitatory neurotransmitter and the all-purpose counterpart to GABA

- **Norepinephrine**, which affects levels of alertness; a lack of norepinephrine is implicated in depression

- **Endorphins**, which are the body's natural painkillers

ENDOCRINE SYSTEM

The **endocrine system** provides another way by which various parts of our bodies relay information to one another. This system works through groups of cells known as glands, which release substances called hormones. Hormones affect cell growth and proliferation. The primary gland is the **pituitary gland**, which is also known as the master gland. The pituitary releases **hormones**, which in turn control hormonal release by many other glands. Hormones are different from neurotransmitters in many ways. Neurotransmitters are released locally, while hormones are not. Hormones coordinate a wide range of responses, while neurotransmitters trigger highly localized and specific reactions. Hormones are present in the bloodstream, while neurotransmitters work in the synapse. Hormones also affect the body for long periods of time compared with neurotransmitters. The pituitary is located just under the part of the brain that controls it—the hypothalamus. Stressful situations cause the pituitary to release **adrenocorticotropic hormone (ACTH)**, which stimulates the **adrenal glands**, resulting in fight-or-flight reactions. The adrenal glands secrete **epinephrine** (adrenaline) and **norepinephrine** (noradrenaline). The **thyroid gland**, located at the front of the neck, produces **thyroxine**, which is important for regulating cellular metabolism.

GENETICS

Behavioral genetics is the application of the principles of evolutionary theory to the study of behavior. **Traits** are distinctive characteristics or behavior patterns that are determined by genetics. Genes are the basic biological elements responsible for carrying information about traits between successive generations. A **dominant trait** is more likely to be expressed in offspring than is a **recessive trait**. A **genotype** comprises all of the possible combinations of genes. Whenever a dominant gene is paired with a recessive gene, the dominant one typically will be shown in the **phenotype**, the observable result. The phenotype tends to show the recessive trait only when two recessive genes are paired together. Genes reside on rod-shaped chromosomes. Humans have 46 chromosomes, with one set of 23 inherited from each parent, so that half of our genetic makeup comes from each parent.

Some disorders are the result of genetic abnormalities. **Down syndrome** occurs when there are three copies of the 21st chromosome, which generally causes some degree of intellectual disability. **Huntington's chorea** is a genetic disorder that results in muscle impairment that does not typically occur until after

Nature vs. Nurture

As mentioned earlier, the behavioral-genetics approach examines the ways in which we are different from one another. The term **heritability** is used here to discuss the degree of variance among individuals that can be attributed to genetic variations. Many physical and psychological characteristics are inherited. However, genes do not determine everything about us. **Environmentality** is the degree to which a trait's expression is caused by the environment in which an organism lives. Psychology has long been concerned with the relative influences of genetics and environment. This controversy is known as the **nature versus nurture debate**. Today, the common view is that nature and nurture work together; our psychological makeup is largely the result of the interaction of these two forces.

age 40. It is caused by the degeneration of the structure of the brain known as the basal ganglia, and it is fatal. Because of the late onset of the disease, it is frequently passed down to the next generation before its symptoms are manifested. New genetic mapping techniques are revealing other relationships between specific genes and disorders, and scientists are trying to address ways to correct genetic flaws and provide genetic counseling.

It is important to note that the brain can reorganize itself by forming or severing neural connections throughout one's life. This important ability, called **neuroplasticity**, allows the brain to compensate for injury or disease, in order to continue responding adaptably to the environment. **Michael Gazzaniga** has not only done pioneering research in this area, focusing on split-brain patients, he has also published works in cognitive neuroscience for the general reader.

KEY TERMS

Physiological Techniques

physiological psychology
electroencephalogram
(EEG)
computerized axial tomography
(CAT) scan
magnetic resonance imaging
(MRI) scan
functional MRI (fMRI)
positron emission tomography
(PET) scan

Functional Organization of the Nervous System

nervous system
central nervous system
(CNS)
peripheral nervous system
(PNS)
neurons
afferent neurons
efferent neurons
reflexes
somatic nervous system
autonomic nervous system
sympathetic nervous system
fight-or-flight reaction
parasympathetic nervous
system

Neuroanatomy

hindbrain
midbrain
forebrain
cerebellum
medulla oblongata
reticular activating system
(RAS)
pons
tectum
tegmentum
limbic system
thalamus
hippocampus
anterograde amnesia
amygdala
hypothalamus
lateral hypothalamus
ventromedial hypothalamus
cerebral cortex
sensory cortex
motor cortex
left and right cerebral
hemispheres
corpus callosum
Paul Broca
expressive aphasia
Broca's area
Carl Wernicke

receptive aphasia
Wernicke's area
Roger Sperry
split-brain patients
contralateral processing
frontal lobe
parietal lobe
temporal lobe
occipital lobe
optic chiasm
association areas
apraxia
agnosia
alexia
agraphia
neuroplasticity
Michael Gazzaniga

Neural Transmission
nerves
neurons
soma
dendrites
axons
myelin sheath
nodes of Ranvier
terminal buttons
synapse
neurotransmitters
resting membrane potential
leak channels
action potential
nerve impulse
excitatory
inhibitory

enzymes
reuptake
acetylcholine
serotonin
dopamine
GABA
glutamate
norepinephrine
endorphins

Endocrine System
pituitary gland
hormones
adrenocorticotropic
    hormone (ACTH)
adrenal glands
epinephrine
norepinephrine
thyroid gland
thyroxine

Genetics
trait
dominant trait
recessive trait
genotype
phenotype
heritability
environmentality
nature versus nurture
    debate
Down syndrome
Huntington's chorea

Chapter 7 Drill

See Chapter 19 for answers and explanations.

1. Damage to the Broca's area in the left cerebral hemisphere on the brain would likely result in which of the following?

    (A) A repetition of the speech of others
    (B) A loss of the ability to speak
    (C) A loss of the ability to visually integrate information
    (D) A loss of the ability to comprehend speech
    (E) An inability to solve verbal problems

2. In the neuron, the main function of the dendrites is to

    (A) release neurotransmitters to signal subsequent neurons
    (B) preserve the speed and integrity of the neural signal as it propagates down the axon
    (C) perform the metabolic reactions necessary to nourish and maintain the nerve cell
    (D) receive input from other neurons
    (E) connect the cell body to the axon

3. Veronica is having trouble balancing as she walks, and her muscles seem to have lost strength and tone. A neuroanatomist looking into her condition would most likely suspect a problem with Veronica's

    (A) medulla oblongata
    (B) right cerebral hemisphere
    (C) cerebellum
    (D) occipital lobes
    (E) thalamus

4. Which of the following neurotransmitters is generally associated with the inhibition of continued neural signaling?

    (A) Dopamine
    (B) Adrenaline
    (C) GABA
    (D) Serotonin
    (E) Acetylcholine

5. A phenotype is best defined as

    (A) an observable trait or behavior that results from a particular genetic combination
    (B) the underlying genetic composition of a species
    (C) a biological unit within which genetic information is encoded
    (D) a recessive genetic combination that remains physically unexpressed
    (E) the genetic combination given by a parent to his or her offspring

6. John is constantly overeating and can't seem to control his appetite, no matter how hard he tries. It is possible that John may have damage in which of the following brain structures?

    (A) Thalamus
    (B) Pons
    (C) Hypothalamus
    (D) Amygdala
    (E) Association areas

7. A demyelinating disorder, such as multiple sclerosis, would cause all of the following symptoms EXCEPT

    (A) a reduction of white matter in the central nervous system
    (B) an increased rate of neuronal conduction
    (C) a slower propagation of signals along the axon
    (D) a deficiency of sensation
    (E) a decreased neuronal insulation

8. Which area of the brain is responsible for coordinating complex motor functions?

    (A) Frontal lobe
    (B) Occipital lobe
    (C) Reticular activating system
    (D) Cerebellum
    (E) Temporal lobe

9. All of the following brain areas are associated with the experience of emotion EXCEPT the

    (A) temporal lobe
    (B) amygdala
    (C) hypothalamus
    (D) pons
    (E) frontal lobe

10. The correct order of a nerve impulse is

    (A) resting potential, depolarization, hyperpolarization, repolarization, resting potential
    (B) resting potential, depolarization, repolarization, resting potential, hyperpolarization
    (C) resting potential, depolarization, repolarization, hyperpolarization, resting potential
    (D) depolarization, resting potential, repolarization, hyperpolarization, resting potential
    (E) depolarization, resting potential, repolarization, resting potential, hyperpolarization

REFLECT

Respond to the following questions:

- Which topics in this chapter do you hope to see on the multiple-choice section or essay?

- Which topics in this chapter do you hope not to see on the multiple-choice section or essay?

- Regarding any psychologists mentioned, can you pair the psychologists with their contributions to the field? Did they contribute significant experiments, theories, or both?

- Regarding any theories mentioned, can you distinguish between differing theories well enough to recognize them on the multiple-choice section? Can you distinguish them well enough to write a fluent essay on them?

- Regarding any figures given, if you were given a labeled figure from within this chapter, would you be able to give the significance of each part of the figure?

- Can you define the key terms at the end of the chapter?

- Which parts of the chapter will you review?

- Will you seek further help, outside of this book (such as a teacher, Princeton Review tutor, or AP Students), on any of the content in this chapter—and, if so, on what content?

Chapter 8
Biological Bases:
Consciousness

CONSCIOUSNESS

Consciousness is defined as the awareness that we have of ourselves, our internal states, and the environment. A **state of consciousness** enables us to evaluate the environment and to filter information from the environment through the mind, while being aware of the occurrence of this complex process. One state of consciousness is that of being alert. Alertness and the associated state of arousal involve the ability to remain attentive to our surroundings. It is something that we often take for granted; however, many patients who arrive in an emergency room are not alert for various reasons, arriving in a so-called altered state of consciousness. This can be due to head injuries, toxins, or other medical conditions. The ability to be alert is impaired in a variety of disorders, including narcolepsy, attention deficit disorder, depression, and chronic fatigue syndrome. Even without these disorders, it is not possible to maintain a heightened state of alertness indefinitely, and alertness varies over a 24-hour cycle. Alertness and arousal are controlled by structures within the brainstem. These structures are known as the reticular formation (also known as the reticular activating system, or RAS).

Philosophers and psychologists have debated the nature of consciousness for centuries. **William James** referred to consciousness as the **stream of thought**. The cognitive psychologist **Robert Sternberg** refers to consciousness as a **mental reality** that we create in order to adapt to the world. It serves to establish our personal identity. **The unconscious** level commonly refers to automatic processes, such as breathing or the beating of the heart. These are occurring because the brain is telling them to occur, but they are not happening as a result of conscious intervention.

Consciousness serves two important functions. First, consciousness is responsible for monitoring, or keeping track of ourselves, our environment, and our relationship with the environment. Additionally, consciousness serves a controlling role, planning our responses to the information gathered by monitoring. We typically think of ourselves as fully conscious, but there are lower levels of consciousness, specifically the preconscious and unconscious levels.

The **preconscious level** contains information that is available to consciousness but is not always in consciousness. It can be retrieved when needed. This is where directions to frequently visited places might be stored. The preconscious is also where many automatic behaviors are stored. You use these behaviors in tasks that you can do nearly without thought, such as riding a bicycle.

Consciousness exists on a continuum—starting from **controlled processing**, where we are very aware of what we are doing, and moving on to **automatic processing**, where we perform tasks mechanically, such as brushing our teeth. The continuum proceeds through daydreaming, a state in which we can regain consciousness in a moment, and meditation. Next, comes sleep and dreaming and, at the far end of the spectrum, coma and unconsciousness.

SLEEP AND DREAMING

Sleep is an altered state of consciousness. Interestingly, scientists still do not precisely understand the function of sleep. One theory holds that sleep is necessary for restorative processes. If this theory is correct, then some chemical in the body should be associated with sleep. Researchers have discovered some neurochemicals, notably **melatonin**, that play a role in sleep, yet a definitive cause-and-effect relationship between a brain chemical and the control of sleep has not been demonstrated.

Sleep and Evolution

Another theory of sleep is based on evolution. According to this point of view, our ancestors who survived to pass on their genes were diurnal (awake during the day and asleep at night). Our nocturnal ancestors were more likely to meet with disaster and die off before passing on their genes, as their visual system was not built to survive at night and avoid nocturnal predators.

In addition to conducting chemical investigations of sleep, psychologists investigate the functions of sleep by depriving animals or humans of it. It is difficult to deprive organisms of sleep, as the need for sleep is very strong. One 24-hour cycle without sleep is tolerable, but the second such cycle is considerably more difficult. By the third 24-hour cycle, **hallucinations** can begin, as well as **illusions**. Four 24-hour cycles of sleep deprivation can lead to paranoia and other psychological disturbances. All of the symptoms of sleep deprivation disappear when the deprived person is allowed to sleep again.

Another approach to the study of sleep is to investigate the pattern of sleeping. Sleeping generally occurs in humans during the time their area of the world is in darkness—that is, at night. People who live in extreme northern or southern exposures, where it may be light for close to 24 hours, generally try to create conditions of darkness in order to sleep. Our body temperature and other physiological markers follow a day-to-night type of pattern, known as a **circadian rhythm.** Body temperature rises as the morning approaches, is at a high during the day, dips in early afternoon, and then begins to drop again before sleep at night. Although this is a general description of the flow of alertness throughout the day, it varies by individual, and circadian rhythms also vary with age. Newborns can spend two-thirds of a day asleep. Older adults tend to peak in the morning and decline as the day progresses, while adolescents and young adults tend to be more energetic in the mid to late evening.

circa = around

dia = day

circadian = around the day

Light, both natural and artificial, also influences the biological clock by activating light-sensitive photoreceptors in the retina. Photoreceptors send signals to the brain's pineal gland, which is the region responsible for the production of melatonin. Because of the nature of the relationship of the Earth and the Sun, this natural day-night rhythm is a 24-hour one. Our circadian rhythms generally match this pattern. However, if all time cues (such as sunlight, clocks, and television) are removed, then we tend to follow roughly a 25-hour rhythm, called free-running rhythm.

External stimuli are important to setting our circadian rhythms. Rapidly changing these stimuli, such as in the case of traveling across time zones, can disturb circadian rhythms. In this example, the result can be the unpleasant feelings associated with jet lag.

Sleep itself is not a uniform process. Rather, sleep can be divided into stages based on brain-wave patterns. Brain waves are usually measured with **electroencephalograms (EEGs)**, which provide a picture of the electrical activity of the brain. When we are awake and focused, **beta wave** activity is happening. While still awake but more relaxed, we drift into **alpha waves**. Then, when we drift off to sleep, **theta wave** activity takes over. In stage 2 sleep, a pattern of waves known as **sleep spindles** appears. These spindles are occasionally broken up by **K complexes**, which are large, slow waves. The skeletal muscles relax during this portion of sleep. In stages 3 and 4, **delta waves** are most common, with a larger proportion of delta waves occurring during stage 4 sleep. The last stage of sleep is called **REM (rapid eye movement)** sleep. In all other stages of sleep, which often are referred to collectively as NREM or non-REM sleep, the eyes are relatively still. Researchers **Aserinsky** and **Kleitman** discovered that the eyes move vigorously during the REM stage. This stage of sleep is typically associated with dreaming, although it is not the only stage of sleep in which dreaming occurs. In REM sleep, our brain waves are mostly theta and beta. The fact that this is a very deep stage of sleep, characterized by suppressed skeletal muscle tone, but in which our brain waves resemble those observed when we are nearly awake, has led investigators to refer to REM sleep as **paradoxical sleep**.

Each sleep cycle is approximately 90 minutes long; therefore, if we sleep seven and one-half hours we will experience 5 cycles. We drift through the stages of sleep as follows:

- Stage 1: for up to 5 minutes

- Stage 2: for about 20 minutes

- Stage 3: for another 10 minutes

- Stage 4: for about 30 minutes

- Then back up through stage 3 for 10 minutes

- Stage 2: for 10 minutes

- Stage 1: for 1 or 2 minutes

- Then into REM sleep for 10 minutes

As the period of sleep progresses, stages 3 and 4 diminish and eventually disappear. Meanwhile, the REM or dream sleep gets longer until near morning when the dreams are approximately one hour long. Because of their proximity to an awakened state and their length, dreams occurring toward the end of sleep are more easily remembered. Psychologists note that the big difference in sleep is between REM and non-REM.

Sleep researcher **William Dement** studied the effects of the deprivation of REM sleep. By depriving participants of REM sleep (waking them every time they entered a REM period) and then allowing them to sleep normally after the experimental period, participant's REM periods increased from the normal 90 minutes of REM per night to 120 minutes of REM sleep in the period immediately following the deprivation. This is known as **REM rebound**, and it helps reinforce the idea that we need to sleep.

Given that sleep is such an important factor in our lives, it is not surprising that psychologists are interested in disorders of sleep. **Dyssomnias** are abnormalities in the amount, quality, or timing of sleep, and they include insomnia, narcolepsy, and sleep apnea. **Insomnia** is the most common of the sleep disorders and represents the inability to fall asleep or to maintain sleep. Chronic stress can cause temporary insomnia, as can the use of alcohol or stimulants such as caffeine.

Narcolepsy is the inability to stay awake. A narcoleptic has irresistible and persistent urges to sleep throughout the day and at inappropriate times, such as when driving. Interestingly, when narcoleptics fall asleep, it is typically only for a few minutes, and the sleep is almost all REM sleep. Although narcolepsy can be treated, the cause of the disorder is unknown. However, recent research suggests that the cause of narcolepsy is a dysfunction in the region of the hypothalamus that produces the neurotransmitter hypocretin (also called orexin).

Sleep apnea is a disorder in which a person repeatedly stops breathing while sleeping, which results in awakening after a minute or so without air. This disorder can occur hundreds of times in a night, leaving the sufferer exhausted during the day. Sleep apnea is associated with obesity and also may be linked to alcohol consumption. **Sudden infant death syndrome (SIDS)** may also be linked to sleep apnea.

Sleepwalking, or **somnambulism**, occurs when an individual walks around and sometimes even talks, while sleeping. Scientists have shown that sleepwalking is not simply acting out dreams, as it occurs during stage 3 and 4 sleep, not during REM.

Dreams, like sleep itself, are mysterious. We all dream every night, yet we do not always remember our dreams, and the function of dreams remains unknown. Freud hypothesized that dreams are the expression of unconscious wishes or desires. In psychoanalytic theory, the **manifest content**, or storyline and imagery of the dream, offers insight into and important symbols relating to unconscious processes. The **latent content** is the emotional significance and underlying meaning of the dream. The **activation-synthesis hypothesis of dreaming** postulates that dreams are the product of our awareness of neural activity due to sensory input while we are sleeping. Thus, if it starts raining while you are sleeping, you may dream of a waterfall. The **problem-solving theory of dreaming** holds that dreams provide a chance for the mind to work out issues that occupy its attention during waking hours. Neural repair, consolidation of memories, and protein synthesis seem to occur during dreams.

A **nightmare** is an elaborate dream sequence that produces a high level of anxiety or fear for the dreamer. The dreamer may experience a sense of physical danger to himself or his loved ones or a strong sense of embarrassment about doing something unacceptable. These dreams are vivid and can often be elaborately described by the dreamer upon awakening; they generally occur during REM sleep. In contrast, **night terrors** occur in much deeper sleep states; these involve actual behaviors such as screaming, crying, and jerking/lunging movements while asleep. This state is thought to overlap with somnambulism, as a person suffering a night terror may also be quite mobile, going through all the motions of being attacked by some horror, and yet be fully asleep. Nevertheless, there is usually no memory of these actions later on.

The Clinical Uses of Hypnosis

Hypnosis has some clinical applications. In some types of psychotherapy, hypnotism is used to extract memories so terrible that they were repressed from the conscious into the unconscious mind. It is controversial whether such repressed memories really exist. Such reports of repressed memories may be dubious in a legal setting and have been used to falsely accuse people of crimes they did not commit. People who are hypnotized may also be susceptible to **posthypnotic suggestion**. Posthypnotic suggestions are instructions given to people when they are hypnotized that are to be implemented after they wake. Such suggestions have had limited success in treating chronic pain, reducing blood pressure, and even in helping people quit smoking.

HYPNOSIS

Hypnosis is an altered state of consciousness in which the hypnotized person is very relaxed and open to suggestion. Hypnotized people can be convinced that they see things that are not there or that they are having experiences that they are not having. Hypnotized individuals can sometimes also recall things that they could not recall when they were in a normal state of consciousness. Typically, a person who is hypnotized has no recollection of the hypnosis upon returning to normal consciousness. Some theories hold that hypnosis is a state of deep relaxation, whereas other theories hold that hypnosis is not a real effect at all, but is rather a form of the participant's living up to the expectations of the hypnotist or experimenter. Another theory of hypnosis is the **neodissociative theory**. According to **Hilgard's theory of the hidden observer**, hypnosis somehow divides or dissociates the mind into two parts. One part obeys the hypnotist, while the other part, referred to as the hidden observer, silently observes everything. While this theory may explain the phenomenology of hypnotism, the physiology of hypnotism remains unexplained. Explaining hypnosis is made more difficult by the finding that hypnotic suggestibility varies on a normally distributed curve—in other words, some people are more susceptible to hypnosis than others.

MEDITATION

Meditation refers to a variety of techniques, many of which have been practiced for thousands of years, and which usually involve learning to train one's attention. Meditators may focus intensely on a single thing, such as their breathing, or they may broaden their attention and be aware of multiple stimuli, such as anything in their auditory field. Meditation has been utilized successfully to manage pain, stress, and anxiety disorders. Mindfulness-based stress reduction (MBSR) is a protocol commonly used in the medical setting to help alleviate stress. Meditators have increased alpha and theta waves while they are meditating (and to some extent have increased above their baseline after stopping), with more experienced meditators showing greater improvements.

PSYCHOACTIVE DRUG EFFECTS

Q: Why are narcotics effective?

Answer on page 149.

Drug	Effect on CNS	Effect on the Brain	Effect on Behavior
Alcohol	Depressant	Decreases dopamine levels	Dizziness, slurred speech, impaired judgment High doses can result in respiratory depression and death.
Barbiturates Examples: Seconal, Nebutal	Depressant	Inhibits neural arousal centers	Decreases anxiety; increases relaxation High doses can result in respiratory depression and death. Can be very addictive and dangerous when mixed with other depressants or alcohol
Tranquilizers Examples: Xanax, Valium, Librium	Depressant	Inhibits neural arousal centers	Reduces anxiety without inducing sleep
Caffeine	Stimulant	Accelerates heart rate; constricts blood vessels Reduces levels of adenosine, a neurochemical regulator of norepinephrine release	Can lead to irritability, anxiety, insomnia
Amphetamines Examples: diet pills, Ritalin	Stimulant	Increases body temperature and heart rate Increases production of dopamine and norepinephrine	Can be addictive Produces feelings of euphoria High doses can lead to motor dysfunction.

Drug	Effect on CNS	Effect on the Brain	Effect on Behavior
Cocaine	Stimulant	Stimulates heart rate and blood pressure Increases dopamine, serotonin, and norepinephrine release	Users feel as though they have increased mental abilities and social ability. Can be highly addictive
Nicotine	Stimulant	Stimulates acetylcholine transmission Increases heart rate	Has depressant behavioral effects such as decreasing appetite while increasing heart rate and respiration Can sometimes cause euphoria and dizziness
Narcotics Example: Oxycodone, Heroin	Depressant	Activates receptors for endogenous endorphins	Induces relaxation and euphoria; can relieve pain May cause impaired cognitive ability, sweating, nausea, and respiratory depression Highly addictive and available only by prescription or through illicit means
Hallucinogens Examples: LSD and marijuana	Distort sensory perceptions	May increase serotonin levels	May induce sensory synesthesia, in which stimuli from one sense, such as hearing, produce sensory effects in other modalities, such as vision Occasionally, the perceptual alterations are extremely unpleasant and terrifying. This state may also be accompanied by paranoia.

In discussing psychoactive drugs, it is important to distinguish among dependence, tolerance, and withdrawal. **Dependence** occurs when an individual continues using a drug despite overarching negative consequences in order to avoid unpleasant physical and/or psychological feelings associated with not taking it. (This term has generally replaced the term *addiction* in psychological and health circles.) Like physical dependence, psychological dependence is biologically based. Enjoyable behaviors produce activity in dopamine circuits in the brainstem, most notably in the nucleus accumbens, the "pleasure center" of the brain. This dopaminergic pathway naturally leads to feelings of reward and pleasure. Many addictive drugs share the characteristic of stimulating the release of dopamine in the nucleus accumbens.

A person has developed **tolerance** to a drug when increasingly larger doses are needed in order for the same effect to occur. It is possible to develop tolerance without being dependent. **Withdrawal** refers to the process of weaning off a drug one has become dependent upon; this often involves physical and psychological symptoms of a highly unpleasant nature. It can be said those dependent on drugs are, among other things, avoiding symptoms of withdrawal.

A: They are effective because they bear a striking resemblance to the endogenous endorphins, neurochemicals responsible for pain relief, and are implicated in pleasant feelings and euphoria.

KEY TERMS

Consciousness
> state of consciousness
> William James
> stream of thought
> Robert Sternberg
> mental reality
> unconscious level
> preconscious level
> controlled processing
> automatic processing

Sleep and Dreaming
> sleep
> melatonin
> hallucinations
> illusions
> circadian rhythm
> electroencephalograms
>   (EEGs)
> beta waves
> alpha waves
> theta waves
> sleep spindles
> K complexes
> delta waves
> rapid eye movement
>   (REM)
> Aserinsky and Kleitman
> paradoxical sleep
> William Dement
> REM rebound

> dyssomnias
> insomnia
> narcolepsy
> sleep apnea
> sudden infant death
>   syndrome (SIDS)
> sleepwalking
>   (somnambulism)
> manifest content
> latent content
> activation-synthesis
>   hypothesis of dreaming
> nightmare
> night terrors

Hypnosis
> neodissociative theory
> Hilgard's theory of the
>   hidden observer
> posthypnotic suggestion

Psychoactive Drug Effects
> depressants
> stimulants
> barbiturates
> tranquilizers
> amphetamines
> narcotics
> hallucinogens
> dependence
> tolerance
> withdrawal

Chapter 8 Drill

See Chapter 19 for answers and explanations.

1. The brain wave patterns known as "sleep spindles" are most characteristic of which stage of sleep?

   (A) Stage 1 sleep
   (B) Stage 2 sleep
   (C) Stage 3 sleep
   (D) Stage 4 sleep
   (E) REM sleep

2. Subliminal perception is a form of preconscious processing that occurs when stimuli are presented too rapidly for us to be consciously aware of them. The fact that these stimuli were perceived and processed on some level can be demonstrated by

   (A) immediate recognition of these stimuli
   (B) subtle influence to do or say something that has been presented subliminally
   (C) inability of the stimuli to be subject to the tip-of-the-tongue phenomenon
   (D) greater tendency of these stimuli to be subject to proactive interference
   (E) slower recall of these stimuli in a matched-pairs trial

3. If all external time cues are removed or blocked, the human circadian "free-running" rhythm tends to cycle every

   (A) 20 hours
   (B) 24 hours
   (C) 25 hours
   (D) 27 hours
   (E) 36 hours

4. All of the following are differences between nightmares and night terrors EXCEPT

   (A) nightmares typically occur during REM sleep, while night terrors typically occur during other sleep stages
   (B) nightmares are often recalled vividly and in detail upon waking, whereas night terrors are not
   (C) people are usually relatively still during nightmares, while they may move around quite a lot, even sleepwalk, during night terrors
   (D) while people may vocalize during nightmares, night terrors are more likely to involve screaming, crying, or shouting
   (E) nightmares are generally expressions of the dreamer's conscious issues, while night terrors reflect unconscious concerns

5. Which of the following is NOT a member of the class of psychoactive drugs collectively known as narcotics?

   (A) Codeine
   (B) Morphine
   (C) Heroin
   (D) Opium
   (E) Cocaine

6. Alcohol withdrawal syndrome occurs when an individual with a dependence on alcohol suddenly limits or stops his or her consumption of alcohol. Nervous symptoms of withdrawal include seizures and uncontrollable shaking of the extremities. What is the most plausible mechanism of action for these physical symptoms?

   (A) Chronic alcohol consumption causes down-regulation of GABA receptors, leading to a reduction in CNS inhibition, and excito-neurotoxicity.
   (B) Long-term alcohol abuse stimulates the autonomic nervous system, causing tremors.
   (C) Cessation of alcohol consumption leads to a reduction in dopamine production in the nucleus accumbens.
   (D) Alcohol is a hallucinogenic, and withdrawal causes the body to respond by relaxing, disinhibiting, and amplifying sensory information.
   (E) Alcohol is a depressant, decreasing inhibitory GABA-binding activity in the central nervous system.

7. A patient goes to the doctor's office citing symptoms of wakefulness in the night and tiredness during the day. Given these symptoms, which of the following might be a correct diagnosis?

    (A) Narcolepsy
    (B) Sleep apnea
    (C) Somnambulism
    (D) Paradoxical sleep
    (E) Night terrors

8. A 62-year-old female is on hypertension medication. Over the past three years, her dosage has increased twice. If she forgets to take her medication, her blood pressure increases dramatically. This increase in her blood pressure is an example of

    (A) addiction
    (B) psychological dependence
    (C) physical dependence
    (D) tolerance
    (E) diuretics

9. Paradoxical sleep occurs during

    (A) stage 1 sleep
    (B) stage 2 sleep
    (C) stage 3 sleep
    (D) stage 4 sleep
    (E) REM sleep

10. Over the course of the night, which is true about the sleep cycles?

    (A) Stages 3 and 4 eventually disappear while REM cycles lengthen to approximately one hour long.
    (B) Stages 2 and 3 eventually disappear while REM cycles lengthen to approximately 30 minutes long.
    (C) Stages 3 and 4 eventually disappear while stages 1 and 2 lengthen to approximately 20 minutes each.
    (D) REM cycles eventually disappear while stages 3 and 4 lengthen to approximately one hour long.
    (E) Stages 1 and 2 eventually disappear while stages 3 and 4 lengthen to approximately 20 minutes each.

REFLECT

Respond to the following questions:

- Which topics in this chapter do you hope to see on the multiple-choice section or essay?

- Which topics in this chapter do you hope not to see on the multiple-choice section or essay?

- Regarding any psychologists mentioned, can you pair the psychologists with their contributions to the field? Did they contribute significant experiments, theories, or both?

- Regarding any theories mentioned, can you distinguish between differing theories well enough to recognize them on the multiple-choice section? Can you distinguish them well enough to write a fluent essay on them?

- Regarding any figures given, if you were given a labeled figure from within this chapter, would you be able to give the significance of each part of the figure?

- Can you define the key terms at the end of the chapter?

- Which parts of the chapter will you review?

- Will you seek further help, outside of this book (such as a teacher, Princeton Review tutor, or AP Students), on any of the content in this chapter—and, if so, on what content?

Chapter 9
Sensation and Perception

INTRODUCTION TO SENSATION AND PERCEPTION

To study **sensation** is to study the relationship between physical stimulation and its psychological effects. Sensation is the process of taking in information from the environment. **Perception** refers to the way in which we recognize, interpret, and organize our sensations.

THRESHOLDS

In **psychophysics**, the branch of psychology that deals with the effects of physical stimuli on sensory response, researchers determine the smallest amount of sound, pressure, taste, or other stimuli that an individual can detect. Psychologists conducting this type of experiment are attempting to determine the **absolute threshold**—the minimal amount of stimulation needed to detect a stimulus and cause the neuron to fire 50 percent of the time. At the absolute threshold, we cannot detect lower levels of stimuli, but we can detect higher levels.

In a typical absolute-threshold experiment, an experimenter plays a series of tones of varying volume to determine at exactly what volume the participant first reports that she can hear the tone. Another approach to measuring **detection thresholds** involves **signal detection theory (SDT)**. This theory takes into consideration that there are four possible outcomes on each trial in a detection experiment: the signal (stimulus) is either present or it is not, and the participants respond that they can detect a signal or they cannot. Therefore, we have the following four possibilities:

- **Hit**—the signal was present, and the participant reported sensing it.

- **Miss**—the signal was present, but the participant did not sense it.

- **False alarm**—the signal was absent, but the participant reported sensing it.

- **Correct rejection**—the signal was absent, and the participant did not report sensing it.

SDT takes into account response bias, moods, feelings, and decision-making strategies that affect our likelihood of having a given response.

Another type of threshold is the **discrimination threshold**, which is the ability to distinguish the difference between two stimuli. The minimum amount of distance between two stimuli that can be detected as distinct is called the **just noticeable difference (JND)** or **difference threshold**.

Weber's Law

Ernst Weber (1795–1878) noticed that at low weights, say one ounce, it was easy to notice one-half-ounce increases or decreases in weight; however, at high weights, say 32 ounces, participants were not well able to judge one-half-ounce differences. The observation that the JND is a proportion of stimulus intensity is called **Weber's law**. Simply put, this law states that the greater the magnitude of the stimulus, the larger the differences must be to be noticed.

In this case, the experiment might involve playing pairs of tones of varying volumes. The participants would try to determine if the tones that they heard were the same or different.

Subliminal perception is a form of preconscious processing that occurs when we are presented with stimuli so rapidly that we are not consciously aware of them. When later presented with the same stimuli for a longer period of time, we recognize them more quickly than stimuli we were not subliminally exposed to. Clearly, there was some preconscious processing, known as **priming**, occurring even if we were not aware of it. Another example of preconscious information processing can be seen in the **tip-of-the-tongue phenomenon**, in which we try to recall something that we already know is available but is not easily available for conscious awareness. This phenomenon demonstrates that certain preconscious information may be available to the conscious mind but quite difficult to access.

That moment at the optometrist's when they ask which is better — lens 1 or lens 2? lens 1 or lens 2? — and you freak out because they seem the same. Don't worry! You're right at the JND!.

RECEPTOR PROCESSES

Sensory organs have specialized cells, known as **receptor cells**, which are designed to detect specific types of energy. For example, the visual system has specialized receptor cells for detecting light waves. The area from which our receptor cells receive input is the **receptive field**. Incoming forms of energy to which our receptors are sensitive include mechanical (such as in touch), electromagnetic (such as in vision), and chemical (such as in taste). No matter what the form of the input at the level of the receptor, it must first be converted, or **transduced**, into the electrochemical form of communication used by the nervous system. Through a process called **transduction**, the receptors convert the input, or stimulus, into neural impulses, which are sent to the brain. For example, when we hear something, tiny receptor cells in the inner ear first convert mechanical vibrations into electrochemical signals. These signals are then carried by neurons to the brain. Transduction takes place at the level of the receptor cells, and then the neural message is passed to the nervous system. The incoming information from all of our senses, except for smell, travels to the sensory neurons of the thalamus. The thalamus, as you may recall from the neuroanatomy section, redirects this information to various sensory cortices in the cerebral cortex where it is processed. It is at the level of the thalamus that the **contralateral shift** occurs, in which much of the sensory input from one side of the body travels to the opposite side of the brain. Olfaction, or the sense of smell, travels in a more direct path to the cerebral cortex, without stopping at or being relayed by the thalamus.

SENSORY MECHANISMS

Sensory receptors deal with a wide range of stimuli, and we experience a wide variety of input within each given sensory dimension. Imagine, for example, the gamut of colors and intensities that the eye can sense and relate to the brain. **Sensory coding** is the process by which receptors convey such a range of information to the brain.

Every stimulus has two dimensions: what it is (its **qualitative dimension**) and how much of it there is (its **quantitative dimension**). The qualitative dimension is coded and expressed by which neurons are firing. For example, neurons firing in the occipital lobe would indicate that the sensory information is light, and neurons firing in the temporal lobe might indicate that the sensory stimulus is sound. In contrast, the quantitative information is coded by the number of cells firing. Bright lights and loud noises involve the excitation of more neurons than those brought on by dim lights and quiet noises. The wavelengths of light and frequency of sound are perceived as hue and pitch, respectively. The physical characteristic of amplitude is perceived as brightness for light and loudness for sound. Similarly, the physical trait of complexity is known as saturation, when dealing with light, and timbre, when referring to sound. Sensory neurons respond to differing environmental stimuli by altering their firing rate and the regularity of their firing pattern. **Single-cell recording** is a technique by which the firing rate and pattern of a single receptor cell can be measured in response to varying sensory input.

Visual Mechanisms

Sensation occurs in differing ways for the various sensory systems. **Visual sensation** occurs when the eye receives light input from the outside world. Note that the object as it exists in the environment is known as the **distal stimulus**, whereas the image of that object on the retina is called the **proximal stimulus**. Because of the shape of the retina and the positions of the cornea and the lens, the proximal stimulus is inverted. The brain, through perceptual processes, is then capable of interpreting this image correctly.

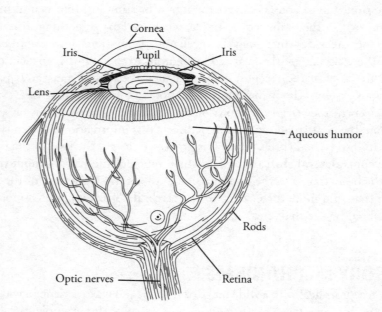

Visual sensation is a complex process. First, light passes through the **cornea**, which is a protective layer on the outside of the eye. Just under the cornea is the **lens**. The curvature of the lens changes to accommodate for distance. These changes are called, logically, **accommodations**. The **retina** is at the back of the eye and serves as the screen onto which the proximal stimulus is projected. The retina is covered with receptors known as **rods** and **cones**. Rods, located on the periphery of the retina, are sensitive in low light. Cones, concentrated in the center of the retina, or **fovea**, are sensitive to bright light and color vision. After light stimulates the receptors, this information passes through horizontal cells to **bipolar** and **amacrine cells**. Some low-level information processing may occur here. The stimulation then travels to the ganglion cells of the **optic nerves**. The optic nerves cross at the **optic chiasm**, sending half of the information from each visual field to the opposite side of the brain. Each visual field includes information from both the left and right eye. From here, information travels to the primary visual cortex areas for processing. The brain processes the information received from vision—color, movement, depth, and form—in parallel, not serial, fashion. In other words, the brain is simultaneously identifying the patterns of what is seen. **Serial processing** occurs when the brain computes information step-by-step in a methodical and linear matter, while **parallel processing** happens when the brain computes multiple pieces of information simultaneously. Over time and through practice, serial processes can turn into parallel processes, just as riding a bike initially requires a person to consider each decision, but later is done seemingly automatically. **Feature detector** neurons "see" different parts of the pattern, such as a line set at a specific angle to the background. Like pieces of a jigsaw puzzle, these parts are amalgamated to produce the pattern in the environment. This process starts at the back of the occipital lobe and moves forward. As the information moves forward, it becomes more complex and integrated. This process, by which information becomes more complex as it travels through the sensory system, is known as **convergence** and occurs across all sensory systems. Once lines and colors have been sensed, the information travels through two pathways: the dorsal stream and the ventral stream. The ventral stream is the "what" pathway that connects to the prefrontal cortex, allowing a person to recognize an object. The dorsal stream is the "where" pathway that integrates visual information with the other senses through a connection to the somatosensory cortex at the top of the brain.

Two different processes contribute to our ability to see in color. The first is based on the **Young-Helmholtz** or **trichromatic theory**. According to this theory, the cones in the retina of the eyes are activated by light waves associated with blue, red, and green. We see all colors by mixing these three, much as a television does. However, this does not tell the whole story. Another theory, known as **opponent process theory**, contends that cells within the thalamus respond to opponent pairs of receptor sets—namely, black/white, red/green, and blue/yellow. If one color of the set is activated, the other is essentially turned off. For example, when you stare at a red dot on a page and then you turn away to a blank piece of white paper, you will see a green dot on the blank piece of paper because the red receptors have become fatigued and, in comparison, the green receptors are now more active. This is known as an **afterimage**. **Color blindness** responds to this theory, as well.

Tip!
Think C for cones and C for color.

Most color blindness occurs in males, which provides strong evidence that this is a sex-linked genetic condition. **Dichromats** are people who cannot distinguish along the red/green or blue/yellow continuums. **Monochromats** see only in shades of black and white (this is much more rare). Most color blindness is genetic.

Auditory Mechanisms

Auditory input, in the form of sound waves, enters the ear by passing the outer ear, the part of the ear that is on the outside of your head, and into the ear canal.

Q: What are the ossicles?

Answer on page 160.

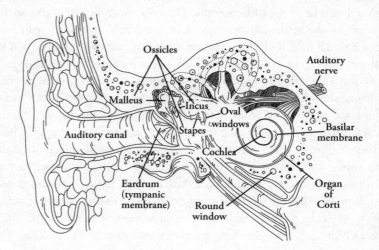

The outer ear collects and magnifies sound waves. The vibrations then enter the middle ear, first vibrating the **tympanic membrane**. This membrane abuts the **ossicles**, the three tiny bones that comprise the middle ear. Vibration of the tympanic membrane vibrates the ossicles. The last of the three ossicles is the **stapes**, which vibrates against the oval window. The oval window is the beginning of the inner ear. The vibrations further jiggle the **cochlea**. Within the cochlea are receptor cells, known as hair cells, so named for their hair-like cilia which move in response to the vibrations. The hair cells line a structure in the cochlea called the basilar membrane. From the cochlea, sound energy is transferred to the auditory nerve and then to the temporal lobe of the auditory cortex. The inner ear is also responsible for balance and contains **vestibular sacs**, which have receptors sensitive to tilting.

Various theories have been suggested for how hearing occurs. Current thinking relies on the work of Georg von Békésy, which asserts that a traveling wave energizes the basilar membrane. As frequencies get higher, so do the peaks of the traveling wave, increasing the stimulation of the receptors for hearing. This accounts for recognition of sound above 150 Hz. However, humans can hear from 20 to 20,000 Hz. The volley principle—which states that receptor cells fire alternatively, increasing their firing capacity—appears to account for the reception of sound in the lower ranges. **Place theory** asserts that sound waves generate activity at different places along the basilar membrane. **Frequency theory** in hearing states that we sense pitch because the rate of neural impulses is equal to the frequency of a particular sound. **Deafness** can occur from damage to the ear structure or the neural pathway.

Conductive deafness refers to injury to the outer or middle ear structures, such as the eardrum. Impairment of some structure or structures from the cochlea to the auditory cortex results in **sensorineural**, or nerve, deafness.

Other Sensory Mechanisms

Olfaction (smell) is a chemical sense. Scent molecules reach the olfactory epithelium, deep in the nasal cavity. The scent molecules contact receptor cells at this location. Axons from these receptors project directly to the olfactory bulbs of the brain. From there, information travels to the olfactory cortex and the limbic system. Because the amygdala and hippocampus connect to olfactory nerves, it is easy to understand why certain smells trigger memories.

Gustation (taste) is also a chemical sense. The tongue is coated with small protrusions known as papillae. Located on the papillae are the taste buds, the receptors for gustatory information. There are five basic tastes: sweet, salty, bitter, sour, and umami (savory). These five tastes may have evolved for specific reasons. For example, sweetness, which we tend to like, is often accompanied by calories. Most poisonous plants, in contrast, taste bitter, a taste we generally do not like. Information from the taste buds travels to the medulla oblongata and then to the pons and the thalamus. This information is then relayed to the gustatory areas of the cerebral cortex, as well as the hypothalamus and limbic system.

The skin has **cutaneous** and **tactile receptors** that provide information about pressure, pain, and temperature. The receptor cells sensitive to pressure and movement are fast-conducting myelinated neurons, which send information to the spinal cord. From here, the information goes to the medulla oblongata, the thalamus, and finally, to the somatosensory cortex. Pain information is sent via two types of neurons; C fibers are unmyelinated and responsible for the throbbing sense of chronic pain, while myelinated A-delta fibers send information about acute pain. The pain signal first reaches the spinal cord and triggers the release of "substance P" (a neuropeptide, or chemical signal similar to a neurotransmitter, that alerts the spinal cord to the presence of a painful stimulus). The signal then travels to the thalamus and to the cingulate cortex, which is responsible for attention. Once pain is perceived, the brain begins to reduce the intensity of the signal through a process known as "pain-gating." A signal is sent from the brain to opiate receptors in the spinal cord, which reduces the sensation of pain. This information projects to the limbic system and then to the somatosensory cortex. The receptor cells for temperature can be divided into **cold fibers**, which fire in response to cold stimuli, and **warm fibers**, which are sensitive to warm stimuli.

Other senses include the **vestibular sense**, which involves the sensation of balance. This sense is located in the semicircular canals of the inner ear. **Kinesthesis**, found in the joints and ligaments, transmits information about the location and position of the limbs and body parts.

Use this table to compare and contrast different sensory systems.

Sensory System	Receptor Cells Location	Type of Energy	Transduction	Processing Center Location
Visual	Eye	Light	Rods and cones in the retina	Occipital lobe
Auditory	Ear	Sound	Cochlea	Temporal lobe
Tactile	Tactile and cutaneous cells on the skin	Pressure	Tactile cells	Somatosensory cortex
Olfaction (smell)	Nose	Chemical	Olfactory receptor cells	Olfactory bulb
Gustation (taste)	Tongue	Chemical	Taste buds	Cerebral cortex

A: The ossicles are three tiny bones in the middle ear, called the malleus, incus, and stapes, that connect the eardrum to the oval window.

SENSORY ADAPTATION

Our sensory systems need to do more than simply detect the presence and absence of stimulation. They also need to do more than detect the intensity or quality of stimuli. A key feature of our sensory systems is that they are dynamic, that is, they detect changes in stimuli intensity and quality. Two processes are used in responding to changing stimuli: adaptation and habituation.

Adaptation is an unconscious, temporary change in response to environmental stimuli. An example of this process is our adaptation to being in darkness. At first, it is difficult to see, but our visual system soon adapts to the lack of light. Sensory adaptation to differing stimuli leaves our sensory systems at various adaptation levels. The adaptation level is the new reference standard of stimulation against which new stimuli are judged. A familiar example is that of the swimming pool. If you enter a 75-degree swimming pool directly from an air-conditioned room, it will feel warm, as your adaptation level is set for the cold room. If, however, you are on a hot beach and then enter the same pool, it will feel cold, as your adaptation level is set for the heat of the beach.

Habituation is the process by which we become accustomed to a stimulus, and notice it less and less over time. **Dishabituation** occurs when a change in the stimulus, even a small change, causes us to notice it again. Dishabituation also occurs when a stimulus is removed and then re-presented. A good example of this pair of processes is in the noise from an air conditioner. We may notice a noisy air conditioner when we first enter a room, but after a few minutes, we barely even notice it; we have habituated to the noise. However, when the air conditioner's compressor turns on, slightly altering the sound being generated, we once again notice the noise. This noticing is dishabituation. Although habituation is not typically a conscious process, we can control it under certain circumstances. If, in the examples above, we are unaware of the air-conditioner noise, but then someone asks us if the noise of the air conditioner sounds like something else, we can force ourselves to dishabituate, and again notice the noise. This control over our information processing is the key to distinguishing habituation from sensory adaptation: you cannot control sensory adaptation; for example, you cannot force your eyes to adapt to darkness by mere force of will. You can, however, force yourself to pay attention to things to which you have habituated.

ATTENTION

The term **attention** refers to the processing through cognition of a select portion of the massive amount of information incoming from the senses and contained in memory. In common terms, attention is what allows us to focus on one small aspect of our perceptual world, such as a conversation, while constantly being assailed by massive input to all of our sensory systems. Attention serves as a bottleneck, or funnel, that channels out some information in order to focus on other information. This process is essential because the brain is not equipped to process and pay attention to all of the information it is presented with at a particular moment. The fact that the brain must take shortcuts and focus on particular information is a key issue in perception, which explains why the brain can be tricked through illusions. A good example of attention in action is **selective attention**, by which we try to attend to one thing while ignoring another. For example, we try to attend to a movie, while trying to ignore the people having a conversation behind us. An example of selective attention is called the "**cocktail party phenomenon**," which refers to our ability to carry on and follow a single conversation in a room full of conversations. At the same time, our attention can quickly be drawn to another conversation by key stimuli, such as someone saying our name. This recognition of our name is a demonstration that, although we are not paying very much attention to those other conversations, we are definitely attending to information we are not consciously aware of at that moment. This phenomenon has been studied in the laboratory with headphones, by playing a different message in each of a participant's ears. The participant is instructed to repeat only one of the conversations. This repetition is referred to as **shadowing**. The message played into the nonshadowed ear is largely ignored, however. Changes in that message or key words, like names, can draw attention to that message. There are two main types of theories explaining selective attention: filter theories and attentional resource theories. **Filter theories** propose that stimuli must pass through some form of screen or filter to enter into attention. Donald Broadbent proposed a filter at the receptor level. However, the notion of a filter at this level has generally been discarded, based on findings showing that meaningful stimuli, such as our own names, can catch our attention. Therefore, the filter must be at a higher processing level than that of the receptors because meaning has already been processed.

Attentional resource theories, in contrast, posit that we have only a fixed amount of attention, and this resource can be divided up as is required in a given situation. So, if you are deeply engrossed in this book, you are giving it nearly all of your attentional resources. Only strong stimulation could capture your attention. This theory is also inadequate, however, because all attention is not equal. For example, a conversation occurring near you is more likely to interfere with your reading than is some other nonverbal noise.

Differentiating Messages
It is easiest for people to tell the difference between messages when they are physically different, such as when one message is spoken by a woman and the other by a man.

Divided attention, trying to focus on more than one task at a time, is most difficult when attending to two or more stimuli that activate the same sense, as in watching TV and reading. The ability to successfully divide attention declines with age.

PERCEPTUAL PROCESSES

When we were describing sensory mechanisms, we talked about how environmental stimuli affect the receptor systems. This section deals with **perceptual processes**—how our mind interprets these stimuli. There are two main theories of perception—bottom-up and top-down.

Remember This!
Sensation = bottom-up process
Perception = top-down process

Bottom-up processing achieves recognition of an object by breaking it down into its component parts. It relies heavily on the sensory receptors. Bottom-up processing is the brain's analysis and acknowledgement of the raw data. **Top-down processing**, by contrast, occurs when the brain labels a particular stimulus or experience. For example, let's think about the first time a person tastes the sourness of a lemon. In this example, the neurons firing to alert the brain of the presence of some taste in the mouth is a bottom-up process, whereas labeling it "sour" is the top-down process. However, the next time the person sees a lemon, they might salivate or wince before ever tasting the lemon. This is top-down processing because the expectation based on experience influences the perception of the lemon.

Visual perception is quite complex. We need to perceive depth, size, shape, and motion. Depth perception is facilitated by various perceptual cues. Because of the limited ability of the brain to process information, it must take certain shortcuts and educated guesses based on how the world is normally structured. As such, the brain uses these cues but can also fall victim to illusions.

Visual perception cues can be divided into monocular and binocular cues. **Monocular depth cues** are those that we need only one eye to see. As such, they can be depicted in two-dimensional representations. **Relative size** refers to the fact that images that are farther from us project a smaller image on the retina than do those that are closer to us. Therefore, we expect an object that appears much larger than another to be closer to us. Related to this idea is the idea of **texture gradient**. Textures, or the patterns of distribution of objects, appear to grow more dense as distance increases. If we are looking at pebbles in the distance, they appear smooth and uniform, but close up may appear jagged and rough. Another monocular depth cue is **interposition**, also known as occlusion, which occurs when a near object partially blocks the view of an object behind it. **Linear perspective** is a monocular cue based on the perception that parallel lines seem to draw closer together as the lines recede into the distance. Picture yourself standing on a train track, looking at the two rails. As the rails move away from you, they appear to draw closer together. The place where the rails seem to join is called the **vanishing point**. This is the point at which the two lines become indistinguishable from a single line and then disappear. Objects present near the vanishing point are assumed to be farther away than those along the tracks at a point where they diverge greatly. **Aerial perspective**, another perceptual cue, is based on the observation that atmospheric moisture and dust tend to obscure objects in the distance more than they do nearby objects. An example of this notion occurs when one is driving in the fog; a far-off building looks more distant than it really is through the fog, but its image quickly becomes clearer and clearer as you approach. **Relative clarity** is a perceptual clue that explains why less distinct, fuzzy images appear to be more distant. **Motion parallax** is the difference in the apparent movement of objects at different distances, when the observer is in motion. For example, when riding on a train, a person sees distant objects out of a window as seeming to move fairly slowly; they may appear to move in the same direction as the train. Nearer objects seem to move more quickly and in the opposite direction to the movement of the train. Note that motion parallax differs from other monocular depth cues in that it requires motion and cannot be represented in a two-dimensional image.

Binocular depth cues rely on both eyes viewing an image. They result from the fact that each eye sees a given image from a slightly different angle. **Stereopsis** refers to the three-dimensional image of the world resulting from binocular vision. **Retinal convergence** is a depth cue that results from the fact that your eyes must turn inward slightly to focus on near objects. The closer the object, the more the eyes must turn inward. The complement to stereopsis is **binocular disparity**, which results from the fact that the closer an object is, the less similar the information arriving at each eye will be. This process can be demonstrated by covering one eye, then the other, while looking at something directly in front of you. This procedure reveals two very different views of the object. Repeat this procedure with an object across the room, however, and the two views appear more similar.

Nature, Nurture, and the Visual Cliff

Together, the binocular cues for vision enable us to have depth perception. To test whether depth perception was innate (nature) or learned (nurture), researchers **Eleanor Gibson and Richard Walk** developed the **visual cliff** to test depth perception. The visual cliff was a glass tabletop that appeared to be clear on one side and had a checkerboard design visible on the other side. Infants were placed on the checkerboard side of the "cliff," and researchers tracked whether they would crawl onto the clear side, thus going "over the cliff." Most infants refused to do so, which implies that depth perception is at least partially innate. Because the infant had to be a few months old, it was unclear how much learning had influenced depth perception. With other animals tested (chicks, pigs, kittens, turtles), it was concluded that the animal's visual skills depended on the importance of vision to the organism's survival.

As previously stated, the visual system also needs to perceive and recognize form, that is, size and shape. The **Gestalt approach** to form perception is based on a **top-down theory**. This view holds that most perceptual stimuli can be broken down into figure-ground relationships. Figures are those things that stand out, whereas the ground is the field against which the figures stand out. The famous vase-face example shows us that figure and ground are often reversible.

Some basic Gestalt principles of figure detection include the following:

- **Proximity**—the tendency to see objects near each other as forming groups

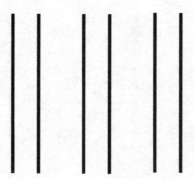

The Gestalt Principle of Proximity: We tend to see these as three pairs of lines, rather than six individual lines.

- **Similarity**—the tendency to prefer grouping like objects together

The Gestalt Principle of Similarity: We tend to see these as rows of circles and rows of squares, rather than columns of circles and squares.

- **Symmetry**—the tendency to perceive forms that make up mirror images

The Gestalt Principle of Symmetry: We tend to see the top figures as a single circle, and the lower figures as forming a single triangle.

- **Continuity**—the tendency to perceive fluid or continuous forms, rather than jagged or irregular ones

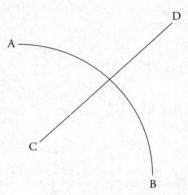

The Gestalt Principle of Continuity: We tend to see this as two lines, one from point A to point B, the other from C to D, rather than seeing it as A to D and C to B.

- **Closure**—the tendency to see closed objects rather than those that are incomplete

The Gestalt Principle of Closure: We tend to see this as three rectangles, even though there is actually only one rectangle that is completely visible.

These Gestalt principles represent the **Law of Prägnanz**, or minimum tendency, meaning that we tend to see objects in their simplest forms.

A different theory of form recognition is based on a **feature detector approach**. This approach differs from the Law of Prägnanz, which reduces an image to its simplest form, by positing that organisms respond to specific aspects of a particular stimulus. For example, when driving a car, we use feature detection to anticipate the movement of other cars and pedestrians that demand our immediate attention, helping us to be more aware of the environment.

Constancy is another important perceptual process. Constancy means that we know that a stimulus remains the same size, shape, brightness, weight, and/or volume even though it does not appear to. People who have never seen airplanes on the ground will have trouble perceiving the actual size of a plane because of their experience with the size of the object when airborne. The *ability* to achieve constancy, which is innate, and the *experience*, which is learned, both contribute to our development of the various types of constancy.

One of the most complex abilities we have is **motion detection**. We perceive motion through two processes. One records the changing position of the object as it moves across the retina. The other tracks how we move our head to follow the stimuli. In both cases, the brain interprets the information with special motion detectors. A related issue is the perception of **apparent motion**. Examples of apparent movement include blinking lights on a roadside arrow, which give the appearance of movement (**phi phenomenon**); a motion picture, where still pictures move at a fast enough pace to imply movement (**stroboscopic effect**); and still light that appears to twinkle in darkness (**autokinetic effect**).

KEY TERMS

Thresholds

sensation
perception
psychophysics
absolute threshold
detection thresholds
signal detection theory (SDT)
hit
miss
false alarm
correct rejection
discrimination thresholds
just noticeable difference (JND)
difference threshold
Ernst Weber
Weber's law
subliminal perception
priming
tip-of-the-tongue phenomenon

Receptor Processes

receptor cells
receptive field
transduced
transduction
contralateral shift

Sensory Mechanism

sensory coding
qualitative dimension
quantitative dimension
single-cell recording
visual sensation
distal stimulus
proximal stimulus
cornea
lens
accommodations
retina
rods
cones
fovea
bipolar cells
amacrine cells
optic nerves
optic chiasm
serial processing

parallel processing
feature detector
convergence
Young-Helmholtz theory
    (trichromatic theory)
opponent process theory
afterimage
color blindness
dichromats
monochromats
auditory input
tympanic membrane
ossicles
stapes
cochlea
vestibular sacs
place theory
frequency theory
deafness
conductive deafness
sensorineural
olfaction
gustation
cutaneous receptors
tactile receptors
cold fibers
warm fibers
vestibular sense
kinesthesis

Sensory Adaptation

adaptation
habituation
dishabituation

Attention

selective attention
cocktail party phenomenon
shadowing
filter theories
attentional resource theories
divided attention

Perceptual Processes

bottom-up processing
top-down processing
visual perception
monocular depth cues
relative size
texture gradient
interposition
linear perspective
vanishing point
aerial perspective
relative clarity
motion parallax
binocular depth cues
stereopsis
retinal convergence
binocular disparity
Eleanor Gibson and
    Richard Walk

visual cliff
Gestalt approach
top-down theory
proximity
similarity
symmetry
continuity
closure
Law of Prägnanz
feature detector approach
constancy
motion detection
apparent motion
phi phenomenon
stroboscopic effect
autokinetic effect

Chapter 9 Drill

See Chapter 19 for answers and explanations.

1. If a person is supposed to press a button when he sees a red triangle but instead presses the button when he sees a green triangle, what is this called?

    (A) Opponent process
    (B) Hit
    (C) False alarm
    (D) Miss
    (E) Correct rejection

2. The five basic gustatory sensations that most animals possess are

    (A) bitter, salty, sweet, tangy, sour
    (B) salty, sweet, bitter, sour, umami
    (C) smooth, grainy, cold, hot, prickly
    (D) grain, fruit, meat, vegetable, dairy
    (E) salty, sharp, umami, sour, bitter

3. Cats tend to notice slight movements under low lighting conditions with greater ease than do humans; they do not, however, find it easy to distinguish colors. This is primarily due to their retinas containing, in comparison to humans,

    (A) relatively fewer amacrine cells and relatively more bipolar cells
    (B) relatively fewer ganglion cells and relatively more osmoreceptors
    (C) relatively fewer cilia and relatively more optic nerve cells
    (D) relatively fewer cones and relatively more rods
    (E) relatively fewer mechanoreceptors and relatively more ossicles

4. The Gestalt concept of perceptual continuity refers to

    (A) our tendency to see objects near to each other as belonging to the same group
    (B) our tendency to see objects that are closer to us as larger than objects that are farther away
    (C) our tendency to see fluid or complete forms rather than irregular or incomplete ones
    (D) our tendency to see similar-looking objects as part of the same group
    (E) our tendency to see two slightly different images from each of our eyes

5. Which of the following would be the best illustration of Weber's law?

    (A) Most people can recognize the difference between a 40- and 80-decibel sound, but not an 80- and 82-decibel sound.
    (B) A person can recognize an imperceptible amount of perfume in a ten-foot-by-ten-foot room.
    (C) People cannot attend to more than one stimulus at a time.
    (D) A person has the ability to tell the difference between a 20-watt bulb and a 100-watt bulb 50 percent of the time.
    (E) All auditory stimuli above a certain frequency "sound" as if their frequencies are the same.

6. What structure in the middle ear generates vibrations that match the sound waves striking it?

    (A) Basilar membrane
    (B) Tympanic membrane
    (C) Cochlea
    (D) Malleus
    (E) Stapes

7. In the human visual pathway, what cell type comprises the bundle of fibers called the optic nerve?

    (A) Rods
    (B) Bipolar cells
    (C) Ganglion cells
    (D) Fovea cells
    (E) Cones

8. Instead of perceiving a series of lines, humans perceive two shapes: a circle and a rectangle. What best accounts for this phenomenon?

    (A) The principles of Gestalt psychology
    (B) Bottom-up processing
    (C) Parallel processing
    (D) Weber's law
    (E) Summation

9. Claire views the figure above and reports seeing a triangle in the center supported by some concentric discs. Which Gestalt principle does Claire rely on most heavily to render this description?

    (A) Proximity
    (B) Symmetry
    (C) Similarity
    (D) Closure
    (E) Continuity

10. Laretta walks into a classroom and notices a strange odor. She sits down for class and, over time, forgets about the smell. When she returns to class the next day, she notices the odor again. This phenomenon is known as

    (A) habituation
    (B) dishabituation
    (C) adaptation
    (D) sensitization
    (E) desensitization

REFLECT
Respond to the following questions:

- Which topics in this chapter do you hope to see on the multiple-choice section or essay?

- Which topics in this chapter do you hope not to see on the multiple-choice section or essay?

- Regarding any psychologists mentioned, can you pair the psychologists with their contributions to the field? Did they contribute significant experiments, theories, or both?

- Regarding any theories mentioned, can you distinguish between differing theories well enough to recognize them on the multiple-choice section? Can you distinguish them well enough to write a fluent essay on them?

- Regarding any figures given, if you were given a labeled figure from within this chapter, would you be able to give the significance of each part of the figure?

- Can you define the key terms at the end of the chapter?

- Which parts of the chapter will you review?

- Will you seek further help, outside of this book (such as a teacher, Princeton Review tutor, or AP Students), on any of the content in this chapter—and, if so, on what content?

Chapter 10
Learning

LEARNING: AN OVERVIEW

Learning is a relatively permanent or stable change in behavior as a result of experience. Such changes may be associated with certain changes in the connections within the nervous system. Learning occurs by various methods, including classical conditioning, operant conditioning, and social learning. Cognitive factors are also implicated in learning, particularly in humans.

NONASSOCIATIVE LEARNING

Nonassociative learning occurs when an organism is repeatedly exposed to one type of stimulus. Two important types of nonassociative learning are **habituation** and **sensitization**. A habit is an action that is performed repeatedly until it becomes automatic, and habituation follows a very similar process. Essentially, a person learns to "tune out" the stimulus. For example, suppose you live near train tracks, and trains pass by your house on a regular basis. When you first move into the house, the sound of the trains passing by is annoying and loud, and it always makes you cover your ears. However, after living in the house for a few months, you become used to the sound and stop covering your ears every time the trains pass. You may even become so accustomed to the sound that it becomes background noise, and you don't even notice it anymore.

Dishabituation occurs when the previously habituated stimulus is removed or altered. More specifically, after a person has been habituated to a given stimulus, and the stimulus is removed, this leads to dishabituation—the person is no longer accustomed to the stimulus. If the stimulus is then presented again, the person will react to it as if it were a new stimulus and is likely to respond even more strongly to it than before. In the train example above, dishabituation could occur when you go away on vacation for a few weeks to a quiet beach resort. The train noise is no longer present, so you become dishabituated to that constant noise. Then, when you return to your home and the noisy train tracks, the first time you hear the train after you return, you notice it again, and you may start covering your ears again or have an even more severe reaction.

Sensitization is, in many ways, the opposite of habituation. During sensitization, there is an increase in responsiveness due to either a repeated application of a stimulus or a particularly aversive or noxious stimulus. Instead of being able to "tune out" or ignore the stimulus so as to avoid reacting at all (as in habituation), the stimulus actually produces a more exaggerated response. Imagine that instead of trains passing by your house, you attend a rock concert and sit near the stage. The feedback noise from the amplifier may at first be merely irritating, but as the aversive noise continues, instead of getting used to it, it actually becomes much more painful, to the point at which you have to cover your ears and perhaps even move. Sensitization may also cause you to respond more vigorously to similar stimuli. For example, as you leave the rock concert, an ambulance passes. The siren, which usually doesn't bother you, seems particularly loud and abrasive, as you've been sensitized to the noise of the rock concert. Thankfully, sensitization is usually temporary and unlikely to result in any long-term behavior change. **Desensitization** refers to a decreased responsiveness to an aversive stimulus after repeated exposure. This phenomenon may occur on its own or in the context of **desensitization therapy**. For example, if you have a phobia against snakes, you might engage in **systematic desensitization**: you look at a picture of a snake until your reaction is normal; then you come into a room with a snake until your reaction is normal. In various therapy sessions, you get closer and closer to the snake, eventually even handling it. By being exposed to the stimulus but having no bad outcomes, you can become desensitized to the stimulus and thus overcome your phobia.

CLASSICAL CONDITIONING

Classical conditioning was first described by **Ivan Pavlov** and is sometimes called **Pavlovian conditioning**. Classical conditioning occurs when a neutral stimulus, paired with a previously meaningful stimulus, eventually takes on some meaning itself. For example, if you shine a light in your fish tank, the fish will ignore it. If you put food in the tank, they will all typically swim to the top to get the food. If, however, each time you feed the fish, you shine the light in the tank before putting in the food, the fish will begin to learn about the light. Eventually, the light alone will cause the fish to swim to the top, as if food had been placed in the tank. The previously neutral light has now taken on some meaning. If you are having a difficult time understanding the different parts of classical conditioning, note that *conditioning* is another word for *learning*. For instance, *unconditioned response* is just another way of saying *unlearned response*.

Psychologists use specific terms for the various stimuli in classical conditioning. The **conditioned stimulus (CS)** is the initially neutral stimulus—in our example, the light. The **unconditioned stimulus (US)** is the initially meaningful stimulus. In our example, the US is food. The response to the US does not have to be learned; this naturally occurring response is the **unconditioned response (UR)**. In our example, the UR is swimming to the top of the tank. The **conditioned response (CR)** is the response to the CS after conditioning. Again, in our example, the CR is swimming to the top.

What has just been presented is the simplest case of classical conditioning. The CS and the US can be paired into classical conditioning in a number of ways. **Forward conditioning**, in which the CS is presented before the US, can be further divided into **delay conditioning**, in which the CS is present until the US begins, and **trace conditioning**, in which the CS is removed some time before the US is presented. For the most part, the CS, or neutral stimulus, should come before the US. In the fish example above, this point is true because if the US was present first, the fish could be distracted from noticing the presence of the CS and will therefore not learn the association. Forward conditioning has been found to be the most effective at modifying behavior.

John Watson and his assistant Rosalie Rayner demonstrated classical conditioning with a child known now as Little Albert. Albert was first tested and found to have no fear of small animals, though he did show fear whenever a steel bar was banged loudly with a hammer. Watson then presented Albert repeatedly with a small, harmless white rat, and at the same time, banged the steel bar, making the child cry. Afterward, Albert cringed and cried any time he was presented with the rat—even if the noise wasn't made. Furthermore, Albert showed that he was afraid of other white fluffy objects; the closer they resembled the white rat, the more he cried and cringed. This is known as **generalization**. If Albert could distinguish among similar but distinct stimuli, he would be exhibiting **discrimination**. We can use this example to demonstrate other terms related to classical conditioning. **Acquisition** takes place when the pairing of the natural and neutral stimuli (the loud noise and the rat) have occurred with enough frequency that the neutral stimulus alone will elicit the conditional response (cringing and crying). **Extinction**, or the elimination of the conditioned response, can be achieved by presenting the CS without the US repeatedly (in other words, the white rat without the loud noise). Eventually, the white rat will not produce the unpleasant response. However, **spontaneous recovery**, in which the original response disappears on its own, but then is elicited again by the previous CS at a later time, is also possible under certain circumstances. Returning to the fish: if after having taught them to associate a light with feeding, you shine a light and give no food a number of times, the fish will initially swim to the top looking for food, but will eventually ignore the light. However, after a period of time of not shining the light, if you shine the light again, the fish will again swim to the top. Notice that they do so spontaneously, without having been taught again. Of course, if there is no food, then the fish will even more quickly stop responding to the light.

Spontaneous recovery demonstrates that even though the learning is not evident during the extinction period, the association between the CS and CR is still stored in the brain.

In **second-order conditioning**, a previous CS is used as the US. In our example, the fish would now be trained with a new CS, such as a tone, which would be paired with the light, which would now serve as the US. If the conditioning were successful, the fish would learn to swim to the top in response to the tone. Second-order conditioning is a special case of higher-order conditioning, which, in theory, can go up to any order as new CSs are linked to old ones. In practice, higher-order conditioning is rarely effective beyond the second order.

There are two distinct theories as to why classical conditioning works. Pavlov and Watson believed that the pairing of the neutral (eventual CS) and the natural (US) stimuli occurred because they were paired in time. This is the **contiguity approach**. Robert Rescorla believes that the CS and US get paired because the CS comes to predict the US. The fish from the initial example come to expect food upon seeing the light. This is known as the **contingency approach**.

OPERANT CONDITIONING

Operant conditioning (also called **instrumental conditioning**) involves an organism's learning to make a response in order to obtain a reward or avoid punishment. The response is an action not typically associated with obtaining a particular reward. **B.F. Skinner** pioneered the study of operant conditioning, although the phenomenon first was discovered by **Edward L. Thorndike**, who proposed the law of effect, which states that a behavior is more likely to recur if reinforced. Skinner ran many operant conditioning experiments. He often used a specially designed testing apparatus known as an operant conditioning chamber, or a Skinner Box.

This box typically was empty except for a lever and a hole through which food pellets could be delivered. Skinner trained rats to press the lever (not a typical behavior for rats) in order to get food. To get the rats to learn to press a lever, the experimenter would use a procedure called **shaping**, in which a rat first receives a food reward for being near the lever, then for touching the lever, and finally for pressing the lever. In the end, the rat is rewarded only for pressing the lever. This process is also referred to as **differential reinforcement of successive approximations**.

In a typical operant conditioning experiment, pressing the bar is the type of response (also called an operant), and food is the reinforcer. Food is a form of **natural reinforcement**; you don't have to learn to like it. These types of natural reinforcers, such as food, water, and sex, provide **primary reinforcement**. **Secondary reinforcement** is provided by learned reinforcers. Money is a good example of a secondary reinforcer. In nature, money is just paper or metal; it has no intrinsic value. We have learned, however, that money can be exchanged for primary reinforcers.

Reinforcement can be divided into positive and negative reinforcement. **Positive reinforcement** is a reward or event that increases the likelihood that a particular type of response will be repeated. For example, picture an experiment in which a rat is given a food pellet every time it presses a lever. The food provides positive reinforcement, increasing the likelihood that the rat will press the lever again. **Negative reinforcement** is the removal of an aversive event in order to encourage the behavior. An example of negative reinforcement occurs in an experiment in which a rat is sitting on a mildly electrified cage floor. Pressing a bar in the cage turns off the electrical current. The removal of the negative experience (shock) is rewarding. **Omission training** also seeks to decrease the frequency of behavior by withholding the reward until the desired behavior is demonstrated.

	reinforcement (think **re**ward)	punishment
positive (think addition!)	giving food, giving praise, giving money, giving a good grade, giving gold stars	giving pain, giving a chore, giving extra homework, giving a bad grade
negative (think subtraction!)	taking away a chore, ending a punishment, removing pain, cancelling homework	taking away food, taking away money (a fine), taking away freedom (being grounded, getting a time-out)

Behaviorists use various schedules of reinforcement in their experiments. A **schedule of reinforcement** refers to the frequency with which an organism receives reinforcement for a given type of response. In a **continuous reinforcement schedule**, every correct response that is emitted results in a reward. This produces rapid learning, but it also results in rapid extinction, where extinction is a decrease and eventual disappearance of a response once the behavior is no longer reinforced.

Schedules of reinforcement in which not all responses are reinforced are called **partial (or intermittent) reinforcement schedules**. A **fixed-ratio schedule** is one in which the reward always occurs after a fixed number of responses. For example, a rat might have to press a lever 10 times in order to receive a food pellet. This schedule is called a 10:1 ratio schedule. Fixed-ratio schedules produce strong learning, but the learning extinguishes relatively quickly, as the rat quickly detects that the reinforcement schedule no longer is operative. A **variable-ratio schedule** is one in which the ratio of responses to reinforcement is variable and unpredictable. A good example of this is slot machines. The response, putting in money and pulling the lever, is reinforced with a payoff in a seemingly random manner. Reinforcement can come at any time. This type of schedule takes longer to condition a response; however, the learning that occurs is resistant to extinction, which helps explain why people can become addicted to gambling. A **fixed-interval schedule** is one in which reinforcement is presented as a function of fixed periods of time, as long as there is at least one response. This schedule is similar to being a salaried employee. Every two weeks, the paycheck arrives regardless of your work performance (as long as you show up at all). Finally, in the **variable-interval schedule**, reinforcement is presented at differing time intervals, as long as there is at least one response. Variable-interval, like variable-ratio, is more difficult to extinguish than fixed schedules.

Variable Interval in the Classroom

This schedule of reinforcement is illustrated by a teacher who gives pop quizzes. The time at which the quiz will be given is always changing.

Like reinforcement, **punishment** is also an important element of operant conditioning, but the effect is the opposite: reinforcement increases behavior, while punishment decreases it. Punishment is the process by which a behavior is followed by a consequence that decreases the likelihood that the behavior will be repeated. Like reinforcement, punishment can be both positive AND negative. Positive punishment involves the application, or pairing, of a negative stimulus with the behavior. For example, if cadets speak out of turn in military boot camp, the drill sergeant makes them do 20 push-ups. On the contrary, negative punishment involves the removal of a reinforcing stimulus after the behavior has occurred. For example, if a child breaks a window while throwing a baseball in the house, he loses TV privileges for a week. Positive punishment adds and negative punishment subtracts. Commonly, reinforcement and punishment are used in conjunction when shaping behaviors; however, it is uncommon for punishment to have as much of a lasting effect as reinforcement. Once the punishment has been removed, it is no longer effective. Furthermore, punishment instructs only what not to do, whereas reinforcement instructs what to do. Reinforcement is therefore a better alternative to encourage behavioral changes and learning. Additionally, the processes described for classical conditioning (acquisition, extinction, spontaneous recovery, generalization, and discrimination) occur in operant conditioning, as well.

Note that the term "negative reinforcement" is often used incorrectly; colloquially, people use that term when they mean punishment.

Let's further examine two specific types of operant learning: **escape** and **avoidance**. In escape, an individual learns how to get away from an aversive stimulus by engaging in a particular behavior. This helps reinforce the behavior so he or she will be willing to engage in it again. For example, a child does not want to eat her vegetables (aversive stimulus), so she throws a temper tantrum. If the parents respond by not making the child eat the vegetables, then she will learn that behaving in that specific way will help her escape that particular aversive stimulus. On the other hand, avoidance occurs when a person performs a behavior to ensure an aversive stimulus is not presented. For example, a child notices Mom cooking vegetables for dinner and fakes an illness so Mom will send him to bed with ginger ale and crackers. The child has effectively avoided confronting the aversive stimulus (the offensive vegetables) altogether. As long as either of these techniques work (meaning the parents do not force the child to eat the vegetables), the child is reinforced to perform the escape and/or avoidance behaviors.

Operant conditioning techniques are used quite frequently in places that have controlled populations, such as in a prison or mental institution. These institutions set up a **token economy**—an artificial economy based on tokens. These tokens act as secondary reinforcers, in that the tokens can be used for purchasing primary reinforcers, such as food. The participants in a token economy are reinforced for desired behaviors (responses) with tokens; this reinforcement is designed to increase the number of positive behaviors that occur.

Learned helplessness occurs when consistent efforts fail to bring rewards. If this situation persists, the subject will stop trying. Psychologist Martin Seligman's original experiment placed dogs in a room with an electrified floor. At first, the dogs would try to escape the room or avoid the floor, but they ultimately learned that there was nothing they could do to prevent being shocked. Eventually, when the dogs' leashes were removed, they still stayed on the electrified floor, even though they could have escaped. This fact shows that they have learned to be helpless. Seligman sees this condition as possibly precipitating depression in humans. If people try repeatedly to succeed at work, school, and/or relationships, and find their efforts are in vain no matter how hard they try, depression may result.

BIOLOGICAL FACTORS

The biological basis of learning is of great interest to psychologists. Neuroscientists have tried to identify the neural correlates of learning. In other words, what physiological changes are brought about when we learn?

In the 1960s, psychologists noticed that neurons themselves could be affected by environmental stimulation. Experiments were conducted in which some rats were raised in an enriched environment, while others were raised in a deprived environment. The enriched environment included things to explore and lots of room in which to move, whereas the deprived environment was just a small, empty cage. At the end of the experiment, the rats were sacrificed, and their brains were examined. The experimenters found that the rats from the enriched environment had thicker cortexes, higher brain weight, and greater neural connectivity in their brains. This pattern of results suggests that neurons can change in response to environmental stimuli.

Donald Hebb proposed that human learning takes place by neurons forming new connections with one another or by the strengthening of connections that already exist. To study how learning affects specific neurons, scientists study the sea slug aplysia. This is a good animal to study because it has only about 20,000 neurons, whereas humans have millions. Aplysia can be classically conditioned to withdraw their gill, a protective response. **Eric Kandel**, a neuroscientist, examined classical conditioning in aplysia. Kandel paired a light touch (CS) with a shock (US). This pairing causes the aplysia to withdraw its gill (UCR). After training, the light touch alone can elicit the gill withdrawal (now a CR). Kandel found that when a strong stimulus, such as a shock, happens repeatedly, special neurons called modulatory neurons release neuromodulators. **Neuromodulators** strengthen the synapses between the sensory neurons (the ones that sense the touch) and the motor neurons (the ones that withdraw the gill) involved. Additionally, new synapses were created. In other words, the neurons sensing shock and those that withdrew the gill became more connected than they were before. This experiment illustrated a neural basis for learning, namely, a physiological change that correlates with a relatively stable change in behavior as a result of experience. This is known as **long-term potentiation** (LTP). The same basic process has been shown to be the neural basis of learning in mammals. An easy way to remember this information is that "neurons that fire together, wire together."

At a given synapse, long-term potentiation involves both presynaptic and postsynaptic neurons. For example, dopamine is one of the neurotransmitters involved in pleasurable or rewarding actions. In operant conditioning, reinforcement activates the limbic circuits that involve memory, learning, and emotions. Because reinforcement of a good behavior is generally intrinsically pleasurable (like food or praise), the circuits are strengthened as dopamine floods the system, making it more likely the behavior will be repeated.

After long-term potentiation has occurred, passing an electrical current through the brain doesn't disrupt the memory associations between the neurons involved, although other memories will be wiped out. For example, when people receive a blow to the head resulting in a concussion, they lose their memory for events shortly preceding the concussion. This is due to the fact that long-term potentiation has not had a chance to occur (and leave traces of memory connections), while old memories, which were already potentiated, remain.

Long-term memory storage involves more permanent changes to the brain, including structural and functional connections between neurons. For example, long-term memory storage includes new synaptic connections between neurons, permanent changes in pre- and postsynaptic membranes, and a permanent increase or decrease in neurotransmitter synthesis. Furthermore, visual imaging studies suggest that there is greater branching of dendrites in regions of the brain thought to be involved with memory storage. Other studies suggest that protein synthesis somehow influences memory formation; drugs that prevent protein synthesis appear to block long-term memory formation.

The neural processes described above occur when animals or people learn new behaviors or change their behaviors based on experience (that is, environmental feedback). However, not all behaviors are learned: some are innate. These are the things we know how to do instinctively (or our body just does without us consciously thinking about it), not because someone taught us to do them (for example, breathing or pulling away from a hot stove). Further, innate behaviors are always the same between members of the species, even for those performing them for the first time.

SOCIAL LEARNING

Classical and operant conditioning obviously do not account for all forms of learning. A third kind of learning is **social learning** (also called observational learning), which is learning based on observing the behavior of others as well as the consequences of that behavior. Because this learning takes place by observing others, it is also referred to as **vicarious learning**.

Albert Bandura conducted some of the most important research on social learning. In a classic study, Bandura had children in a waiting room with an adult **confederate** (someone who was "in" on the experiment). For one group of children, the adult would simply wait. For another group of children, the adult would punch and kick an inflatable doll (thus the experiment is now nicknamed the **Bobo Doll Experiment**). In both groups, the children were then brought into another room to play with interesting toys, but after a short time, the experimenters told the children they had to stop playing with the interesting toys, and were brought back to the initial waiting room. The idea was to frustrate the children, and then see how they managed their frustration. Many of the children who had witnessed an adult abusing the doll proceeded to abuse the doll themselves. But most of the children who had witnessed an adult quietly waiting proceeded to quietly wait themselves. This experiment illustrated the power of **modeling** in affecting changes in behavior. This finding calls into question the behaviorist assertion that learning must occur through direct experience.

Bandura concluded that four conditions must be met for observational learning to occur. First, the learner must pay attention to the behavior in question. Second, there must be retention of the observed behavior, meaning that it must be remembered. Third, there must be a motivation for the learner to produce the behavior at a later time. Finally, the potential for reproduction must exist, that is, the learner must be able to reproduce the learned behavior.

Observational learning is a phenomenon frequently discussed in the debate over violence in the media. This issue is a particularly relevant one for television programs designed for children, as studies have shown that young children are particularly likely to engage in observational learning. However, even toddlers have shown unsolicited helping behaviors in experimental settings, suggesting that observational learning occurs in both positive and negative directions.

Building on recent views that there are multiple types of intelligence, including emotional intelligence, a number of schools have developed programs in **social and emotional learning**. These programs are designed to help develop empathy and conflict resolution in students.

COGNITIVE PROCESSES IN LEARNING

The behaviorist view, championed by Skinner, is that behavior is a series of behavior-reward pairings, and cognition is not as important to the learning process. In more recent years, many psychologists have abandoned this view. One more recent view of learning posits that organisms start the learning process by observing a stimulus; then they continue the process by evaluating that stimulus; then they move on to a consideration of possible responses; and finally, they make a response. Various lines of evidence indicate that cognitive factors play a role in both animal and human learning. For example, if humans could be conditioned to salivate to the word *style*, they also would be likely to salivate to the word *fashion*. These words are not acoustically similar, but rather semantically similar, meaning they have a related meaning instead of sounding alike, so this pattern of behavior results from **cognitive** evaluation.

Perhaps a more profound demonstration of a similar phenomenon comes from work with pigeons. Pigeons were shown pictures containing either trees or no trees. They were trained to peck a key for food, but only when a picture of a tree was shown. As you might expect, they would peck the key only when tree pictures were shown, even after reinforcement stopped. They even pecked at pictures of trees that they had never seen before. Therefore, the birds must have formed a concept of trees, in which a concept is defined as a cognitive rule for categorizing stimuli into groups. Any new stimuli were categorized according to the concept.

Q: What is CTA?

Answer on page 184.

An example of classical conditioning worthy of special mention is **conditioned taste aversion (CTA)**, also known as the **Garcia effect**, after the psychologist who discovered it. John Garcia demonstrated that animals that eat a food that results in nausea induced by a drug or radiation will not eat that food if they ever encounter it again. This effect is profound and can be demonstrated with forward or backward conditioning. It is also highly resistant to extinction. A notable feature of this phenomenon is that it works best with food. It is hard to condition an aversion to a light paired with illness, for example. Psychologists have used this finding as evidence that animals are biologically predisposed to associate illness with food, as opposed to, say, light. This predisposition is a useful feature for a creature that samples many types of food, such as a rat. Humans also experience CTA. If you have ever eaten a food and vomited afterward, you may never want to eat that food again, even if you know that the food itself did not cause you to be ill.

CTA demonstrates another learning phenomenon: **stimulus generalization**. Let's say that you eat a peach and get sick. You may never want to eat a peach again, but you may also develop an aversion to other similar fruits, such as nectarines. The two fruits are similar, so you generalize from one stimulus (the peach) to the other (the nectarine).

Garcia's research is profound for two reasons: (1) it shows that certain species are built to learn certain associations more easily than others; (2) it shows that classical conditioning might be occurring through the access of some concept. The fact that someone might get sick from eating a peach, then refuses to eat all fruit, suggests that this person has attached that negative feeling to the concept of fruit. If it was simple classical conditioning, this effect would not occur because the person did not have a direct experience getting sick while eating other types of fruit. There must be some concept at work, which discredits the "black box" theory of the brain held by behaviorists. It also calls into question the assertion that direct experience is necessary to learn and associate. Looking at this learning as cognitive provides the explanation for why someone would develop food aversion even though that person doesn't become sick until hours after she has eaten the food. That person must access the concept of what she ate earlier and attach the association with getting sick. Finally, this is a cognitive issue because sometimes people develop food aversion to a food item they think made them ill, such as sushi, even though it could have been something else that brought upon the illness, such as bacteria in the water at the sushi restaurant.

Other evidence for a cognitive component to learning derives from the work of **Edward Tolman**. Rats permitted to explore a maze without being reinforced would find the exit after following an indirect path; the time it took them to exit the maze without reinforcement decreased quite slowly. However, when reinforcers were applied after several trials without reinforcement, the rats' time to exit the maze decreased dramatically, indicating that the rats knew how to navigate to a specific location within the maze and so had formed a **cognitive map**, or mental representation of the maze. This demonstrates **latent learning**, or learning that is not outwardly expressed until the situation calls for it.

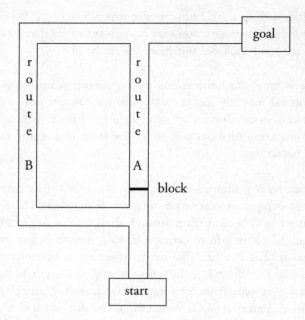

A: CTA, or conditioned taste aversion, can occur when animals eat a food that results in nausea induced by a drug or radiation; the animals often will not eat that food if they ever encounter it again.

Another form of learning is **insight learning**. This occurs when we puzzle over a solution to a problem, unsuccessfully, and then suddenly the complete solution appears to us. As discussed in the next chapter, this can be quite useful for solving problems.

KEY TERMS

Nonassociative Learning

learning

habituation

sensitization

dishabituation

desensitization

desensitization therapy

systematic desensitization

Classical Conditioning

Ivan Pavlov

Pavlovian conditioning

conditioned stimulus

unconditioned stimulus

unconditioned response

conditioned response

forward conditioning

delay conditioning

trace conditioning

generalization

discrimination

acquisition

extinction

spontaneous recovery

second-order conditioning

contiguity approach

contingency approach

Operant Conditioning

operant conditioning
  (instrumental conditioning)

B.F. Skinner

Edward L. Thorndike

shaping

differential reinforcement
    of successive
    approximations

natural reinforcement

primary reinforcement

secondary reinforcement

positive reinforcement

negative reinforcement

omission training

schedule of reinforcement

continuous reinforcement
    schedule

partial (or intermittent)
    reinforcement schedule

fixed-ratio schedule

variable-ratio schedule

fixed-interval schedule

variable-interval schedule

punishment

escape

avoidance

token economy

learned helplessness

Biological Factors

Donald Hebb

Eric Kandel

neuromodulators

long-term potentiation

Social Learning

social learning
    (observational learning)

vicarious learning

Albert Bandura

Bobo Doll Experiment

modeling

social and emotional learning

Cognitive Processes in Learning

cognitive

conditioned taste aversion

Garcia effect

stimulus generalization

Edward Tolman

cognitive map

latent learning

insight learning

Chapter 10 Drill

See Chapter 19 for answers and explanations.

1. After having been struck by a car, a dog now exhibits fear responses every time a car approaches. The dog also exhibits a fear response to the approach of a bus, a truck, a bicycle, and even a child's wagon. The dog has undergone a process of

    (A) stimulus discrimination
    (B) stimulus generalization
    (C) spontaneous recovery
    (D) backward conditioning
    (E) differential reinforcement

2. Which of the following would be an example of second-order conditioning?

    (A) A cat tastes a sour plant that makes it feel nauseated and will not approach that plant again.
    (B) A horse that is fed sugar cubes by a particular person salivates every time that person walks by.
    (C) A pigeon that has received food every time a red light is presented exhibits food-seeking behavior when a yellow light is presented.
    (D) A rabbit that has repeatedly seen a picture of a feared predator paired with a musical tone exhibits a fear response to the musical tone as well as to a flashed light alone that had been repeatedly paired with the tone.
    (E) Wild rats instinctively avoid canine predators, but domesticated rats show little fear of the domesticated dogs they encounter, and may even join them in exploration or play.

3. The reinforcement schedule that generally provides the most resistance to response extinction is

    (A) fixed-ratio
    (B) fixed-interval
    (C) variable-ratio
    (D) variable-interval
    (E) continuous

4. The importance of enrichment and stimulation of the brain during critical periods in development can be seen in all of the following EXCEPT

    (A) an increase in the number of neurons
    (B) an increase in the number of connections between neurons
    (C) strengthening of already existing connections between neurons
    (D) an increase in the size of neurons
    (E) higher levels of neurotransmitters

5. According to Albert Bandura, observational learning can occur even in the absence of

    (A) observed consequences of behavior
    (B) direct attention to the behavior
    (C) retention of the observed behavior over time
    (D) ability to reproduce the behavior
    (E) motivation to reproduce the behavior at a later time

6. Jay joins a social media website to lose weight. He receives points based on the intensity of his daily exercise and praise from fellow users for each workout he logs on the website. This increases his exercise frequency and intensity. Eventually he stops logging onto the website, but continues to exercise with increased frequency. This is an example of

    (A) vicarious reinforcement
    (B) operant conditioning
    (C) innate behavior
    (D) classical conditioning
    (E) observational learning

7. Which of the following scenarios is an example of negative reinforcement?

    (A) After staying out past her curfew, Stephanie is grounded the next weekend.
    (B) When Toni finishes her homework, she does not have to take out the trash.
    (C) When Ben received an A for his research project, his family treated him to dinner at his favorite restaurant.
    (D) When Lola the dog jumps on her owner, the owner takes a step away from her.
    (E) When the rat in a Skinner Box presses the lever, it delivers an electric shock.

8. Chemotherapy is well-known to cause nausea and vomiting. A chemotherapy patient's care team cautions the patient to eat only "novel" or new foods before treatment as opposed to food staples, like chicken, rice, or pasta. This is most likely due to

   (A) operant conditioning
   (B) taste aversion
   (C) Yerkes-Dodson Law
   (D) observational learning
   (E) stimulus generalization

9. Leigha, who is expecting college acceptance letters, knows the mailman comes every day around 1:30 P.M. Hoping that the mail arrives early, she checks the mailbox at 12:45, 1:15, and 1:40. She does not check again until the next day around the same time. This is an example of which reinforcement schedule?

   (A) Fixed-interval
   (B) Variable-interval
   (C) Fixed-ratio
   (D) Variable-ratio
   (E) Continuous

10. Kevin tries to teach his dog Muka to roll over. First, he teaches her to lie down. Then, he teaches her to lie on her side. Eventually, Kevin gets Muka to roll onto her back and, finally, all the way around. He gives her a treat with every step. This process is known as

   (A) habituation
   (B) discrimination
   (C) generalization
   (D) shaping
   (E) sensitization

REFLECT

Respond to the following questions:

- Which topics in this chapter do you hope to see on the multiple-choice section or essay?

- Which topics in this chapter do you hope not to see on the multiple-choice section or essay?

- Regarding any psychologists mentioned, can you pair the psychologists with their contributions to the field? Did they contribute significant experiments, theories, or both?

- Regarding any theories mentioned, can you distinguish between differing theories well enough to recognize them on the multiple-choice section? Can you distinguish them well enough to write a fluent essay on them?

- Regarding any figures given, if you were given a labeled figure from within this chapter, would you be able to give the significance of each part of the figure?

- Can you define the key terms at the end of the chapter?

- Which parts of the chapter will you review?

- Will you seek further help, outside of this book (such as a teacher, Princeton Review tutor, or AP Students), on any of the content in this chapter—and, if so, on what content?

Chapter 11
Cognitive Psychology: Memory, Language, and Problem-Solving

MEMORY

According to the **modal model**, memory is divided into three separate storage areas: **sensory**, **short-term**, and **long-term**. Each type of memory has four components: storage capacity, duration of code, nature of code, and a way by which information is lost. Consider each type of memory in turn.

Sensory Memory

Sensory memory is the gateway between perception and memory. This store is quite limited. Information in sensory memory is referred to as **iconic** if it is visual and **echoic** if it is auditory. The iconic store lasts for only a few tenths of a second while the echoic store lasts for three or four seconds. The items in sensory memory are constantly being replaced by new input, with only certain items entering into short-term memory.

The nature of sensory memory is clarified by certain types of events. If you have ever watched someone jump rope quickly, you may have noticed the perception of the rope being at many points in its rotation at once. A quickly moving fan also may generate such a perception. This phenomenon is called **visual persistence**. Sensory information in sensory memory remains in attention briefly; the speed of the rope or fan causes the sensory information to run together.

In 1960, researcher **George Sperling** experimented on memory and **partial report**. He first presented participants with a matrix of three rows of four letters each for just milliseconds.

$$\begin{array}{cccc} G & Z & E & P \\ R & K & O & D \\ B & T & X & F \end{array}$$

Next, he asked participants to either recite the entire matrix or to recollect just one of the rows. He found that while participants were not able to recall all twelve letters presented due to the rapid decay of iconic memory, they were generally able to accurately recall the cued row, meaning they had an image of the entire matrix stored in memory. Sperling called this ability to recall these lines of letters **iconic memory** or **short-term visual memory.** This suggests that the capacity for iconic memory is quite large, but the duration is incredibly short, and the information is not easily manipulable. Additionally, further studies emphasized the brief window for retention—the longer the amount of time between seeing the matrix and being cued to recall the row, the worse the participants performed.

Short-Term Memory (STM)

Short-term memory holds information from a few seconds up to about a minute. Psychologist **George Miller** found that the information stored in this portion of memory is primarily acoustically coded, despite the nature of the original source. Short-term memory can hold about seven items, plus or minus two (convenient for telephone numbers). Items in the short-term store are maintained there by rehearsal. Rehearsal can be divided into two types: **maintenance rehearsal** and **elaborative**

rehearsal. Maintenance rehearsal is simple repetition to keep an item in short-term memory until it can be used (as when you say a phone number to yourself over and over again until you can dial it). Elaborative rehearsal involves organization and understanding of the information that has been encoded in order to transfer the information to long-term memory (as when you try to remember the name of someone you have just met at a party). Elaborative rehearsal is more effective than maintenance rehearsal for ensuring short-term memory information is sent to long-term memory; therefore, it is a preferred way to study.

There is some evidence that the depth of processing is important for encoding memories. Information that is thought about at a deeper level is better remembered. For example, it is easier to remember the general plot of a book than the exact words, meaning that semantic information (meaning) is more easily remembered than grammatical information (form) when the goal is to learn a concept. On the other hand, rhyme can be useful in aiding phonological processing. Another useful **mnemonic device** is to use short words or phrases that represent longer strings of information. For example, ROYGBIV is an acronym that is helpful in memorizing the colors of the rainbow (red, orange, yellow, green, blue, indigo, violet). A mnemonic device is any technique that makes it easier to learn and remember something.

The **dual-coding hypothesis** indicates that it is easier to remember words with associated images than either words or images alone. By encoding both a visual mental representation and an associated word, there are more connections made to the memory and more of an opportunity to process the information at a deeper level. For this reason, imagery is a useful mnemonic device. One aid for memory is to use the **method of loci**. This involves imagining moving through a familiar place, such as your home, and in each place, leaving a visual representation of a topic to be remembered. For recall, then, the images of the places could be called upon to bring into awareness the associated topics.

It is also easier to remember things that are personally relevant, known as the **self-reference effect**. We have excellent recall for information that we can personally relate to because it interacts with our own views or can be linked to existing memories. A useful tool for memory, then, is to relate new information to existing knowledge by making it personally relevant.

Items in short-term memory may be forgotten or they may be **encoded** (stored and able to be recalled later) into long-term memory. Items that are forgotten exit short-term memory either by **decay**—that is, the passage of time—or by **interference**—that is, they are displaced by new information. One type of interference is **retroactive interference**, in which new information pushes old information out of short-term memory. The opposite of retroactive interference is **proactive interference**, in which old information makes it more difficult to learn new information.

An additional feature of short-term memory is that it seems to store items from a list sequentially. This sequential storage leads to our tendency to remember the first few and last few items in a list better than the ones in the middle. These effects are called the **primacy** (remembering the first items) and **recency** (remembering the last items) **effects**. The recency effect tends to fade in about a day; the primacy effect tends to persist longer. The overall effect is called the **serial position effect**.

The Serial Position Effect

An interesting feature of short-term memory is that its limit of about seven items is not as limiting as it would seem. The reason is that what constitutes an item need not be something as simple as a single digit. In fact, it can be a fairly large block of information. George Miller defined grouping items of information into units as **chunking**. For example, when learning a friend's phone number (typically seven digits), you probably chunk the information into a 3-digit and a 4-digit number in order to better retain the information.

Long-Term Memory (LTM)

Long-term memory is the repository for all of our lasting memories and knowledge, and it is organized like a gigantic network of interrelated information. It is capable of permanent retention for the duration of our lives. Evidence suggests that information in this store is primarily **semantically encoded**—that is, encoded in the form of word meanings. However, certain types of information in this store can be either **visually encoded** or **acoustically encoded.**

Everyday Example
Remembering song lyrics is an example of acoustic encoding.

Information in the long-term store can be stored in different ways, depending on the type of information it is. One kind of storage is through **episodic memory**, or memory for events that we ourselves have experienced. Another kind is through **semantic memory**, also known as declarative, which comprises facts, figures, and general world knowledge. A third type is **procedural memory**—that is, consisting of skills and habits. Because these memories are stored in the striatum, they are frequently not subject to damage and injury. A final way to classify memory is into categories based on whether or not it can be accessed consciously or not. **Declarative (or explicit) memory** is a memory a person can consciously consider and retrieve, such as episodic and semantic memory. In contrast, **nondeclarative (or**

implicit) memory is beyond conscious consideration and would include procedural memory, priming, and classical conditioning.

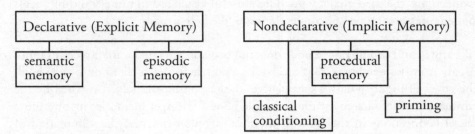

Recalling items in long-term memory is subject to **state-dependent memory**. This principle states that information is more likely to be recalled if the attempt to retrieve it occurs in a situation similar to the situation in which it was encoded. For example, if you memorize information about psychology while in a classroom, you should remember it better in that same classroom than if the information was memorized at home. State-dependent learning also applies to states of mind, meaning that information memorized when under the influence of a drug is easier to access when in a similar state than when not on that drug.

The process of retrieval is thought to involve the activation of semantic networks. If our long-term memories contained isolated pockets of information without any organization, they might be more difficult to access. A person might have numerous memories for directions, people's faces, the definitions of tens of thousands of words, and other such content; with that much information, it could be nearly impossible to find anything. Just as hierarchies are useful for handling information during the encoding process, it is believed that information is stored in long-term memory as an organized network. In this network exist individual ideas called nodes, which can be thought of like cities on a map. Connecting these nodes are associations, which are like roads connecting the cities. Not all roads are created equal; some are superhighways while others are dirt roads. For example, for a person living in a city, there may be a stronger association between the nodes "bird" and "pigeon" than between "bird" and "penguin." According to this model, the strength of an association in the network is related to how frequently and how deeply the connection is made. Processing material in different ways leads to the establishment of multiple connections. In this model, searching through memory is the process of starting at one node and traveling the connected roads until one arrives at the idea one

Working Memory

Some psychologists believe there is an additional type of memory called **working memory**. Within the modal model, it is argued that working memory would fall between the sensory registry and short-term memory, and it can last up to about 30 seconds before decaying or being transferred into either short- or long-term memory. It is believed that the information stored in working memory can be manipulated in a way that iconic or echoic memory would not be, which helps distinguish working memory from other more evanescent forms of memory. For example, iconic memory would allow a person to remember five letters presented visually, whereas working memory would allow a person to remember those five letters and rearrange them in alphabetical order. While some psychologists are certain that working memory is a distinct part of the memory system, other psychologists believe that working memory is simply a part of short-term memory.

is looking for. Retrieval of information can be improved by building more and stronger connections to an idea. Because all memories are, in essence, neural connections, the road analogy provides a useful visual aid in understanding access to memories: strong neural connections are like better roads.

Like any neural connection, a node does not become activated until it receives input signals from its neighbors that are strong enough to reach a response threshold. The effect of input signals is cumulative: the response threshold is reached by the summation of input signals from multiple nodes. Stronger memories involve more neural connections in the form of more numerous dendrites, the stimulation of which can summate more quickly and powerfully to threshold. Once the response threshold is reached, the node "fires" and sends a stimulus to all of its neighbors, contributing to their activation. In this way, the activation of a few nodes can lead to a pattern of activation within the network that spreads onward. This process is known as **spreading activation**. It suggests that when trying to retrieve information, we start the search from one node. We do not then "choose" where to go next; rather, that activated node spreads its activation to other nodes around it to an extent related to the strength of association between that node and each other. This pattern continues, with well-established links carrying activation more efficiently than more obscure ones. The network approach helps explain why hints may be helpful. They serve to activate nodes that are closely connected to the node being sought after, which may therefore contribute to that node's activation. It also explains the relevance of contextual cues in state-dependent memory.

A phenomenon that many psychologists believe occurs in the long-term store is the **flashbulb memory**, which is a very deep, vivid memory in the form of a visual image associated with a particular emotionally arousing event. For example, many people remember exactly what they were doing when they heard that planes had crashed into the World Trade Center on September 11, 2001. However, some psychologists believe that recall of such events is no more accurate than recall of other memories.

Sometimes what we remember happened only in part or even not at all. Memory **reconstruction** occurs when we fit together pieces of an event that seem likely. **Source amnesia** is one likely cause of memory reconstruction. In this case, we attribute the event to a different source than it actually came from. For example, if children read and reread a story, they may come to think the events of the story happened to them rather than to the character. Similarly, childhood memories of both trivial and serious events can be reconstructed (falsified) by repeated suggestion. **Elizabeth Loftus** and other psychologists are studying the existence of false or implanted memories. They have demonstrated that repeated suggestions and misleading questions can create false memories. This is called **framing**. Similarly, eyewitness accounts, thought to be very strong evidence in courts of law, are accurate only about half the time. This is particularly true when dealing with children as eyewitnesses. The degree of confidence in the testimony of the witness does not necessarily correlate to accuracy of the account.

Before we move on, let's mention types of interference that we discussed briefly in the short-term memory section. Retroactive interference occurs when newly memorized information interferes with the ability to remember previously memorized information. Proactive interference occurs when previously memorized information interferes with the ability to learn and memorize new information. To give an example of retroactive interference, when you learn a new language (such as Spanish), it can interfere with your memory of a language that you learned previously (for example, Italian).

LANGUAGE

Language is the arrangement of sounds or written symbols to communicate ideas. Language has several key features.

- First, language is arbitrary—that is, words rarely sound like the ideas that they convey.

- Second, language has a structure that is additive in a certain sense. For example, words are added together to form sentences, sentences to form paragraphs, and so on.

- Third, language has multiplicity of structure, meaning that it can be analyzed and understood in a number of different ways.

- Fourth, language is productive, meaning that there are nearly endless meaningful combinations of words.

- Finally, language is dynamic, meaning that it is constantly changing and evolving.

Language can be broken down into subcomponents. **Phonemes** are the smallest units of speech sounds in a given language that are still distinct in sound from each other. Phonemes combine to form **morphemes**, the smallest semantically meaningful parts of language. **Grammar**, the set of rules by which language is constructed, is governed by syntax and semantics. **Syntax** is the set of rules used in the arrangement of morphemes into meaningful sentences; this can also be thought of as word order. **Semantics** refers to word meaning or word choice. **Prosody** is the rhythm, stress, and intonation of speech.

Children acquire language in stages. Infants make cooing noises, which consist of the utterance of phonemes that do not correspond to actual words, until roughly 4 months of age. The next stage after cooing is babbling, which is the production of phonemes only within the infants' own to-be-learned language. Sounds not relevant to this language drop out at this stage, which usually lasts until the first year of life. Soon the infant uses single words to convey demands and desires. These single words filled with meaning are called **holophrases**. Holophrases are single terms that are applied by the infant to broad categories of things. For example, it is not uncommon to hear an infant call any passing woman "mama." This type of error is known as an **overextension**, and it results from the infant not knowing enough words to express something fully. **Underextension** is when a child thinks that his or her "mama" is the only "mama." Infants develop vocabulary as time goes on and tend to have up to 100 words in their vocabulary by 18 months.

At about two years of age, infants start combining words. Two- or three-word groups are termed **telegraphic speech**. This speech lacks many parts of speech. For example, a two-year-old would say, "mommy food," which means "mommy, give me food." This is called "telegraphic speech" because people used to remove what they deemed unnecessary words when sending telegrams, in order to save money.

Vocabulary is increasing rapidly at this point. By age 3, children know more than 1,000 words, but they frequently make **overgeneralization** errors. These are errors in which the rules of language are overextended, such as in saying, "I goed to the store." *Go* is an irregular verb, but the child applies the standard rules of grammar to it. By age 5, most grammatical mistakes in the child's speech have disappeared, and the child's vocabulary has expanded dramatically. At 10 years old, a child's language is essentially the same as an adult's.

Noam Chomsky postulated a system for the organization of language based on the concept of what he referred to as **transformational grammar**. Transformational grammar differentiates between the **surface structure of language**—the superficial way in which the words are arranged in a text or in speech—and the **deep structure of language**—the underlying meaning of the words. Chomsky was struck by the similarities between the grammars of different languages, as well as by the similarities of language acquisition in children, regardless of the language they were learning. Based on this similarity, he proposed an innate **language acquisition device**, which facilitates the acquisition of language in children, and a **critical period** for the learning of language. **B.F. Skinner**, a noted behaviorist, countered Chomsky's argument for language acquisition. Skinner explored the idea of the "language acquisition support system," which is the language-rich or language-poor environment the child is exposed to while growing up. Chomsky's language acquisition device (LAD) provides the foundational structure of language, while the language acquisition support system (LASS) provides the scaffolding to help young children learn language.

Language and thought are interactive processes. Language can influence thought, and cognition can influence language. **Benjamin Lee Whorf**, in collaboration with **Edward Sapir**, proposed a **theory of linguistic relativity**, according to which speakers of different languages develop different cognitive systems as a result of their differences in language. A popularly cited example of this idea is illustrated by the Garo people of Burma, who have many words for rice. English speakers have only a few words to describe rice. The hypothesis is that rice is critical to the Garo way of life and so involves more categorization and complexity of thought than it does for someone in an English-speaking culture.

CONCEPTS

We are constantly being inundated with information about our surroundings. In order to organize all of this information, we devise concepts. A **concept** is a way of grouping or classifying the world around us. For example, chairs come in a large variety of sizes and shapes, yet we can identify them as chairs. The concept of chairs allows us to identify them without learning every possible trait of all chairs. **Typicality** is the degree to which an object fits the average. What are the average characteristics of a chair? When we picture "chair," an image emerges in our brain. This typical picture that we envision is referred to as a **prototype**. But we can imagine other images of a chair that are distant from the prototype to varying degrees.

Concepts can be small or large, more or less inclusive. A **superordinate concept** is very broad and encompasses a large group of items, such as the concept of "food." A **basic concept** is smaller and more specific—for example, "bread." A **subordinate concept** is even smaller and more specific, such as "rye bread." Concepts are essential for thinking and reasoning. Without such categorization, we would be so overwhelmed by our surroundings that we would be incapable of any deeper thought.

COGNITION

Cognition encompasses the mental processes involved in acquiring, organizing, remembering, using, and constructing knowledge.

Reasoning, the drawing of conclusions from evidence, can be further divided into deductive and inductive reasoning. **Deductive reasoning** is the process of drawing logical conclusions from general statements. **Syllogisms** are deductive conclusions drawn from two premises. For example, consider the following argument:

> All politicians are trustworthy.
>
> Janet is a politician.
>
> Therefore, Janet is trustworthy.

The logical conclusion is that Janet is trustworthy. This is drawn from the general statements that all politicians are trustworthy and that Janet is a politician. In general, statements can be sound (the conclusion follows from the premises), unsound, valid (the conclusion is true—Janet is trustworthy), or invalid.

Inductive reasoning is the process of drawing general inferences from specific observations. For example, you might notice that everybody on the football team seems to be a good student. You could infer that all people who play football are good students. However, this is not necessarily true. You are drawing an inference based on a common occurrence. Inductive reasoning, while useful, is not as airtight as deductive reasoning.

PROBLEM-SOLVING AND CREATIVITY

Problem-solving involves the removal of one or more impediments to the finding of a solution in a situation. The problems to be solved can be either well-structured, with paths to solution (for example, "What is the square footage of my room?"), or ill-structured, with no single, clear path to solution (for example, "How can I succeed in school?"). In order to solve problems, we must decide whether the problem has one or more solutions. If many correct answers are possible, we use a process known as **divergent thinking**. Brainstorming is an example of divergent thinking. If the problem can be solved only by one answer, **convergent thinking** must be used. Convergent thinking, then, requires narrowing of the many choices available.

When solving well-structured problems, we often rely on **heuristics**, or intuitive rules of thumb that may or may not be useful in a given situation. There are a number of types of heuristics and all may lead to incorrect conclusions. The **availability heuristic** means that the rule of thumb is judged by what events come readily to mind. For example, many people mistakenly believe that air travel is more dangerous than car travel because airplane crashes are so vividly and repeatedly reported. The **representativeness heuristic** also can lead to incorrect conclusions. In this case, we judge objects and events in terms of how closely they match the prototype of that object or event. For example, many people view high school athletes as less intelligent. However, most high school athletes must meet certain academic standards in order to participate in sports. A person's particular view of the athlete will determine whether the representativeness heuristic is leading to a correct or incorrect conclusion. Unfortunately, such erroneous conclusions are how racism, sexism, and ageism persist. Heuristics contrast with **algorithms**, which are systematic, mechanical approaches that guarantee an eventual answer to a problem.

Insight and Köhler's Chimps

A famous example of insight is the example of Köhler's chimps. **Wolfgang Köhler** had a chimp in a cage with two sticks. Outside of the cage were some bananas. The chimp wanted the bananas but could not reach them with either stick. After struggling for a while, the chimp took the two sticks, and put the thinner end of one into the hollow end of the other, making one long stick of sufficient length to reach the bananas. The novel approach of combining the sticks was presumably the result of an insight.

Ill-structured problems often require insight to be solved. **Insight** is the sudden understanding of a problem or a potential strategy for solving a problem that usually involves conceptualizing the problem in a new way. Recent studies have demonstrated that insight is more likely to occur when the problem-solvers are able to create some mental and/or physical space between themselves and the problem.

Problems requiring insight are often difficult to solve because we have a **mental set**, or fixed frame of mind, that we use when approaching the problems. An example of a mental set is **functional fixedness**, which is the tendency to assume that a given item is useful only for the task for which it was designed. For example, many people might see this AP Psychology book as a source of information for the AP Exam, but it can also serve as a bed support, a writing surface, a source of kindling, or much more!

Other obstacles to problem-solving include confirmation bias, hindsight bias, belief perseverance, and framing. **Confirmation bias**, the search for information that supports a particular view, also hinders problem-solving by distorting objectivity. The **hindsight bias**, or the tendency after the fact to think you knew what the outcome would be, also distorts our ability to view situations objectively. Similarly, **belief perseverance** affects problem-solving. In this mental error, a person sees only the evidence that supports a particular position, despite evidence presented to the contrary. **Framing**, or the way a question is phrased, can alter the objective outcome of problem-solving or decision-making.

Creativity can be defined as the process of producing something novel yet worthwhile. The elusive nature of creativity makes it a difficult topic to study. For example, what is truly novel, and who is the judge of what is or is not worthwhile? Briefly, creative people tend to be motivated to create, primarily for the sheer joy of creation, rather than for financial or material gain. Creative people also seem to exhibit care and consideration when choosing a specific area of interest to pursue. Once they have chosen that area, they tend to immerse themselves in it and to develop extensive knowledge of all aspects of the topic. Creativity seems to correlate with nonconformity to the rules governing the area of creativity. For example, Copernicus had to disregard the common belief that the Earth was the center of the solar system to make his discoveries about planetary motion.

KEY TERMS

Memory

modal model
sensory memory
short-term memory
long-term memory
iconic
echoic
visual persistence
George Sperling
partial report
short-term visual memory
   (iconic memory)
George Miller
maintenance rehearsal
elaborative rehearsal
mnemonic device
dual-coding hypothesis
method of loci
self-reference effect
encoded
decay
interference
retroactive interference
proactive interference
primacy effect
recency effect
serial position effect
chunking
semantically encoded
visually encoded
acoustically encoded
episodic memory
semantic memory
procedural memory
declarative (or explicit) memory
nondeclarative (or implicit)
   memory
state-dependent memory
working memory
spreading activation
flashbulb memory
reconstruction
source amnesia
framing
Elizabeth Loftus

Language

phoneme
morpheme
grammar
syntax
semantics
prosody
holophrases
overextension
underextension
telegraphic speech
overgeneralization
Noam Chomsky
transformational grammar
surface structure of language
deep structure of language
language acquisition device
critical period
B.F. Skinner
Benjamin Lee Whorf
Edward Sapir
theory of linguistic relativity

Concepts

concept
typicality
prototype
superordinate concept
basic concept
subordinate concept

Cognition

cognition
reasoning
deductive reasoning
syllogisms
inductive reasoning

Problem-Solving and Creativity
    divergent thinking
    convergent thinking
    heuristics
    availability heuristic
    representativeness
        heuristic
    algorithms
    insight
    Wolfgang Köhler
    mental set
    functional fixedness
    confirmation bias
    hindsight bias
    belief perseverance
    framing
    creativity

Chapter 11 Drill

See Chapter 19 for answers and explanations.

1. The main difference between auditory and visual sensory memory is that

    (A) visual memory dominates auditory memory
    (B) visual sensory memory lasts for a shorter period of time than auditory sensory memory
    (C) visual sensory memory has a higher storage capacity than auditory sensory memory
    (D) a phone number read to an individual will be lost before a phone number that was glanced at for 15 seconds
    (E) if both visual and auditory stimuli are presented at the same time, the visual stimulus is more likely to be transferred to the long-term memory than is the auditory stimulus

2. The greater likelihood of recalling information from memory while in the same or similar environment in which the memory was originally encoded is an example of

    (A) retroactive interference
    (B) chunking
    (C) elaborative rehearsal
    (D) encoding specificity
    (E) procedural memory

3. The term given to that part of language composed of tones and inflections that add or change meaning without alterations in word usage is

    (A) syntax
    (B) grammar
    (C) phonemics
    (D) semantics
    (E) prosody

4. Which of the following would NOT be an example of a two-year-old's usage of telegraphic speech?

    (A) "Where ball?"
    (B) "Boy hurt."
    (C) "Milk."
    (D) "Mommy give hug."
    (E) "Go play group."

5. Students are given a reasoning task in which they are asked, in 60 seconds, to come up with as many ways as possible to use a spoon that do not involve eating or preparing food. The number and diversity of responses could most accurately reflect the students'

    (A) divergent thinking abilities
    (B) convergent thinking abilities
    (C) intelligence quotients
    (D) working memories
    (E) subordinate concepts

6. Recalling the fact that Abraham Lincoln was the president of the United States during the Civil War is an example of

    (A) procedural memory
    (B) implicit memory
    (C) semantic memory
    (D) episodic memory
    (E) nondeclarative memory

7. Stefano tries his hardest to learn German, but he continues to replace words with Spanish words by accident. This is most likely a result of

    (A) proactive interference
    (B) retroactive interference
    (C) telegraphic speech
    (D) surface structure of language
    (E) semantic encoding

8. Ben continues to get stuck on a physics problem, approaching it the same way every time. This is an example of

    (A) functional fixedness
    (B) a mental set
    (C) a representativeness heuristic
    (D) insight learning
    (E) framing

9. Which of the following is an example of a representativeness heuristic?

(A) Kelly creates a perfect mental image of a rose in her mind.

(B) Malik thinks that cancer is more deadly than heart disease because he sees advertisements for cancer research frequently.

(C) Priscilla uses a box as a stepstool to reach the highest shelf.

(D) In an effort to prove her theory true, Jennifer interprets the otherwise objective facts as supporting evidence for her claims.

(E) Looking back, Justino feels he should have been able to predict the ending of the horror movie all along.

10. Sheldon memorizes organic chemistry functional groups by relating them to his passion and understanding of landscaping. This memorization technique is known as

(A) functional fixedness

(B) chunking

(C) maintenance rehearsal

(D) state-dependent memory

(E) self-referential effect

REFLECT

Respond to the following questions:

- Which topics in this chapter do you hope to see on the multiple-choice section or essay?

- Which topics in this chapter do you hope not to see on the multiple-choice section or essay?

- Regarding any psychologists mentioned, can you pair the psychologists with their contributions to the field? Did they contribute significant experiments, theories, or both?

- Regarding any theories mentioned, can you distinguish between differing theories well enough to recognize them on the multiple-choice section? Can you distinguish them well enough to write a fluent essay on them?

- Regarding any figures given, if you were given a labeled figure from within this chapter, would you be able to give the significance of each part of the figure?

- Can you define the key terms at the end of the chapter?

- Which parts of the chapter will you review?

- Will you seek further help, outside of this book (such as a teacher, Princeton Review tutor, or AP Students), on any of the content in this chapter—and, if so, on what content?

Chapter 12
Cognitive Psychology: Intelligence and Testing

STANDARDIZATION AND NORMS

When we use tests designed to measure psychological characteristics, we need to know what the scores mean. For example, if a tester measures your IQ, and you score a 125 on this IQ test, how do you know what your IQ is relative to the rest of the world? To determine such relative standing, tests are standardized. Standardization is accomplished by administering the test to a **standardization sample,** a group of people who represent the entire population. The data collected from the standardization sample is compared against **norms,** which are standards of performance against which anyone who takes a given test can be compared. Tests need to be restandardized when a new, different population takes the test. The **Flynn effect** supports the need to restandardize because the data indicates that the population has become smarter over the past 50 years. Thus, an IQ of 100 may mean different things in different years, depending on the standardization sample.

RELIABILITY AND VALIDITY

More Reliability Methods

Other methods of testing reliability include **split-half**, in which one group takes half the test (perhaps only the odd-numbered questions) and another group takes the other half, and **equivalent form**, in which different but similar tests covering the same concepts are given to different groups.

Tests used to measure any psychological trait or ability must be both reliable and valid. **Reliability** is a measure of how consistent a test is in the measurements it provides. In other words, reliability refers to the likelihood that the same individual would get a similar score if tested with the same test on separate occasions (disallowing for practice effects or effects due to familiarity with the test items from the first testing). In fact, reliability is often assessed by giving participants a test and later—preferably after they have forgotten the specific items—administering the same test again. The two sets of scores are compared and a correlation coefficient is computed between them. This is called the **test-retest method**. Tests that are perfectly reliable have a reliability coefficient of one. Reliabilities apply only to groups, however, so that even though a given test is highly reliable, a given individual may show substantial fluctuations in scores.

Validity refers to the extent that a test measures what it intends to measure. Validity is calculated by comparing how well the results from a test correlate with other measures that assess what the test is supposed to predict. So, for example, if you just developed a new IQ test, and you wanted to know if it was valid, you might compare your results to those that the same participants had achieved on other IQ measures. Even better, you might correlate the IQ test scores with school grades, on the notion that IQ test scores should predict school grades. It is possible to have a test that is reliable but not valid. Such a test consistently measures something, but not what it is intended to measure. However, it is impossible to have a test that is valid but not reliable. If individuals' scores fluctuate wildly, then they cannot consistently correlate with others' scores, whatever these other scores may be. **Internal validity** is the degree to which the subject's results are due to the questions being asked and not another variable. **External validity** is true validity—that is, the degree to which results from the test can be generalized to the "real world." In this case, a test would be externally valid if it does, in fact, measure intelligence.

TYPES OF TESTS

Tests used in psychology can be **projective tests**, in which ambiguous stimuli, open to interpretation, are presented, or **inventory-type tests**, in which participants answer a standard series of questions.

Two popular projective tests are the **Rorschach Inkblot Test** and the **Thematic Apperception Test (TAT)**. The Rorschach is a sequence of 10 inkblots, each of which the participant is asked to observe and then characterize. For example, a participant might see one inkblot as a bat or another as two people staring at each other. Sometimes, people see multiple images in a single inkblot. Different aspects of the participant's descriptions, such as form and movement of objects, are scored to yield an evaluation of the individual's personality.

The TAT is a series of pictures of people in ambiguous relationships with other people. The participant's task is to generate a story to accompany the picture. The story includes both what led up to the scene in the picture and what will occur next. Again, the participant's responses are used to make judgments about his/her personality. Both of these tests are used by followers of the psychoanalytic view of personality. The major criticism of projective personality tests is that the assessment of the responses can be too subjective.

Inventory-type tests contain fixed answers to questions. They typically do not allow free responses. A classic example is the MMPI-2-RF mentioned in Chapter 14. This test presents the participant with a variety of statements. The participant's task is to answer "true," "false," or "can't say." This test, too, yields a characterization of personality. It is often used to diagnose abnormalities.

Other Test Types

There are many other types of tests. **Power tests** gauge abilities in certain areas. These are usually extremely difficult tests in which it is unlikely that a person could answer all the questions correctly. At the other end of the spectrum are **speed tests**. These have very easy items, but the test is timed, making completion difficult. **Achievement tests** assess knowledge gained; the Advanced Placement exams are of this type. In contrast to these are **aptitude tests**, which evaluate a person's abilities. A road test before getting a driver's license is an example of an aptitude test.

INTELLIGENCE

Intelligence can be defined as goal-directed adaptive thinking. Such thinking is difficult to measure on a standardized test. In fact, the nature of intelligence itself is an issue of contention among psychologists. Few psychologists would claim that the popular "intelligence" tests measure all aspects of intelligence. **Alfred Binet** was a French psychologist who first began to measure children's intelligence for the French government. Binet's test measured the "mental age" of school-age children so that children needing extra help could be placed in special classrooms. An American psychologist and Stanford University professor named **Lewis Terman** modified Binet's test to create a test commonly referred to as the **Stanford-Binet Test**. The Stanford-Binet became the first widely administered intelligence test during World War I when the United States Army used it to rank recruits. Most modern psychologists measure an aspect of intelligence, called the IQ or **intelligence quotient**.

This quotient originally was conceived of as a ratio of mental age over chronological (physical) age, multiplied by 100. Mental age is a measure of performance based on comparing the participant's performance to that of an "average" person of a given age. Therefore, if you take a test and your score is comparable to that of an average 10-year-old, then your mental age is 10. IQ scores are normally distributed, with a mean, median, and mode of about 100, and a standard deviation of 15 or 16 points.

Measuring IQs Today
Today, IQs are rarely computed as quotients, but rather are computed on the basis of the extent to which a person's score is above or below the average.

The most common intelligence tests given to children today are the **Stanford-Binet Intelligence Scale** and the **Wechsler Intelligence Scale for Children** (WISC-IV). There is also a version of the Wechsler specifically geared toward adults, the **Wechsler Adult Intelligence Scale** (WAIS). The WISC-IV and WAIS generally have six types of questions: information (how many wings does a bird have?), comprehension (what is the advantage of keeping money in a bank?), arithmetic (if 3 pencils cost $1, what will be the cost of 15 pencils?), similarities (in what ways are seals and sea lions alike?), vocabulary (what does "retain" mean?), and digit span questions in which subjects are asked to hold information in short-term memory.

There has been an ongoing debate as to whether intelligence is one specific set of abilities or many different sets of abilities. In the early part of the 20th century, **Charles Spearman** proposed that there was a general intelligence (or g factor) that was the basis of all other intelligence. The g factor is the intelligence applied across mental activities, which is close to the standard definition for "intelligence." The s factor is the breakdown of this intelligence into a specific component, such as one's ability to process math equations or linguistic puns. Spearman used **factor analysis**, a statistical measure for analyzing test data. **Robert Sternberg** proposed that intelligence could be more broadly defined as having three major components: **analytical, practical,** and **creative intelligence**. **Louis Thurstone**, a researcher in the field of intelligence, posited that we need to think of intelligence more broadly because intelligence can come in many different forms. The most famous proponent of the idea of multiple intelligences is **Howard Gardner** of Harvard University. Gardner has identified the following types of intelligence: **verbal** and **mathematical** (these are the two traditionally measured by IQ tests) as well as **musical, spatial, kinesthetic, environmental, interpersonal** (people perceptive), and **intrapersonal** (insightful, self-awareness). **Daniel Goleman**, a psychologist at Rutgers, has done recent work on the importance of **emotional intelligence** (being able to recognize people's intents and motivations) and has created programs for enhancing one's emotional intelligence.

Heredity/Environment and Intelligence

Nature and nurture interact in the formation of human intelligence. One way to measure the influence of inheritance on IQ is through a **heritability coefficient**. This coefficient, which ranges from 0 to 1, is a rough measure of the proportion of variation among individuals that can be attributed to genetic effects. Heritability is sometimes computed by comparing the IQs of identical twins who were raised separately. The assumption is that because the identical twins have identical genes, all variation in identical twins reared apart must be due to environment. Of course, the assumption is rarely completely met because identical twins are usually not separated at birth and even if they are, they still have shared the intrauterine environment of the mother. This type of analysis typically yields heritability quotients of about 0.6–0.8 (on a scale of 0–1.0). The percentage not due to heritability can be contributed to the environmentality of a particular trait. When psychologists compare the IQs of identical twins raised together to those of fraternal twins raised together, the resulting heritability quotient is about 0.75. This analysis assumes that families and people outside families treat identical and fraternal twins in the same way, an assumption that seems questionable. Many psychologists believe that the true heritability quotient for IQ is about 0.5. Thus, half of the variation among people is due to heredity, half to environment. It is important to realize that the heritability of a trait has nothing to do with its modifiability. For example, height is highly heritable, but heights have been increasing over the past several generations, especially in certain Asian countries such as Japan, as a result of changing diet. Here's a helpful analogy to illustrate modifiability of intelligence and the interplay of nature and nurture: think of nature as the soil in which intelligence can grow and nurture as the degree of care for the crop.

HUMAN DIVERSITY

As previously stated, IQs are roughly normally distributed. As a result, a large majority of people will have an IQ near 100. However, in a normal distribution, there will also be a small number of people at the high and low ends of the IQ range.

Very high IQs are one basis for considering people to be intellectually gifted. Sometimes, an IQ in the 99th percentile (higher than about 135) is considered "gifted," although there is no set standard. Moreover, other measures besides IQ should be used in assigning a label of "gifted." Louis Terman conducted a study of gifted children, following them into adulthood. Many of the participants went on to be very successful; however, part of their success may have been due to the socioeconomic status of their parents. Other factors unrelated to IQ may also have influenced the ability of the participants to succeed.

Intellectual disability refers to low levels of intelligence and adaptive behavior. Low IQ alone does not signify this. To be classified as intellectually disabled, a person must also demonstrate a low level of adaptive competence, or the ability to get along in the world. Intellectual disability can be categorized by severity ranging from mild, with an IQ range of 50–70, to profound, characterized by an IQ lower than 25.

Between the *DSM-IV* and *DSM-5*, the term "mental retardation" became "intellectual disability." It's unlikely that you'll see the outdated former term on the AP Psychology Exam, but better safe than sorry!

ETHICS IN TESTING

Those who are involved in **psychometrics**, or psychological testing, must be sure that they follow certain guidelines. Confidentiality must be protected. The purposes of the test must be clear to those administering and those taking the test. A group of individuals at each research institution sit on the Institutional Review Board, which combs through the proposed methodology of a study to determine if there may be any unethical behavior or adverse consequences of a scientist's research before he or she is granted permission to perform any experiments. Questions should be asked and answered concerning who will see the results of the test and how the scores will be used. Furthermore, the impact of the scores should be ascertained before the test is given.

KEY TERMS

Standardization and Norms

    standardization sample

    norms

    Flynn effect

Reliability and Validity

    reliability

    test-retest method

    split-half reliability

    equivalent-form reliability

    validity

    internal validity

    external validity

Types of Tests

    projective tests

    inventory-type tests

    Rorschach Inkblot Test

    Thematic Apperception Test

    power tests

    speed tests

    achievement tests

    aptitude tests

Intelligence

    Alfred Binet

    Louis Terman

    Stanford-Binet Test

    intelligence quotient (IQ)

    Stanford-Binet Intelligence Scale

    Wechsler Intelligence Scale for Children

    Wechsler Adult Intelligence Scale

    Charles Spearman

    g factor

    factor analysis

    Robert Sternberg

    analytical intelligence

    practical intelligence

    creative intelligence

    Lewis Thurstone

    Howard Gardner

    verbal intelligence

    mathematical intelligence

    musical intelligence

    spatial intelligence

    kinesthetic intelligence

    environmental intelligence

    interpersonal intelligence

    intrapersonal intelligence

    Daniel Goleman

    emotional intelligence

    heritability coefficient

Ethics in Testing

    psychometrics

Chapter 12 Drill

See Chapter 19 for answers and explanations.

1. In the context of psychometric testing, content validity is defined as

   (A) the extent to which the test actually measures what it is purported to measure
   (B) the degree to which there is a correlation between results on the test and future performance on another measure
   (C) the degree to which the test will yield similar results across administrations
   (D) the extent to which scores on two versions of the test are highly correlated
   (E) the degree to which scores on two sections of the same test are consistent with each other

2. Which of the following is an example of a projective test?

   (A) The Stanford-Binet Intelligence Scale
   (B) The Thematic Apperception Test (TAT)
   (C) The Minnesota Multiphasic Personality Inventory (MMPI)
   (D) The Strong Vocational Interest Blank
   (E) The F-scale

3. On a normal score distribution, an IQ score of 85 would be located

   (A) approximately one standard deviation above the mean
   (B) approximately one standard deviation below the mean
   (C) approximately two standard deviations above the mean
   (D) approximately two standard deviations below the mean
   (E) in a variable position—it would depend on the age of the respondent

4. Test standardization is accomplished by

   (A) administering the test to a sample chosen to reflect the characteristics of the population in question
   (B) administering different parts of the test to different samples meant to reflect different populations
   (C) correlating the results on the test with results on other tests that claim to measure the same dimension
   (D) correlating the consistency of scores given by different sets of graders
   (E) equilibrating the number of times each answer choice appears

5. Which of the following is NOT a dimension of intelligence in Howard Gardner's theory of multiple intelligences?

   (A) Environmental
   (B) Mathematical
   (C) Spatial
   (D) Musical
   (E) Emotional

6. Reliability measures

   (A) how consistently the test holds up over time
   (B) how well the test measures what it means to test
   (C) a way in which you can be sure that an experiment tests only one variable at a time
   (D) how consistently an individual will score on the same test on subsequent occasions
   (E) to what extent the findings of a study can be generalized to the whole population

7. A multiple-choice or a true/false question test is an example of a(n)

   (A) projective test
   (B) inventory-type test
   (C) intelligence test
   (D) hereditary test
   (E) environment test

8. Which of the following is necessary for a test to be ethical?

   (A) Confidentiality
   (B) Full disclosure of deception
   (C) Double-blind design
   (D) Internal validity
   (E) Generalization

REFLECT

Respond to the following questions:

- Which topics in this chapter do you hope to see on the multiple-choice section or essay?

- Which topics in this chapter do you hope not to see on the multiple-choice section or essay?

- Regarding any psychologists mentioned, can you pair the psychologists with their contributions to the field? Did they contribute significant experiments, theories, or both?

- Regarding any theories mentioned, can you distinguish between differing theories well enough to recognize them on the multiple-choice section? Can you distinguish them well enough to write a fluent essay on them?

- Regarding any figures given, if you were given a labeled figure from within this chapter, would you be able to give the significance of each part of the figure?

- Can you define the key terms at the end of the chapter?

- Which parts of the chapter will you review?

- Will you seek further help, outside of this book (such as a teacher, Princeton Review tutor, or AP Students), on any of the content in this chapter—and, if so, on what content?

Chapter 13
Developmental
Psychology

LIFE-SPAN APPROACH

The life-span approach to **developmental psychology** takes the view that development is not a process with a clear ending. For decades, development was thought to end with the onset of adolescence. Rather, it is now viewed as a process that continues from birth to death. From this perspective, developmental psychology can be defined as the study of the changes that occur in people's abilities and behaviors as they age. It is important to differentiate between **life-span psychologists** and **child psychologists**. Although both study development, the child psychologist has decided to focus on a particular earlier portion of the typical life span. **Erik Erikson** was the first to successfully champion the view that development occurs across an entire lifetime.

Research Methods

Research methods in developmental psychology vary according to the questions being asked by the researcher. Some developmental psychologists are interested in studying **normative development**, which is the typical sequence of developmental changes for a group of people. For example, some developmental psychologists talk about development occurring in a series of stages, universal to human development. Other developmental psychologists are more interested in individual development, or the individual pattern of development, including differences among individuals during development. Often, the techniques and research methods useful for studying one type of development are not useful for studying other types of development.

Normative development is often studied using the **cross-sectional method**. The cross-sectional method seeks to compare groups of people of various ages on similar tasks. So, for example, a cross-sectional study might involve administering cognitive tests to a group of two-year-olds, a group of four-year-olds, and a group of six-year-olds, and then compare the means of the groups. This approach can reveal the average age at which certain skills or abilities appear. However, the data collected in cross-sectional studies tells us little about the actual development of any single individual.

To research the developmental process, many developmental psychologists use the **longitudinal method**. The longitudinal method involves following a small group of people over a long portion of their lives, assessing change at set intervals. As you might imagine, longitudinal research is more difficult and more expensive to conduct and, therefore, is conducted less frequently than cross-sectional research. However, the longitudinal method does have some benefits because the study of individuals over time rules out the differences between subjects that other studies include. They also allow for the study of the temporal order of events.

DEVELOPMENTAL ISSUES

Developmental psychology, like most aspects of psychology, must deal with the so-called **nature-nurture debate**. **Maturationists** emphasize the role of genetically programmed growth and development on the body, particularly on the nervous system. **Maturation** can best be defined as biological readiness. From their point of view, greater preprogrammed physiological development of the brain allows for more complex conceptualization and reasoning.

The opposing position is the learning perspective, and adherents to this position are sometimes referred to as **environmentalists**. The extreme form can be found in Locke's idea, which states that almost all development is the direct result of learning—infants are born like a blank slate onto which experience etches its lessons. The organism develops more complex behaviors and cognition because it acquires more associations through learning.

There are other issues to be considered when studying development. One is whether development is **continuous** or **discontinuous**—gradual or stage-oriented. Evidence of growth spurts and leaps of cognition support the discontinuous approach, but other studies show gradual development, particularly in social skill building. A **critical period** refers to a time during which a skill or ability must develop; if the ability does not develop during that time, it probably will never develop or may not develop as well. An example of this is language. Scientists believe that, if not exposed to language by roughly age 12, the ability to learn language significantly diminishes or disappears.

Culture also impacts development in important ways. A **collectivist culture** is one in which the needs of society are placed before the needs of the individual. Conversely, **individualist cultures** promote personal needs above the needs of society. It is important to realize that a developing child's relationship with her environment and culture is bidirectional, meaning that just as a child's social environment plays a role in how she develops, she also contributes to the society in which she is born.

The Feral Child
One famous example in favor of the critical period is Genie, the "feral child" who was isolated from other humans from infancy until age 13, preventing her from learning spoken language.

DEVELOPMENTAL THEORIES

Developmental theories can be divided into two broad classes: those that conceptualize development as a single, continuous, unitary process and those that view it as occurring in discrete stages. **Stages** are patterns of behavior that occur in a fixed sequence. Each stage has a unique set of cognitive structures, or sets of mental abilities, that build on the cognitive structures established in the previous stage. Quite likely, some aspects of development may occur in stages at the same time that others occur along a continuum. Psychologists typically agree that the edges of stages are blurred and may overlap for various domains within a stage.

> **Dimensions of Development**
>
> Development typically occurs within three realms: physical, cognitive, and social.

Physical Development

Physical development starts at conception. The **zygote**, or fertilized egg, goes through three distinct phases of gestation prior to birth. The first stage is the **germinal stage**, in which the zygote undergoes cell division, expanding to 64 cells and implanting itself in the uterine wall. This stage lasts about two weeks. The **embryonic stage** consists of organ formation and lasts until the beginning of the third month. In the **fetal stage**, sexual differentiation occurs and movement begins to develop. Growth is rapid in this stage. Various harmful environmental agents, known as **teratogens**, may affect fetal development. One such agent is alcohol. Some fetuses exposed to alcohol develop **fetal alcohol syndrome (FAS)**, resulting in physical abnormalities and cognitive deficiencies.

A newborn baby, or **neonate**, is nearly helpless, but is equipped with a few reflexes. The **sucking reflex** can be triggered by placing something in the baby's mouth. The **palmar reflex** is the automatic grabbing elicited by something being placed in one of the neonate's hands. Stroking the bottom of the foot causes the toes to splay out. This is known as the **Babinski reflex**. The **head-turning reflex** (also called the rooting reflex) is the response elicited by touching the baby's cheek, and the **Moro reflex** is the splaying out of the limbs in response to loss of support, such as when a baby believes it is suddenly falling. Finally, neonates have an **orienting reflex**, which is activated when they orient themselves to sudden changes in their surroundings. For example, if there is a loud crash, infants will search for the origin of the noise to orient themselves. This reflex persists into adulthood. However, most of the reflexes mentioned above disappear months after birth as the child matures and develops.

Infants also seem to have innate likes and dislikes. Infants prefer to look at face-like patterns over other more or less complex patterns. Infants have a developed sense of taste. Neonates will make **stereotyped ingestive responses**, sucking and smacking their lips, if someone places a drop of sugar water in their mouths. If one uses lemon juice, the neonate will gape—allowing the fluid to come out of the mouth—will stick out the tongue, and will probably cry. This behavior makes evolutionary sense given that sour and bitter flavors are often associated with harmful bacteria that can make the baby ill.

Much of the research on the physical development of children focuses on the refinement of motor control and perceptual abilities. Humans undergo a fairly predictable course of motor development, beginning with rudimentary reflexes and progressing through the learning of specialized movements to assist with daily living and recreational activities.

Reflexive movements are primitive, involuntary movements that serve to "prime" the neuromuscular system and form the basis for the more sophisticated movements to come. For example, the palmar grasp reflex primes the nervous system for the more controlled grasping learned at later stages. Reflexes, and learning to inhibit reflexes, occur during the first year of a child's life and overlap with the stage in which rudimentary movements are learned.

Rudimentary movements serve as the first voluntary movement performed by a child. They occur in very predictable stages from birth to age 2, and they include rolling, sitting, crawling, standing, and walking. These form the foundation on which the fundamental movements are built and are primarily dictated by genetics (that is, these movements are more or less "pre-programmed").

The **fundamental movement** stage occurs from age 2 to age 7; during this time, the child is learning to manipulate his or her body through actions such as running, jumping, throwing, and catching. This stage is highly influenced by environment, much more so than the rudimentary movement stage that precedes it. Children are typically in school at this stage, and physical activity and games are necessary for proper motor development. Movements initially start out uncoordinated and poorly controlled, but as the child advances in age, movements become more refined, coordinated, and efficient.

During the stage of **specialized movement**, children learn to combine the fundamental movements and apply them to specific tasks. This stage can be subdivided into two shorter stages: a **transitional substage** and an **application substage**. During the transitional substage, a combination of movements occurs; for example, grasping, jumping, and throwing are combined to take a shot in basketball. The application substage is defined more by conscious decisions to apply these skills to specific types of activity; for example, one child might choose to play basketball, whereas another might use the same set of skills and abilities to play baseball. Additionally, the application of strategy to movement is now possible; for example, a child choosing to delay shooting the basketball until she has a clear shot at the basket.

Ultimately, children progress to a lifelong application stage, typically beginning in adolescence and progressing through adulthood. During this time, movements are continually refined and applied to normal daily activities as well as recreational and competitive activities.

Both of these processes are dependent on neural development. There is evidence that the brain is still organizing itself in the months after birth. In fact, nervous system development continues into early adulthood. It is important to note that although perceptual and motor development depend on the development of the nervous system, the development of the nervous system depends on **environmental interaction** on the part of the child. It has been demonstrated that children raised in situations in which their ability to crawl or walk is restricted have impaired motor skills. This occurs, for example, in some institutions in countries without regulation of childcare facilities. Additionally, perceptual development can be delayed by lack of stimulation. An important theme in developmental psychology is that of the critical period—that for some parts of the brain, the phrase "use it or lose it" holds true.

Experiments with animals have shown that depriving an eye of stimuli by covering it at the very beginning of life will lead to the underdevelopment of the part of the occipital lobe responsible for vision in that eye. As a result, that section of the brain will be allocated to another function. This plasticity, or changeability, of the brain is illustrated in an experiment in which a third eye was added to a frog. The occipital lobe flexibly responded by dividing the processing power of the occipital lobe into three eyes rather than two. This experiment worked only if the eye was introduced very close to birth, demonstrating the limited critical period during which some experience must occur for the brain to develop in a particular way.

Nature, Nurture, and the Critical Period

This phenomenon is informative with regard to the nature-nurture issue. The child is not born as a blank slate: it has some innate reflexes. However, the physiological development of the child depends on its interactions with the environment. Nature and nurture play complementary roles in development.

Puberty is another landmark of physical development. Growth spurts in height and weight, development of secondary sex characteristics, and menstruation in girls or nocturnal emissions in boys characterize this stage. There are also social and cognitive changes that are discussed later in this section.

Most people peak physically in early adulthood. One just needs to look at professional athletes to recognize this fact. Adulthood is marked by gradual decrease of physical abilities, although a healthy lifestyle will slow this process. At approximately 50 years old, women experience menopause, a change in estrogen production causing menstruation to cease.

In the elderly population, the gradual diminution of adulthood reaches noticeable proportions. The senses lose much of their efficacy. For example, half of those over age 80 have lost their sense of smell. Diseases such as Alzheimer's can affect memory, cognition, and personality.

Cognitive Development

Cognitive development refers to the development of learning, memory, reasoning, problem-solving, and related skills.

Piaget

Jean Piaget proposed an influential theory of the cognitive development of children. Piaget's developmental theory is based on the concept of **equilibration**. Equilibration is a child's attempt to reach a balance between what the child encounters in the environment and what cognitive structures the child brings to the situation. Children try to reach equilibration through **assimilation**, incorporating new ideas into existing schemas. For example, a child may develop a **schema**, or mental representational model, for animals after encountering dogs and cats. When he goes to the zoo and sees more exotic four-legged animals like elephants or giraffes, he must assimilate this new information into his existing category of animals. However, when facing information that does not easily fit into an existing schema, the child must modify the schema to include the new information. This process is called **accommodation**. For example, this child's schema of animal might go through a process of accommodation if he encountered a kangaroo that hopped on two legs.

According to Piaget, children go through a series of developmental stages. Piaget believed that these stages occur in a fixed order, and a child can be in only one stage at any given time. The following are the four stages Piaget proposed, first presented as a chart and then in more detail.

Each stage can be categorized by the presence/absence of schemas, the types of mental operations the child can perform, and the presence or absence of theoretical thought.

Q: What are the typical age ranges for Piaget's stages of development?

Answer on page 223.

Stage	Explanation	Schemas	Mental Operations	Theoretical thinking
Sensorimotor	Act on objects that are present and begin to develop schemas but incapable of operations			
Preoperational	Able to use schemas not present (symbolic thought) but lacks ability to perform mental operations	X		
Concrete Operational	Able to access schemas and perform mental operations but still limited to experiences	X	X	
Formal Operational	Able to use schemas, understand operations, and apply both to theoretical questions not based on experiences	X	X	X

- **Sensorimotor Stage.** This stage usually occurs during the first two years of life and is typified by reflexive reactions and then circular reactions, which are repeated behaviors by which the infant manipulates the environment. For example, if an infant kicks its legs and hits the mobile on its crib with its foot, stimulating movement, the infant is likely to repeat the action in the future. **Object permanence**, which develops during this stage, is the knowledge that objects continue to exist when they are outside the field of view. For example, if a ball rolls under a chair, the child will continue to look for it. At this age, the child lacks the ability to access mental schemas or solve problems through performing a mental operation, which is the ability to represent and manipulate information in a person's mind. Schemas are acquired in the preoperational stage, while mental operations become accessible during the concrete operational stage. Another hallmark of the sensorimotor stage is the development of goal-oriented behavior. For example, a very young child who is able to roll over at will, but not yet able to crawl, may consciously roll over multiple times to reach a favorite toy.

- **Preoperational Stage.** The preoperational stage typically occurs from ages two to seven. Children generally begin this stage with the development of language. Language represents a shift to **symbolic thinking**, or the ability to use words to substitute for objects. Other characteristics of the stage are **egocentrism**, seeing the world only from one's own point of view, **artificialism**, believing that all things are human-made, and **animism**, believing that all things are living.

- **Concrete Operational Stage.** Typically occurring from ages seven to eleven, this is the stage when children develop the ability to perform a mental operation and then reverse their thinking back to a starting point, a concept called **reversibility**. Another important concept is **conservation**—the idea that the amount of a substance does not change just because it is arranged differently. For example, conservation of mass might be demonstrated by taking a large ball of clay and using it to create several smaller balls of clay. A child in the concrete operational stage will understand that the total amount of clay has not changed, while a child in the preoperational stage might think that there is more clay because there are more balls.

Criticism of Piaget

Piaget's theory is not universally accepted. Other researchers have found flaws in his research methods and his underestimation of children's abilities especially at ages four to five. Critics attest that some children that age can take another's perspective and are not so egocentric. Other criticisms include the failure of Piaget to recognize the environmental factors pushing child development.

- **Formal Operational Stage.** This stage begins at about age 12. At this level, children are fully capable of understanding abstractions and symbolic relationships. They are also capable of **metacognition**, or the ability to recognize one's cognitive processes and adapt those processes if they aren't successful. The formal operational stage is also the point at which a child acquires hypothetical reasoning, which is the ability to figure out answers to problems with which a person does not have direct experience. For example, a child in the concrete operational stage would have great difficulty imagining how the world might change as a result of an alien invasion, while a 12-year-old could posit numerous theories on the issue.

Theory of Mind (TOM) and the False Belief Task

A key cognitive ability that develops in childhood around the age of four is theory of mind. TOM allows children to understand that other people see the world differently than they do. It is the opposite of egocentrism. Psychologists test theory of mind through the "false belief task." For example, in this test, a child under the age of four opens a container that is labeled "pencils" and finds gumballs instead. The child is asked what another child, who is not present, would think is in the container. The correct answer is "pencils," but because a child under the age of four does not have TOM, that child will answer "gumballs." Psychologists now believe that the absence of theory of mind helps to explain the actions of people with autism, which is discussed in Chapter 16.

A: Sensorimotor:
0–2 years old
Preoperational:
2–7 years old
Concrete Operational:
7–11 years old
Formal Operational:
12 years +

Vygotsky

Another influential theory of cognitive development was proposed by **Lev Vygotsky**. Piaget believed that biological maturation is the driving force in development. Vygotsky, on the other hand, stressed social factors as critical to the developmental process. Vygotsky believed that much of development occurs by **internalization**, the absorption of knowledge into the self from environmental and social contexts. Vygotsky also proposed the concept of a **zone of proximal development**, which is the range between the developed level of ability that a child displays and the potential level of ability of which the child is actually capable. These two levels are often referred to as the **actual development level** versus the **potential development level**, respectively. Actual development rarely lives up to its potential because ability depends on input from the environment, and environmental input is rarely truly optimal. According to Vygotsky, the way by which a child realizes his potential is through the process of scaffolding. Scaffolding is the support system that allows a person to move across the zone of proximal development incrementally, with environmental supports, such as teachers and parents. If a person fails to advance, it might mean that the scaffolding steps are too high above the person's current abilities.

Life-span psychologists have realized that cognitive development continues into adulthood. Childhood and early adulthood are times marked by relatively rapid neural growth. However, we lose a small percentage of brain weight between our early 20s and our 80s. In the later years, many adults show a decrease in **fluid intelligence**—that is, the ability to think in terms of abstract concepts and symbolic relationships. This decrease, however, is accompanied by increased **crystallized intelligence**, or specific knowledge of facts and information.

Older but Wiser

A related feature of adult cognitive development is **wisdom**. It is assumed in many cultures that older members of a society have a perspective or level of accumulated knowledge that gives them wisdom. Wisdom is a form of insight into life situations and conditions that results in good judgments about difficult life problems.

Social Development

Social development involves the ability to interact with others and with the social structures in which we live. Erik Erikson tried to capture the complexities of social development in his psychosocial theory. This theory is important not only for its description of the developmental process as a series of stages marked by the resolution of specific developmental "tasks," but also because it was the first theory to assert that development is a life-span process. Erikson's stages of **psychosocial development** include the following.

Trust vs. Mistrust

This stage occurs during the first year of life. Infants decide whether the world is friendly or hostile, depending on whether or not they can trust that their basic needs will be met. Trust and hopefulness are the outcomes of positive resolutions of this stage.

Autonomy vs. Shame and Doubt

Between the ages of one and three, the child must develop a sense of control over bodily functions as well as over the environment. Successful resolution of this stage involves mastery of toilet training, walking, and others skills related to control of the self.

Initiative vs. Guilt

This is the stage that occurs at about three to six years of age and often corresponds with a child's entry into a broader social world outside the home. Children at this stage must take initiative and learn to assert themselves socially, without overstepping their bounds. The successful resolution of this stage results in the development of a sense of purpose.

Industry vs. Inferiority

Children from ages six to twelve are in this stage. They are now in school and are becoming accustomed to receiving feedback for their work. Thus, they must gain a sense of accomplishment and pride in their work. They begin to understand what they are capable of doing. The successful resolution of this stage produces a sense of competence.

Identity vs. Role Confusion

This stage involves the adolescent search for identity. Adolescents question what type of person they are and begin to develop their own values at this stage. The resolution of this stage is **fidelity**, or truthfulness to one's self.

Intimacy vs. Isolation

This is the stage of early adulthood when we attempt to form loving, lasting relationships. The successful resolution of this stage results in one's learning how to love in a mature, giving way. If this stage is not successfully resolved, feelings of isolation or a lack of intimacy may result.

Generativity vs. Stagnation

This stage occurs during middle adulthood and brings with it the struggle to be productive in both career and home, and to contribute to the next generation with ideas and possibly with children. Being productive in these ways is called **generativity**. This is the stage where we try to leave our "mark" on the world. Failure to resolve this stage can result in feelings of **stagnation** or isolation.

Integrity vs. Despair

This stage occurs during old age and brings with it the struggle to come to terms with one's life, which involves accepting both successes and failures. The positive outcome of this stage is wisdom, whereas the failure to resolve this stage can lead to bitterness and despair.

Erikson's is not the only social development theory. In the 1950s, **Harry and Margaret Harlow** demonstrated that rhesus monkey infants need comfort and security as much as food. Through the use of artificial, inanimate surrogate mothers, Harlow ascertained that these infants become more attached to soft "mothers" without food than to wire ones with food. **Attachment** is defined as the tendency to prefer specific familiar individuals to others. **John Bowlby** is considered the father of attachment theory. He devoted extensive research to the concept of attachment and pioneered the psychoanalytic view that early experiences in childhood have an important influence on development and behavior later in life. Bowlby believed that a close and loving relationship between a child and a caregiver is critical to the infant's healthy development and provides a model that the growing child will use to build mutually beneficial relationships in his or her life. In contrast, a lack of responsiveness and physical support on the part of the parent will hurt the child in the short-term and his or her relationships in the long-term. In the 1970s, **Mary Ainsworth** studied human infant attachment. Using the **strange situation,** in which a parent or primary guardian leaves a child with a stranger and then returns, Ainsworth recognized four attachment patterns.

- **Secure**—The child is generally happy in the presence of the primary caretaker, is distressed when he or she leaves, but can be consoled again quickly after he or she returns.

- **Avoidant**—The child may be inhibited in the presence of the primary caretaker, and may pretend to not be distressed when he or she leaves. (Blood pressure and cortisol analyses show that the child is in fact quite stressed out.)

- **Ambivalent**—The child may have a "stormy" relationship with the primary caretaker, is distressed when he or she leaves, and has difficulty being consoled after his or her return.

- **Disorganized**—The child has an erratic relationship with the primary caretaker and with other adults. This attachment style is more common in cases of severe neglect and/or abuse.

Diana Baumrind has identified the following three types of parenting styles.

- **Authoritarian**—Parents have high expectations for their child to comply with rules without debate or explanation. This style is the most likely to use corporal punishment (like spanking) for disobedience. Children of these parents are socially withdrawn, lack decision-making capabilities, and lack curiosity. Authoritarian parents will exert a high level of control and low level of warmth.

- **Authoritative**—Parents also expect compliance to rules but explain rules and encourage independence. Parents set limits, give out punishments, and forgive. Children of these parents have high self-esteem, are independent, and are articulate. Authoritative parents will exert a high level of control and high level of warmth.

- **Permissive**—Parents have few expectations and are warm and non-demanding. Children are rarely punished, and parents consider themselves friends of the child. Children of these parents are not good at accepting responsibility, controlling their impulses, or being generous in social relationships. Permissive parents will exert a low level of control and high level of warmth.

Another theory of social development concerns the stages of death and dying developed by **Elisabeth Kubler-Ross**. She identified the following ways people tend to come to terms with terminal illnesses—denial, anger, bargaining, depression, and acceptance. Later psychologists have acknowledged these as well as other emotions involved in grieving and have shown that the stages are not necessarily ordered.

Moral Development

The most influential theory of **moral development** was advanced by **Lawrence Kohlberg**, who expanded on an early theory proposed by Piaget. Kohlberg's theory can be divided into levels, each of which has two distinct stages.

Kohlberg's Level I

Level I encompasses ages seven to ten and is the level of preconventional morality. **Preconventional morality** is a two-stage system of moral judgment. In the first stage, it is based on avoiding punishment and receiving rewards. In this stage, children often will mention a fear of being punished as a reason why rules should not be broken. As children age, preconventional morality changes slightly. The second stage of preconventional morality is characterized by a focus on individualism and exchange. Children work for their own interest at this stage, and while they will strike deals with others to satisfy the other person, their primary interest is a selfish one. In summary, in stage 1 of preconventional morality, children make judgments motivated by fear; in stage 2, they make judgments by evaluating the benefit for themselves.

Kohlberg's Level II

Level II typically occurs from about ages 10 to 16 and sometimes beyond. This is the stage of **conventional morality**. Conventional morality is the internalizing of society's rules and morals. The motivation to follow these rules is generated by the child's knowing that it is "right" to do so. The first stage of this level (stage 3) is typified by the child's trying to live up to what others, especially authority figures, expect of him or her. The child understands that the rules set forth by society are important, and the child tries to conform to these rules. The second stage of conventional morality (stage 4) involves the development of conscience. Young teens at this stage obey rules and feel moral, societal obligations.

Kohlberg's Level III

Level III occurs from age 16 and onward. This is the level of **postconventional morality**. At this level, societal rules are still important, but an internal set of values has developed that may generate occasional conflict with societal values. The first stage of this level (stage 5) is characterized by a belief in individual rights and social contracts. Individual rights, such as those of life and liberty, may outweigh social contracts. In general, however, a balance must be maintained between individual interests and societal rules. The second stage of postconventional morality (stage 6) represents the highest stage of moral development in Kohlberg's model. This stage involves the belief in universal principles of justice. Universal principles of justice are universal rules of morality that typically do, but occasionally do not, agree with the rules of society. An individual at stage 6 believes that the universal principles of justice outweigh societal rules and acts accordingly. Few people reach this level, according to Kohlberg.

> ### Criticism of Kohlberg
> Although Kohlberg's theory is an important and influential one, it has been challenged as being inadequate for describing the moral development of people who live in non-Western culture and of women. **Carol Gilligan** has developed a revised version of Kohlberg's theory. Rather than focusing on the awareness and development of the concept of justice, as Kohlberg did, Gilligan's theory places the development of caring relationships as central to moral progress.

SEX ROLES, SEX DIFFERENCES

Psychosexual development is the development of an awareness of one's own sexuality, including the identification of the self with a particular gender. There are differences between the sexes at birth, and, although most observable sexual development occurs during adolescence, psychosexual development starts at a much younger age.

Children develop **gender identity**, the awareness that they are boys or girls, by age two or three. The acquisition of sex-related roles, called **gender typing**, also occurs very early, from the ages of two to seven. This age range is also when children come to understand that there is **gender constancy**—that is, that gender is a fixed, unchangeable characteristic. At this age, children begin to understand that gender is a characteristic of the individual and that items such as clothes or even behavior do not define the sex of the individual. **Androgyny** may develop as children begin to blur the lines between stereotypical male and female roles in society. For example, androgynous individuals can be assertive and aggressive when necessary, but they can also be gentle and nurturing.

Attempting to understand the **fixations** of his patients, **Sigmund Freud** elaborated a theory of psychosexual development. This is a stage theory in which attention was given to parts of the body that were especially significant for the developing person. During the **oral stage**, from birth to about two, the primary source of pleasure for the infant comes from sucking, as well as using the voice to cry out for caretakers. People who develop fixations during this stage may become addicted to gum, cigarettes, or alcohol, or may become verbally abusive people. During the **anal stage**, from about two to three, toddlers learn that they are praised when they do well with toilet training, and are not praised (or even scolded) when they do not. People who develop fixations during this stage may have issues with control, either being overcontrolling (he's so anal!) or being willfully messy (she throws her crap everywhere!). During the **phallic stage**, from about three to six, children realize that they are boys or girls, and begin to puzzle out what that means. Although Freud wrote later (non-judgmentally) about bisexuality and homosexuality, this early theory focused on heterosexual development. Accordingly, the opposite-sex parent is taken as an ideal for future partner choices. People who develop fixations during this stage may be extremely picky about their partner choices, only selecting people who are similar to their parent. During the **latency stage**, from about six to twelve, there is no one particular part of the body that has the most importance for the developing mind. Children in this stage are partly focused on gender identification, which is why many boys associate primarily with other boys, and many girls associate primarily with other girls, and the two groups regard each other with a mixture of interest and suspicion. This is the age of "cooties." People who develop fixations in this stage primarily socialize with their own gender as adults, even though they are heterosexual. During the **genital stage**, from about twelve until death, the genital region becomes the primary source of sensual/sexual pleasure, unless traumas in prior stages have resulted in fixations.

A later psychoanalyst, Erik Erikson, developed another stage theory, one that focused on social and interpersonal factors. Thus, his theory is referred to as one of psychosocial development. Although you may not need to know the details of his eight stages, you should know that he focused on issues of identity. For example, he recognized that teenagers struggle not only with hormones (as Freud talked about), but also with identity and with roles. After all, the teenager no longer has the child identity he or she used to have, but does not yet have the adult identity he or she will have in a few years. As popular singers have recognized, the teen is no longer a girl, but not yet a woman; the teen is somewhere from Boyz to Men. Erikson is also known for extending developmental psychology to include life after 13, including the concept of the "mid-life crisis," another moment of identity reformation.

Another theory of how sex roles develop has been proposed by **Albert Bandura**. Bandura felt that, like violent behavior, sexual roles could be acquired through social or vicarious learning. Young boys see older boys being rewarded for being masculine and punished for being feminine. This pattern creates a self-perpetuating cycle, according to Bandura, with each successive generation providing the model for the following generation. This view has been supported by research showing that parents reward independence and competition in boys, while they reward nurturing and caring behaviors in girls.

It is important to consider that biological, social, and cognitive factors all play a role in sexual development. Additionally, we must consider that, when discussing sexual development, there is much disagreement on what is "normal." Theories of sexual development are often products of the culture and time in which they were developed and do not always reflect what is considered normal in modern society.

KEY TERMS

Life-Span Approach

developmental psychology
life-span psychologists
child psychologists
Erik Erikson
normative development
cross-sectional method
longitudinal method

Developmental Issues

nature-nurture debate
maturationists
maturation
environmentalists
continuous
discontinuous
critical period
culture
collectivist culture
individualist culture

Developmental Theories

stages
physical development
zygote
germinal stage
embryonic stage
fetal stage
teratogens
fetal alcohol syndrome (FAS)
neonate
sucking reflex
palmar reflex
Babinski reflex
head-turning reflex
Moro reflex
orienting reflex
stereotyped ingestive responses
reflexive movement
rudimentary movement
fundamental movement
specialized movement
transitional substage
application substage
environmental interaction
Jean Piaget
equilibration
assimilation

schema
accommodation
sensorimotor stage
object permanence
preoperational stage
symbolic thinking
egocentrism
artificialism
animism
concrete operational stage
reversibility
conservation
formal operational stage
metacognition
Lev Vygotsky
internalization
zone of proximal development
actual development level
potential development level
fluid intelligence
crystallized intelligence
wisdom
psychosocial development
fidelity
generativity
stagnation
Harry and Margaret Harlow
attachment
John Bowlby
Mary Ainsworth
strange situation
child attachment patterns:
    secure, insecure,
    avoidant, disorganized
Diana Baumrind
parenting styles:
    authoritarian, authoritative,
    permissive
Elizabeth Kubler-Ross
moral development
Lawrence Kohlberg
preconventional morality
conventional morality
postconventional morality
Carol Gilligan

Sex Roles, Sex Difference
> psychosexual development
> gender identity
> gender typing
> gender constancy
> androgyny
> fixation
> Sigmund Freud
> stages of psychosexual develop-
> > ment: oral, anal, phallic,
> > latency, genital
> Albert Bandura

Chapter 13 Drill

See Chapter 19 for answers and explanations.

1. In neonates, the response to a feeling of lost bodily support (like falling) that involves a splaying out of the limbs is called the

   (A) palmar reflex
   (B) Babinski reflex
   (C) orienting reflex
   (D) Moro reflex
   (E) rooting reflex

2. The belief that there is often a discrepancy between a child's outward cognitive abilities and his or her true cognitive abilities is most closely associated with which of the following theorists?

   (A) Jean Piaget
   (B) Lev Vygotsky
   (C) Leon Festinger
   (D) Sigmund Freud
   (E) Julian Rotter

3. According to Erik Erikson, the major developmental task of school-age children before puberty is to develop

   (A) a sense of competence in their efforts
   (B) the ability to form stable intimate relationships
   (C) a feeling of trust that their basic needs will be met
   (D) control over basic bodily functions
   (E) a consistent self-view of identity and roles

4. Shyera, approaching the age of five, believes that all things, from people to animals to plants to objects, are alive, but she has trouble understanding circumstances from these other "living" things' points of view. Piaget's theory would place Shyera

   (A) at the sensorimotor stage
   (B) at the preoperational stage
   (C) at the concrete operational stage
   (D) at the formal operational stage
   (E) at the latency stage

5. Lawrence Kohlberg's theory of moral development posits that a child at the first stage of preconventional morality

   (A) is motivated primarily by the evaluation of self-benefit
   (B) is motivated primarily by the desire to live up to expectations
   (C) is motivated primarily by a belief in balancing individual rights with social contracts
   (D) is motivated primarily by the desire to maintain a "just world"
   (E) is motivated primarily by the desire to receive reward and avoid punishment

6. An infant cries when his mother leaves the room but is quickly consoled when she returns. The infant feels comfortable to explore and wander around when the mother is in the room. Mary Ainsworth would describe this infant as having

   (A) insecure attachment
   (B) avoidant attachment
   (C) secure attachment
   (D) disorganized attachment
   (E) generalized attachment

7. A school-age student is able to recognize that the water she poured from a short wide cup is still the same amount of water in a tall, skinny vase. This concept is known as

   (A) conservation
   (B) object permanence
   (C) conditioning
   (D) crystalized intelligence
   (E) egocentrism

8. Trivial Pursuit, a board game that asks for answers to random facts, relies most heavily on which form of knowledge?

   (A) Assimilation
   (B) Crystalized intelligence
   (C) Internalization
   (D) Wisdom
   (E) Fluid intelligence

9. In a modern art museum, Mira comes across an abstract furniture exhibit. She sees one particular piece that looks like a desk, but is later told it is actually a bookshelf. After looking at the furniture piece a little longer, she then sees it can be a bookshelf. This concept of learning is called

    (A) functional fixedness
    (B) object permanence
    (C) a mental set
    (D) accommodation
    (E) assimilation

10. Bandura believed which of the following statements about gender development?

    (A) Gender is a learned behavior that has a critical period right before puberty.
    (B) Gender is genetically based and does not have to do with socialization.
    (C) Gender is a result of hormonal fluctuations that happen during puberty.
    (D) Gender roles are a result of cognitive development only.
    (E) Gender roles are at least in part observed and rewarded through socialization.

REFLECT

Respond to the following questions:

- Which topics in this chapter do you hope to see on the multiple-choice section or essay?

- Which topics in this chapter do you hope not to see on the multiple-choice section or essay?

- Regarding any psychologists mentioned, can you pair the psychologists with their contributions to the field? Did they contribute significant experiments, theories, or both?

- Regarding any theories mentioned, can you distinguish between differing theories well enough to recognize them on the multiple-choice section? Can you distinguish them well enough to write a fluent essay on them?

- Regarding any figures given, if you were given a labeled figure from within this chapter, would you be able to give the significance of each part of the figure?

- Can you define the key terms at the end of the chapter?

- Which parts of the chapter will you review?

- Will you seek further help, outside of this book (such as a teacher, Princeton Review tutor, or AP Students), on any of the content in this chapter—and, if so, on what content?

Chapter 14
Motivation and Emotion

BIOLOGICAL BASES

Motivation is defined as a need or desire that serves to energize or direct behavior.

Learning is motivated by biological and physiological factors. Without motivation, action and learning do not occur. Animals are motivated to act by basic needs critical to the survival of the organism. For a given organism to survive, it needs food, water, and sleep. For the genes of the organism to replicate, reproductive behavior is needed to produce offspring and to foster their survival. Hunger, thirst, sleep, and reproduction needs are **primary drives**. The desire to obtain learned reinforcers, such as money or social acceptance, is a **secondary drive**.

The interaction between the brain and motivation was noticed when **Olds and Milner** discovered that rats would press a bar in order to send a small electrical pulse into certain areas of their brains. This phenomenon is known as intracranial self-stimulation. Further research demonstrated that if the electrode was implanted into certain parts of the limbic system, the rat would self-stimulate nearly constantly. The rats were motivated to stimulate themselves. This finding also suggests that the limbic system, particularly the nucleus accumbens, must play a pivotal role in motivated behavior, and that dopamine, which is the prominent neurotransmitter in this region, must be associated with reward-seeking behavior.

> Four primary theories attempt to explain the link between neurophysiology and motivated behavior: instinct theory, arousal theory, opponent process theory, and drive-reduction theory.

Instinct theory, supported by evolutionary psychology, posits that the learning of species-specific behavior motivates organisms to do what is necessary to ensure their survival. For example, cats and other predatory animals have an instinctive motivation to react to movement in their environment to protect themselves and their offspring.

Arousal theory states that there is an optimum level of arousal—that is, of alertness and activation—at which performance on a given task is optimal. Arousal is a direct correlate of nervous system activity. A moderate arousal level seems optimal for most tasks, but keep in mind that what is optimal varies by person as well as task. The **Yerkes-Dodson law** states that tasks of moderate difficulty, neither too easy nor too hard, elicit the highest level of performance. The Yerkes-Dodson law also posits that high levels of arousal for difficult tasks and low levels of arousal for easy tasks are detrimental, while high levels of arousal for easy tasks and low levels of arousal for difficult tasks are preferred.

The **opponent process theory** is a theory of motivation that is clearly relevant to the concept of addiction. It posits that we start off at a motivational baseline, at which we are not motivated to act. Then we encounter a stimulus that feels good, such as a drug or even a positive social interaction. The pleasurable feelings we experience are the result of neuronal activity in the pleasure centers of the brain (the nucleus accumbens). We now have acquired a motivation to seek out the stimulus that made us feel good. Our brains, however, tend to revert back to a state of emotional neutrality over time. This reversion is a result of an opponent process, which works in opposition to the initial motivation toward seeking the stimulus. In other words, we are motivated to seek stimuli that make us feel emotion, after which an opposing motivational force brings us back in the direction of a baseline. After repeated exposure to a stimulus, its emotional effects begin to wear off; that is, we begin to habituate to the stimulus. The opponent process, however, does not habituate as quickly, so what used to cause a very positive response now barely produces one at all. Additionally, the opponent process overcompensates, producing withdrawal. As with drugs, we now need larger amounts of the formerly positive stimuli just to maintain a baseline state. In other words, we are addicted.

The **drive-reduction theory** of motivation posits that psychological needs put stress on the body and that we are motivated to reduce this negative experience. Another way to view motivation is using the homeostatic regulation theory, or homeostasis. **Homeostasis** is a state of regulatory equilibrium. When the balance of that equilibrium shifts, we are motivated to try to right the balance. A key concept in the operation of homeostasis is the negative feedback loop. When we are running out of something, like fuel, a metabolic signal is generated that tells us to eat food. When our nutrient supply is replenished, a signal is issued to stop eating. The common analogy for this process is a home thermostat in a heating-cooling system. It has a target temperature, called the **set point**. The job of the thermostat is to maintain the set point. If body weight rises above the set point, the action of the **ventromedial hypothalamus** will send messages to the brain to eat less and to exercise more. Conversely, when body weight falls below the set point, the brain sends messages to eat more and exercise less through the **lateral hypothalamus**.

Homeostasis in Action
A good example of homeostasis is hunger. The body needs fuel, namely, food. If you do not eat for a while, you may notice that you feel hungry. Avoid eating for too long, and soon you will be famished and very motivated to eat.

HUNGER, THIRST, AND SEX

The homeostatic regulation model provides a biological explanation for the efficacy of primary reinforcers such as hunger and sex. The brain provides a large amount of the control over feeding behavior. Specifically, the **hypothalamus** has been identified as an area controlling feeding. This control can be demonstrated by lesion studies in animals. If the ventromedial hypothalamus (VMH) is lesioned, the animal eats constantly. The negative feedback loop that should turn off eating has been disrupted. If we damage a neighboring portion of the hypothalamus, the lateral hypothalamus (LH), then the animal stops eating, often starving to death. In more normal circumstances, **leptin** plays a role in the feedback loop between signals from the hypothalamus and those from the stomach. Leptin is released in response to a buildup of fat cells when enough energy has been consumed. This signal is then interpreted by the satiety center in the hypothalamus, working as a safety valve to decrease the feeling of hunger.

The feedback loop that controls eating can be broken by damaging the hypothalamus, but the operation of this mechanism raises the question of what is actually monitored and regulated in normal feeding behavior. Two prime candidates exist. The first candidate hypothesis is **blood glucose**. This idea forms the basis for the **glucostatic hypothesis**. Glucose is the primary fuel of the brain and most other organs. When **insulin** (a hormone produced by the pancreas to regulate glucose) rises, glucose decreases. To restore glucostatic balance, a person needs to eat something. If cellular fuel gets low, then it needs to be replenished. The glucostatic theory of energy regulation gains support from the finding that the hypothalamus has cells that detect glucose.

The glucostatic theory is not without flaws, however. Blood glucose levels are very transient, rising and falling quite dramatically for a variety of reasons. How could it be, then, that such a variable measure could control body weight, which remains relatively stable from early adulthood onward? Another phenomenon inconsistent with a glucostatic hypothesis is diabetes, a disorder of insulin production. Diabetics have greatly elevated blood glucose, but they are no less hungry than everyone else.

A second candidate hypothesis is called the **lipostatic hypothesis**. As you might have guessed, this theory states that fat is the measured and controlled substance in the body that regulates hunger. Fat provides the long-term energy store for our bodies. The fat stores in our bodies are fairly fixed, and any significant decrease in fat is a result of starvation. The lipostatic hypothesis gained support from the discovery of leptin, which is a hormone secreted by fat cells. Leptin may be the substance used by the brain to monitor the amount of fat in the body.

There are several disorders related to eating habits, body weight, and body image that have their roots in psychological causes. **Anorexia nervosa**, which is more prevalent in females, is an eating disorder characterized by an individual being 15 percent below ideal body weight. **Body dysmorphia**, or a distorted body image, is key to understanding this disorder. Another related eating disorder is **bulimia nervosa,** which is characterized by alternating periods of binging and purging.

As mentioned earlier, biological drives are those that ensure the survival not only of the individual, but also the survival of the individual's genes. Like that of feeding and drinking, the motivation to reproduce relies on the hypothalamus, which stimulates the **pituitary gland** and which results in the production of androgens and estrogens. **Androgens** and **estrogens** are the primary sexual hormones in males and females, respectively. Without these hormones, sexual desire is eliminated in animals and is greatly reduced in humans.

The Long and the Short of It

In reality, both glucose and body fat are probably monitored, with glucostatic homeostasis responsible for the starting and stopping of individual meals and lipostatic homeostasis responsible for larger long-term patterns of eating behavior.

The Great Motivator: Thirst

Another great motivator of action in humans and animals is thirst. A human can live for weeks without food, but only for a few days without water. Water leaves the body constantly through sweat, urine, and exhalation. This water needs to be replaced, and the body regulates our patterns of intake so that water is consumed before we are severely water depleted. The lateral hypothalamus is implicated in drinking. Lesions of this area greatly reduce drinking behavior. Another part of the hypothalamus, the preoptic area, is also involved. Lesions of the preoptic area result in excessive drinking.

THEORIES OF MOTIVATION

Biological Theory

As discussed in the "biological bases" of motivation, early theories on motivation relied on a purely biological explanation of motivated behavior. Animals, especially lower animals, are thought to be motivated by **instinct**, genetically programmed patterns of behavior. These early theories, along with arousal theory and drive-reduction theory, have given us an understanding of nature's role in motivating behavior.

Humanistic Theory

Abraham Maslow proposed a hierarchical system for organizing needs. This hierarchy can be divided into five levels. Each lower-level need must be met in order for an attempt to be made to fill the next category of needs in the hierarchy, which is illustrated in the diagram below.

Needs arise both from unsatisfied physiological drives as well as higher-level psychological needs, such as the need for safety, belonging and love, and achievement. Along with instincts, drives, and arousal, needs provide an additional explanation for motivation. Maslow's hierarchy is somewhat arbitrary—it comes from a Western emphasis on individuality, and some individuals have shown the ability to reorganize these motives (for example, hunger strikes or eating disorders). Nevertheless, it has been generally accepted that we are only motivated to satisfy higher-level needs once certain lower-level needs have been met. The inclusion of higher-level needs, such as self-actualization and the need for recognition and respect from others, also explains behaviors that the previous theories do not.

Self-actualization occurs when people creatively and meaningfully fulfill their own potential. This is the ultimate goal of human beings according to Maslow's theory.

Cognitive Theories

Cognitive psychologists divide the factors that motivate behavior into **intrinsic** and **extrinsic factors**: that is, factors originating from within ourselves and factors coming from the outside world, respectively. A single type of behavior can be motivated by either intrinsic or extrinsic factors. Extrinsic motivators are often associated with the pressures of society, such as getting an education, having a job, and being sociable. Intrinsic motivators, in contrast, are associated with creativity and enjoyment. Over time, our intrinsic motivation may decrease if we receive extrinsic rewards for the same behavior. This phenomenon is called the **overjustification effect**. For example, a person may love to play the violin for fun but when he is a paid concert performer, he will play less for fun and view using the violin as part of his job.

Intrinsic or Extrinsic?

We may read because we enjoy it. In this case, reading is a behavior motivated by an intrinsic need. However, we may read because we need to know some information that will be on a test. Here, reading is driven by extrinsic motivation.

An important intrinsic motivator is the need for **self-determination**, or the need to feel competent and in control. This need frequently conflicts with the pressures brought to bear by extrinsic motivators. The goal is to seek a balance between the fulfillment of the two categories of need. Related to the concept of self-determination is **self-efficacy**, or the belief that we can or cannot attain a particular goal. In general, the higher the level of self-efficacy, the more we believe that we can attain a particular goal and the more likely we are to achieve it, as well.

Although physiological needs form the basis for motivation, humans are not automatons, simply responding to biological pressures. Various theories have attempted to describe the interactions among motivation, personality, and cognition. **Henry Murray** believed that, although motivation is rooted in biology, individual differences and varying environments can cause motivations and needs to be expressed in many different ways. Murray proposed that human needs can be broken down into 20 specific types. For example, people have a **need for affiliation**. People with a high level of this need like to avoid conflicts, like to be members of groups, and dislike being evaluated.

Social Theory

Another cognitive theory of motivation concerns the need to avoid **cognitive dissonance**. People are motivated to reduce tension produced by conflicting thoughts or choices. Generally, they will change their attitude to fit their behavioral pattern, as long as they believe they are in control of their choices and actions. This will be discussed further in the Social Psychology chapter.

Sometimes, motives are in conflict. **Kurt Lewin** classified conflicts into four types. In an **approach-approach** conflict, one has to decide between two desirable options, such as having to choose between two colleges of similar characteristics. **Avoidance-avoidance** is a similar dilemma. Here, one has to choose between two unpleasant alternatives. For example, a person might have to choose between the lesser of two evils. In **approach-avoidance** conflicts, only one choice is presented, but it carries both pluses and minuses. For example, imagine that only one college has the major the student wants but that college is also prohibitively expensive. The last set of conflicts is **multiple approach-avoidance**. In this scenario, many options are available, but each has positives and negatives. Choosing one college out of many that are suitable, but not ideal, represents a multiple approach-avoidance conflict.

THEORIES OF EMOTION

Emotions are experiential and subjective responses to certain internal and external stimuli. These experiential responses have both physical and behavioral components. Various theories have arisen to explain emotion.

Emotion consists of three components: a physiological (body) component, a behavioral (action) component, and a cognitive (mind) component. The physical aspect of emotion is one of physiological arousal, or an excitation of the body's internal state. For example, when being startled at a surprise party, you may feel your heart pounding, your breathing becoming shallow and rapid, and your palms becoming sweaty. These are the sensations that accompany emotion (in this instance, surprise). The behavioral aspect of emotion includes some kind of expressive behavior: for example, spontaneously screaming and bringing your hands over your mouth. The cognitive aspect of emotion involves an appraisal or interpretation of the situation. Upon first being startled, the thought "dangerous situation" or "fear" may arise, only to be reassessed as "surprise" and "excitement" after recognizing the circumstances as a surprise party. This describes how the situation is interpreted or labeled. Interestingly, many emotions share the same or very similar physiological and behavioral responses; it is the mind that interprets one situation that evokes a quickened heart rate and tears as "joyful" and another with the same responses as "fearful."

One class of theories relies on physiological explanations of emotion. The **James-Lange theory** posits that environmental stimuli cause physiological changes and responses. The experience of emotion, according to this theory, is a result of a physiological change. In other words, if an argument makes you angry, it is the physiological response (increased heart rate, increased respiratory rate) that prompts the experience of emotion.

There are many reasons why we now know that this theory is incorrect. We know that a given state of physiological arousal is common to many emotions. For example, a person might feel tenseness in his or her body as a result of being nervous, scared, or even excited. How, then, is it possible that the identical physiological state could lead to the rich variety of emotions that we experience? Another common experience that conflicts with the logic of the James-Lange theory is cutting onions. The physiological response to cutting onions is watering eyes; however, this physiological response does not make us sad.

The **Cannon-Bard theory** arose as a response to the James-Lange theory. The Cannon-Bard theory asserts that the physiological response to an emotion and the experience of emotion occur simultaneously in response to an emotion-provoking stimulus. For example, a tarantula, which acts as an emotion-provoking stimulus, would stimulate the thalamus. The thalamus would send simultaneous messages to both the autonomic nervous system and the cerebral cortex. Messages to the cortex produce the experience of emotion (fear), and messages to the autonomic nervous system produce physiological arousal (running, heart palpitations).

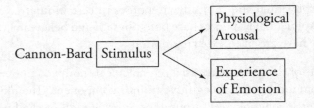

The **two-factor theory,** proposed by **Schachter and Singer,** adds a cognitive twist to the James-Lange theory. The first factor is physiological arousal; the second factor is the way in which we cognitively label the experience of arousal. Central to this theory is the understanding that many emotional responses involve very similar physiological properties. The emotion that we experience, according to this theory, is the result of the label that we apply. For example, if we cry at a wedding, we interpret our emotion as happiness, but if we cry at a funeral, we interpret our emotion as sadness.

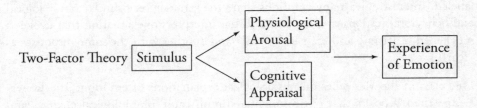

According to more recent studies by Zajonc, Le Doux, and Armony, some emotions are felt before being cognitively appraised. A scary sight travels through the eye to the thalamus, where it is then relayed to the amygdala before being labeled and evaluated by the cortex. According to these studies, the amygdala's position relative to the thalamus may account for the quick emotional response. There are several parts of the brain implicated in emotional processing. The main area of the brain responsible for emotions is the limbic system, which includes the amygdala. The amygdala is most active when processing negative emotions, particularly fear.

Although theorists have disagreed over time about how emotions are processed, there has been a great deal of agreement about the universality of certain emotions. Darwin assumed that emotions had a strong biological basis. If this is true, then emotions should be experienced and expressed in similar ways across cultures, and in fact, this has been found to be the case. A scientist and pioneer in the study of emotions, **Paul Ekman** observed facial expressions from a variety of cultures and pointed out that, regardless of where two persons were from, their expressions of

Processing Emotions
Different sides of the brain also seem to be responsible for different emotional states. That is, the right brain is dominant in processing negative emotions, while the left brain seems to be more involved in processing positive emotions.

certain emotions were almost identical. In particular, Ekman identified six basic emotions that appeared across cultures: anger, fear, disgust, surprise, happiness, and sadness. These findings suggest that emotions and how they are expressed are innate parts of the human experience.

The evolutionary basis for emotion is thought to be related to its adaptive roles. It enhances survival by serving as a useful guide for quick decisions. A feeling of fear one experiences when walking alone down a dark alley while a shadowy figure approaches can be a valuable tool to indicate that the situation may be dangerous. A feeling of anger may enhance survival by encouraging one to fight back against an intruder. Other emotions may have a role in influencing individual behaviors within a social context. For example, embarrassment may encourage social conformity. Additionally, in social contexts, emotions provide a means for nonverbal communication and empathy, allowing for cooperative interactions.

On a more subtle level, emotions are a large influence on our everyday lives. Our choices often require consideration of our emotions. A person with a brain injury to their prefrontal cortex (which plays a role in processing emotion) has trouble imagining their own emotional responses to the possible outcomes of decisions. This can lead to making inappropriate decisions that can cost someone a job, a marriage, or his or her savings. Imagine how difficult it could be to refrain from risky behaviors, such as gambling or spending huge sums of money, without the ability to imagine your emotional response to the possible outcomes.

THE ROLE OF THE LIMBIC SYSTEM IN EMOTION

The limbic system is a collection of brain structures that lie on both sides of the thalamus; together, these structures appear to be primarily responsible for emotional experiences. The main structure involved in emotion in the limbic system is the amygdala, an almond-shaped structure deep within the brain. The amygdala serves as the conductor of the orchestra of our emotional experiences. It can communicate with the hypothalamus, a brain structure that controls the physiological aspects of emotion (largely through its modulating of the endocrine system), such as sweating and a racing heart. It also communicates with the prefrontal cortex, located at the front of the brain, which controls approach and avoidance behaviors—the behavioral aspects of emotion. The amygdala plays an especially key role in the identification and expression of fear and aggression.

Emotion, Memory, Decision-Making, and the Autonomic Nervous System

Emotional experiences can be stored as memories that can be recalled by similar circumstances. The limbic system also includes the hippocampus, a brain structure that plays a key role in forming memories.

When memories are formed, the emotions associated with these memories are often also encoded. Take a second to close your eyes and imagine someone whom you love very much. Notice the emotional state that arises with your memory of that person. Recalling an event can bring about the emotions associated with it. Note that this isn't always a pleasant experience. It has an important role in the suffering of patients who have experienced traumatic events. Similar circumstances to a traumatic event can lead to recall of the memory of the experience, referred to as **"flashback."** Sometimes this recall isn't even conscious; for example, for someone involved in a traumatic car accident, driving past the intersection where the incident occurred might cause an increase in muscle tension, heart rate, and respiratory rate.

The **prefrontal cortex** is critical for emotional experience, and it is also important in temperament and decision-making. It is associated with a reduction in emotional feelings, especially fear and anxiety, and is often activated by methods of emotion regulation and stress relief. The prefrontal cortex is like a soft voice, calming down the amygdala when it is overly aroused. The prefrontal cortex also plays a role in executive functions—higher-order thinking processes such as planning, organizing, inhibiting behavior, and decision-making. Damage to this area may lead to inappropriateness, impulsivity, and trouble with initiation. This area is not fully developed in humans until they reach their mid-twenties, explaining the sometimes erratic and emotionally charged behavior of teenagers. The most famous case of damage to the prefrontal cortex occurred to a man in the 1800s named Phineas Gage. Gage was a railroad worker who, at age 25, suffered an accident in which a railroad tie blasted through his head, entering under his cheekbone and exiting through the top of his skull. After the accident, Gage was described as "no longer himself," prone to impulsivity, unable to stick to plans, and unable to demonstrate empathy. The accident severely damaged his prefrontal cortex, and while the reports about the change to his personality and behavior have been debated, this case led to the discovery of the role of the prefrontal cortex in personality.

The **autonomic nervous system (ANS)** is responsible for controlling the activities of most of the organs and glands, and it controls arousal. As mentioned earlier, it answers primarily to the hypothalamus. The **sympathetic nervous system (SNS)** provides the body with brief, intense, vigorous responses. It is often referred to as the fight-or-flight system because it prepares an individual for action. It increases heart rate, blood pressure, and blood sugar levels in preparation for action. It also directs the adrenal glands to release the stress hormones epinephrine and norepinephrine. The **parasympathetic nervous system (PNS)** provides signals to the internal organs during a calm resting state when no crisis is present. When activated, it leads to changes that allow for recovery and the conservation of energy, including an increase in digestion and the repair of body tissues.

Many physiological states associated with emotion have been discussed. These include heart rate, blood pressure, respiratory rate, sweating, and the release of stress hormones. An increase in these physiological functions is associated with the sympathetic (fight-or-flight) response. In order to measure autonomic function, clinicians can measure heart rate, finger temperature, skin conductance (sweating), and muscle activity. Keep in mind that different patterns tend to exist during different emotional states, but states such as fear and sexual arousal may display very similar patterns.

STRESS

A concept related to emotion is the feeling of stress. **Stress** causes a person to feel challenged or endangered. Although this definition may make you think of experiences such as being attacked, in reality, most **stressors** (events that cause stress) are everyday events or situations that challenge us in more subtle ways. Stressors can be significant life-changing events, such as the death of a loved one, a divorce, a wedding, or the birth of a child. There are also many smaller, more manageable stressors, such as holidays, traffic jams, and other nuisances. Although these situations are varied, they share a common factor: they are all challenging for the person experiencing them.

As you may have inferred, the same situation may have different value as a stressor for different people. The perception of a stimulus as stressful may be more consequential than the actual nature of the stimulus itself. For example, some people find putting together children's toys or electronic items quite stressful, yet other people find relaxation in similar tasks, such as building models.

What is most important for determining the stressful nature of an event is its appraisal, or how the individual interprets it. When stressors are appraised as being challenges, as one may perceive the AP Psychology Exam, they can actually be motivating. On the other hand, when they are perceived as threatening aspects of our identity, well-being, or safety, they may cause severe stress. Additionally, events that are considered negative and uncontrollable produce a greater stress response than those that are perceived as negative but controllable.

Some stressors are **transient**, meaning that they are temporary challenges. Others, such as those that lead to job-related stress, are **chronic** and can have a negative impact on one's health. The physiological response to stress is related to what is referred to as a **fight-or-flight response**, a concept developed by **Walter Cannon** and enhanced by Hans Selye into the **general adaptation syndrome**. The three stages of this response to prolonged stress are alarm, resistance, and exhaustion. **Alarm** refers to the arousal of the sympathetic nervous system, resulting in the release of various stimulatory hormones, including **corticosterone,** which is used as a physiological index of stress. In the alarm phase, the body is energized for immediate action, which is adaptive for transient, but not chronic, stressors. **Resistance** is the result of parasympathetic rebound. The body cannot be aroused forever, and the parasympathetic system starts to reduce the arousal state. If the stressor does not relent, however, the body does not reduce its arousal state to baseline. If the stressor persists for long periods of time, the stress response continues into the **exhaustion** phase. In this phase, the body's resources are exhausted, and tissue cannot be repaired. The immune system becomes impaired in its functioning, which is why we are more susceptible to illness during prolonged stress.

Richard Lazarus developed a cognitive theory of how we respond to stress. In this approach, the individual evaluates whether the event appears to be stressful. This is called primary appraisal. If the event is seen to be a threat, a secondary appraisal takes place, assessing whether the individual can handle the stress. Stress is minimized or maximized by the individual's ability to respond to the stressor.

Research into stress has revealed that people generally show one of two different types of behavior patterns based on their responses to stress. The **Type-A pattern** of behavior is typified by competitiveness, a sense of time urgency, and elevated feelings of anger and hostility. The **Type-B pattern** of behavior is characterized by a low level of competitiveness, low preoccupation with time issues, and a generally easygoing attitude. People with Type-A patterns of behavior respond to stress quickly and aggressively. Type-A people also act in ways that tend to increase the likelihood that they will have stressful experiences. They seek jobs or tasks that put great demands on them. People with a Type-B pattern of behavior get stressed more slowly, and their stress levels do not seem to reach those heights seen in people with the Type-A pattern of behavior. There is some evidence that people with Type-A behavior patterns are more susceptible to stress-related diseases, including heart attacks, but may survive them more frequently than Type-Bs.

KEY TERMS

Biological Bases

- motivation
- primary drives
- secondary drives
- Olds and Milner
- instinct theory
- arousal theory
- Yerkes-Dodson law
- opponent process theory
- drive-reduction theory
- homeostasis
- set point
- ventromedial
  hypothalamus
- lateral hypothalamus

Hunger, Thirst, and Sex

- hypothalamus
- leptin
- blood glucose
- glucostatic hypothesis
- insulin
- lipostatic hypothesis
- anorexia nervosa
- body dysmorphia
- bulimia nervosa
- pituitary gland
- androgens
- estrogens

Theories of Motivation

- instinct
- Abraham Maslow
- self-actualization
- intrinsic factors
- extrinsic factors
- overjustification effect
- self-determination
- self-efficacy

- Henry Murray
- need for affiliation
- cognitive dissonance
- Kurt Lewin
- approach-approach
- avoidance-avoidance
- approach-avoidance
- multiple approach-avoidance

Theories of Emotion

- James-Lange theory
- Cannon-Bard theory
- two-factor theory
- Schachter and Singer
- Paul Ekman

**The Role of the Limbic System
in Emotion**

- flashback
- prefrontal cortex
- autonomic nervous system
- sympathetic nervous system
- parasympathetic nervous
  system

Stress

- stressors
- transient
- chronic
- fight-or-flight response
- Hans Selye
- general adaptation syndrome
- alarm
- corticosterone
- resistance
- exhaustion
- Richard Lazarus
- Type-A pattern
- Type-B pattern

Chapter 14 Drill

See Chapter 19 for answers and explanations.

1. An example of a secondary drive is

   (A) the satisfying of a basic need critical to one's survival
   (B) an attempt to get food to maintain homeostatic equilibrium related to hunger
   (C) an attempt to act only on instinct
   (D) an effort to obtain something that has been shown to have reinforcing properties
   (E) an effort to continue an optimal state of arousal

2. An example of the Yerkes-Dodson law is

   (A) the need to remain calm and relaxed while taking the SAT while letting adrenaline give a little boost
   (B) performing at the highest level of arousal in order to obtain a primary reinforcer
   (C) a task designed to restore the body to homeostasis
   (D) the need to remain calm and peaceful while addressing envelopes for a charity event
   (E) working at maximum arousal on a challenging project

3. A substance that can act directly on brain receptors to stimulate thirst is

   (A) angiotensin
   (B) endorphin
   (C) thyroxin
   (D) lipoprotein
   (E) acetylcholine

4. Rhoni is a driven woman who feels the need to constantly excel in her career in order to help maintain the lifestyle her family has become accustomed to and in order to be seen as successful in her parents' eyes. The factors that motivate Rhoni's career behavior can be described as primarily

   (A) intrinsic
   (B) extrinsic
   (C) hierarchical
   (D) self-determined
   (E) instinctual

5. Which of the following is less likely to be characteristic of a Type-A personality than of a Type-B personality?

   (A) A constant sense of time urgency
   (B) A tendency toward easier arousability
   (C) A greater likelihood to anger slowly
   (D) A higher rate of stress-related physical complaints
   (E) A need to see situations as competitive

6. Sanju is hungry and buys a donut at the nearby donut shop. According to drive-reduction theory, she

   (A) has returned her body to homeostasis
   (B) will need to eat something else, since a donut is rich in nutrients
   (C) will continue to feel hungry
   (D) will have created another imbalance and feel thirsty
   (E) has raised her glucose levels to an unhealthy level

7. Jorge walks into a dark room, turns on the light, and his friends yell "Surprise!" Jorge's racing heartbeat is interpreted as surprise and joy instead of fear. This supports which theory of emotion?

   (A) The opponent-process theory
   (B) The James-Lange theory
   (C) The Cannon-Bard theory
   (D) The Schachter-Singer theory
   (E) The Yerkes-Dodson law

8. A person addicted to prescription drugs started by taking the prescribed amount, but then increased the dosage more and more to feel the same effect as when they first started. This progression is consistent with the

   (A) instinct theory
   (B) arousal theory
   (C) two-factor theory
   (D) drive-reduction theory
   (E) opponent-process theory

9. All of the following are symptoms of chronic stress
EXCEPT

(A) hypertension
(B) immunosuppression
(C) chronic fatigue
(D) tissue damage
(E) suppressed appetite

10. The hypothalamus does which of the following?

(A) Serves as a relay center
(B) Regulates homeostasis
(C) Aids in encoding memory
(D) Regulates most hormones to be secreted
(E) Regulates fear and aggression

REFLECT

Respond to the following questions:

- Which topics in this chapter do you hope to see on the multiple-choice section or essay?

- Which topics in this chapter do you hope to not see on the multiple-choice section or essay?

- Regarding any psychologists mentioned, can you pair the psychologists with their contributions to the field? Did they contribute significant experiments, theories, or both?

- Regarding any theories mentioned, can you distinguish between differing theories well enough to recognize them on the multiple-choice section? Can you distinguish them well enough to write a fluent essay on them?

- Regarding any figures given, if you were given a labeled figure from within this chapter, would you be able to give the significance of each part of the figure?

- Can you define the key terms at the end of the chapter?

- Which parts of the chapter will you review?

- Will you seek further help, outside of this book (such as a teacher, Princeton Review tutor, or AP Students), on any of the content in this chapter—and, if so, on what content?

Chapter 15
Personality

PERSONALITY THEORIES AND APPROACHES

Personality can be defined as a person's enduring general style of dealing with others and with the world around them. Personality theories can be divided into four broad categories: psychoanalytic, humanistic, social-cognitive, and trait theories.

Psychoanalytic Theories

Sigmund Freud and those who followed his basic beliefs and practices typify **psychoanalytic** theories of personality. The term **psychodynamic** means a psychological approach based on a marriage of Freudian concepts, such as the unconscious, with more modern ideas. Freud, the first and most influential personality psychologist, believed that the mind can be divided broadly into the conscious and the unconscious. The unconscious, according to Freud, plays a major role in behavior; however, the contents of the unconscious mind are not readily accessible. People's motivations and the source of their problems lie within the unconscious. Although the unconscious is typically not open to scrutiny, certain events, according to Freud, allow for glimpses into the unconscious mind. When people make slips of the tongue or reveal the latent content of dreams, they provide brief looks into their unconscious minds. Freud also discovered that free association is a way to get a glimpse of the unconscious mind. A popular metaphor of the mind is to imagine it as an iceberg with the "conscious" brain sitting above the water and the dark recesses of the "unconscious" lying below. In **free association**, a therapist actively listens, while the patient relaxes and reports anything that comes into his mind, no matter how absurd it might seem. The therapist then analyzes this seemingly random jumble of thoughts, looking for themes that may demonstrate some of what lies in the unconscious.

Freud was also a pioneer in the analysis of dreams, which he viewed as a window into the unconscious mind. Freud believed that the remembered parts of the dream, or the manifest content, amounted to a coded version of the real conflict, or the latent content. For example, knives and stabbing might symbolize male genitalia and intercourse, while boxes, ships, or other containers might symbolize the female uterus. Freud further described the mind as consisting of three distinct components: the id, the superego, and the ego. (Freud actually used regular German words to describe these mental structures; his English translators came up with these Latin terms. Since AP will test you on the Latin terms, we'll retain them.)

Q: According to Freud, what are the three components of the mind?

Answer on page 254.

The **id** is the source of mental energy and drive. It encompasses all of the basic human needs and desires, including those for food and sex. The id operates on the **pleasure principle**, which is the desire to maximize pleasure while minimizing pain.

The **superego** is the internal representation of all of society's rules, morals, and obligations. The superego represents the polar opposite of the id.

The **ego**, according to Freud, is the part of the mind that allows a person to function in the environment and to be logical. It operates on the **reality principle**, which is that set of desires that can be satisfied only if the means to satisfy them exists and is available. The ego works as an intermediary between the id and the superego.

Freud hypothesized that the ego deals with the anxiety produced by the id-superego conflict using various defense mechanisms. Defense mechanisms often serve a useful purpose in helping the individual reduce tension and maintain a healthy outlook, even if it means using self-deception. Repression is one of these defense mechanisms. **Repression** is the process by which memories or desires that provoke too much anxiety to deal with are pushed into the unconscious. For example, some people involved in terrible accidents have no memory of the accidents at all. The memory, according to Freudian theory, has been repressed.

Displacement is a defense mechanism that directs anger away from the source of the anger to a less threatening person or object. A boy who is angry with his father may not want to show hostility directly to his father; instead, he may yell at a friend or stuffed animal, thereby displaying his rage but in a way that does not make his situation worse.

Reaction formation is another defense mechanism by which the ego reverses the direction of a disturbing desire to make that desire safer or more socially acceptable. For example, a person who unconsciously hates the poor might consciously experience this feeling as a strong desire to help the homeless. Or a lawmaker who is gay but closeted may speak and vote against gay rights. Other defense mechanisms include the following:

- **Compensation**—making up for failures in one area by success in others

- **Rationalization**—creating logical excuses for emotional or irrational behavior

- **Regression**—reverting to childish behaviors

- **Denial**—the refusal to acknowledge or accept unwanted beliefs or actions

- **Sublimation**—the channeling or redirecting of sexual or aggressive feelings into a more socially acceptable outlet

Freud's theory paved the way for a variety of psychodynamic theories, many of which were developed in direct response to Freud's own. **Karen Horney**, for example, pointed out the inherent male bias in Freud's work. She developed a theory of personality based on the need for security. According to Horney's theory, **basic anxiety**, or the feeling of being alone in an unfamiliar or hostile world, is a central theme in childhood. The interactions between the child and the parent, as the child deals with this anxiety, form the basis for adult personality. Children who find security in their relationships with their parents will find security in other adult relationships. Children who lack security in their relationships with their parents and their surroundings will grow up insecure and distrusting, and they are likely to end up with various unhealthy personality styles.

Carl Jung formulated another theory of personality that was, in part, a response to Freud's theory. Jung believed that the mind comprises pairs of opposing forces.

The ego is most involved in conscious thought and attempts to balance the interaction with the environment along with the opposing forces of the id and superego.

For example, each person has a **persona,** the mask the person presents to the outside world, and a **shadow**, the deep, passionate, inner person (including the person's "dark side"). Jung also proposed that we each have an **anima** and an **animus**, a female and male side to our personality. Jung believed that all of the opposing forces and desires of the mind were balanced by a force called the **Self**. Jung also divided the unconscious differently than Freud. Jung proposed that each of us has a **personal unconsciousness** comprised of repressed memories and clusters of thought and a **collective unconscious** of behavior and memory common to all humans and passed down from our ancient and common ancestors. **Archetypes** are the behaviors and memories in the collective unconscious. Reverence for motherhood is an example of an archetype.

Alfred Adler, like other psychoanalytic psychologists, believed that childhood is the crucial formative period. He also thought, however, that all children develop feelings of inferiority because of their size and level of competence. He speculated that people spend the rest of their lives trying to overcome this inferiority and develop lifestyles suited to this purpose. Adler thought the best way to overcome inferiority is to develop a lifestyle of social interest; that is, one of contribution to society. Failure to make these accommodations may result in the development of an **inferiority complex**. Adler also saw personality as a product of birth order.

Humanistic Theories

Humanistic theories of personality emphasize the uniqueness and richness of being human. These theories arose partially in response to behaviorism (see Chapter 5). As a result, they focus on subjective reality and subjective mental events. In contrast to behaviorism's attempts to reduce behavior to its smallest components, humanistic theories take a holistic view. They view people as unitary, not separable into learned reactions, and certainly not divisible into compartments such as the ego and superego. The final and most important concept in humanistic theories is the concept of self-actualization. **Self-actualization** is becoming, in a creative way, the person you are capable of being. According to humanistic theories, self-actualization is the ultimate purpose for existence.

Two humanistic theorists whose work typifies this school of thought are **Abraham Maslow** (discussed in Chapter 14) and **Carl Rogers**.

A: The id, the ego, and the superego

Rogers believed that the self constitutes the most important aspect of personality. Our **self-concept** is our mental representation of who we feel we truly are. Internal conflicts arise when we experience **incongruence**, or discrepancies between our self-concept and our actual thoughts and behavior, as well as from feedback from our surroundings. Rogers believed that **conditions of worth**, or, other people's evaluations of our worth, distort our self-concept. Parents and teachers play a critical role in child development, Rogers hypothesized, and should not impose conditions of worth on children. Instead, people should be treated with **unconditional positive regard**. This means that people, particularly children, should be loved despite failures. Saying, for example, "I love you only when you're good," creates poor self-concept.

Social-Cognitive Theories

Social-cognitive theories of personality are based on the assumption that cognitive constructs are the basis for personality. We bring constructs, such as expectations, to every social situation. These constructs are developed and modified through learning in social environments.

A representative example of a social-cognitive theory of personality was developed by **Albert Bandura**. Bandura focuses on the concept of self-efficacy as central to personality. **Self-efficacy** refers to a person's beliefs about his or her own abilities in a given situation. Basically, the belief that you can do a particular task greatly increases the chances that you actually can do it. People have different **explanatory styles,** or ways in which people explain themselves or react in different situations. Explanatory styles can be either positive or negative.

Another important social-cognitive theory is the **locus of control theory**. **Julian Rotter** proposed that the extent to which people believe that their successes or failures are due to their own efforts plays a major role in personality. People who have an **internal locus of control** believe that successes or failures are a direct result of their efforts, whereas people with an **external locus of control** are more likely to attribute success or failure to luck or chance.

Self-Efficacy and Success

Bandura has proposed that this theory has implications for education. Emphasizing accomplishments rather than failures should, according to self-efficacy theory, increase the likelihood of future successes.

Trait Theories

Trait theories of personality provide quantitative systems for describing and comparing traits or stable predispositions to behave in a certain way. A particular trait theory stipulates that certain traits are part of the person and are not typically environmentally dependent. Additionally, we each have traits in some degree or another. Trait theorists generally believe that traits are largely inherited, rather than acquired through experience. Trait theorists are divided over how to categorize traits. A relatively recent and influential theory focuses on the **Big Five** personality traits, which are introversion-extroversion, neuroticism-stability, agreeableness-antagonism, conscientiousness-undirectedness, and openness-nonopenness.

Two ways of researching traits are by **nomothetic** and **idiographic analysis**. Nomothetic traits such as the Big Five are thought to be universal. Idiographic traits are those that are unique to the individual, such as openness or curiosity. **Gordon Allport**, a trait theorist, identified three types of traits: **cardinal** (traits that override a person's whole being), **central** (the primary characteristics of the person), and **secondary** (traits that constitute interests). **Raymond Cattell** saw traits differently because he believed that 16 **source traits** were the basis of personality.

Evaluation of the Various Personality Theories

Each of the personality theories provides some insight into the formation of personality, but each also has its flaws. The main problem with the psychoanalytic theory is that it was not developed through empirical testing, although recent psychologists have subjected Freud's theories to the scientific method. Testing supports some of his theories but not others. The humanistic theories also suffer from lack of empirical evidence in addition to what some believe is an overly optimistic outlook on life. Nevertheless, they are frequently the basis of counseling today. Cognitive theories, also popular in today's world, describe personality as a function of environmental perception and rational thought. However, critics suggest that this approach does not take into account the breadth of humanness. Trait theories face criticism that they are unable to explain the origin of personality.

Source traits are the person's underlying characteristics. They give rise to clusters of **surface traits**, those readily seen in the individual. **Walter Mischel** recognized that traits are not necessarily consistent across various situations but often vary depending upon the circumstances.

ASSESSMENT TECHNIQUES

Techniques used for assessing personality vary. The psychoanalytic approach has traditionally involved the classic one-on-one therapist and patient relationship. In this situation, the therapist's role is to use various techniques, such as free association and dream recall, to gain access to the unconscious.

The humanistic theorists fall short in the area of assessment. Maslow described the characteristics of self-actualizing people, but the characteristics were chosen by Maslow himself, and are not necessarily quantifiable or useful for assessment. The very personal nature of the self makes it nearly impossible for a test or assessment tool to measure the levels at which someone is being true to his or her self. Rogers and others relied primarily on interviews.

Social-cognitive theorists have the benefit of questionnaire-type assessment tools. Rotter developed a locus-of-control questionnaire, versions of which are still used in psychological assessment today. There are also a number of scales or questionnaires designed to evaluate people's level of self-efficacy. These measures have been used to look at the validity of Maslow's hypothesis by computing correlations between people's levels of self-efficacy and their actual performance levels.

Trait Theory Assessments

If there were a competition among the various kinds of theorists as to who had the most complete tools for assessment, the trait theorists would win hands down. **Hans Eysenck** developed the **Eysenck Personality Inventory**, a questionnaire designed to examine people's personalities based on their traits. Raymond Cattell also developed a questionnaire to quantify traits. Cattell named his assessment tool the **16 PF (Personality Factor) Questionnaire**, signifying the 16 traits or personality factors it measures. These are just two of a number of questionnaires designed to evaluate personality traits.

Perhaps the most widely used assessment tool that measures traits is the **MMPI-2-RF** (Minnesota Multiphasic Personality Inventory-2, Restructured Form). This test is frequently used as a prepackaged assessment tool, measuring everything from traits to mental disorders.

SELF-CONCEPT, SELF-ESTEEM

Self-concept refers to how we view ourselves, whereas **self-esteem** refers to how much we value ourselves. Self-understanding can be divided into two parts: the *me* and the *I*.

The *me* is comprised of the following:

- **The physical self**—our body, our name, and the like

- **The active self**—how we behave

- **The social self**—how we interact with others

- **The psychological self**—our feelings and personalities

The self-knower, the *I*, is responsible for the coordination and interpretation of the four parts of the *me*. The *I* is responsible for how we perceive ourselves as consistent over time, as individuals, and as having free will. The *I* allows us to reflect on ourselves and to have a self-concept.

Self-esteem develops and differentiates as we age. As children, we are able only to make judgments about ourselves in the general domains of cognitive, physical, social, and behavioral competence. Young children also make errors of self-evaluation due to the **halo effect**, which refers to the error by which we generalize a high self-evaluation from one domain to another. (It also applies to evaluations of others, such as when one assumes a successful athlete would also be articulate.) Domains continue to emerge as we age and are faced with increasingly differentiated areas in which to test ourselves. Low self-esteem can result in reluctance to try new tasks and to persist at tasks already started. Self-esteem is also related to whom we compare ourselves to, which is posited by Leon Festinger in his **social comparison theory.** People can also inflate their self-esteem by basking in reflective glory, which is when someone takes pride in the accomplishments of an individual or group that the person strongly affiliates with in his or her life.

11 Domains of Competency

By the time we reach adulthood, self-esteem can be broken into 11 domains of competency within which we evaluate ourselves. These domains are morality, sociability, intimacy, athleticism, intelligence, sense of humor, nurturance, job competence, adequacy as a provider, physical appearance, and household management.

TEMPERAMENT

Temperament is the early appearing set of individual differences in reaction and regulation that form the "nucleus" of personality. For a trait to be considered part of temperament, it must be early appearing, stable, and constitutionally based, meaning that it is rooted in the physiology of the child. According to developmental psychologist **Mary Rothbart**, temperament is generally assessed on three scales: **surgency** (amount of positive affect and activity level), **negative affect** (amount of frustration and sadness), and **effortful control** (ability of a child to self-regulate moods and behavior). **Jerome Kagan's** work on the physiology of young children showed that children classified as low in effortful control were more likely to have higher baseline heart rates, more muscle tension, and greater pupil dilation. The stability of temperament is also quite remarkable, with surgency at 21 months correlating with the person's behavior at 18 years old.

KEY TERMS

Personality Theories and Approaches

personality
Sigmund Freud
psychoanalytic
psychodynamic
free association
Freudian components
id
pleasure principle
superego
ego
reality principle
repression
displacement
reaction formation
compensation
rationalization
regression
denial
sublimation
Karen Horney
basis anxiety
Carl Jung
persona
shadow
anima
animus
Self
personal unconscious
collective unconscious
archetypes
Alfred Adler
inferiority complex
humanistic
self-actualization
Abraham Maslow
Carl Rogers
self-concept
incongruence
conditions of worth
unconditional positive regard

social-cognitive theories
Albert Bandura
self-efficacy
explanatory styles
locus of control theory
Julian Rotter
internal locus of control
external locus of control
Big Five
nomothetic analysis
idiographic analysis
Gordon Allport
Raymond Cattell
Walter Mischel

Assessment Techniques

Hans Eysenck
Eysenck Personality
    Inventory
16PF (Personality Factor)
    Questionnaire
MMPI-2-RF

Self-concept, Self-esteem

self-concept
self-esteem
physical self
active self
social self
psychological self
halo effect
social comparison theory

Temperament

Mary Rothbart
surgency
negative affect
effortful control
Jerome Kagan

Chapter 15 Drill

See Chapter 19 for answers and explanations.

1. According to Freudian theory, which part of the mind operates according to the reality principle?

   (A) The superego
   (B) The ego
   (C) The id
   (D) The archetype
   (E) The shadow

2. The defense mechanism of reaction formation is defined as

   (A) directing angry feelings away from the source of the anger to a less threatening object
   (B) reverting to behaviors more characteristic of childhood
   (C) attempting to make up for failures in certain areas by overcompensating efforts in other areas
   (D) creating excuses for irrational feelings or behaviors that sound logical
   (E) reversing the direction of a disturbing feeling or desire to make it safer or more socially acceptable

3. All of the following personality theorists can be considered psychodynamic in approach EXCEPT

   (A) Karen Horney
   (B) Carl Jung
   (C) Alfred Adler
   (D) Albert Bandura
   (E) Erik Erikson

4. According to Maslow and Rogers, the process by which human beings attain their full creativity and potential is termed

   (A) self-esteem
   (B) self-amplification
   (C) self-efficacy
   (D) self-actualization
   (E) self-reflection

5. A psychologist interested in demarcating and measuring traits would most likely use which of the following?

   (A) The 16 PF Questionnaire
   (B) The WAIS
   (C) The *DSM-5*
   (D) The ANOVA
   (E) The WISC

6. Anne is terrible at riding a bike, but she knows that she has the ability to get better if she practices more often. This is an example of

   (A) high self-efficacy and an external locus of control
   (B) low self-efficacy and an internal locus of control
   (C) high self-efficacy and an internal locus of control
   (D) low self-efficacy and an external locus of control
   (E) low self-efficacy and learned helplessness

7. Lukas is a handsome guy who gets great grades and is the star of the football team. Ian assumes he is trustworthy, as well. This is most likely an example of

   (A) gender bias
   (B) an archetype
   (C) an inferiority complex
   (D) self-actualization
   (E) the halo effect

8. Tanya is a competitive figure skater trying to land her quadruple salchow. She gets frustrated with herself and her coach for not landing it and kicks the ice. This is an example of

   (A) displacement
   (B) sublimation
   (C) denial
   (D) regression
   (E) compensation

9. Carl Jung's theory of the anima and animus posits that

   (A) the self is a collection of archetypes from the collective unconscious
   (B) a person must first learn to trust his or her caregiver as an infant to thrive
   (C) there is both a male and female side to each personality
   (D) a positive self-worth comes from a balanced Self
   (E) individuals should not overcompensate for their weaknesses, but rather embrace them

10. Cara feels good about herself because she is going to become a doctor. This is an example of

    (A) self-efficacy
    (B) self-esteem
    (C) self-concept
    (D) rationalization
    (E) reaction formation

REFLECT

Respond to the following questions:

- Which topics in this chapter do you hope to see on the multiple-choice section or essay?

- Which topics in this chapter do you hope not to see on the multiple-choice section or essay?

- Regarding any psychologists mentioned, can you pair the psychologists with their contributions to the field? Did they contribute significant experiments, theories, or both?

- Regarding any theories mentioned, can you distinguish between differing theories well enough to recognize them on the multiple-choice section? Can you distinguish them well enough to write a fluent essay on them?

- Regarding any figures given, if you were given a labeled figure from within this chapter, would you be able to give the significance of each part of the figure?

- Can you define the key terms at the end of the chapter?

- Which parts of the chapter will you review?

- Will you seek further help, outside of this book (such as a teacher, Princeton Review tutor, or AP Students), on any of the content in this chapter—and, if so, on what content?

Chapter 16
Clinical
Psychology:
Disorders

DEFINITIONS OF DISORDER

When is behavior disordered? The definition of **disordered behavior** is composed of four components. First, disordered behavior is unusual—it deviates statistically from typical behavior. Second, disordered behavior is maladaptive, that is, it interferes with a person's ability to function in a particular situation. Third, disordered behavior is labeled as abnormal by the society in which it occurs. Finally, disordered behavior is characterized by perceptual or cognitive dysfunction. In order for behavior to be disordered, it should meet all of these criteria. Behavior must be compared with the behavior of the society in which it occurs. So, for example, self-mutilation in this country is behavior that stands apart from what society considers normal. In other parts of the world, however, scarring is an important part of certain rituals.

THEORIES OF PSYCHOPATHOLOGY

Different schools of psychology have attempted to understand the causes of disordered behavior in different ways. Sigmund Freud engaged in careful observation and analysis of people with varying degrees of behavioral abnormalities. Freud and the **psychoanalytic school** hypothesized that the interactions among conscious and especially unconscious parts of the mind were responsible for a great deal of disordered behavior. The power of unconscious motives drives behavior. To protect the ego, painful or threatening impulses are repressed into the unconscious. The source of this repression stems from issues that arose during childhood. Generally speaking, if intrapsychic conflicts are not resolved, they may lead us to act abnormally. Much of Freud's writing described his analyses of maladaptive behavior.

The **humanistic school** of psychology suggests that disordered behavior is, in part, a result of people being too sensitive to the criticisms and judgments of others. This tendency is related to people being unable to accept their own nature and having low self-esteem. This lack of acceptance may result, according to the humanistic view, from feelings of isolation due to a lack of unconditional positive regard received as a child.

The **cognitive perspective** views disordered behavior as the result of faulty or illogical thoughts. Distortions in the cognitive process, according to this point of view, lead to misperceptions and misinterpretations of the world, which in turn lead to disordered behavior. The cognitive approach to treatment involves changing the contents of thought or changing the ways in which those contents are processed.

The **behavioral approach** to disordered behavior is based on the notion that all behavior, including disordered behavior, is learned. Disordered behavior has, at some point, been rewarded or reinforced, and has now been established as a pattern of behavior. Treatment involves the unlearning of the maladaptive behavior, or the modification of the learned responses to certain stimuli.

The **biological view** of disordered behavior, which is a popular one in the United States at the present time, views disordered behavior as a manifestation of abnormal brain function, due to either structural or chemical abnormalities in the brain. This point of view supports medication as providing appropriate treatment for various types of disordered behavior.

The **sociocultural approach** holds that society and culture help define what is acceptable behavior.

There are commonalities among theories on psychopathology, though. Psychologists of all perspectives realize that disorders have multiple causes. One part of explaining a disorder is to look at the predisposing causes, which are the environmental or genetic influences that exist before the disorder begins and makes people vulnerable to the disorder. The next factors to consider are the precipitating causes, which are the triggering events that bring about the disorder. Lastly, psychologists consider the maintaining causes, which are the factors that make the disorder more likely to continue.

Causes of Disorder					
Psycho-analytic	Humanistic	Cognitive	Behavioral	Biological	Socio-cultural
Negative, early childhood experiences or a conflict between the superego and id	Low self-esteem or negative self-regard	Maladaptive thought processes	Reinforcement of depressive behavior	Neurons or neuro-transmitters	Cultural and environmental influences

DIAGNOSIS OF PSYCHOPATHOLOGY

The *Diagnostic and Statistical Manual of Mental Disorders (DSM-5)* is the American Psychiatric Association's handbook for the identification and classification of behavioral disorders. The *DSM-5* calls for the separate notation of important social factors and physical disabilities, in addition to the diagnosis of mental disorder. There are overarching categories in which a specific disorder will be classified. Below are some of the major categories, though be sure to do some extra research, as this list does not cover all.

NEURODEVELOPMENTAL DISORDERS

The term *neurodevelopmental* refers to the developing brain. Related disorders manifest early in development, and may be due to genetic issues, trauma in the womb, or brain damage acquired at birth or in the first years of life. These disorders can range from very specific learning deficits to very global impairments to social skills or intelligence.

Intellectual disability (formerly known as mental retardation) is characterized by delayed development in general mental abilities (reasoning, problem-solving, judgment, academic learning, etc.). These delays translate into an impairment of adaptive functioning in aspects of daily life such as self-care, communication, or occupation. The severity can range from mild to moderate to severe to profound.

Autism spectrum disorder is a neurodevelopmental disorder that often manifests early on in childhood development. This may manifest itself in social communication deficits, both verbal and nonverbal, in which the individual has difficulty noticing social cues and has difficulty engaging others. ASD can also manifest itself in the form of restrictive or repetitive behaviors, difficulty coping with change, or difficulty with accepting change in activity. The spectrum varies widely from person to person, ranging from mild to severe. The term *Asperger's disorder* is no longer used.

Attention-deficit hyperactivity disorder (ADHD) is described as patterned inattention and/or hyperactivity-impulsivity. While everyone experiences spurts of inattention or impulsivity, ADHD interferes with an individual's ability to function at home, work, school, activities, etc. It may sometimes interfere with friends and relationships, and at least some symptoms must have been present before the age of 12 for diagnosis.

Other neurodevelopmental disorders include **communication disorders** such as language disorder, speech sound disorder, and fluency disorder (stuttering); **motor disorders** such as developmental coordination disorder, stereotypic movement disorder, and tics; and **specific learning disorders**.

SCHIZOPHRENIA SPECTRUM AND OTHER PSYCHOTIC DISORDERS

Although the term **schizophrenia** literally means "split brain," these disorders have nothing to do with what used to be called Multiple Personality Disorder. Rather, these disorders are marked by disturbances in thought, perception and speech, as well as motor behavior and emotional experience.

It is important to distinguish between delusions and hallucinations. **Delusions** are beliefs that are not based in reality, such as believing that one can fly, that one is the president of a country, or that one is being pursued by the CIA (assuming that these things are not true). **Hallucinations** are perceptions that are not based in reality, such as seeing things or hearing voices that are not there, or feeling spiders on one's skin (assuming they are not really there).

Disorganized thinking and **disorganized speech** are typical. A person with such a disorder may switch from one topic to another in illogical fashion, may respond to questions with irrelevant answers, and may produce streams of speech that have little or no coherence ("word salad").

It is important to distinguish between **positive symptoms** and **negative symptoms**. Just like with Skinner's learning theory, the terms *positive* and *negative* here have nothing to do with good or bad, but rather they refer to adding and subtracting. A positive symptom of schizophrenic disorders refers to something that a person has, which typical people do not. Thus, delusions and hallucinations are positive symptoms. A negative symptom refers to something that typical people do have, but that one does not have. In schizophrenic disorders, a limited range of emotion and the lack of desire to initiate activities are both particularly noticeable. A number of antipsychotic medications can alleviate the positive symptoms of schizophrenia spectrum disorders.

BIPOLAR AND RELATED DISORDERS

Bipolar disorders, as the name suggests, involves movement between two poles: depressive states on the one hand, and manic states on the other hand. Because manic states often have psychotic features, the *DSM-5* now regards bipolar disorders as a bridge between the psychoses and the major depressive disorders.

DEPRESSIVE DISORDERS

Unlike the everyday-language use of the term ("I'm so depressed about that test"), **depressive disorders** involve the presence of a sad, empty, or irritable mood, combined with changes in thinking and bodily functioning that significantly impair one's ability to function. These disorders go far beyond normal sadness or grief, and last longer than usual periods of sadness. Separate or combined treatments such as psychotherapy (in particular cognitive-behavioral therapy) and anti-depressant medications may assist in recovery.

ANXIETY DISORDERS

Fear is an emotional response to something present; anxiety is a related emotional response, but to a future threat or a possibility of danger. In a state of anxiety, the nervous system wants to get into fight-or-flight mode, but there is nothing there to fight and nothing to flee from. Physical effects of anxiety may include but are not limited to muscle tension, hyperalertness for danger signs, and avoidance behaviors. Sleep disturbances, irritability, and inability to concentrate are common related symptoms.

Treatments vary from behavioral modification in the case of specific phobias to cognitive-behavioral therapy to psychotherapy to medical treatment through **anxiolytics**, anti-anxiety medications.

Panic disorder is an anxiety disorder characterized by recurring **panic attacks**, as well as the constant worry of another panic attack occurring. While panic attacks last only a few minutes, they are debilitating. They are accompanied by sweating, increased heart rate, and a general feeling of being paralyzed with fright.

Generalized anxiety disorder (GAD) is an anxiety disorder characterized by an almost constant state of autonomic nervous system arousal and feelings of dread and worry.

Obsessive-compulsive disorder (OCD) is another anxiety disorder, characterized by involuntary persistent thoughts or obsessions, as well as by compulsions, or repetitive behaviors that are time-consuming and maladaptive, that an individual believes will prevent a particular (usually unrelated) outcome.

Post-traumatic stress disorder (PTSD) is caused by exposure to trauma, such as war or violence, which leads to recurring thoughts and anxiety linked to the trauma. These symptoms, in turn, lead to a decreased ability to function as well as to a general detachment from reality.

Phobias, or persistent, irrational fears of common events or objects, are also anxiety disorders. Phobias include fear of objects, such as snakes, and fear of situations. **Agoraphobia**, for example, is the fear of being in open spaces, public places, or other places from which escape is perceived to be difficult.

OBSESSIVE-COMPULSIVE AND RELATED DISORDERS

As the name suggests, these disorders involve **obsessions** and/or **compulsions**. Be clear on the difference between these terms: obsessions are thoughts; compulsions are actions. Specifically, obsessions are intrusive (unwanted) thoughts, urges, or images that plague the individual. Compulsions are repetitive behaviors (or mental acts) that one feels compelled to perform, often in relation to an obsession. For example, intrusive thoughts about germs could lead to repeated hand-washing.

This is the textbook example for **obsessive-compulsive disorder (OCD)**. Related disorders include **body dysmorphic disorder** and **hoarding disorder**, which involve obsessive thoughts about bodily defects or the need to save possessions. Some specific disorders involve hair-pulling and skin-picking.

TRAUMA- AND STRESSOR-RELATED DISORDERS

By definition, these disorders follow a particularly disturbing event or set of events (the trauma or the stressor). Although it is completely normal for people to respond to a stressful event with stress symptoms, some people recover naturally, whereas others develop symptoms. The best-known such disorder is **post-traumatic stress disorder**, which can involve intrusive thoughts or dreams related to the trauma, irritability, avoidance of situations that might recall the traumatic event, sleep disturbances, diminished interest in formerly pleasurable activities, and social withdrawal. Other disorders include **reactive attachment disorder**, which can occur in seriously neglected children being unable to form attachments to their adult caregivers, and **adjustment disorders**, or maladaptive responses to particular stressors.

DISSOCIATIVE DISORDERS

What gets dissociated in dissociative disorders is primarily consciousness or identity. In many cases, these disorders appear following a trauma, and may be seen as the mind's attempt to protect itself by splitting itself into parts. Thus, one might experience **derealization**, the sense that "this is not really happening," or **depersonalization**, the sense that "this is not happening to me." Significant gaps in memory may be related to **dissociative amnesia**, an inability to recall life events that goes far beyond normal forgetting. Perhaps the most extreme of these disorders is **dissociative identity disorder** (formerly known as multiple personality disorder), in which one may not only "lose time," but also manifest a separate personality during that lost time. This disorder is most often associated with significant trauma or abuse in childhood.

SOMATIC SYMPTOM AND RELATED DISORDERS

Soma means "body." **Somatic symptom disorder** involves, as one might expect, bodily symptoms combined with disordered thoughts, feelings, and/or behaviors connected to these symptoms. It is not the symptoms themselves, but how the individual experiences them, that is striking and seems maladaptive. That is, the level of worry seems out of proportion to the symptom itself. Related worries appear in **illness anxiety disorder**, in which one worries excessively about the possibility of falling ill. **Conversion disorder** (formerly known as hysteria) involves bodily symptoms like changed motor function or changed sensory function that are incompatible with neurological explanations. There may be a suspicion that the symptoms are **psychogenic**, meaning created by the mind. This may prompt some people to say, "It's all in your mind." However, a symptom can originate from the mind but actually end up in the body. According to an old joke, the difference between Americans and Russians is that if an American doesn't want to go to a dinner, he or she will pretend to have a headache; the Russian has to actually have the headache. In conversion disorder, the individual may be completely unaware of the mental origin of the physical symptoms. Finally, there is also **factitious disorder**, in which an individual knowingly falsifies symptoms in order to get medical care, or sympathy or aid from others. This disorder differs from simple lying in that the deception occurs even when there are no obvious rewards.

FEEDING AND EATING DISORDERS

Anorexia nervosa (commonly called anorexia) involves not only restriction of food intake, but also intense fear of gaining weight and disturbances in self-perception, such as thinking one looks fat, when one does not. The self-starvation behavior associated with this disorder can lead to life-threatening medical conditions. **Bulimia nervosa** (commonly called bulimia) involves recurrent episodes of **binge-eating**: eating large amounts of food in short amounts of time, followed by inappropriate behaviors to prevent weight gain, such as self-induced vomiting (**purging**), using laxatives, or intense exercising. There is usually a heightened sense of shame in connection with both binging and purging. Self-image is also unduly affected by body shape and weight. **Binge-eating disorder** might be thought of as bulimia without purging. But this occurs in both normal-weight and overweight/obese people. There is a loss of control associated with the binge-eating in this disorder. Finally, **pica** refers to regular consumption of non-nutritive foods (plastic, paper, dirt, string, chalk, etc.). This occurs more often in children, but can occur in adults. Pica is occasionally seen in pregnant women and individuals with iron deficiency. While it is not clear why this occurs, it is most likely a result of biochemical, physiological, and cultural factors.

PERSONALITY DISORDERS

Consider data that suggests that 15% of U. S. adults have at least one personality disorder. This is roughly one in seven people. While we do not encourage you to start diagnosing people without training, you might think about the people you have met as you study personality disorders.

A personality disorder refers to a stable (and inflexible) way of experiencing and acting in the world, one that is at variance with the person's culture, that starts in adolescence or adulthood, and leads to either personal distress or impairment of social functioning. (It is important to note that, by definition, children cannot have personality disorders. Think of it this way: children are still developing their personalities.) Ten personality disorders are organized into three clusters. You might think of them as the three Ws: the weird, the wild, and the worried.

Cluster A includes paranoid, schizoid, and schizotypal personality disorders. These individuals appear to be markedly odd or eccentric. With **paranoid personality disorder**, there may be a pattern of general distrust of others that is not justified by real circumstances. **Schizoid personality disorder** is marked by disturbances in feeling (detachment from social relationships, flat affect, does not enjoy close relationships with people), whereas **schizotypal personality disorder** is marked by disturbances in thought (odd beliefs that do not quite qualify as delusions, such as superstitions, belief in a "sixth sense," etc.; odd speech; eccentric behavior or appearance).

Cluster B includes antisocial, borderline, histrionic, and narcissistic personality disorders. These individuals appear to be dramatic, emotional, or erratic. Terms like *psychopath* or *sociopath* have been used to describe people with **antisocial personality disorder**, which is characterized by a persistent pattern of disregard for, and violation of, the rights of others. Lying, cheating, stealing, and having no remorse are common. **Borderline personality disorder** involves a very stormy relationship with the world, with others, and with one's own feelings. People with this disorder have a regular pattern of instability in relationships, often involving frantic efforts to avoid abandonment (imagined or real), alternating between extremes of idealization and devaluation ("You're the best ever!" → "I hate you!") with the same person, identity disturbance, impulsivity, chronic feelings of emptiness, and anger control issues. **Histrionic personality disorder** involves a pattern of excessive emotionality and attention-seeking, beyond what might be considered normal (even in a "culture of selfies"). **Narcissistic personality disorder** involves an overinflated sense of self-importance, fantasies of success, beliefs that one is special, a sense of entitlement, a lack of empathy for others, and a display of arrogant behaviors or attitudes.

Cluster C includes avoidant, dependent, and obsessive-compulsive personality disorders. These individuals appear to be anxious or fearful. **Avoidant personality disorder** involves an enduring pattern of social inhibition, feelings of inadequacy, and hypersensitivity to real or perceived criticism, which lead to avoidance behavior in relation to social, personal, and intimate relationships. **Dependent personality disorder** is marked by an excessive need to be cared for, leading to clingy and submissive behavior and fears of separation. People with this disorder may feel unable to make everyday decisions without constantly consulting others and getting their advice and approval. Finally, **obsessive-compulsive personality disorder (OCPD)** is marked by a rigid concern with order, perfectionism, control, and work, at the expense of flexibility, spontaneity, openness, and play. These people may be described using Freud's term "anal." In distinction to OCD, which involves unwanted or intrusive thoughts along with unwanted or intrusive compulsions, OCPD can involve similar thoughts and compulsions, but they are not seen by the person as intrusive. Rather, the person with OCPD may think that the problem lies with other people, who do not see the need for things to be ordered in a certain way.

In many cases, people do not seek treatment for their personality disorder. But if their disorder leads them to become depressed or anxious, due to social or occupational impairments, they may seek help for depression or anxiety, and may become diagnosed in that way.

IN ADDITION

We have only given an overview and selection of the disorders listed in the *DSM-5*. Other disorders include the following: elimination disorders; sleep-wake disorders; sexual dysfunctions; gender dysphoria; disruptive, impulse-control and conduct disorders; substance-related and addictive disorders; neurocognitive disorders; paraphilic disorders; and others.

KEY TERMS

Diagnosis of Psychopathology
DSM-5

Neurodevelopmental Disorders
intellectual disability
autism spectrum disorder
attention-deficit hyperactivity
disorder (ADHD)
communication disorders
motor disorders
specific learning disorders

Schizophrenia Spectrum and Other Psychotic Disorders
schizophrenia
delusions
hallucinations
disorganized thinking
disorganized speech
positive symptoms
negative symptoms

Bipolar and Related Disorders
depressive disorder

Anxiety Disorders
anxiolytics
panic disorder
panic attack
generalized anxiety disorder
(GAD)
obsessive-compulsive disorder
(OCD)
post-traumatic stress disorder
(PTSD)
phobias
agoraphobia

Obsessive-Compulsive and Related Disorders
obsessions
compulsions
obsessive-compulsive disorder
(OCD)
body dysmorphic disorder
hoarding disorder

Trauma- and Stressor-Related Disorders
post-traumatic stress disorder
reactive attachment disorder
adjustment disorders

Dissociative Disorders
derealization
depersonalization
dissociative amnesia
dissociative identity disorder
(DID)

Somatic Symptom and Related Disorders
somatic symptom disorder
illness anxiety disorder
conversion disorder
psychogenic
factitious disorder

Feeding and Eating Disorders
anorexia nervosa
bulimia nervosa
binge eating
purging
binge-eating disorder
pica

Personality Disorders
Cluster A
paranoid personality disorder
schizoid personality disorder
schizotypal personality disorder
Cluster B
antisocial personality disorder
borderline personality disorder
histrionic personality disorder
narcissistic personality disorder
Cluster C
avoidant personality disorder
dependent personality disorder
obsessive-compulsive personality disorder

Definitions of Disorder
    disordered behavior

Theories of Psychopathology
    psychoanalytic school
    humanistic school
    cognitive perspective
    behaviorism approach
    biological view
    sociocultural approach

Chapter 16 Drill

See Chapter 19 for answers and explanations.

1. A man claims to hear voices telling him to run for president. He is most likely experiencing

   (A) delusions
   (B) obsessions
   (C) hallucinations
   (D) compulsions
   (E) inceptions

2. The disorder characterized by psychological difficulties that manifest themselves as physical symptoms is

   (A) bipolar disorder
   (B) conversion disorder
   (C) organic disorder
   (D) undifferentiated disorder
   (E) paranoid disorder

3. Which of the following are most characteristic of a dissociative disorder?

   (A) A persistent, irrational fear of objects or situations
   (B) Difficulties in forming lasting personal relationships
   (C) Involuntary and persistent thoughts that interfere with daily activity
   (D) Auditory and tactile hallucinations
   (E) Memory dysfunction and/or altered perceptions of identity

4. Depression has been associated with low levels of the neurotransmitter

   (A) acetylcholine
   (B) GABA
   (C) serotonin
   (D) chlorpromazine
   (E) dopamine

5. Which of the following is NOT characterized by the *DSM-5* as an anxiety disorder?

   (A) Phobia
   (B) Social phobia
   (C) Anxious personality disorder
   (D) Panic disorder
   (E) Generalized anxiety disorder

6. A high-school girl goes missing, and when she is found in a town 100 miles away a week later, she has assumed a new personality and has no apparent recollection of her life at home. Which category of disorder is she most likely suffering from?

   (A) Somatoform disorder
   (B) Delusional disorder
   (C) Personality disorder
   (D) Dissociative disorder
   (E) Schizophrenia

7. Conversion disorder is best characterized by

   (A) a constant fear of being ill
   (B) panic attacks and severe anxiety
   (C) frequent vague complaints about physical symptoms
   (D) functional impairment of a limb or sensory ability with no apparent physical cause
   (E) religious obsessions

8. All of the following are Cluster B personality disorders EXCEPT

   (A) borderline personality disorder
   (B) schizoid personality disorder
   (C) histrionic behavior disorder
   (D) narcissistic personality disorder
   (E) antisocial personality disorder

9. A child shows difficulty engaging with other children and needs to follow a very strict routine every day to function properly. If the routine is broken, he cries and has a very difficult time adjusting. These symptoms may satisfy which of the following diagnoses?

   (A) Attention-deficit hyperactivity disorder
   (B) Reactive attachment disorder
   (C) Obsessive-compulsive disorder
   (D) Adjustment disorder
   (E) Autism spectrum disorder

10. All of the following are classified as feeding and eating disorders EXCEPT

    (A) pica
    (B) binge-eating disorder
    (C) bulimia nervosa
    (D) body dysmorphic disorder
    (E) anorexia nervosa

REFLECT

Respond to the following questions:

- Which topics in this chapter do you hope to see on the multiple-choice section or essay?

- Which topics in this chapter do you hope not to see on the multiple-choice section or essay?

- Regarding any psychologists mentioned, can you pair the psychologists with their contributions to the field? Did they contribute significant experiments, theories, or both?

- Regarding any theories mentioned, can you distinguish between differing theories well enough to recognize them on the multiple-choice section? Can you distinguish them well enough to write a fluent essay on them?

- Regarding any figures given, if you were given a labeled figure from within this chapter, would you be able to give the significance of each part of the figure?

- Can you define the key terms at the end of the chapter?

- Which parts of the chapter will you review?

- Will you seek further help, outside of this book (such as a teacher, Princeton Review tutor, or AP Students), on any of the content in this chapter—and, if so, on what content?

Chapter 17
Clinical
Psychology:
Treatment

TREATMENT APPROACHES

The various disordered behaviors described in the previous chapter can be viewed from varying perspectives. Often, insight into the true nature of a disorder can be derived from examining the strategy that is most effective in treating the disorder.

Insight Therapies: Psychoanalytic and Humanistic Approaches

The psychoanalytic approach to the treatment of disordered behavior is rooted in the concept of **insight**. Insight into the cause of the problem, according to this theory, is the primary key to eliminating the problem.

Psychoanalysis

Psychoanalysis, or psychoanalytic therapy, as it is sometimes called, was first developed by Freud and focuses on probing past defense mechanisms of repression and rationalization to understand the unconscious cause of a problem. A primary tool for revealing the contents of the unconscious is **free association**, in which the patient reports any and all conscious thoughts and ideas. Within the pattern of free associations are hints to the nature of the unconscious conflict. The insight process does not occur quickly, however, as patients exhibit resistance to the uncovering of repressed thoughts and feelings.

In psychoanalytic therapy, the therapist strives to remain detached from the patient, resisting emotional or personal involvement. This detachment is intended to encourage **transference**, which occurs when the patient shifts thoughts and feelings about certain people or events onto the therapist. This process is thought to help reveal the nature of the patient's conflicts. **Countertransference** may occur if the therapist transfers his or her own feelings onto the patient. In order to avoid countertransference, psychotherapists have typically undergone analysis themselves and many continue to do so while practicing therapy.

Freud and Dreams

According to psychoanalytic theory, another window into the unconscious is provided by dreams. Freud believed that the images and occurrences in dreams—the **manifest content** of dreams—are actually symbols representing the **latent**, or truly meaningful, **content** of dreams.

Humanistic Therapy

The humanistic school of psychology takes a related, yet different approach to the treatment of disordered behavior. Rather than treating the person seeking help as a patient, the humanistic approach treats the individual as a client. **Client-centered therapy** was invented by **Carl Rogers** and involves the assumption that clients can be understood only in terms of their own reality. This approach differs from the Freudian approach in its focus on the client's present perception of reality, rather than the past and its analysis of conscious, instead of unconscious, motives. The goal of the therapy is to help the client realize full potential through self-actualization.

In order to accomplish this, the client-centered therapist takes a somewhat different approach from that of the Freudian. Rather than remaining detached, the therapist is open, honest, and expressive of feelings with the client (an active listener). Rogers referred to this way of relating to the client as **genuineness**.

The next key for successful client-centered therapy, according to Rogers, is **unconditional positive regard**. You may recall from previous chapters that Rogers believed that unconditional positive regard for the child by the parent was critical for healthy development. The therapist provides this unconditional positive regard to help the client reach a state of unconditional self-worth.

The final key to successful therapy is **accurate empathic understanding**. Rogers used this term to describe the therapist's ability to view the world from the eyes of the client. This empathy is critical to successful communication between the therapist and client.

A different type of approach toward treatment is **Gestalt therapy**, which combines both physical and mental therapies. **Fritz Perls** developed this approach to blend an awareness of unconscious tensions with the belief that one must become aware of and deal with those tensions by taking personal responsibility. Clients may be asked to physically "act out" psychological conflicts in order to make them aware of the interaction between mind and body.

Behavioral Therapy

Behavioral therapy stands in dramatic contrast to the insight therapies. First, behavioral therapy is a short-term process, whereas the insight approaches are extended over long periods of time, often spanning years. Secondly, behavior therapy treats symptoms because, in this school of thought, there is no deep underlying cause of the problem. The disordered behavior itself is both the problem and symptom. To change behavior, behavioral therapists use specific techniques with clearly defined methods of application and clear ways to evaluate their efficacy.

Counterconditioning is a technique in which a response to a given stimulus is replaced by a different response. For example, if a patient seeks behavioral therapy to stop drinking alcohol, the therapist must take the learned responses, the positive feelings generated by drinking alcohol, and replace them with a new reaction, namely, negative feelings concerning alcohol.

Counterconditioning can be accomplished in a few ways. One is to use **aversion therapy**, in which an aversive stimulus is repeatedly paired with the behavior that the client wishes to stop. So, to use our alcohol example, the therapist might administer a punishment to the patient each time the patient drinks alcohol.

Alcoholics and Aversion Therapy

This approach is sometimes used in treating alcoholism. Patients are administered a drug called Antabuse, which makes them violently ill if they consume alcohol.

Another method used for counterconditioning is **systematic desensitization**. This technique involves replacing one response, such as anxiety, with another response, such as relaxation. In order to achieve this goal, a therapist constructs, with the help of the client, a hierarchical set of mental images related to the stressful stimulus. These mental images are laid out in an order such that each one is slightly more anxiety-inducing than the previous one. The patient then learns a deep-relaxation technique. Next, the therapist asks the patient to bring to mind the least stressful of the mental images. As the client imagines the scene, he or she may become anxious. The client is instructed to practice the relaxation technique the moment the feelings of anxiety begin and to continue using the relaxation technique until he or she feels fully relaxed while imagining the scene. The therapist, over time, systematically helps the client work up the hierarchy until he or she is able to imagine the most stressful scene in the hierarchy without experiencing anxiety. This technique relies on learning mechanisms to associate the formerly anxiety-provoking stimuli with relaxation.

Changing It Up
A variation of systematic desensitization can occur when a therapist introduces the client to increasingly more anxiety-inducing stimuli instead of relying solely on his or her imagination.

Other forms of behavioral therapy involve **extinction procedures**, which are designed to weaken maladaptive responses. One way of trying to extinguish a behavior is called **flooding**. Flooding involves exposing a client to the stimulus that causes the undesirable response. If, for example, a client has come to a therapist to try to overcome a fear of spiders, the therapist will actually expose the client to spiders. Of course, the client will have a high anxiety level, but after a few minutes of being near the spider without any negative consequences, the client will presumably realize that the situation is not dangerous.

Implosion is a similar technique, in which the client imagines the disruptive stimuli rather than actually confronting them.

Operant conditioning is a behavior-control technique that we discussed in the chapter on learning. A related approach is **behavioral contracting**, in which the therapist and the client draw up a contract to which they both agree to abide. The client must, according to the contract, act in certain ways, such as not exhibiting undesirable behaviors; meanwhile, the therapist must provide stated rewards if the client holds up his or her end of the bargain.

Modeling is a therapeutic approach based on Bandura's social learning theory. This technique is based on the principle of vicarious learning. Clients watch someone act in a certain way and then receive a reward. Presumably, the client will then be disposed to imitate that behavior.

Cognitive Therapy

Cognitive approaches to the treatment of disordered behavior rely on changing cognitions, or the ways people think about situations, in order to change behavior. One such approach is **rational-emotive behavior therapy (REBT)** (sometimes called simply **RET**, for **rational-emotive therapy**), formulated by **Albert Ellis**. REBT is based on the idea that when confronted with situations, people recite statements to themselves that express maladaptive thoughts. The maladaptive thoughts result in maladaptive emotional responses. The goal of REBT is to change the maladaptive thoughts and emotional response by confronting the irrational thoughts directly. Incorrect thoughts are changed in a simple way: the patient is told that he or she is incorrect and why. An example of a maladaptive thought is, "I always have to be perfect in everything I do" or "Other people's opinions are crucial to my happiness."

Another cognitive approach is **cognitive therapy,** formulated by **Aaron Beck**, in which the focus is on maladaptive schemas. These schemas cause the client to experience cognitive distortions, which in turn lead them to feel worthless or incompetent. Beck asserted that there is a **negative triad** of depression that involves a negative view of self, of the world, and of the future. This view is learned through experiences and then becomes a cycle of response that needs to be addressed through cognitive therapy. Maladaptive schemas include **arbitrary inference**, in which a person draws conclusions without evidence, and **dichotomous thinking**, which involves all-or-none conceptions of situations. An example might be that of a person, faced with the stress of a job interview, who thinks, "If I don't get this job, I'll be a complete failure." The goal of cognitive therapy is to eliminate or modify the individual's maladaptive schemas.

Biological Therapies

Biological therapies are medical approaches to behavioral problems. Biological therapies are typically used in conjunction with one of the previously mentioned forms of treatment.

Electroconvulsive therapy (ECT) is a form of treatment in which fairly high voltages of electricity are passed across a patient's head. This treatment causes temporary amnesia and can result in seizures. It has been successful in the treatment of major depression, but today it is used only when all other means of treating depression have failed because of the risks involved with memory loss.

Another form of biological treatment is **psychosurgery**. Perhaps the most well-known form of psychosurgery is the **prefrontal lobotomy**, in which parts of the frontal lobes are cut off from the rest of the brain. This surgery was a popular treatment for violent patients from the 1930s to the 1950s. It frequently left patients in a zombie-like or catatonic state. Its use marked a controversial chapter in the history of psychotherapy.

Psychopharmacology is the treatment of psychological and behavioral maladaptations with drugs. There are four broad classes of **psychotropic**, or psychologically active drugs: antipsychotics, antidepressants, anxiolytics, and lithium salts.

Antipsychotics like Clozapine, Thorazine, and Haldol reduce the symptoms of schizophrenia by blocking the neural receptors for dopamine. You may recall that dopamine is implicated in schizophrenia and in movement disorder. Unfortunately, jerky movements, tremors, and muscle stiffness are among the side effects of these drugs. The clinician must decide which is worse—the psychological disorder being treated or the side effects of the drugs.

Antidepressants can be grouped into three types: monoamine oxidase (MAO) inhibitors, tricyclics, and selective reuptake inhibitors. **MAO inhibitors,** like Eutron, work by increasing the amount of serotonin and norepinephrine in the synaptic cleft. They produce this increase by blocking monoamine oxidase, which is responsible for the breakdown of many neurotransmitters. These drugs are effective but toxic and require special dietary modifications. **Tricyclics,** like Norpramin, Amitriptyline, and Imipramine are tricyclics that increase the amount of serotonin and norepinephrine.

The third class of antidepressants, **selective reuptake inhibitors** (often called the selective serotonin reuptake inhibitors, or SSRIs, for the neurotransmitter most affected by them) also work by increasing the amount of neurotransmitter at the synaptic cleft, in this case by blocking the reuptake mechanism of the cell that released the neurotransmitters. Prozac (Fluoxetine) is one example of such a drug. The indirect mechanism of action of these drugs means that they have fewer side effects. They are the most frequently prescribed class of antidepressant drugs in the United States.

Anxiolytics depress the central nervous system and reduce anxiety while increasing feelings of well-being and reducing insomnia. A commonly prescribed anti-anxiety medication is Xanax. Anxiolytics also include barbiturates, which are rarely used because of their potential for addiction and their danger when mixed with other drugs. **Benzodiazepines**, which also include Valium (Diazepam) and Librium (Chlordiazepoxide), cause muscle relaxation and a feeling of tranquility.

Lithium carbonate, a salt, is effective in the treatment of bipolar disorder. The mechanism of action is not known, however.

MODES OF THERAPY

Not all forms of therapy involve an individual client seeing a therapist. **Group therapy**, in which clients meet together with a therapist as an interactive group, has some advantages over individual therapy. It is less expensive, and the group dynamic may be therapeutic in and of itself. Of course, the psychological effect of the therapist also may be diluted across the members of the group because attention is focused on the group rather than on a specific individual. One area in which group therapy has gained popularity is in the treatment of substance abuse. **Twelve-step programs** are one form of group therapy, although they are usually not moderated by professional psychotherapists. These programs, modeled after Alcoholics Anonymous, are a combination of spirituality and group therapy. The twelve-step programs focus on a strong social support system of people who are experiencing or who have experienced addictions or other types of maladaptive adjustments to life.

Another therapy in which there is more than a single client is **couples** or **family therapy**. This type of treatment arose out of the simple observation that some dysfunctional behavior affects the afflicted person's loved ones. Couples therapy approaches the couple dyad as a system that involves complex interactions. Family therapy has distinct advantages in that it allows family members to express their feelings to one another and to the therapist simultaneously. This behavior, in turn, encourages family members to listen to one another in a way that might not occur in other settings.

KEY TERMS

Treatment Approaches

insight
psychoanalysis
free association
manifest content
latent content
transference
countertransference
client-centered therapy
Carl Rogers
genuineness
unconditional positive regard
accurate empathetic understanding
Gestalt therapy
Fritz Perls
behavioral therapy
counterconditioning
aversion therapy
systematic desensitization
extinction procedures
flooding
implosion
operant conditioning
behavioral contracting
modeling

rational-emotive behavior therapy (REBT)
Albert Ellis
cognitive therapy
Aaron Beck
negative triad
arbitrary inference
dichotomous thinking
electroconvulsive therapy (ECT)
psychosurgery
prefrontal lobotomy
psychopharmacology
psychotropic drugs
antipsychotics
antidepressants
MAO inhibitors
tricyclics
selective reuptake inhibitors (SSRIs)
anxiolytics
benzodiazepines
lithium carbonate

Modes of Therapy

group therapy
twelve-step programs
couples therapy
family therapy

Chapter 17 Drill

See Chapter 19 for answers and explanations.

1. The concept of *accurate empathic understanding* is most closely associated with which of the following therapeutic approaches?

   (A) Psychoanalytic therapy
   (B) Inductive therapy
   (C) Client-centered therapy
   (D) Implosion therapy
   (E) Reductionist therapy

2. Behavioral therapeutic approaches, such as systematic desensitization, have been most often used with those experiencing or diagnosed with

   (A) fugue
   (B) dementia
   (C) dissociative disorder
   (D) schizophrenia
   (E) phobia

3. A psychoanalytically oriented therapist would most likely be in accord with which of the following criticisms regarding behaviorally oriented therapies?

   (A) Behaviorally oriented therapies often take years to complete and create an onerous financial burden for the patient.
   (B) Behaviorally oriented therapies are concerned solely with the modification of troubling behavioral symptoms and do not address the underlying problems which may have produced those symptoms.
   (C) Behaviorally oriented therapies can be performed only by therapists who have had the longest and most rigorous training and, as a result, can never impact as many people as can other treatment approaches.
   (D) Behaviorally oriented therapies are relatively uninterested in the development of an egalitarian client-therapist relationship and miss opportunities to promote emotional growth and empowerment.
   (E) Behaviorally oriented therapies avoid the technique of role-playing and may not be suitable for group or family therapy situations.

4. The cognitively oriented therapeutic approach known as rational-emotive behavior therapy is most closely associated with

   (A) Julian Rotter
   (B) Albert Ellis
   (C) Abraham Maslow
   (D) Raymond Cattell
   (E) Rollo May

5. Which of the following is NOT a major class of drugs used for psychotherapeutic effect?

   (A) Anticoagulants
   (B) Anxiolytics
   (C) Monoamine oxidase inhibitors
   (D) Lithium salts
   (E) Selective reuptake inhibitors

6. Judy has acrophobia, a fear of heights. A behavioral therapist creates a treatment plan to take her to the top of the Empire State Building on the first session, where she will remain until her reaction to the stimulus subsides. This technique is known as

   (A) systematic desensitization
   (B) aversion therapy
   (C) flooding
   (D) implosion
   (E) behavior contracting

7. A behavioral therapist uses which of the following techniques?

   (A) Free association
   (B) Dream analysis
   (C) Hypnosis
   (D) Extinction procedures
   (E) Unconditional positive regard

8. Selective Serotonin Reuptake Inhibitors, more commonly known as SSRIs, are generally effective in treating which of the following?

   (A) Depressive disorders
   (B) Anxiety disorders
   (C) Bipolar disorder
   (D) Feeding and eating disorders
   (E) Schizophrenic disorders

9. A psychotherapist would most likely use which of the following therapies?

    (A) Implosion
    (B) Systematic desensitization
    (C) Free association
    (D) Flooding
    (E) Positive self-talk

10. Carl Rogers is most closely identified with which of the following therapy perspectives?

    (A) Humanistic therapy
    (B) Psychoanalytic therapy
    (C) Behavioral therapy
    (D) Cognitive behavioral therapy
    (E) Biological therapy

REFLECT

Respond to the following questions:

- Which topics in this chapter do you hope to see on the multiple-choice section or essay?

- Which topics in this chapter do you hope not to see on the multiple-choice section or essay?

- Regarding any psychologists mentioned, can you pair the psychologists with their contributions to the field? Did they contribute significant experiments, theories, or both?

- Regarding any theories mentioned, can you distinguish between differing theories well enough to recognize them on the multiple-choice section? Can you distinguish them well enough to write a fluent essay on them?

- Regarding any figures given, if you were given a labeled figure from within this chapter, would you be able to give the significance of each part of the figure?

- Can you define the key terms at the end of the chapter?

- Which parts of the chapter will you review?

- Will you seek further help, outside of this book (such as a teacher, Princeton Review tutor, or AP Students), on any of the content in this chapter—and, if so, on what content?

Chapter 18
Social
Psychology

Social psychology refers to the study of psychology within the context of social or interpersonal interactions. Sociology, the study of cultures and societies, has a large effect on an individual's environment, which can influence cognition and behavior. Here are a few theories and important concepts of sociology and how they relate to the intersecting discipline of social psychology.

IDENTITIES AND GROUPS

Societies, organizations of individuals, have a shared **culture**, a common set of beliefs, behaviors, values, and material symbols. Therefore, identities begin to form as collective **social identities** that are placed upon individuals from others, and individuals form their own **personal identities** about themselves. Personal identities are generally words that describe personality, such as kind, generous, thoughtful, insightful, etc., while social identities are how individuals are seen in the context of their society. Social identities can be related to religion, work, appearance, disability, gender, sexual orientation, immigration status, or any other label that societies have come to understand through their shared culture. For instance, someone's social identities might be lawyer, young adult, Muslim, and female. These traits do not have anything to do with personality traits, yet they are factors of how individuals are seen by others in society, which may color social interactions. These identities can give some individuals an inherent advantage in some societies while other identities can be a disadvantage. For instance, those who have citizenship in a certain country have more power and rights than those who are considered immigrants, noncitizens, or undocumented. Similarly, in the United States, adults tend to hold more power in society than children or the very elderly. Individuals hold multiple social identities, and the effects and nature of these overlapping identities is referred to as **intersectionality**. Someone who identifies as female, Latina, and bisexual can provide a window into each of these social identities and how they intersect and create complexity when combined.

The closest group that individuals create with one another is called the **primary group**, which usually consists of family and close friends. These relationships are generally long lasting and emotionally deep. Individuals spend time with others in their primary groups for the sake of spending quality time with them, not for any other gain. Most others fall into a **secondary group**, a group of friends and acquaintances who perhaps have shared interests or values. For instance, a person may take classes at school with classmates who have a shared interest in the material or take part in a running group with others who share that passion for running. Within societies, these identities form the idea of sameness or difference, which generate **in-groups** and **out-groups**. In-groups refer to groups of individuals with a shared identity. For example, teachers share an in-group with other teachers, while accountants would be considered an out-group.

While this example is harmless, in- and out-groups can create harmful situations when one group believes it is superior to another. **Ethnocentrism** refers to holding values or beliefs of one's own in-group as better than those of another's, which can lead to conflict, prejudice, and more. On the other hand, **cultural relativism** is the idea that the beliefs and values of one's in-group may be different than those of another, but that they are not necessarily better or worse: just different. Sometimes, individuals try to enter a new in-group through **assimilation**, a process of taking on another's culture in order to fit in to a new society. Assimilation is common amongst immigrants and individuals settling into a new culture. Individuals who do not shed their former identities, but rather keep elements of their own culture and take on elements of their new culture show **multiculturalism**.

As individuals immigrate or emigrate, study abroad, or even visit other societies and cultures, they may experience **culture shock** or **cultural lag**. Culture shock refers to the way in which behaviors and values can be seen differently across cultures. Language barriers are common examples of culture shock, as are small social faux pas that get lost in translation or contain different meanings across cultures. **Cultural lag** refers to the time it takes for cultures to catch up to technological innovations or practices.

Individuals play **roles** within groups and societies, some of which may change or conflict with each other over the course of a lifetime. Someone could have roles of father, husband, son, and teacher simultaneously. **Role conflict** occurs when two or more of these roles are at odds with each other: imagine the man described receives a phone call at work to say that his child went home from school sick. Does he stay at work and fulfill his role as a teacher or does he leave work early to tend to his child? Similarly, **role strain** can occur within the same role: college students are in college to study, but are also at school to meet friends from around the world and learn to take care of themselves on their own. The balance of study and experience can create strain within that role. **Role exit** occurs when a person leaves behind a role to take on another: graduating from college and starting the workforce means the person leaves the role of student and takes on the role of employee.

SOCIAL INSTITUTIONS

In societies, there are a variety of **social institutions** designed to promote and transmit social norms to its members through a variety of constructs.

Family, religion, government, economy, politics, health, medicine, and education are all social institutions and have an impact on the way individuals interact with each other and within their respective societies. Family is an important institution that provides kinship and belonging within a society, while religion provides belonging as well as a sense of purpose and connection to the supernatural. Governments create laws to maintain order in societies, and various structures of governments can directly affect individuals' quality of life. Economies manage transactions between individuals, organizations, and groups. Health and medicine are interesting institutions that can change dramatically from culture to culture, especially with regard to mental health. Some cultures may treat a condition as a sickness, while other cultures may not recognize that same condition as abnormal. Finally, education is an institution that transmits knowledge from generation to generation and teaches individuals about the values of that country.

Even though education is free for all, not everyone has the same opportunities, depending on where individuals live. **Institutionalized discrimination** is a particular type of discrimination that refers to unfair treatment of certain groups by organizations. Zoning laws, government, and other organizations can create rules that, unintentionally or intentionally, put certain groups at a social disadvantage. Institutionalized discrimination can lead to unequal opportunities of access to quality education and healthcare, as well as suppressed attainment of wealth.

Closely related to institutionalized discrimination are the concepts of **availability** and **accessibility**. Availability refers to whether something even exists for a person to use. If, for example, a low-income housing complex does not have any grocery stores within 5 miles, this would be an issue of availability, in which it might be more difficult for these people to be able to get to the grocery stores. This particular scenario of not having good grocery stores (except maybe convenience stores that sell chips and candy) is called a **food desert**. Because people may not have cars or ways of reaching these grocery stores, the healthy food is not available to them, and this can have resounding health consequences. Accessibility refers to whether a person can actually use the tools and resources that are available to them. For instance, a class uses a particular textbook for readings, but one student is visually impaired. Even though that book is available to the student for purchase, it is not usable to him or her as is. The book would have to be made accessible, either through braille or voice-over computer programs.

GROUP DYNAMICS

Group dynamics is a general term for some of the phenomena we observe when people interact. For example, **social facilitation** is an increase in performance on a task that occurs when that task is performed in the presence of others. You may have experienced this effect if you play sports. The opposite effect is called **social inhibition**, which occurs when the presence of others makes performance worse. Many people experience social inhibition when they give a speech. People experience social facilitation when they find a task to be easy or well-practiced, and they suffer from social inhibition when a task is overly difficult or novel.

Another effect that occurs when people interact in groups is **social loafing**, or the reduced effort group members put into a task as a result of the size of the group. For example, when you are assigned a group project, you may put in less effort than you would if it were an individual project, hoping that the other group members will pick up some of your slack. People are prone to social loafing when they believe their performance is not being assessed or monitored.

Another interesting effect of being in groups is the exaggeration of our initial attitudes. This effect is known as **group polarization**. Group polarization occurs when a judgment or decision of a group is more extreme than what individual members of the group would have reached on their own. For example, if people with negative racial attitudes are placed into a group and told to discuss racial issues, those who started off the experiment with high prejudice often end up with an even higher prejudice after the discussion.

Research has been conducted on the resolution of conflicts within groups. The most effective method to resolve a conflict between two groups is to have them cooperate toward a superordinate goal. For example, in the Robbers Cave experiment, campers who had been feuding for weeks were able to overcome their differences when they cooperated to solve problems, such as a water leak that threatened the whole camp. Another effective technique is **GRIT (Graduated and Reciprocated Initiatives in Tension-Reduction)**. This approach encourages groups to announce intent to reduce tensions and show small, conciliatory behaviors, as long as these reduced tensions and behaviors are reciprocated.

ATTRIBUTION

Attribution refers to the way in which people assign responsibility for certain outcomes. Typically, attribution falls into two categories— dispositional (or individual) and situational. **Dispositional attribution** assumes that the cause of a behavior or outcome is internal. **Situational attribution** assigns the cause to the environment or external conditions. When students fail a test, they might attribute that failure to their own poor work habits or lack of intellectual abilities (a dispositional attribute), or they could attribute their failure to some external factor such as bad instruction (a situational attribute).

A **self-serving bias** sees the cause of actions as internal (or dispositional) when the outcomes are positive or external (or situational) when the results are negative. When a teacher's class fails a test, that teacher blames the students for their lack of initiative and motivation. However, when the class does very well, the teacher attributes the students' success to his or her superior teaching and motivational ability. When your class gets back a paper, think about how often you've heard fellow students say things like, "I got an A" but "He gave me a C." A related concept is the **fundamental attribution error**. In this process of judging the behavior of others, people are more likely to overestimate the role of dispositional attributes and to underestimate the role of the situation. For example, if you are waiting for your friend to meet you at the movies and she is so late that the movie has already started, you would be more likely to blame your friend's lateness on her laziness or

The Power of Groupthink

Another interesting phenomenon that may occur when people are in groups is what **Irving Janis** has referred to as "groupthink." **Groupthink** occurs when members of a group are so driven to reach unanimous decisions that they no longer truly evaluate the repercussions or implications of their decisions. Groupthink may be observed when the groups making decisions are isolated and homogeneous, when there is a lack of impartial leadership inside or outside the group, and when there is a high level of pressure for a decision to be made. Often, groups experiencing groupthink start to acquire feelings of invulnerability and omnipotence. They do not believe they can make a mistake and as a result, often do. A **mindguard** in the group may take on the responsibility of criticizing or even ostracizing members of the group who do not agree with the rest. The groupthink hypothesis has been applied to understand political situations, such as how political leaders can make decisions that seem, in retrospect, so obviously bad to people outside of the group.

procrastination than on a traffic jam or car accident. Your judgment exemplifies a fundamental attribution error.

Some attributions actually affect the outcome of the behavior, as in the case of the **self-fulfilling prophecy**. Because Person A expects Person B to achieve or fail, Person B is likely to do just that. This is especially true in education and is known as the **Rosenthal Effect**. When teachers are told that certain children are expected to achieve in the following year, those children tend to do better than others, even when there is actually no difference in ability levels.

INTERPERSONAL PERCEPTION

Psychologists have studied **interpersonal attraction**, the tendency to positively evaluate a person and then to gravitate to that person. Interpersonal attraction is obviously based on characteristics of the person to whom we are attracted, but it may be subject to environmental and social influences, as well. Factors leading to interpersonal attraction include positive evaluation, shared opinions, good physical appearance, familiarity, and proximity of the individuals to each other. **Positive evaluation** refers to the fact that we all like to be positively evaluated, and therefore, we tend to prefer the company of people who think highly of us. **Shared opinions** as a basis for interpersonal attraction are typically thought of as a form of social reinforcement. If we are praised and rewarded by a person for our opinions, then we tend to prefer their company. It is important to note that similarity across other factors, such as age and race, also tends to be a good predictor of interpersonal attraction. The variability of proximity is an interesting factor. It has been shown that people are more likely to be attracted to those in close physical proximity to them. Studies have shown that apartment building residents are much more likely to have friends who live on their floor than they are to have friends who live on other floors. This is an example of the **mere exposure effect**, which states that people tend to prefer people and experiences that are familiar.

CONFORMITY, COMPLIANCE, OBEDIENCE

Conformity is the modification of behavior to make it agree with that of a group. **Solomon Asch** performed studies on the nature of conformity. In these studies, participants thought that they were being evaluated on their perceptual judgments. Small groups of people sitting together were shown stimuli, such as lines of differing lengths. Each member of the group was to report which of several comparison lines matched a standard line in length. Each individual in the group was asked to respond orally in turn. The participants did not know that the other members of a given group were not naïve participants, but rather were confederates of the experimenter. The correct answers in the experiment were obvious. However, the confederates, pretending to be naïve participants, would purposely respond incorrectly. Asch found that, in general, the naïve participants agreed with the other

Q: What factors may lend themselves to interpersonal attraction?

See answer on page 292

Conformity Factors
Factors influencing conformity include group size, the cohesiveness of the group opinion, gender, social status, culture, and the appearance of unanimity.

members of the group, even though the answer they gave was obviously incorrect. Furthermore, Asch demonstrated that the participants knew that the answers they gave were wrong, but said them anyway.

Generally speaking, three or more members of a group are sufficient for conformity effects to occur. The desire to conform seems higher if the participants see themselves as members of a cohesive group. In general, women are more likely to conform than are men. People who view themselves as being of medium or low social status are more likely to conform than are those who perceive themselves as being of high social status. The cultural influence on conformity is interesting; people in more collective societies tend to conform more than do those in individualistic societies. Finally, unanimity is important. A participant is much less likely to conform if even one other person in the group did not conform.

Compliance is the propensity to accede to the requests of others, even at the expense of your own interests. One method of eliciting compliance is justification, in which you present reasons why a person should comply. Another method is **reciprocity**, which involves creating the appearance that you are giving someone something in order to induce that individual to comply with your wishes. Salespeople have perfected the **foot-in-the-door phenomenon**, which involves making requests in small steps at first (to gain compliance), in order to work up to big requests. The opposite of this phenomenon is called the **door-in-the-face phenomenon**, in which a large request is made first, making subsequent smaller requests more appealing. The likelihood of compliance to a particular request also depends on our regard for the person making the request. Generally speaking, the more highly we regard the person making the request, the more likely we are to comply with the person's request. In general, there are two reasons why people will resist compliance. One reason is because people have been exposed to a weak version of an argument and are, therefore, inoculated to further attempts to get them to comply. This theory is known as the **inoculation hypothesis**. Another reason people resist is because they feel that they are being forced against their will to comply, which is known as **psychological reactance**.

Obedience was studied by **Stanley Milgram** in a series of famous experiments. The basic paradigm was as follows: participants were led to believe that their job was to administer shocks of increasing intensity to another participant if that participant performed poorly on a given learning task. The other participant was actually a confederate, intentionally performing badly, so that the real participant would be obliged to administer shock. The confederate also acted as if the shocks were painful, pleading with the participant to stop. (In fact, no shocks were given.) The participant was instructed by the experimenter to continue the shocks, despite the obvious pain the "other participant" was enduring. You might think that you would not administer painful shocks in this paradigm, but a very high percentage of people did just that. Through additional studies, Milgram found that several factors were critical to whether or not the person would obey. The first was the perceived authority of the test administrator. For example, when the person overseeing the experiment introduced himself as a graduate student instead of as a scientist, the subject was much less likely to comply. Another factor was physical distance. If the subject was forced to sit in the room with the person receiving the shocks, his level of obedience dropped; the subject was also less likely to obey if the experimenter communicated the commands by phone instead of in person. Obedience also tended to go down if the subject was told that he was responsible for the outcome, if the subject witnessed someone else disobeying the experimenter, and if the experimenter instructed the subject to immediately apply a high level of voltage to the "learner." The major conclusion from this study was that people tended to be obedient to a figure of authority, but only if certain criteria were met. It also demonstrated that people are much less likely to obey when they feel that they have an ally in standing up to the pressure.

ATTITUDES AND ATTITUDE CHANGE

Attitudes are combinations of affective (emotional) and cognitive (perceptual) reactions to different stimuli. The affective component is the emotional response an item or issue arouses, whereas the cognitive component is what we think about the item or issue. Attitudes are acquired, in part, by vicarious conditioning. If, for example, we observe a person being bitten by a dog, we form an attitude about that dog. In this case, the affective component might be fear, and the cognitive component might be the understanding that this particular dog bites.

Cognitive dissonance occurs when attitudes and behaviors contradict each other. Generally, such tension is not pleasant, and people tend to change in order to achieve cognitive consistency. **Leon Festinger** studied this phenomenon and came to the conclusion that people are likely to alter their attitude to fit their behavior. For example, law-abiding citizens speed frequently. A cognitive conflict exists. Which is going to change—their attitude toward the law or their over-the-limit driving? Generally, people adjust their attitudes and continue their behavior. Cognitive dissonance tends to occur only when the person feels that he has a choice in the matter. If someone feels that he is being forced to speed, his attitude will remain intact.

Persuasion is the process by which a person or group can influence the attitudes of others. The efficacy of persuasion derives in part from the characteristics of the persuader. People who have positions of authority or who appear to be experts on a given topic are more likely to be viewed as persuasive. The motive of the persuader is also critical. If an author tries to convince you that authors are poor, and that you should donate five dollars to the poor authors' fund, you probably would not believe the author. Your disbelief would stem from your confidence that the author's motive is selfish. However, if an author asks for five dollars for disaster relief, you might be more likely to be persuaded because the motive seems more altruistic.

An additional factor affecting persuasive ability is interpersonal attractiveness. More attractive, likeable, trustworthy, and knowledgeable people are viewed as more persuasive. Most people are also swayed by the presentation of facts.

A: Interpersonal attraction may occur as a result of positive evaluation, shared opinions, good physical appearance, familiarity, or proximity.

Another factor influencing the persuasion process is the nature of the message. Repetition is an effective technique for achieving persuasion, which is why the same advertisements run so frequently. Fear is another motivator of attitudinal change. A prime example of the use of fear in persuasive attempts is the practice of putting cars wrecked in DWI (driving-while-intoxicated) accidents on display. The idea is that seeing the result of such an accident will induce an attitudinal change about drunk driving.

The **elaboration likelihood model** explains when people will be persuaded by the content of a message (or the logic of its arguments), and when people will be influenced by other, more superficial characteristics like the length of the message, or the appearance of the person delivering it. Because persuasion can be such a powerful means for influencing what people think and do, much research has gone into studying the various elements of a message that might have an impact on its persuasiveness.

The three key elements are message characteristics, source characteristics, and target characteristics.

1. The message characteristics are the features of the message itself, such as its logic and the number of key points in the argument. This category also includes more superficial things, such as the length and grammatical complexity.

2. The source characteristics of the person or group delivering the message, such as expertise, knowledge, and trustworthiness, are also of importance. People are much more likely to be persuaded by a major study described in the *New England Journal of Medicine* than by something in the pages of the local supermarket tabloid.

3. Finally, the target characteristics of the person receiving the message (such as self-esteem, intelligence, and mood) have an important influence on whether a message will be perceived as persuasive. For instance, some studies have suggested that those with higher intelligence are less easily persuaded by one-sided messages.

The two cognitive routes that persuasion follows under this model are the **central route** and the **peripheral route**. Under the central route, people are persuaded by the content of the argument. They ruminate over the key features of the argument and allow those features to influence their decision to change their point of view. The peripheral route functions when people focus on superficial or secondary characteristics of the speech or the orator. Under these circumstances, people are persuaded by the attractiveness of the orator, the length of the speech, whether the orator is considered an expert in his field, and other features. The elaboration likelihood model then argues that people will choose the central route only when they are both motivated to listen to the logic of the argument (they are interested in the topic) and they are not distracted, thus focusing their attention on the argument. If those conditions are not met, individuals will choose the peripheral route,

Marketing and Persuasion
Market researchers refer to the use of facts as the **central route to persuasion**.

and they will be persuaded by more superficial factors. Messages processed via the central route are more likely to have longer-lasting persuasive outcomes than messages processed via the peripheral route.

Finally, some people can be influenced to change their attitudes more easily than others. In general, people with high self-esteem are less easily persuaded than are those with low self-esteem. Thus, many hate groups recruit people who are considered outsiders or who have few friends. These people with low self-esteem are susceptible to having their attitudes on issues, such as race, changed to match those of the hate group.

ATTRACTION

While there are many factors that lead to attraction between individuals, there are three main factors: proximity, similarity, and physical attractiveness. It has been found in research that people who are in close proximity with each other are more likely to be attracted to one another. They are more often exposed to one another and therefore can more readily develop attraction. Proximity can also lead people to places of shared interest. These shared interests create similarities that the individuals have in common, and this also can lead to attraction. Finally, physical attractiveness is the most salient of the three components, but it is worth noting. While physical attractiveness is not the only component to attraction, it plays into internal social biases in society. The halo effect is a term that correlates physical attractiveness to other good traits that do not have anything to do with physicality. According to the halo effect, a person who is more physically attractive is often assumed to also be kind, honest, and caring.

ALTRUISM AND HELPING BEHAVIOR

Q: What is the bystander effect?

See answer on page 296.

Some psychologists are interested in **altruism** and **helping behavior**. Research into these topics emerged in part as a result of the case of Kitty Genovese, a woman who was murdered outside of her apartment complex. According to media reports, between 15 and 41 neighbors saw or heard part of the attack, but many did not intervene or contact the police. Psychologists refer to this failure to act as the **bystander effect**. It occurs as a result of **diffusion of responsibility**. Simply put, each person assumes that someone else will (or should) help or call the police.

Altruism can help reduce the tendency toward the bystander effect. Altruism is selfless sacrifice, and it occurs more frequently than it might appear. Altruism has been explained in terms of an empathic response to the plight of others. People place themselves in the position of others in distress, and they act toward others as they would like others to act toward them.

ORGANIZATIONAL PSYCHOLOGY

This area of social psychology deals primarily with the workplace. The **equity theory** proposes a view whereby workers evaluate their efforts versus their rewards. Job satisfaction is often based on this concept. **Human factors research** deals with the interaction of person and machine. Many job-related accidents are caused by design flaws in equipment related to the expectancy of the worker. The **Hawthorne effect** indicates that workers being monitored for any reason work more efficiently and productively. This was demonstrated in an experiment that took place in a Western Electric plant. The study was intended to test whether levels of light increased or decreased worker productivity. The outcome, however, showed that worker productivity increased at all levels of light simply because of the presence of the monitors.

AGGRESSION/ANTISOCIAL BEHAVIOR

Antisocial behavior, behavior that is harmful to society or others, can be divided roughly into two kinds: **prejudice** and **aggression**.

Prejudice is a negative attitude toward members of a particular group without evidentiary backing. Quite literally, prejudice is the result of prejudging members of a group. Note that bias and prejudice are not the same. Bias simply refers to a tendency or preference, and biases are not necessarily negative. Whereas prejudice refers to a belief, **discrimination** refers to an action. That is, discrimination involves treating members of a group differently from members of another group.

People tend to categorize things into groups based on common attributes. One theory of this phenomenon is that classification occurs when people compare new stimuli or people to preexisting prototypes in order to determine the group to which the novel stimuli belong. **Stereotypes** are prototypes of people. Although stereotypes can be useful for categorization, they can be harmful by leading us from incorrect assumptions to incorrect conclusions. One assumption we tend to make is **outgroup homogeneity**, that is, that every member of a group other than our own is similar. A false conclusion is **illusory correlation**, in which we tend to see relationships where they don't actually exist. An example of illusory correlation is noticing that people of a certain ethnic group are apprehended for crimes while ignoring that people of the same ethnic group also do positive things for the society.

Aggression is behavior directed toward another, with the intention of causing harm. Aggression occurs for multiple reasons. **Hostile aggression** is emotional and

The Contact Hypothesis

Attempts to understand how to reduce prejudice and stereotyping have included the **contact hypothesis**, which posits that groups with stereotypes about each other would lose these stereotypes if the groups were exposed to each other. This hypothesis has not been supported by data because contact can also serve merely to reinforce existing stereotypes. Factors such as the different social status of the two groups or a lack of common interests, may stand in the way of groups reducing stereotypes through contact. These factors are also illustrated in the Robbers Cave experiment, discussed previously.

impulsive, and it is typically induced by pain or stress. **Instrumental aggression**, in contrast, is aggression committed to gain something of value. For example, a child pushing another child on a playground to get a prized toy is an example of instrumental aggression.

Biological factors play a role in aggression in all species, including humans. Aggression is sensitive to hormonal fluctuations, particularly fluctuations of the androgen, testosterone, which increases aggressive tendencies. Steroid abusers, who use large quantities of synthetic hormones, may experience uncontrollable aggression.

As **Albert Bandura's** work has demonstrated, aggression has a strong learned component. If children see adults rewarded for aggression, it is likely that they will learn that aggression is an effective strategy for coping with problems. Additionally, pornography frequently depicts violence toward women. Again, vicarious learning theory tells us that watching pornographic films can lead to learning that might result in violence at a later time.

Environmental factors also can lead to aggression. Experiencing pain and being surrounded by aggressive behavior, discomfort, and frustration have all been shown to be possible causes of aggressive behavior. Additionally, we have the ability to view the victims of violence as somehow less than human, a process called **dehumanization**. This phenomenon was demonstrated in a study by **Philip Zimbardo,** which tested the effect of **role-playing** in the subject of obedience and conformity. In the experiment, he randomly selected participants to play "jailed" roles while others were randomly selected to act as guards. The prisoners had numbers, not names. The guards wore uniforms and mirrored glasses. Within a short period of time, the participants in each group began to act as though they hated the participants in the other group. The two groups, when stripped of their individual identity, turned to mob identity and violence. In effect, what started out as role-playing became serious identification with the roles. The experiment got out of hand and had to be stopped prematurely to preserve the participants' well-being.

Research on reducing aggression has identified some successful techniques. Punishment, which is frequently used as a treatment for aggression, is not particularly effective in reducing aggression. Rather, the observation of nonaggressive models of conflict resolution or the diffusion of aggression with humor or empathy are more effective at disrupting violent behavior.

A: The bystander effect asserts that the more people there are witnessing a crime, the less likely any one of them is to help the victim.

KEY TERMS

Identities and Groups

society
culture
social identity
personal identity
primary group
secondary group
in-group
out-group
intersectionality
culture shock
cultural lag
role
role conflict
role strain
role exit

Social Institutions

institutionalized discrimination
availability
accessibility
food desert

Attraction

attraction
the halo effect

Group Dynamics

social facilitation
social inhibition
social loafing
group polarization
GRIT (Graduated and
    Reciprocated Initiatives in
    Tension-Reduction)
Irving Janis
groupthink
mindguard

Attribution

dispositional attribution
situational attribution
self-serving bias
fundamental attribution error
self-fulfilling prophecy
Rosenthal Effect

Interpersonal Perception

interpersonal attraction
positive evaluation
shared opinions
mere exposure effect

Conformity, Compliance, Obedience

conformity
Solomon Asch
compliance
reciprocity
foot-in-the-door phenomenon
door-in-the-face phenomenon
inoculation hypothesis
psychological reactance
obedience
Stanley Milgram

Attitudes and Attitude Change

attitude
persuasion
central route to
    persuasion
elaboration likelihood model
central route
peripheral route
cognitive dissonance
Leon Festinger

Altruism and Helping Behavior
> altruism
> helping behavior
> bystander effect
> diffusion of responsibility

Organizational Psychology
> equity theory
> human factors research
> Hawthorne effect

Aggression/Antisocial Behavior
> prejudice
> aggression
> discrimination
> stereotypes
> outgroup homogeneity
> illusory correlation
> contact hypothesis
> hostile aggression
> instrumental aggression
> Albert Bandura
> dehumanization
> Philip Zimbardo
> role-playing

Chapter 18 Drill

See Chapter 19 for answers and explanations.

1. The "fundamental attribution error" phenomenon can best be seen in which of the following examples?

    (A) John blames his failure to get a job on his lack of appropriate skills and ill-preparedness.
    (B) Phyllis doesn't get the lead in the school play and blames her drama teacher for this failure.
    (C) Jane blames herself for forgetting that she has a term paper due in two days.
    (D) Bill doesn't hire John because he believes that John's lateness is a result of John's laziness and lack of respect for the job. In reality, John was late because he got a flat tire on the way to the interview.
    (E) Karen understands that her friend is late because she was caught in rush-hour traffic.

2. In the Asch conformity experiments, which of these was NOT a consistent factor influencing the degree to which conformity to the group answer would be shown by the experimental subject?

    (A) Unanimity of group opinion
    (B) Size of the group
    (C) The subject's perception of his/her social status compared with that of group members
    (D) Age of the subject
    (E) Gender of the subject

3. Students are randomly designated by experimenters as likely to experience significant jumps in academic test scores in the coming semester, and this designation is communicated to their teachers. When actual test scores are examined at the end of the semester, it is found that these randomly designated students did indeed tend to experience jumps in performance. This phenomenon is known as

    (A) the Hawthorne effect
    (B) the Kandel effect
    (C) cognitive dissonance
    (D) self-fulfilling prophecy
    (E) the Ainsworth effect

4. An old woman carrying a number of packages trips and falls on a busy urban sidewalk and is having trouble getting back up. The fact that few people are likely to stop and offer her help is referred to by social psychologists as an example of

    (A) illusory correlation
    (B) diffusion of responsibility
    (C) cognitive dissonance
    (D) altruistic orientation
    (E) just-world hypothesis

5. Which of the following would illustrate the "foot-in-the-door" technique of facilitating compliance with a request?

    (A) A professional fundraiser, needing to get $10,000 from a foundation, first requests four times that amount, expecting to be turned down so that she can then ask for the lesser amount.
    (B) A teenager, wanting to extend his curfew from 10:00 P.M. to midnight, first asks if it can be extended to 11:00 P.M. for a specific "special" occasion; he then plans to ask for the further extension at a later date after pointing out to his parents he was able to handle the 11:00 P.M. curfew.
    (C) A mother wishing to get her twins to do their homework each day upon coming home from school and before other activities tells each of them separately that the other twin has agreed to do just that.
    (D) An interviewee desperately needing to get a new job researches the mode of dress in each company he lands an interview with and always shows up at the meeting in that exact mode of dress.
    (E) A teacher wishing all her students to get their assignments in on time promises her class extra grading points for turning them in early.

6. According to Attribution Theory, which of the following is an example of the self-serving bias?

(A) A man does not have health insurance, but is not worried because he is young and healthy.

(B) A woman knows a man who does not have insurance. That man gets into a car accident, and medical expenses cause him to lose his home. She wonders why he didn't have insurance.

(C) A toddler builds a tall tower with blocks and says "Me good!" when she completes the tower. However, she bumps it and it falls down. She frowns and says, "Bad blocks!"

(D) Yuan's teacher believes he is well prepared for his history exam and offers encouragement to him as he approaches the final. Yuan continues to study hard for the exam and gets an A on the final.

(E) A hurricane devastates an area of Mississippi and many residents seek grief counseling.

7. A group of five students and a group of three students, all roughly the same size and strength, engage in a game of tug of war. The game is equal for a long while, neither side immediately gaining an advantage. This is most likely an example of

(A) social loafing
(B) dehumanization
(C) conformity
(D) group polarization
(E) social facilitation

8. A child tries to get a raise on his weekly allowance. When he first approaches his parents, he asks for $100 per week. His parents scoff and tell him this is out of the question. Then, he asks for $50 per week, and receives the same reply. Finally, he asks for $10 per week and his parents agree. This is an example of

(A) foot-in-the-door phenomenon
(B) central route of persuasion
(C) peripheral route of persuasion
(D) door-in-the-face phenomenon
(E) elaboration likelihood model

9. Stanley Milgram's study involving the "teacher," "learner," and "experimenter" tested which of the following principles?

(A) Conformity
(B) Dehumanization
(C) Groupthink
(D) Role-playing
(E) Obedience

10. Albert Bandura's famous Bobo Doll experiment shows the power of

(A) observation
(B) conformity
(C) hostile aggression
(D) dehumanization
(E) instrumental aggression

REFLECT

Respond to the following questions:

- Which topics in this chapter do you hope to see on the multiple-choice section or essay?

- Which topics in this chapter do you hope not to see on the multiple-choice section or essay?

- Regarding any psychologists mentioned, can you pair the psychologists with their contributions to the field? Did they contribute significant experiments, theories, or both?

- Regarding any theories mentioned, can you distinguish between differing theories well enough to recognize them on the multiple-choice section? Can you distinguish them well enough to write a fluent essay on them?

- Regarding any figures given, if you were given a labeled figure from within this chapter, would you be able to give the significance of each part of the figure?

- Can you define the key terms at the end of the chapter?

- Which parts of the chapter will you review?

- Will you seek further help, outside of this book (such as a teacher, Princeton Review tutor, or AP Students), on any of the content in this chapter—and, if so, on what content?

Chapter 19
Chapter Drills:
Answers and
Explanations

CHAPTER 1

Understand the Question/Key Words Drill

3. What's a scientist who's into the (physical basis) of (psychological phenomena) called?

10. One of the (primary tools) of the school of (structuralism) was

18. Binocular cues help you see (depth) because

35. What type of effect is this: person (only remembers) words from the (beginning and end) of a list?

47. The (recognition-by-components) theory asserts that we categorize objects by breaking them down into their component parts and then

   We break stuff down and then do what?

56. The fact that V. can (ignore) the crowd is called what?

70. Which of the following was (true) of Stanley (Milgram's studies of obedience?)

88. In their discussions of the (process of development,) the advocates of (the importance of nurture) in the (nature-nurture controversy) emphasize which of the following?

   Nurture emphasizes what?

Easy Questions Drill

1. Understand the Question/Key Words:
   Predict the Answer:
   Answer:

   Freud = which perspective?
   Psychoanalytic
   (B) Easy enough.

2. Understand the Question/Key Words:
   Predict the Answer:
   Answer:

   When you stop using a drug, you go through what?
   Withdrawal
   (C) Be careful not to rush through and accidentally pick another answer.

3. Understand the Question/Key Words: Conditioning: when the dog salivates at what?
   Predict the Answer: The light without the food
   Answer: **(B)** Watch for (A) and (C). Both are wrong, but close enough to trip up someone who is rushing. If you picked (D) or (E), better hit the books.

4. Understand the Question/Key Words: Circle *basic unit* and *nervous system*.
   Predict the Answer: Neuron
   Answer: **(D)** Watch out for the others—they are all parts of the neuron.

5. Understand the Question/Key Words: Circle *methods of research* and *central to behaviorist*.
   Predict the Answer: Experimenting
   Answer: **(E)** Again, if you don't know, start reviewing. POE should easily get rid of (B), (C), and (D).

Medium Questions Drill

33. Understand the Question/Key Words: What regulates hunger and thirst?
    Predict the Answer: I'm not sure, but I know what it's not (use POE).
    Answer: **(C)** Using POE, you should have been able to get rid of at least (D) and (E), and most likely (A) (review Chapter 12).

34. Understand the Question/Key Words: Which psychologists were into viewing things as part of a whole?
    Predict the Answer: Don't remember, but I know all the main perspectives well (use POE).
    Answer: **(D)** If you know your perspectives well, you could easily have gotten rid of at least (A), (B), and (C). Cognitive socialist doesn't make sense, so the answer must be (D).

35. Understand the Question/Key Words: What's wrong with the study: Survey comp sci class to find out who in the school has computers.
    Predict the Answer: The sample is biased.
    Answer: **(B)** It's the closest answer to yours. Use POE for the rest.

36. Understand the Question/Key Words: Looking out the window stimulates which two parts of the brain?
    Predict the Answer: Occipital and another (use POE)
    Answer: **(E)** Knowing occipital gets it down to two answer choices. If you don't know it from there, guess and move on (review Chapter 7).

37. Understand the Question/Key Words: Circle *behaviorism* and *true of.*
    Predict the Answer: Experimenting, everything is learned, consequences
    Answer: **(C)** It's the closest answer to yours. Choice (A) is psychodynamic, (B) is a sort of cognitive behaviorism, (D) is wrong, and (E) is silly.

CHAPTER 2

Put It All Together

Our Sample Essay

Stress can have serious psychological and physiological consequences. Although one cannot completely avoid stress, it is essential to our health and well-being that we learn effective coping strategies to better manage stress. Many things in our lives are very stress-inducing. These stressors can range from major life-changing events such as marriage, divorce, moving, or the death of a loved one to simple daily hassles like traffic or family arguments.

From a physiological standpoint, when an individual is stressed, the sympathetic nervous system responds with readiness for "fight or flight." In normal circumstances, this elevated level of stimulation abates when the perceived danger disappears. But what if it doesn't disappear? Then, the body does allow some systems to return to normal—breathing, heart rate—but other systems remain at the ready—elevated levels of sugar and adrenaline in the blood, for example. The greatest danger of prolonged exposure to stress, according to Hans Selye's general adaptation syndrome, is that the strain placed on the body, coupled with elevated hormone levels caused by stress reactions, can lead to cardiovascular disease and can weaken a person's immunity to disease.

From a psychological standpoint, stress represents a challenge to the way that we think and the way that we behave. It is very easy, when struggling with major and minor stresses, to feel defeated or overwhelmed by what it might take to overcome the challenge. Stress is more than just the occurrence of a stressful event. It is also an individual's vulnerability to stress and, according to Richard Lazarus, the importance of the stressful event to the individual. For example, the death of a grandparent can be a highly stressful occurrence. However, if the death occurs after a long illness, it may be more of a relief.

There are three main types of events that contribute to stress in an individual's life: daily hassles, life events, and catastrophes. Daily hassles typically have a low level of personal importance, yet individuals may still react strongly to these minor stressors if they are, at the time, highly vulnerable to stress. If a person already endured a great deal of stress that day, new stress becomes, in a sense, cumulative, serving to increase already present physiological stress responses.

A life event is any event that requires change and adaptation. Again, the level of importance and the vulnerability of the person will impact the amount of stress the person experiences. Many people experience extreme physiological reactions to life events such as the death of a spouse. They may be unable to eat or sleep, most likely because the body is in this state of pseudo-alertness.

Finally, catastrophes—rare, unexpected disasters such as earthquakes or floods—can lead to physiological stress responses such as post-traumatic stress disorder (for example, nightmares or flashbacks about a past catastrophe). Most individuals tend to experience some degree of stress response to catastrophes, because the events are often so extreme and overwhelming.

To deal with a stressful event such as a catastrophe, many people unconsciously employ a coping strategy such as denial or repression. Denial, not accepting that a catastrophe has actually occurred, is one way that individuals stave off the full impact of what has just happened. Some theorize that having the knowledge of an event such as a catastrophe and denying it allows the body to gradually process the stress that it could not handle all at once.

Repression, the ability of the mind to keep anxiety-producing thoughts in the subconscious, allows individuals to attempt to deal with a catastrophic situation without thinking through the many horrifying ramifications. As a means of coping, repression often allows individuals to function, whereas full awareness might impede their ability to respond as needed.

In conclusion, the body and mind are an amazing team—working together they are able to cope with difficult and stressful situations while still functioning. However, in a society wrought with stress, it is possible that individuals may lose this adaptive strength, breaking down under the "stress" of a constant need to cope with stress.

CHAPTER 4

Drill 1: Understand the Question/Key Words

7. Psychoanalytic vs. behaviorist: How are they different?

22. What technology should you use to look at different regions of the brain?

39. The (somatosensory cortex) is the (primary) area of the

    The circled words mean what?

58. To know what a picture is, the info has to get to which part of the brain?
    (Answer: occipital lobe)

78. What's it called when someone doesn't give false positives—if there is no sound, there is no report?

89. The (lower) the (p-value) of a study, the
    Lower p-value means what?

Drill 2: Predict the Answer

5. How will Thomas learn to make a big meal using the stuff he knows?

   He can link together what he knows (called chaining, if you remember that).

22. What does the endocrine system do?

   It secretes hormones into the body.

35. What big thing did Wilhelm Wundt do for psychology?

    He created the first psychology lab in 1879, and he is considered the father of experimental psychology.

45. Why do taste buds need to be able to replace themselves?

    Otherwise, if you burned your mouth, you would lose your sense of taste forever.

72. What technology should you use to study brain waves?

    Electrosomething...(Electroencephalogram or EEG, if you remember)

Drill 3: Using All Three

15. Of the following (variables,) which typically requires a measurement that is more complex?

Understand the Question/Key Words:	Which variable requires more complex measurement?
Predict the Answer:	The complex one—not categorical.
Answer:	**(B) It's continuous.** Choice (A) is out, (C) doesn't make sense, and (D) and (E) aren't those kinds of variables.

35. Which of the following most accurately states the role of the (iris)?

Understand the Question/Key Words:	What does the iris do?
Predict the Answer:	It opens and closes the pupil (controls amount of light, if you remember).
Answer:	**(B) It says to open and close the iris and regulate the entrance of light.** Choice (A) is way off. Be careful of (C)— the iris does not project light onto the retina. Choices (D) and (E) are not true and not close to your answer.

42. The nature-nurture controversy concerns

Understand the Question/Key Words:	Which is more important: genes or environment?
Predict the Answer:	Inborn and external processes determine behavior.
Answer:	**(C) It's the closest to yours: "inborn processes" (genes) and "external stimuli" environment.** Be careful of (A): it is a similar idea, but not the same. Choice (B) is way off base, (D) is a silly trap answer (using the words *natural* and *nurture* to lure you), and (E) doesn't answer the question at all.

66. Prior to the fall of the Berlin wall, East Berlin schools de-emphasized the (individuality) of the student. As a result, many of the children from those schools tend to have a(n)

Understand the Question/Key Words:	What happens if kids are taught to not be individuals?
Predict the Answer:	They depend on others for their self-identity and self-esteem.
Answer:	**(D) They have an external locus of control— looking to others for their self-esteem and self-identity.** Choices (A) and (B) are not close to yours (no optimism, pessimism). Choice (C) is the opposite of what you want, and (E) is just filler.

85. A (prototypic example) of a (category) is called a(n)

Understand the Question/Key Words:	A major example of something is called what?
Predict the Answer:	I don't know—a major example.
Answer:	**(E) Exemplar—a major example.** Choice (A) does not mean a major example. Choice (B) is only a feature, not an example of the whole category. Choice (C) is weak. Don't pick (D)! It's a verbal trap.

Drill 4: Essay Drill

Here Is Our Work It, Chart It, Count It, and Sketch It:

1. One of the major approaches to learning is classical conditioning.

   A. (Explain) the <u>process of classical conditioning</u>, (defining and illustrating) all necessary terms. Show how

   classical conditioning could be used to

   (1) Condition a monkey to "appreciate" only the works of certain artists

   (2) Teach a group of students a mathematical concept

D and I	Do It
UCS, CS, UCR, CR, and so on. Use Pavlov ex. and create another.	Reward for id-ing Monet, none for Munch. Teach writing out proofs by rewarding through examples.

B. Explain how both (extinction) and (spontaneous recovery) transpire. Use (one) of the above examples to illustrate.

Define	Illustrate How
extinction—loss of learning because of no reinforcement	Substitute teacher so no reward for detailed proofs.
Spon rec.—comes back instantly with reward	Students stop. Return of teacher, spontaneous rec.

Opening
4 points
1.   CS   Pavlov example
2.   UCS
3.   CR
4.   UCR

---

2 points: Monkeys
5.   Use the right terms
6.   Set up the conditioning

---

2 points: Math class
7.   Use the right terms
8.   Set up the conditioning

---

2 points:
9.   Define Extinction and Spontaneous recovery
10.   Use class example with substitute teacher
Closing

Drill 5: POE

4. **B** Can obese people have *fewer* fat cells than average-weight people?

27. **B** Your key word from the question is "connectionist approaches." Would connectionists think things occurred in individual segments or in a bunch of networks simultaneously?

47. **A** Your key word is "chunking." Even if you don't remember this memory technique, (A) sounds more like chunking than (B).

85. **C** Your key word is "person-centered psychotherapy." Even without that clue, suppressing negative feelings of a client or using a didactic approach are not typically the chosen methods of most psychotherapists.

92. **B** Even without a clue, it's understood in the field of psychology that counselors do not do either (A) or (C) for clients.

CHAPTER 5 DRILL

1. **D** A cognitive psychologist is primarily interested in thought processes and products, and (D), involving word association, is most directly connected to such processes and products. Choice (A) is more the province of biological psychologists, (B) that of humanistic psychotherapists, (C) of clinical psychotherapists or behaviorists, and (E) is more of interest to developmental psychologists.

2. **C** The idea of *tabula rasa* is most closely associated with the philosopher John Locke. Choice (A), David Hume, is a philosopher who speculated on the nature of knowledge and perception; (B), Charles Darwin, is more closely identified with the theory of natural selection and evolution of species; (D), Sigmund Freud, was the founder of psychoanalytic theory; and (E), Erich Fromm, was one of the theorists influenced by Freud.

3. **B** The concept of dualism refers to the division of the world and all things in it into two parts: body and spirit. Choice (C) refers to two ways of conceptualizing the structure and function of the mind and (E) to two different types of experimental variables.

4. **D** Humanistic psychologists are primarily concerned with the impact of free will on behavior. Choice (A), the stress on childhood experiences, is emphasized in the psychoanalytic approach. Choice (B), the importance of biological predispositions, refers to either the biological/medical model or the behavioral-genetics approach. Choice (C), the cognitive approach, focuses on how maladaptive thoughts can influence behavior, and (E), the social-cognitive approach, centers on the interaction of culture and behavior.

5. **C** Proponents of the psychoanalytic or psychodynamic approach believe that the source of all current trauma can be traced back to childhood repressed memories. Choice (A), the cognitive approach, stresses the importance of thought processes and schemas in evaluating behaviors. Choice (B), behaviorists, believe in the power of learning and other environmental influences on behavior. Choice (D), the social cultural perspective, focuses instead on the culture of individuals and how it

shapes them into who they are; (E), the medical/biological approach, seeks physiological answers in brain and body chemistry to explain behavior.

6. **B** Circle the key words *behavior* and *learned*. These words indicate that the answer is associated with behaviorism. The person synonymous with behaviorism is B.F. Skinner, (B).

7. **E** First, eliminate anything that is not a defense mechanism: self-actualization, (B), and consciousness, (D). Because denial is a state that dismisses an event as unimportant or trivial and not that the individual does not remember what happened, you can eliminate (A). Projection is placing one's problems onto someone else's actions or emotions. This is not the case in this situation, so cross-out (C). The answer choice left is repression, (E), the correct answer; repression is a defense mechanism in which the subconscious keeps painful memories from surfacing.

8. **C** Carl Rogers is one of the major players in the humanistic approach to psychology. He coined the term *unconditional positive regard* toward his patients, always viewing them in a positive light. However, this is not a psychological approach. Cognitive psychology is focused on cognition and thought processes. While maladaptive thoughts are part of treating the whole person, it is not the only component of what makes up a person, so eliminate (B). The sociocultural components of a person are also another component of an individual's experience, but Carl Rogers sought to treat the individual rather than systemic problems. The correct answer is (C), since behaviorism is associated with B.F. Skinner.

9. **E** According to Maslow's hierarchy of needs, the physiological needs of a person, such as the need for food and water, are at the base of the pyramid. Maslow suggested that if a person cannot have these basic needs satisfied, it is much more difficult to accomplish a sense of belonging, esteem, and potentially self-actualization.

10. **A** Many credit Wilhelm Wundt with discovering the field of psychology in Leipzig, Germany. He opened a laboratory to study consciousness in 1879, and many credit this as the beginning of the field of psychology.

CHAPTER 6 DRILL

1. **D** By definition, a double-blind experimental design is one in which neither the researchers nor the experimental subjects know whether the subjects have been assigned to an experimental group or a control group; this is done to minimize the chance that either the researchers or the subjects will influence the results through their own expectations (researchers) or by trying to act in accordance with what is thought to be desired (subjects). Choice (B) describes a single-blind experimental design; (E) is completely nonsensical.

2. **B** In a normal statistical curve, about 68 percent of all scores will fall within one standard deviation of the mean; this includes scores both above and below the mean. Choice (A) is the percentage that would occur between the mean and one standard deviation above it only; (C) is the percentage that would occur within two standard deviations of the mean.

3. **B**   This is the definition of a Type II error—concluding there is no difference when in fact there is a difference. Choice (A) is the definition of a Type I error. Choice (E) is an erroneous conclusion drawn when, in fact, a Type I error has been made.

4. **C**   All of the other answers are standard tenets for designing and carrying out ethically acceptable research. Choice (C) has nothing to do with ethics, though it would not be very good for the research design in another way—if both the subjects and the researchers knew which of the former would be part of the experimental group, there would be a great likelihood of expectancy effects confounding the study.

5. **B**   A correlation of –0.84 implies that as one variable increases, the other is likely to decrease—positive correlations indicate that two variables vary directly, while negative correlations indicate that two variables vary inversely. Remember the famous research statement, "correlation does not imply causation," and you'll know that neither (D) nor (E) is correct.

6. **C**   The behavior of the subjects is measured here as the outcome of the study. The control and independent variables in this study are the violent vs. nonviolent videogames and the behavior supposedly "depends" on which games were played. Therefore, the behavior of the subjects is the dependent variable, (C). Of course, there are most likely some confounding variables and possibly some sampling bias in this study, but the behavior must be classified as the dependent variable. Perhaps all the subjects were young teens, or that some participants signed up because they enjoy playing videogames. These would be examples of confounding variables.

7. **D**   A categorical variable is one that cannot be measured. Hair color, gender, school attended, and dog breed are all variables that cannot be measured, so they are examples of categorical variables. Height can be measured, so it is not a categorical variable.

8. **D**   Circle the key words here: *different regions* and *socioeconomic statuses*. Since the study seeks to look at different backgrounds and regions of the country, they are seeking to measure a large cross-sectional population. Longitudinal studies measure the same subjects over a long period of time, and there is no lapse in time here, so eliminate (A). There is not enough information about the design of this study to know if it is experimental or not (most likely correlational), so eliminate (B) and (C), as well. Choice (E), a case study, studies only one subject or a few subjects at a time. This is not true of this study, so the correct answer is (D).

9. **E**   As you most likely noticed, there are many things wrong with this method of procuring subjects for a study. Eliminate (A) because there is a pre-screening or advertising bias with weight-loss studies. People who respond to this ad most likely already want to or are trying to lose weight. The answer cannot be (B) because the people inquiring about the ad have control over whether they participate in the study, so they are self-selecting. The selection bias is also present here because these ads are only in New York City buses and subways. Many people visit New York City, but this is not a representative area of the entire country, so there is a selection bias. Therefore, eliminate (C). The healthy user bias may or may not be as large of a factor here. However, potential subjects who already engage in a healthy lifestyle or in the process of losing weight can make this supplement look more effective than with an unhealthy subject. Eliminate (D). A representative bias is not a

real term. What any researcher hopes to have is a representative sample, which will most likely not happen by attracting subjects from a subway ad. Therefore, the correct answer is (E).

10. **B**   A normal curve for a bell curve is to have most of the data around the middle of a graph, creating a symmetrical bell shape. Since this is not the case, eliminate (C). If the peak of a bell curve is not centered but rather in the lower end of the chart, it is called a negative skew. If the curve sits to the right of the graph's center, it is a positive skew. The curve described here is a negative skew since many subjects scored low totals. The correct answer is (B).

CHAPTER 7 DRILL

1. **B**   Damage to Broca's area, which is on the left side on the frontal lobe of the cortex, controls the muscles of speech. Choice (A), repetition of the speech of others, is often referred to as echolalia. Choice (C), the loss of the ability to visually integrate information, or prosopagnosia, is often the result of damage to the occipital lobe. Choice (D), the loss of the ability to comprehend speech, refers to damage in the Wernicke's area of the temporal lobe, and (E), the inability to solve verbal problems, stems from some kind of damage to the left hemisphere.

2. **D**   The dendrites are attached to the cell body, and their purpose is to receive signals and information from other neurons, usually by receiving neurotransmitters; these signals will determine whether or not the neuron will "fire." Choice (A) is the function of the terminal buttons, (B) is that of the myelin sheaths, (C) is that of the cell body, and (E) is that of the axon hillock.

3. **C**   The cerebellum is the part of the brain most involved with maintaining balance and muscular strength and tone. Choice (A) is the part of the brain that controls heart rate, swallowing, breathing, and digestion; (B) is the part, in most people, that is specialized for spatial and intuitive processing; (D) are involved in processing visual input; and (E) is the brain's primary relay station for sensory information.

4. **C**   GABA is the neurotransmitter most associated with inhibitory neural processes; the others generally act to excite neurons further.

5. **A**   The phenotype is the actual observable trait or behavior that results from a specific genetic combination. Due to dominant and recessive trait expressions, the phenotype can represent more than one specific possible genotype, or genetic contribution, which (E) is talking about. Choice (C) is the definition of a gene itself.

6. **C**   The hypothalamus, part of the limbic system, controls motivated behaviors such as hunger, thirst, and sex. Choice (A), the thalamus, routes sensory information to the sensory areas of the brain; (B), the pons, connects the lower brain regions with the higher functioning areas of the brain. Choice (D), the amygdala, controls fear and aggression via the limbic system, and (E), the association areas of the brain, match existing information with incoming information already stored in the brain.

7. **B**   Myelin is an insulating sheath wrapped around the axons of neurons. White matter in the central nervous system is composed of myelinated axons; thus, a reduction in myelination would result in

a decrease in white matter and neuronal insulation—(A) and (E), as symptoms, can be eliminated. Gaps in the myelin sheath (called nodes of Ranvier) allow depolarization of the axon and conduction of neuronal signals along the length of the axon. Myelination speeds the movement of the action potential along the length of the axon in a process called saltatory conduction. Choice (C) would be a symptom and can be eliminated; a reduction in myelination would decrease (not increase) saltatory conduction (which makes (B) the correct answer choice). This would decrease sensation, as sensory information from the peripheral nervous system would be hindered from reaching the central nervous system. Choice (D) is a symptom and can be eliminated.

8. **D** The cerebellum, located behind the pons and below the cerebrum, receives input from the primary motor cortex in the forebrain and coordinates complex motor function, making (D) correct. The frontal lobes contain the primary motor cortices, which are responsible for initiating movement, but do not coordinate complex motor functions, so (A) is wrong. The occipital lobes are responsible for vision, ruling out (B), and the reticular activating system is responsible for arousal and wakefulness, which eliminates (C). The temporal lobes are involved in processing sensory input related to visual memories, language comprehension, and emotion, so it's not (E).

9. **D** The pons is located below the midbrain and above the medulla oblongata, and it connects the brain stem and the cerebellum. Along with the medulla, the pons controls some autonomic functions and plays a role in equilibrium and posture, but it is not associated with the experience of emotion, so (D) is correct. The amygdala, located in the temporal lobe, is part of the limbic system, and it is responsible for processing information about emotion, which means that (A) and (B), which are associated with emotion, can be eliminated. The amygdala and temporal lobe both send projections associated with the experience and regulation of emotional expression to the prefrontal cortices of the frontal lobe, and so (E) can be ruled out. The hypothalamus links the nervous system to the endocrine system, and it also plays a role in emotion, which allows (C) to be cut.

10. **C** The neuron starts at a resting potential, so eliminate (D) and (E). If the neuron reaches the threshold potential, it will depolarize during the action potential and then repolarize to regain stability. Eliminate (A), since hyperpolarization is in between depolarization and repolarization. During the refractory period, there is a period of hyperpolarization, a slight dip below the resting potential, before it returns to the resting potential. This eliminates (B), making (C) the correct answer.

CHAPTER 8 DRILL

1. **B** The specific pattern of brain waves known as sleep spindles is characteristic of stage 2 sleep, and it is associated with a relaxation of the skeletal musculature. Stage 1 sleep and REM sleep characteristically show the smaller, less regular theta waves, and stage 3 and 4 sleep are both more likely to show the longer, slower delta waves.

2. **B** Subliminal information is presented just below the threshold. This information is often referred to as imperceptible, yet it is believed to influence behavior. Choice (A), immediate recognition of

the stimuli, refers to the absolute threshold. Choice (C), the inability of the stimuli to be subject to the tip-of-the-tongue phenomenon, is another kind of preconscious processing, but the inability of a stimulus to be on the tip of the tongue would not be an indication of its presence. There is no evidence that there is proactive interference or that it is slower in a matched-pairs trial, so eliminate (D) and (E).

3. **C**   Though the natural day/night cycle of humans and most other organisms matches the 24-hour cycle of the Earth and Sun, if all cues (such as sunshine) are removed, humans and many other organisms tend to follow a free-running rhythm that cycles approximately every 25 hours, which can be demonstrated through varying body temperature and hormonal levels.

4. **E**   There is no evidence that there is any distinction between what kinds of concerns give rise to nightmares versus night terrors. The hypothesis that one of the functions of dreams is to express conscious or unconscious concerns has its roots in Freudian or psychoanalytic theory, and it is only one of a number of competing theories of dream function, none of which has yet proven conclusive. Choices (A), (B), (C), and (D) all represent characteristic differences between nightmares and night terrors.

5. **E**   Cocaine is a strong stimulant, not a narcotic. Narcotics, such as those mentioned in (A), (B), (C), and (D), are derived originally from the opium poppy and tend to have analgesic and relaxation effects that depress the central nervous system.

6. **A**   Alcohol is a depressant that inhibits neural activity, so eliminate (D). GABA receptors in the central nervous system respond to GABA, an inhibitory neurotransmitter. Alcohol acts on GABA receptors, inhibiting neuronal signaling. Chronic alcohol consumption causes a down-regulation of GABA receptors; therefore, once the artificial depressant (alcohol) is removed from the system, the CNS no longer has an inhibitory influence and excito-neurotoxicity occurs, which can result in seizures and tremors, so (A) is the answer. Alcohol is a depressant and does not stimulate the autonomic nervous system, so (B) cannot be correct. While alcohol consumption does promote dopamine release in the nucleus accumbens (which stimulates the reward pathway in the brain and helps to explain why alcohol is addictive), and cessation of alcohol consumption would surely lead to a decrease in dopamine; this does not explain the physical symptoms of withdrawal described in the question stem, ruling out (C). While alcohol is a depressant, decreasing GABA activity would be excitatory, not inhibitory. Furthermore, this explanation would not account for the symptoms seen in alcohol withdrawal, and so (E) can be eliminated.

7. **B**   The doctor needs to ask more questions before diagnosing the patient, but his or her first thought should be insomnia or sleep apnea. None of the other terms listed in the answer choices constitutes periods of wakefulness during the night. Narcolepsy is overwhelming periods of sleep needed during the day. Somnambulism and night terrors happen during sleep, so even though the person seems to be active, they would not report being awake, eliminating (C) and (E). Paradoxical sleep occurs during dreaming, so eliminate (D). The correct answer is (B), sleep apnea.

8. **C**   The question does not mention that the woman is in any state of psychological dependence or addiction, so eliminate (A) and (B). Her body has grown tolerant to the drug, as shown by her dosage being increased twice, but that is not the reason for this increase in her blood pressure.

Diuretics are one class of hypertension medications, but again, this does not account for her blood pressure increase. You can cross out (D) and (E). The clear reason for this increase is that she forgets to take her medication, and the physical symptom that results is an example of physical dependence, choice (C).

9. **E** Paradoxical sleep occurs during dreaming. The mind is active, but the paradox is when the body remains almost still. REM sleep represents this sleep state.

10. **A** Stages 3 and 4 are the deepest stages of sleep and, over the course of the night, the cycles contain less and less of them until the cycles contain mostly REM. The REM period can last up to approximately an hour toward the morning hours. The correct answer is (A).

CHAPTER 9 DRILL

1. **C** If the individual hits the button to indicate that he has seen a particular stimulus when it was not present, this is called a false alarm.

2. **B** Choice (B) is the only one that contains the five basic taste sensations—bitter, salty, sweet, sour, and umami; relative combinations of these result in the full range of taste sensations. Choice (C) refers to types of touch sensations and (D) to the five basic food groups!

3. **D** Know your retinal receptor cells; the rods are sensitive to low light conditions and to movement, while the cones are responsible for color vision and work best at higher illumination levels. Choice (A) contains two other types of cells found in the retina, but not the ones that make the distinction noted here. The same is true of the ganglion cells, (B), and osmoreceptors sense thirst, anyway. In (E), mechanoreceptors sense physical touch and ossicles are bones of the middle ear.

4. **C** Among the Gestalt principles of perception, continuity refers to our tendency to perceive fluid or continuous forms preferentially, rather than jagged or irregular ones—we would tend to see an image as two lines that "cross" at a point, rather than as two angles sharing a vertex. Choices (A) and (D) are two other Gestalt perceptual principles—proximity and similarity, respectively, and (E) refers to binocular disparity, a depth perception cue.

5. **A** Weber's law relates to the issue of thresholds in sensation and perception. The law states that stimuli need to vary by a constant proportion if we are to distinguish among the stimuli. Recognition of an imperceptible amount of perfume, (B), relates to the issue of absolute threshold. People not attending to more than one stimulus at a time, (C), focuses on selective attention. The ability to tell the difference between 20- and 100-watt bulbs 50 percent of the time refers again to the absolute threshold. All auditory stimuli being the same above a certain frequency, (E), negates frequency theory in audition.

6. **B** The tympanic membrane (also known as the eardrum), located in the middle ear, generates vibrations that match the sound waves striking it, so (B) is correct. Vibrations generated in the tympanic membrane pass through three small bones—the malleus (hammer), the incus (anvil), and the stapes (stirrup); these bones magnify the incoming vibrations by focusing them onto a

structure known as the oval window, which means that (D) and (E) are wrong. Once the vibrations pass through the oval window, they enter the cochlea, a fluid-filled spiral structure in the inner ear, so (C) can be eliminated. The base of the cochlea is lined with a long, fluid-filled duct known as the basilar membrane, which rules out (A). Sound waves passing along the basilar membrane cause it to move up and down, stimulating hair cells in the organ of Corti. These hair cells, in turn, connect with the acoustic, or auditory nerve.

7. **C** The axons of ganglion cells in the retina make up the optic nerve, which carries visual information to the brain, so (C) is correct. Photoreceptors such as rods and cones are specialized cells in the retina that transduce light energy into nerve cell activity and synapse with bipolar cells, but none of those are a part of the optic nerve, which rules out (A), (B), and (E). The fovea is the area of highest visual acuity and contains a high concentration of cones, which are a type of photoreceptor and do not comprise the optic nerve, thereby eliminating (D).

8. **A** Gestalt psychology proposes that humans tend to see objects in their entirety, and our visual processing systems and brain will superimpose a larger organization or structure that makes holistic sense. The "shapes" are technically composed of a series of unconnected lines, but according to Gestalt psychologists, humans are more likely to use both top-down and bottom-up processing to perceive them as a complete circle or a complete rectangle, so (A) is the answer. Bottom-up processing begins with the sensory receptors and works up to the complex integration of information occurring in the brain; while bottom-up processing is a requirement of perceiving the lines in the figure, it does not explain why we see two shapes instead of perceiving many unconnected lines, which makes (B) incorrect. Parallel processing refers to the brain's capability to process multiple sensory inputs simultaneously, and Weber's law explains how much two stimuli must differ in order for their difference to be perceptible; neither accounts for the phenomenon described in the question stem, and so (C) and (D) are both wrong. Summation, also referred to as frequency summation, is related to neuronal signal conduction, when the combined polysynaptic potential of multiple excitatory and inhibitory neurotransmitters determines whether or not an action potential is generated, thereby eliminating (E).

9. **D** Oddly enough, there is not a triangle drawn, but Claire reports seeing a triangle because people have a natural tendency to want to see closed figures as opposed to incomplete figures. This supports the law of closure. She could have said she sees three incomplete concentric discs, but her mind configured it in a way that organizes the information as a closed, complete figure.

10. **B** When Laretta sits down in class and eventually forgets about the odor, this is known as habituation. However, when the stimulus is removed and then re-presented (e.g., when she leaves the class and returns to notice the smell again), this is known as dishabituation. The correct answer is (B).

CHAPTER 10 DRILL

1. **B** The fact that the dog is now exhibiting a fear response to any moving, wheeled vehicle represents a stimulus generalization. Choice (A) is the opposite process—if the dog was originally struck by a blue van of a certain make, for example, and did not show a fear response to any vehicle but that type of blue van. Choice (C) refers to the process whereby a conditioned response was made extinct by removing a conditioned stimulus, but might be elicited by a presentation of that stimulus at a later time. Choice (D), backward conditioning, occurs when an unconditioned stimulus is presented before a conditioned one and has nothing to do with this situation.

2. **D** Second-order conditioning occurs when a previously conditioned stimulus—originally neutral, but now response-eliciting—acts as an unconditioned stimulus and is paired with a new neutral stimulus to be conditioned; eventually, this second stimulus is successful at eliciting a conditioned response. In (D), the rabbit was conditioned to fear the musical tone; then the musical tone was paired with a flashed light; and eventually the flashed light elicited fear even in the absence of the tone. Choice (A) is an example of conditioned taste aversion; (B) is a simple classic conditioning paradigm; (C) is stimulus generalization; and (E), which may be a result of social learning, does not apply to this situation.

3. **C** A variable-ratio reinforcement schedule is one in which the ratio of responses to reward is variable and therefore unpredictable. Although the original conditioning may take longer, the response is quite resistant to extinction. In a fixed-ratio schedule (A), rewards always come after a certain number of correct responses; learning is quick but so is extinction, as it is easy to determine when the reinforcement schedule is no longer operative. This can also be said for (E), a continuous schedule. Choice (B), fixed-interval schedules, with rewards presented after a set time period, have a similar learning/extinction profile to fixed-ratio schedules. Choice (D), variable-interval schedules, with rewards presented at variable time periods, are more resistant to extinction than fixed-interval schedules but not as resistant as variable-ratio schedules.

4. **A** The number of neurons does not increase with learning; in fact, the number of neurons is at its highest for most animals at birth—neurons do not reproduce under normal circumstances. However, they do grow in size and number of connections, alter the strength of already existing connections, and produce higher levels of neurotransmitters as a response to learning. Neurons that wire together, fire together.

5. **A** Though there are many social or observational learning situations that involve rewards or punishments, Bandura's experiments showed that such learning can occur even if there were no rewards or punishments—that is, consequences—to the observed behaviors. According to Bandura, attention to the behavior, retention of it, the ability to reproduce it, and the motivation to reproduce it at some point are what is necessary for observational learning.

6. **B** Operant conditioning is accomplished when someone receives a reward after performing a task; after the person has performed the task and received the reward enough times, they will perform the task without the reward, as (B) asserts. Choice (A), vicarious reinforcement, involves watching another person receive a reward for his or her behavior; there is no mention of Jay being motived by other people getting rewarded. Choice (C), an innate behavior, is one that does not need to be

conditioned and therefore not what is being described in the question stem. Choice (D), classical conditioning, is accomplished by pairing two stimuli, one that is neutral with another that is unconditioned. Over time, the neutral stimulus becomes the conditioned stimulus. Because the question is not describing the pairing of two stimuli, nor is a stimulus presented before the behavior, classical conditioning does not explain the behavior described in the question stem. Choice (E), observational learning, involves the observation of a behavior or set of behaviors and a subsequent modification of behavior on the part of the observer in modeling what they've seen.

7. **B** Negative reinforcement occurs when an unpleasant stimulus is removed. Remember, negative is equivalent to taking something away from a situation and positive is equivalent to adding something in reinforcement terms. Choice (A) describes negative punishment, since Stephanie's weekend privileges are revoked for the next weekend. Choice (B) works because the negative stimulus, taking out the trash, is removed for doing something positive. In (C), Ben receives positive reinforcement because he is rewarded with a pleasant stimulus for having done good work on his project. Choice (D) is another example of negative reinforcement because the dog does an undesirable behavior and the owner removes himself from contact. Choice (E) introduces something unpleasant to the situation, an example of positive punishment. The correct answer is (B).

8. **B** The care team does not want the patient to develop a taste aversion to food staples or favorite foods. The unconditioned stimulus in this case would be the chemotherapy, but the patient would likely associate the foods (a neutral stimulus) with the nausea. While stimulus generalization is part of the concept of taste aversion, the care team is trying to keep the association from occurring in the first place, not that it become generalized before the connection is in place.

9. **A** When dealing with periods of time, always think of "interval" to decipher reinforcement schedules. For number of instances, think "ratio." In this scenario, the mail comes consistently at the same time every day, so it must be an interval schedule, eliminating (C) and (D). Choice (E) is incorrect because continual reinforcement is a reward for every single instance, and she doesn't receive mail every time she goes to the mailbox. Since the time interval between mail deliveries is consistent, this is a fixed-interval schedule. The correct answer is (A).

10. **D** The process of teaching a skill through gradually molding specific behavior is called shaping, (D). Kevin rewards the dog for accomplishing intermediate steps along the way, which shapes Muka's behavior to learn a new trick.

CHAPTER 11 DRILL

1. **B** Visual sensory memory is referred to as *iconic*, and auditory sensory memory is called *echoic*. Iconic memory has a shorter duration than auditory memory, making (A) inaccurate. Visual and auditory memory have approximately the same capacity before encoding, so eliminate (C). The phone number read out loud (echoic) should have a longer duration than visually presented information, so eliminate (D). Choice (E) is wrong because if both auditory and visual information are presented at the same time, auditory information is more likely to be transferred to long-term memory.

2. **D** The principle of encoding specificity states that information is more likely to be recalled if the attempt to retrieve it occurs in a situation similar to the situation in which it was first encoded. Choice (A) refers to the process of new information pushing old information out of short-term memory; (B) to the grouping of items of information in order to better hold them in short-term memory; (C) to organizing short-term memory items in order to transfer them to long-term memory; and (E) to the memory for motoric skills and habits.

3. **E** Prosody is the term given to the tones and inflections added to language that elaborate meaning with no word alterations. Choice (A), syntax, refers to the set of rules in a language for arranging meaningful sounds into words; (B) is one step further up from syntax—the rules that govern the arrangement and formation of words into meaningful phrases and sentences; (C) indicates the smallest units of speech sounds in a language that are still distinct from one another; and (D) refers to the meaning of chosen words, not their expressed tone.

4. **C** Telegraphic speech is a common occurrence in toddlers who are combining words for the first time; it consists of two- or three-word utterances that are composed mostly of salient nouns, verbs, and adjectives with an absence of articles, conjunctions, and prepositions, and a limited use of pronouns. All of the answers except (C) involve two- or three-word utterances that fit that definition; (C) is an example of a holophrase—a single-word utterance of younger children that has a broad meaning.

5. **A** Divergent thinking is the name we give to the problem-solving process used when there are many possible solutions. In contrast, (B) is the process used when the problem has only one solution, such as is the case with most math equations. The intelligence quotient of (C) was originally conceived of as a ratio of mental age over chronological age, multiplied by 100; this was determined by comparing performance to that of others over a range of problem-solving tasks, which might involve both divergent and convergent abilities.

6. **C** This type of knowledge is a fact to be recalled, so it must be part of the explicit memory. Eliminate (A), (B), and (E). Episodic memory refers to memories the person has experienced, and semantic memory is the memory of facts and figures (remember, semantic is meaning-making). No one living today was around to experience Abraham Lincoln's presidency, so it cannot be episodic. The fact is, instead, semantic. The correct answer is (C).

7. **A** Stefano's knowledge of Spanish is interfering with his effort to speak German. In other words, his prior knowledge is hindering his ability to retain new knowledge, so this is an example of proactive interference.

8. **B** Ben cannot get past this physics problem because he is approaching it the same way instead of thinking outside the box. This is known as a mental set, (B). Functional fixedness is a type of mental set; however, it is specifically concerning an object's intended use versus its other creative uses, so eliminate (A). A representativeness heuristic is a prototypical representation of an image or concept, so eliminate (C), and insight learning refers to having a "flash of insight" solving a problem all at once. The question does not state that Ben has solved the problem, so eliminate (D). Framing involves false memories, so eliminate (E), as well. The correct answer is (B).

9. **A** A representativeness heuristic is a prototypical representation. The mental image of a rose is an example of this, so (A) is the correct answer. Choice (B) is an example of an availability heuristic, which pulls upon readily available images or memories, such as seeing advertisements recently. Choice (C) shows someone who is not limited by functional fixedness to solve her dilemma. Choice (D) describes a confirmation bias, and choice (E) describes hindsight bias.

10. **E** Sheldon is relating new knowledge to something he already understands. Functional fixedness refers to only using an object for its intended use, so (A) cannot be the answer. Choice (B) is more related to grouping pieces of information, and there is no evidence of this in the question. Maintenance rehearsal is related to short-term memory only and state-dependent memory depends on where the person is when he or she is learning the information. Choices (C) and (D) can be eliminated. The self-referential effect works here because Sheldon is relating the new information to something he is familiar with. This is choice (E).

CHAPTER 12 DRILL

1. **A** Content validity is a measure of the degree to which material on the test is balanced and is measuring what it is said to measure. Choice (B) refers to another type of validity—predictive validity. Choices (C), (D), and (E) refer not to measures of test validity, but to measures of test reliability.

2. **B** A projective test is one in which ambiguous stimuli, which are open to various kinds of interpretation, are presented, in contrast to the more common inventory-type tests in which participants answer a standard series of questions. The Thematic Apperception Test (TAT) is a well-known projective test; it involves a series of pictures of people in ambiguous relationships with other people, and the respondent's task is to generate a story for each picture, including what led up to the scene in the picture, what is happening now, and what might occur next. All of the other choices are inventory-style tests in which participants are faced with standardized answer choices.

3. **B** IQ scores over a population are distributed along a normal curve, with the mean, median, and modal scores at 100 and a standard deviation of roughly 15 to 16 points; therefore, a score of 85 would be located approximately one standard deviation below the mean. Choice (E) is deceptive, as the original definition of IQ as mental age divided by physical age multiplied by 100 makes it attractive, but physical age would have no effect on where an IQ score is located relative to established means, medians, modes, or standard deviations.

4. **A** Test standardization is used to set the norms for a given population of subjects; these norms can then be used to compare the test results of groups or individuals with specific characteristics to the whole population. In order to set these norms, the test is administered to a (usually fairly large) standardization sample which, as much as is feasible, possesses characteristics reflective of the entire population. Choice (C) actually refers to the measurement of validity, (D) is more of a way of ensuring reliability on tests where scoring is not computerized, and (E) has more to do with the format of the test than the population.

5. **E**   Howard Gardner's theory of multiple intelligences—not just verbal and mathematical, the dimensions measured by most intelligence tests—posits that there are measurable intelligences in all of the dimensions listed except for (E), which is a dimension added by two other theorists, Peter Salovey and John Mayer.

6. **D**   Reliability measures how consistent the results will be if the same subject takes the test multiple times. Choice (A) calls into question current vs. noncurrent practices, while (B) describes validity instead. Choice (C) should be true of any experiment. Choice (E) describes generalizability. The correct answer is (D).

7. **B**   A true/false or other type of multiple-choice question test is one that does not allow for much creativity, so you can eliminate (A). Since there is a very clear-cut answer to each question through multiple-choice responses, the correct answer is (B), inventory-type test. The test could be about the intelligence, environment, or hereditary information, but none of these are the name for a multiple-choice test, eliminating choices (C), (D) and (E).

8. **A**   There are many components to making sure a study is ethical, but the key component is that the subjects must be protected under confidentiality no matter what, (A). The subject should be informed fully as to the nature of the study, but there needs to be a slight element of deception for the experiment to be successful, eliminating (B). A double-blind study does not guarantee an ethical study (perhaps it is testing a drug that is not yet safe for human consumption), so eliminate (C). Validity and generalization have nothing to do with ethics, but rather its effectiveness in what it intends to measure internally and in a general population. Methodology is not included in these two terms, so eliminate (D) and (E). The correct answer is (A).

CHAPTER 13 DRILL

1. **D**   The Moro reflex in newborns is the startle response that involves the splaying of limbs in response to a falling sensation. Choice (A) is the neonatal reflex of grabbing anything placed in the hand; (B), the Babinski reflex, is produced when stroking the bottom of the neonate's foot results in a splaying out of the toes; and (E) is the reflex that causes a newborn to turn in the direction of a touch on the cheek. While the orienting reflex of (C) may be elicited by a loud noise, it occurs whenever there is any other sudden change in the environment, as well.

2. **B**   The cognitive theory of Vygotsky stresses social and environmental, not just biological/maturational, factors as critical to development; he proposed the concept of a zone of proximal development, which is the range between the developed level of ability a child displays and the potential, or latent, level of ability a child is actually capable of. He further theorized that this latent level is hard to elicit due to a lack of optimal environmental circumstances. Choices (A), Jean Piaget, and (D), Sigmund Freud, created alternate theories of development; (C), Leon Festinger, is most closely identified with the theory of cognitive dissonance (see Chapter 18) and (E), Juliann Rotter, with the concept of locus of control (Chapter 14).

3. **A** Erik Erikson's psychosocial theory of development describes a series of "conflicts" or "tasks" at each stage of life, from infancy to old age. In his theory, the successful resolution of each developmental task results in the development of a certain ability or belief, which serves as the foundation for the resolution of the next "task." The developmental task for school-age children is termed "industry vs. inferiority," and the resolution of this stage produces a sense of competence in one's own efforts and work. Choice (B) is the resolution of the task of early adulthood—"intimacy vs. isolation"; (C) is the resolution of the task of infancy—"trust vs. mistrust"; (D) is the resolution of the task of toddlerhood—"autonomy vs. shame/doubt"; and (E) is the resolution of the task of adolescence—"identity vs. role confusion."

4. **B** According to the developmental theory of Jean Piaget, a child of about five would generally be at the preoperational stage, characterized by both animism—the belief that all things are alive—and egocentrism—the ability to see the world only from one's own point of view. Choices (A), (C), and (D) are other stages of Piaget's developmental model. Choice (E) is a developmental stage in Sigmund Freud's theory.

5. **E** The theory of moral development, elaborated by Lawrence Kohlberg, divides such development into three levels—preconventional, conventional, and postconventional—each subdivided into two stages. At the first stage of preconventional morality, generally the first stage young children progress through, moral concerns are primarily motivated by the need to avoid punishment and to receive rewards. Choice (A) characterizes the next stage of the preconventional level; (B) is the first stage of the conventional level; and (C) is the first stage of the postconventional level. Choice (D) refers to the belief that everybody gets what they deserve, which is not one of Kohlberg's levels.

6. **C** An infant who is securely attached will feel secure when he is around his mother, as evidenced by his comfort when his mother is in the room. When she leaves the room, the infant cries, but is easily consoled upon her return. If the child were insecurely attached, his reaction would differ. In the "strange situation" experiment, the insecurely attached children had varied reactions. Some children did not react as much when the mother left the room, and other children did a combination of both behaviors (disorganized behavior). The correct answer is (C).

7. **A** Conservation is a concept that the amount of a material is still the same in different forms. In this case, it is the same amount of water in both the cup and the vase, though the water level may change.

8. **B** Knowledge of certain facts and figures is crystallized intelligence. Perhaps you reasoned your way to a good guess and chose fluid intelligence, but remember, fluid intelligence is mental agility, problem-solving ability, and other qualities that are not necessarily parroting back facts. Assimilation is a type of learning, incorporating information into mental schema. Wisdom is knowledge that comes from life experiences.

9. **D** Since Mira learns to understand that the object is in fact a bookshelf instead of a desk, she is accommodating this information, making adjustments to her already preexisting schema. If it were, in fact, a desk like she originally thought, this would have been assimilation. But it wasn't, so you can cross out (E). Functional fixedness is a type of mental set, but there is no problem-solving in this question, so eliminate (A) and (B). Choice (C) is a milestone from Jean Piaget's preoperational stage. The correct answer is (D).

10. **E**   Bandura's name is synonymous with observational learning. Through this perspective, Bandura posited that gender roles are at least partially observed by the individual. Choice (A) alludes to a behavioral perspective since it involves learning, so eliminate (A). Choice (B) is also incorrect because Bandura was not concerned with genetics apart from socialization. Choice (C) is also an incomplete explanation for the complex subject of gender, aside from it not relating to Bandura's theories. Choice (D) is too extreme with the word "only," and does not address the observational nature of Bandura's work. Only (E) is consistent with Bandura's research.

CHAPTER 14 DRILL

1. **D**   Secondary drives, like secondary reinforcers, are learned by association with primary drives and primary reinforcers. Satisfying basic needs, as in (A), is a primary drive, as is the attempt to maintain homeostatic equilibrium, as in (B). Choice (C), instinct, refers to unlearned behaviors and (E), optimal arousal, refers to biological theory.

2. **A**   The Yerkes-Dodson law relates levels of arousal and task difficulty. Here, a high-difficulty task (SAT) requires low levels of arousal (calm and relaxed). Arousal and obtaining a primary reinforcer, as in (B), is an inaccurate comparison for this theory. Tasks related to homeostasis, as in (C), involve drive-reduction theory. Remaining calm and addressing envelopes, as in (D), is a low-arousal and low-difficulty task.

3. **A**   Angiotensin is a chemical messenger released when the volumetric receptors that monitor extracellular body levels, particularly in the circulatory system, sense low fluid levels, and it acts directly on brain receptors to stimulate thirst. Choice (B) is an opiate-like brain chemical that binds to neural receptor sites, but it has nothing to do with thirst; neither does the neurotransmitter acetylcholine of (E); and (C) is a thyroid, not thirst, hormone.

4. **B**   An extrinsic factor is one that motivates behavior but does not originate within the individual performing the behavior; it instead originates from the outside world. In Rhoni's case, feeling the need to excel at her career in order to keep up her family's lifestyle and her parents' opinion of her qualifies as being primarily from outside of her (though she may enjoy the lifestyle herself). Choice (A) would be a factor that originated within the individual displaying the behavior; (D) and (E) would also describe such internal factors.

5. **C**   As compared to Type-B personalities, Type-As have a greater arousal response overall to stress and a greater tendency to seek it out, as in (B); they also tend to be more competitive, as in (E), more prone to stress-related physical conditions, as in (D), and to feel a greater sense of being pressed for time, as in (A). Type-As also tend to anger more quickly (part of being easier to arouse), so they would be less likely to anger slowly.

6. **A**   According to drive-reduction theory, the drive is hunger in this case, so to reduce the need, Sanju needs to eat something. Since she does this, theoretically, she will return to homeostasis, as in (A). Yes, she may be thirsty as well, but that is not stated in the question, nor will a donut necessarily cause thirst. The donut may increase insulin levels in the body, but it is not certain that they will be raised to unhealthy levels, so choice (A) is the only provable response.

7. **D** The Yerkes-Dodson law and the opponent process theory are not theories of emotion, so eliminate (A) and (E). Jorge is able to cognitively appraise the situation to know he is not in danger. He is experiencing a physiological response to a stimulus, but the cognitive interpretation of that physiological response is the two-factor theory that Schachter and Singer posited. The James-Lange theory would not work here because the physiological response would lead to only one emotional output, most likely fear. Eliminate (B). The Cannon-Bard theory does not connect the cognitive interpretation of the physiological response either, so eliminate (C). The correct answer is (D).

8. **E** The opponent-process theory explains how addiction can create this vicious cycle, in which the user takes increasingly more and more of a drug to achieve the original effect, while the opposite "lows" get lower and lower. Drug use is not an instinct, so eliminate (A). Similarly, you can eliminate (B) because there is nothing in the question concerning arousal. Choice (C) cannot be correct because the two-factor theory is one of emotion, and you can also cross out (D) because this exacerbated cycle would not exist in the drive-reduction theory. This leaves (E), the correct answer.

9. **E** Suppressed appetite is not a symptom of chronic stress, though it may be one of acute stress, which lasts for only a short amount of time. Remember that chronic stress is defined as lasting for weeks, months, or even years.

10. **B** The hypothalamus is mostly in charge of maintaining homeostasis in the body, (B). Choice (A) describes the thalamus, (C) the hippocampus, (D) the pituitary gland, and (E) the amygdala. The correct answer is (B).

CHAPTER 15 DRILL

1. **B** In Freudian theory, the ego is the part of the mind that mediates between the wants/demands of the part of the mind known as the id, (C); the internal representation of rules, morals, and social obligations known as the superego, (A); and the realities of the outside world. The ego involves conscious thought and choice and attempts to find acceptable ways to satisfy desires. Choices (D) and (E) are not parts of the mind in Freudian theory; they are concepts from Jungian theory.

2. **E** Reaction formation is the psychodynamic defense mechanism that involves the ego reversing the direction of a disturbing or unacceptable desire to make that desire safer and more acceptable, as when a person who unconsciously hates children might feel the need to volunteer at a day-care center. The other answers are all definitions of other defense mechanisms: (A) is displacement, (B) is regression, (C) is compensation, and (D) is rationalization.

3. **D** Albert Bandura is identified with a social-cognitive, rather than psychodynamic, theory of personality; his theory does not concern itself very much with unconscious desires and mechanisms, as psychodynamic theories do, but rather focuses on an individual's concepts and beliefs. Horney, Jung, Adler, and Erikson are all psychodynamic theorists who expanded on or modified Freud's original conception of personality.

4. **D**   In the personality and therapeutic theories of Carl Rogers, self-actualization refers to the process by which an individual modifies and grows over time in ways that allow him/her to reach full potential and ability. To humanistic theorists, such as Rogers, self-actualization is the ultimate purpose of human existence. Choice (A) refers to the value we place on ourselves—often a product of self-actualization, but not the actual process. Choice (C), self-efficacy, refers to a person's belief in his/her own competence in a given situation.

5. **A**   The 16PF (Personality Factor) Questionnaire, designed by Raymond Cattell, is designed specifically for investigating the traits, or primarily inherited, enduring, and situationally stable tendencies that govern individual personality. (Cattell theorized there were 16 basic traits, which his instrument purported to measure.) Choices (B) and (E) are intelligence tests—the Weschler Adult Intelligence Scale and the Weschler Intelligence Scale for Children, respectively. Choice (C) is the *Diagnostic and Statistical Manual, Version Five,* currently in use for identification and classification of mental/behavioral disorders, and (D) is analysis of variance, a statistical technique.

6. **B**   Anne is not very competent at riding a bike, which shows she has a low self-efficacy, so eliminate (A) and (C). However, she knows she is in control of getting better at riding a bike if she practices. This means that she has an internal locus of control; she has control over her improvements. The correct answer is (B).

7. **E**   The concept of the halo effect is that multiple positive attributes will surround a person who already possesses some. Since Lukas has good looks, grades, and athleticism, the halo effect suggests that he contains other positive attributes as well, such as being trustworthy. The correct answer is (E).

8. **A**   When Tanya kicks the ice instead of her coach or herself, she is showing displacement, since she directs her anger toward the ice. The correct answer is (A).

9. **C**   Jung's theory of the anima and animus is the male and female qualities that lie in each personality. This supports (C). Beware of the recycled Jungian language in (A) and (D). Neither is true, but test-makers hope that those key words might be enticing. Choice (B) describes Erikson's trust vs. mistrust, and (E) is more of a humanistic viewpoint.

10. **B**   Cara feels good about herself, showing that she is exhibiting positive self-esteem, (B). The question does not show whether she is proficient at a task or not, so eliminate self-efficacy, (A). The self-concept is a larger umbrella to self-esteem, efficacy, schemata, etc., so eliminate (C) as well. Choices (D) and (E) are incorrect because those are defense mechanisms of psychoanalysis. The correct answer is (B).

CHAPTER 16 DRILL

1. **C**   This person is most likely experiencing a psychotic episode. Choices (B) and (D), obsessions and compulsions, refer to a different disorder. Choice (A), delusions, are relevant to psychosis, but they are beliefs not based in reality, and the question stem explicitly says he hears voices, not that he believes anything in particular. Choice (E), inceptions, is not a psychological concept. Only (C), hallucinations, fits the question stem.

2. **B** Conversion disorder occurs when a psychological difficulty manifests itself as a deficit in physiological function in which there is no actual discernable physical problem. Choice (A), bipolar disorder, is characterized by alternating periods of depression and mania, and (E), paranoid disorder, by extreme mistrust and suspicion, often with feelings of persecution. Choice (C), an organic disorder, would be linked to an actual physical deficit, usually of the brain or nervous system.

3. **E** Dissociative disorders, such as amnesia, fugue, or multiple personality disorder, are characterized by dysfunction of memory and disruption in the sense of identity. Choice (A) is more characteristic of phobias, (C) of obsessive disorders, and (D) of certain types of schizophrenia. Choice (B) might be descriptive of some individuals with dissociative disorders, but it is not a diagnostic criterion or a widely seen characteristic of the disorder (many with such disorders have quite extensive social networks).

4. **C** Serotonin is a neurotransmitter that influences mood and seems to be present at lower-than-usual levels in many of those diagnosed with depression (at least, unipolar depression). Choice (A), acetylcholine, has, at least in some studies, been associated with the expression of bipolar behavior when present in greater-than-average amounts. Dopamine deficits have been implicated in Parkinson's disease, and may be implicated in certain instances of schizophrenia, but not depression, so eliminate (E).

5. **C** By *DSM-5* definition, anxiety disorders are characterized by feelings of tension, nervousness, fear, and sometimes panic. All of the choices here qualify except for anxious personality disorder, which is made up.

6. **D** The girl is most likely suffering from dissociative fugue (a type of dissociative disorder), which causes her to experience personal amnesia. Sufferers of dissociative fugue tend to wander or travel and often establish new identities based on who they believe they are, which is (D), dissociative disorder. Choice (A), somatoform disorder, involves physical illness or injury. Choice (B), delusional disorder, is a psychotic illness that is characterized by non-bizarre delusions, with no accompanying hallucinations, mood disturbances, or flattening of affect; furthermore, amnesia is not a symptom of a delusional disorder. Choice (C), personality disorder, is characterized by a set of personality traits that deviates from cultural norms, impairs functioning, and causes distress; there are three major clusters of personality disorders, none of which accurately explain the girl described in the question stem. Although it is possible that the girl's symptoms are feigned in an attempt to seek attention, a possible symptom of histrionic personality disorder, the question stem would need to provide concrete information to draw this conclusion, which it does not. Also, there is no direct evidence of schizophrenia demonstrated in the question stem, so eliminate (E).

7. **D** Conversion disorder is a somatoform disorder in which a person displays blindness, deafness, or other symptoms of sensory or motor failure without a physical cause, as best expressed by (D). Choice (A), a constant fear of illness, refers to hypochondriasis, not conversion disorder. Choice (B), panic attacks and severe anxiety, are symptoms of anxiety disorders, while conversion disorder is a type of somatoform disorder. Frequent vague complaints about physical symptoms, (C), is characteristic of somatization disorder and (E), religious obsessions, may remind you of religious conversion, but that is not the meaning of conversion in this question.

8. **B**   Schizoid personality disorder is classified under Cluster A personality disorders, (B). This person will likely be markedly detached from friends and family members and have a flat affect, whereas Cluster B disorders are more emotional and dramatic.

9. **E**   Many diagnoses like obsessive-compulsive disorder are diagnosed only in adulthood. This is a child, so this must be a neurodevelopmental disorder, narrowing options to (A) and (E). The child is not exhibiting impulsivity/hyperactivity or inattention, but rather restrictive behavior and difficulty in social situations since he is having difficulty engaging with peers. This is descriptive of ASD. The correct answer is (E).

10. **D**   Though body dysmorphic disorder can be interrelated with other diagnoses, such as anorexia nervosa, it is not categorized as a feeding disorder because it does not involve eating. Rather, it is characterized by obsessive thoughts about body parts the person believes are disproportionate or abnormally shaped. This may lead to disordered eating, but it is in the category of obsessive-compulsive and related disorders.

CHAPTER 17 DRILL

1. **C**   Client-centered therapy, as an outgrowth of the humanistic school of psychology, is very concerned with trying to understand the client's view of the world and how it affects him or her, in order to facilitate the client's own tendencies toward growth and fulfillment. Therapists utilizing this approach see accurate empathic understanding—the therapist's ability to view the world through the eyes of the client—as critical to successful communication between client and therapist. While (A), psychoanalytic therapy, also considers communication and understanding the client's view of the world important, it tends to discourage emotional or personal involvement with the patient through such empathy. Psychoanalytic therapists believe a stance of detachment is best for the encouragement of transference, which helps to reveal the nature of the patient's conflicts. Choice (D), implosion therapy, is a behavioral approach with little emphasis on the kind of client-therapist relationship considered essential to client-centered therapy.

2. **E**   Behavioral approaches to therapy are concerned with treating maladaptive or troubling symptoms, rather than underlying causes, and in this school of thought, there are no hidden, "deep" underlying causes—the disordered behavior itself is the problem. As such, behavioral therapies have been most often used with those who seek to change specific behaviors, such as those who suffer from phobias. While behavioral approaches might be tried for individuals with some of the other conditions listed, the more symptom-oriented behavioral techniques are usually not the treatment of choice with conditions that involve more than just a specific maladaptive behavior and/or altered mental states.

3. **B**   Psychoanalytic therapy focuses on probing past defense mechanisms to understand the unconscious roots of problems; indeed, its practitioners believe that troubling behaviors or symptoms cannot possibly cease until a patient gains insight into such unconscious roots. In this approach, treating just symptoms through behavioral methods without addressing the underlying hidden causes will

not result in a lasting "cure" and may instead result in symptoms returning or new ones manifesting. Choices (A) and (C) are not generally criticisms leveled at behavioral therapy by psychoanalysts; indeed, for those it's the other way around—these are criticisms of psychoanalytic approaches often made by behaviorists. The criticism in (D) would more likely be made by humanistic or client-centered therapists.

4. **B**   Rational-emotive behavioral therapy, or simply rational-emotive therapy, is primarily associated with Albert Ellis, who formulated this cognitive approach, which concentrates on modifying incorrect thoughts or cognitions that lead to maladaptive emotional and behavioral responses. Choice (A), Julian Rotter, is associated with the concept of locus of control; (C), Abraham Maslow, with the concepts of hierarchy of needs and self-actualization; (D), Raymond Cattell, with a trait theory of personality and the 16PF Questionnaire; and (E), Rollo May, with the existential approach to psychotherapy.

5. **A**   Anticoagulants are not drugs used for psychotherapeutic purposes; they are, instead, used to modulate the ability of the blood to clot and form vessel blockages. Both (C) and (E) are classes of drugs that belong to the larger family of antidepressants; (B), anxiolytics, as the name implies, are used primarily for the reduction of anxiety; and (D), lithium salts, are useful in the treatment of some cases of bipolar disorder.

6. **C**   There is nothing systematic or progressive about going to the top of the Empire State Building on a first therapy session for acrophobia. Instead, the therapist is choosing a situation in which Judy will most likely have a very strong reaction at first, but will hopefully have less of a reaction the longer she realizes she will not fall off the ledge. This is a technique called flooding, (C). Choice (B) is not the answer because the therapist is not trying to condition Judy not to like something. Choice (D), implosion, is similar to flooding, but it uses visualization techniques instead of physically going to a location or confronting a stimulus. There is not a contract in the question stem either, eliminating (E).

7. **D**   A behavioral therapist will seek to modify behavior by extinguishing maladaptive behaviors and conditioning more adaptive ones. Therefore, extinction procedures will be used to modify behaviors. Choices (A), (B), and (C) are specific to psychoanalysis, while (E) is most closely associated with humanistic therapy. The correct answer is (D).

8. **A**   SSRIs are most commonly used as antidepressants. Therefore, they would most likely be used for depressive disorders.

9. **C**   A psychotherapist would most likely use free association, (C). Choices (A), (B), and (D) are techniques used in behavioral therapy, and (E) is used in humanistic therapy.

10. **A**   Carl Rogers is synonymous with humanistic therapy. If you were unsure, remember that he coined the phrase *unconditional positive regard*, so he was most concerned with treating other humans with the utmost respect and compassion. Hence, the term humanism came forth.

CHAPTER 18 DRILL

1. **D**   The fundamental attribution error is defined as the tendency of people to overestimate a person's disposition and to underestimate the situational circumstances when evaluating another person's behavior. Both (A) and (C) are examples of an internal locus of control. Choice (B), blaming a teacher for one's failures, is an example of an external attribution. In evaluating her friend's behavior, Karen is balancing personal and situational attributes, so eliminate (E) as well.

2. **D**   In the Asch conformity experiments, many factors influenced the degree to which an experimental subject would show conformity to the obviously wrong group opinion, but the subject's age did not show a consistent effect in this regard. Choice (A) certainly did—unanimity was very important; only one dissenting opinion drastically reduced the tendency of the subject to go along with the rest of the group; (B), size of the group, has an influence in that it seems to take a group of at least three members for such conformity to be shown consistently; (C), the subject's perception of his/her own social status versus that of the group, was important—subjects who perceived themselves as of low/medium status were much more likely to conform than those who perceived themselves as of high status; and (E), gender of the subject, was an influencing factor, with females more likely to conform than males.

3. **D**   The self-fulfilling prophecy refers to the scenario in the question—students randomly labeled as likely to experience significant jumps in academic test scores in the coming semester did indeed seem to perform to those expectations on those tests at the end of the semester. Choice (A), the Hawthorne effect, refers to the observation that students or workers who know they are being monitored tend to perform better, even if they do not know why they are being monitored. Choice (B), the Kandel effect, is associated with research into learning and neurophysiology in sea slugs; (C), cognitive dissonance, refers to the discomfort that comes from two conflicting thoughts; and (E), the Ainsworth effect, comes from studies of attachment in human infants.

4. **B**   Diffusion of responsibility, also sometimes referred to as the bystander effect, occurs when every person in a crowded social situation defers to another to make the effort to mount a response to the situation. It can also occur when members of a group perform negative behaviors that no specific individual or individuals will take responsibility for. Choice (D), an altruistic orientation, usually refers to the decision-making paradigm in which individuals wish to maximize the outcome for others, but it could also be applied to this situation as a countervailing force to the diffusion of responsibility. Choice (A), illusory correlation, refers to the false presumption that certain groups are associated with certain stereotypes or behaviors, and (E), the just-world hypothesis, is the belief that because the world is basically fair, people deserve whatever befalls them, positive or negative. Choice (C), cognitive dissonance, deals with conflicting thoughts, not responsibility.

5. **B**   The "foot-in-the-door" technique involves making requests in small increments that people are more likely to initially comply with, and then work from those up to bigger requests; the incremental approach seems to work better than "going for the whole ball of wax all at once." This is what the teenager is trying to do in getting his curfew extended in small increments until he gets the curfew he actually wants. Choice (A) is an example of the "door-in-the-face" technique, in which one asks for much more than what one actually wants, expecting to be turned down; one can then ask for

the smaller, "more reasonable" request, which is more likely to be granted. People also tend to be more likely to comply with or be persuaded by those they feel they are similar to, as in (D), or by those they will receive a desired reward from (hardly a surprise), as in (E).

6. **C**   The man who does not have health insurance in (A) thinks nothing bad will happen to him, which is known as an optimism bias. The woman observing the man who loses his house in (B) most likely feels for the man, but exhibits the just-world bias since she most likely thinks the man failed to act on obtaining health insurance. Choice (C) is the clearest example of the self-serving bias, since the toddler attributes building the block tower to herself, but blames the blocks instead of herself when they tumble to the ground. Remember, the self-serving bias is when a person takes credit for positive achievements and attributes something or someone else as the cause of negative ones. Choice (D) most clearly shows a self-fulfilling prophecy and the Rosenthal Effect, in which the teacher believes in Yuan, and he then goes and studies for his exam. Finally, (E) is an example of a situational attribution, in which the environment causes conditions that affect a large number of the residents described in the answer choice. The correct answer is (C).

7. **A**   Since both groups remained equal for a while, the group that had five members shows evidence of social loafing. The more people assigned to that side of the rope, the less force they thought they needed to exert individually. The three students on the other side of the rope felt more individually responsible and had increased need to contribute.

8. **D**   The child in this question exhibits the door-in-the-face technique to get what he wants from his parents. This technique is named for his parents metaphorically "slamming the door in his face" at his outrageous request of $100 per week. However, when he asks for less money, he is met with less resistance.

9. **E**   Stanley Milgram's study involved a significant amount of deception, tricking the subjects into thinking they were participating in a study on learning. They played roles within the experiment, though this was not the point of the experiment, so eliminate (D). There is not a group in the experiment either, so conformity, dehumanization, and groupthink are not factors here either, eliminating (A), (B), and (C). The point of the experiment was to test obedience to the "experimenter" when he told the subject (the "teacher") to administer what the subject believed to be an electric shock to the "learner" (a confederate to the experimenter in another room). A large percentage of subjects obeyed the experimenter and administered the highest level of electric shock. The correct answer is (E).

10. **A**   Though Bandura was measuring aggressive behavior in the children, the crucial part of the experiment was the children's observation of the adults. If the children observed the adults behaving aggressively toward the bobo doll, they were more apt to act aggressively themselves. If they observed the adults behaving nonaggressively, they were also less likely to act aggressively.

Part VI
Practice Test 2

Practice Test 2

AP® Psychology Exam

SECTION I: Multiple-Choice Questions

DO NOT OPEN THIS BOOKLET UNTIL YOU ARE TOLD TO DO SO.

At a Glance

Total Time
1 hour and 10 minutes
Number of Questions
100
Percent of Total Grade
66.6%
Writing Instrument
Pencil required

Instructions

Section I of this exam contains 100 multiple-choice questions. Fill in only the ovals for numbers 1 through 100 on your answer sheet.

Indicate all of your answers to the multiple-choice questions on the answer sheet. No credit will be given for anything written in this exam booklet, but you may use the booklet for notes or scratch work. After you have decided which of the suggested answers is best, completely fill in the corresponding oval on the answer sheet. Give only one answer to each question. If you change an answer, be sure that the previous mark is erased completely. Here is a sample question and answer.

Sample Question   Sample Answer

Omaha is a

(A) state
(B) city
(C) country
(D) continent
(E) village

Use your time effectively, working as quickly as you can without losing accuracy. Do not spend too much time on any one question. Go on to other questions and come back to the ones you have not answered if you have time. It is not expected that everyone will know the answers to all of the multiple-choice questions.

About Guessing

Many candidates wonder whether or not to guess the answers to questions about which they are not certain. Multiple-choice scores are based on the number of questions answered correctly. Points are not deducted for incorrect answers and no points are awarded for unanswered questions. Because points are not deducted for incorrect answers, you are encouraged to answer all multiple-choice questions. On any questions you do not know the answer to, you should eliminate as many choices as you can and then select the best answer among the remaining choices.

GO ON TO THE NEXT PAGE.

| For more free content, visit PrincetonReview.com

This page intentionally left blank.

GO ON TO THE NEXT PAGE.

PSYCHOLOGY
Section I
Time—1 hour and 10 minutes
100 Questions

Directions: Each of the questions or incomplete statements below is followed by five answer choices. Select the one that is best in each case and then completely fill in the corresponding oval on the answer sheet.

1. Substances that are toxic to humans often taste

   (A) sour
   (B) sweet
   (C) salty
   (D) bitter
   (E) bland

2. Sigmund Freud was the founder of which of the following perspectives in psychology?

   (A) Biological
   (B) Behavioral
   (C) Cognitive
   (D) Psychoanalytic
   (E) Humanistic

3. A behavior that is elicited automatically by an environmental stimulus is called a(n)

   (A) conditioned response
   (B) condition
   (C) aversive stimulus
   (D) reflex
   (E) drive

4. Emotional, cognitive, and behavioral tendencies that constitute underlying personality dimensions on which individuals vary are referred to as

   (A) traits
   (B) moods
   (C) temperaments
   (D) tenets
   (E) personalities

5. The field of psychology arose out of which of the following?

   (A) Biochemistry
   (B) Physics
   (C) Philosophy
   (D) Cross-cultural anthropology
   (E) Statistics

6. Six-month-old Sasha loves to play "peek-a-boo" with her mother, an indication that she has developed a sense of

   (A) play versus learning
   (B) transitivity
   (C) metacognition
   (D) attachment anxiety
   (E) object permanence

7. Studying a few subjects in great depth to investigate a rare condition is known as

   (A) an experiment
   (B) a case study
   (C) naturalistic observation
   (D) correlational research
   (E) longitudinal research

8. Which of the following is the most accurate definition of learning?

   (A) The result of a variety of experiences that temporarily shape behavior
   (B) An enduring change in an organism's behavior based on experience
   (C) The sole result of classical and operant conditioning
   (D) The association of experiences due to their occurrence in close proximity
   (E) A change in behavior that is not susceptible to extinction

GO ON TO THE NEXT PAGE.

9. A group of participants in a sleep study are to be deprived of sleep for four days. After their second sleepless night, participants may begin reporting which of the following?

   (A) Hunger
   (B) Thirst
   (C) Lack of coordination
   (D) Hallucinations
   (E) Increased respiration

10. Conflicting attitudes or behaviors that create tension within a person's mind are referred to in terms of

    (A) persuasion
    (B) general adaptation syndrome
    (C) serial position
    (D) cognitive dissonance
    (E) fluid intelligence

11. Endorphins are chemicals that

    (A) elevate mood and reduce pain
    (B) increase alertness and reduce drowsiness
    (C) lower or raise the threshold for the firing of neurons
    (D) cannot cross the blood-brain barrier
    (E) always elicit an action potential from a neuron

12. Nell decides not to throw her stuffed animal into the toilet after she witnesses her brother Matthew being punished for putting his stuffed animal into the toilet. Nell's decision exemplifies

    (A) prepared conditioning
    (B) tutelage
    (C) scheduled reinforcement
    (D) shaping
    (E) vicarious learning

13. A game show like *Jeopardy!* asks players to demonstrate which of the following types of intelligence?

    (A) IQ
    (B) Crystallized intelligence
    (C) Fluid intelligence
    (D) General intelligence
    (E) Multiple intelligence

14. Which of the following is often true of memory recall?

    (A) People are more likely to recall information that is congruent with their prior schemas.
    (B) People will not recall information unless it is stored in working memory.
    (C) People have no ability to recall information that has been extinguished.
    (D) People will recall nonsense syllables more rapidly than they will sets of numbers.
    (E) People will not recall information for which they did not create a mnemonic device.

15. Objects that absorb light appear

    (A) black
    (B) white
    (C) dark
    (D) bright
    (E) ultraviolet

16. Chantal says that her mother is domineering and overbearing. All of Chantal's friends agree that she is the one that has these characteristics, not her mother. Freud would suggest that Chantal's behavior exemplifies which of the following defense mechanisms?

    (A) Repression
    (B) Regression
    (C) Projection
    (D) Displacement
    (E) Denial

17. A psychologist who believes in the humanistic perspective would be most likely to agree with which of the following statements?

    (A) All behavior can be traced to human biological functions.
    (B) People's behavior is primarily a result of free will.
    (C) Behavior results from conditioning.
    (D) Human behavior is a result of conflicting unconscious motives.
    (E) People are able to understand and analyze the behavior of humans.

GO ON TO THE NEXT PAGE.

18. Which of the following lobes of the brain is central to visual sensation and perception?

    (A) Occipital
    (B) Temporal
    (C) Parietal
    (D) Frontal
    (E) Cerebral

19. In order for the mean, mode, and median of a data set to be equal, the distribution must be

    (A) positively skewed
    (B) asymmetrical
    (C) negatively skewed
    (D) normal
    (E) abnormal

20. The adaptive response of a six-month-old child who shows distress when an attachment figure leaves is known as

    (A) attachment anxiety
    (B) reactive attachment disorder
    (C) object permanence
    (D) separation anxiety
    (E) detachment adaptation

21. B. F. Skinner was well known for his work involving the

    (A) biological perspective
    (B) behavioral perspective
    (C) cognitive perspective
    (D) psychodynamic perspective
    (E) humanistic perspective

22. A researcher has asked participants to complete a questionnaire that will assess how frequently in their lives they experience various emotions using a scale from 1 (never) to 5 (very often). The researcher is particularly interested in the relationship between feelings of guilt and other emotions. This researcher is most likely conducting which of the following types of research?

    (A) Demographic
    (B) Observational
    (C) Correlational
    (D) Experimental
    (E) Statistical

23. Which of the following is the term used to describe a number of psychotic disorders that involve disturbances in nearly every dimension of human psychology including thought, perception, behavior, and communication?

    (A) Schizophrenia
    (B) Intellectual disabilities
    (C) Dissociative disorder
    (D) Depression
    (E) Endorphisms

24. Which of the following most accurately describes the firing of a neuron?

    (A) It occurs gradually as the neuron reaches hyperpolarization.
    (B) It has an all-or-none quality: it either happens, or it does not.
    (C) Its strength diminishes as it travels along the soma.
    (D) It occurs only in the post-synaptic neuron.
    (E) Stronger stimulations make a neuron fire harder.

25. Xavier is beginning his first year of college. He is eager to find a few other freshmen to "hang out" with. Psychologists would say that Xavier is motivated by a(n)

    (A) fraternization need
    (B) assimilation need
    (C) attachment need
    (D) affiliation need
    (E) loneliness need

26. The fact that Will was better able to memorize his lines in the school play after finding out the meanings behind the words best illustrates the influence of

    (A) chunking
    (B) shaping
    (C) maintenance rehearsal
    (D) elaborative rehearsal
    (E) semantic memory

GO ON TO THE NEXT PAGE.

27. The role of the outer ear is to

    (A) transduce sound waves to stimulate the ossicles
    (B) conduct sound by exciting the cilia in the inner ear
    (C) protect the eardrum while it transduces sound
    (D) convey auditory messages to the temporal lobes
    (E) collect and focus sounds from the air

28. At the outset of a study on eating habits, a researcher asks participants a variety of questions, including whether they typically eat breakfast. Whether or not a person eats breakfast is a(n)

    (A) categorical variable
    (B) continuous variable
    (C) dependent variable
    (D) independent variable
    (E) conditioned variable

29. In most people, the left hemisphere of the brain is dominant for

    (A) language
    (B) logic
    (C) analytical reasoning
    (D) mathematical reasoning
    (E) spatial reasoning

30. A piano teacher is helping a student learn a new piece. At first, she praises the student for playing correct notes. After the student begins to show proficiency with the notes, the teacher praises the student only when he adds the proper dynamics and interpretation to the segments he plays. The teacher's method of instruction is an example of which of the following types of training techniques?

    (A) Negative reinforcement
    (B) Negative punishment
    (C) Shaping
    (D) Chaining
    (E) Discriminating

31. After discovering that she was in the early stages of an eating disorder, Maria's parents insisted Maria see a therapist. Although Maria attended the therapy sessions, she was late, uncooperative, and even hostile. After some time, her counselor began to explore Maria's feelings of hostility and found that they actually were feelings she held for her parents. Maria's uncooperativeness and hostility toward her counselor is an example of

    (A) suppression
    (B) conflicting motives
    (C) transference
    (D) countertransference
    (E) reaction formation

32. Tonya runs into an old schoolmate on the street. During their brief conversation, Tonya is unable to recall the schoolmate's name. Days later, she remembers the name out of the blue. To remember the name "out of the blue" is an example of

    (A) tip-of-the-tongue phenomenon
    (B) chunking
    (C) deductive reasoning
    (D) inductive reasoning
    (E) parallelism

33. Hypnosis has been used effectively to diminish

    (A) antisocial personality disorder
    (B) chronic pain
    (C) night terrors
    (D) kinesthetic abilities
    (E) Alzheimer's disease

34. Which of the following best explains why mnemonic devices, such as the method of loci, are typically effective at helping individuals remember information?

    (A) They encode information and store it in STM so that it is easy to retrieve.
    (B) They "file" information in a predictable order so that it is easy to retrieve.
    (C) They enhance memory capacity by augmenting representational fields.
    (D) They encourage individuals to write down everything they wish to remember.
    (E) They connect new information to information already stored in LTM.

GO ON TO THE NEXT PAGE.

35. Quinn awoke from a dream, shaking and covered with sweat. When his wife asked him what had happened, he said he had dreamed he was falling to his death. Quinn's experience is often categorized as a

   (A) hallucination
   (B) phobia
   (C) narcoleptic event
   (D) night terror
   (E) nightmare

36. Which of the following terms describes the behavioral component of negative attitudes toward particular groups?

   (A) Bias
   (B) Conditioning
   (C) Catharsis
   (D) Passive aggression
   (E) Discrimination

37. Which of the following disorders is the result of an abnormality of the twenty-first chromosomal pair?

   (A) Bipolar disorder
   (B) Huntington's chorea
   (C) Down syndrome
   (D) Obsessive-compulsive disorder
   (E) Histrionic personality disorder

38. All of the following are examples of punishment EXCEPT

   (A) grounding a teenager for staying out past curfew
   (B) spanking a child for misbehavior
   (C) permanently revoking the driving privileges of a third-time DWI driver
   (D) refusing to return the boss's phone call after not getting the expected raise
   (E) placing a puppy that has shredded a chair in a confinement cage

39. Carl Jung's concept of a repository of ideas, feelings, and symbols shared by all humans and passed genetically from one generation to another is known as Jung's theory of the

   (A) cultural subconscious
   (B) general awareness
   (C) heritability coefficients
   (D) collective unconscious
   (E) integrated intelligence

40. According to Dr. William Sears, noted authority on infants and child-rearing, infant brain development is, in part, influenced by longer and more frequent periods of active sleeping and dreaming or

   (A) REM sleep
   (B) NREM sleep
   (C) delta sleep
   (D) stage 3 sleep
   (E) stage 4 sleep

41. The rules that govern the placement of words and phrases in a sentence are called

   (A) semantics
   (B) grammar
   (C) syntax
   (D) phonemes
   (E) morphemes

42. An animal is not likely to associate a conditioned stimulus (CS) with an unconditioned stimulus (UCS) if the

   (A) delay between the CS and the UCS is too long
   (B) interval schedule between the two stimuli is variable
   (C) fixed-rational schedule between the two stimuli is altered
   (D) interstimulus ratio is variable
   (E) CS and the UCS occur simultaneously

43. All of the following are examples of secondary drives EXCEPT

   (A) recreation
   (B) sex
   (C) approval
   (D) friendship
   (E) exercise

44. A doctor who smokes cigarettes knows that it is unhealthy, but thinks that he can keep smoking, since he eats healthily. Which concept best explains this thought process?

   (A) Reaction formation
   (B) Affective retraining
   (C) Cognitive dissonance
   (D) Obsessive compulsion
   (E) Psychotic delusion

GO ON TO THE NEXT PAGE.

45. The staggering and slurred speech of a person who has consumed too much alcohol is most likely the result of altered functioning in the

    (A) limbic system
    (B) thalamus
    (C) sensorimotor cortex
    (D) amygdala
    (E) cerebellum

46. After a big Thanksgiving dinner replete with turkey, stuffing, and all, Karmina becomes violently ill. In the weeks that follow this event, Karmina feels an unexplainable aversion to chicken, one of her favorite dishes. Karmina's feeling about chicken reflects

    (A) response generalization
    (B) latent learning
    (C) prepared learning
    (D) unconditioned stimulus response
    (E) stimulus generalization

47. Perception refers to the process by which

    (A) receptors gather information from the environment
    (B) sense organs transmit information to the brain for initial processing
    (C) the brain organizes and interprets sensations
    (D) the brain minimizes responses to stimuli that do not change
    (E) individuals evaluate stimuli

48. The driver of a car that has pulled up next to you at a red light turns up the volume on her radio. The increase in perceived sound that you experience is primarily due to

    (A) neurons firing more intensely
    (B) increased secretions by the pituitary gland
    (C) changing frequency of sound waves
    (D) more neurons firing more frequently
    (E) increased speed of sensations traveling down the "what" pathway

49. Which of the following illustrates why most people can detect the difference between Coke and Pepsi most of the time?

    (A) Subliminal perception
    (B) Absolute threshold
    (C) Signal detection theory
    (D) Difference threshold
    (E) Weber's law

50. Complete the following example using deductive reasoning: All students who attend the Peddie School study Latin. Some students who study Latin also study calculus. Jerome is a student at the Peddie School. It can therefore be determined that

    (A) Jerome studies calculus
    (B) Jerome studies Latin
    (C) Jerome studies both calculus and Latin
    (D) Jerome studies either calculus or Latin
    (E) Jerome studies neither Latin nor calculus

51. Lynda is a confident, capable woman who takes responsibility for her own actions. Lynda has a(n)

    (A) manic coping strategy
    (B) discriminative expectancy
    (C) internal locus of control
    (D) external locus of control
    (E) generalized expectancy

52. Which of the following refers to the benefit of having an emotional release to reduce aggressive tendencies?

    (A) James-Lange theory of emotion
    (B) Counterconditioning
    (C) Catharsis hypothesis
    (D) Transference
    (E) The two-factor theory

53. Which of the following terms refers to the body's tendency to maintain a relatively constant state that permits cells to live and function?

    (A) Perceptual constancy
    (B) Set point
    (C) Homeostasis
    (D) Kinesthesia
    (E) Affect regulation

GO ON TO THE NEXT PAGE.

54. Periods of special sensitivity to specific types of learning that shape the capacity for future development are known as

(A) maturation periods
(B) critical periods
(C) primary development periods
(D) secondary development periods
(E) shaping periods

55. According to researchers Darley and Latanne, bystander intervention decreases when a large number of people witness a crime. What social psychology concept could best explain this phenomenon?

(A) Social loafing
(B) Prejudice
(C) Conformity
(D) Obedience
(E) Diffusion of responsibility

56. Lisa, determined to get away from her abusive father, leaves home and moves in with an abusive boyfriend. Lisa's choice of an abusive boyfriend is most relevant to Sigmund Freud's theory of

(A) psychodynamic conflict
(B) opposing motives
(C) id, ego, and superego
(D) behavioral dysfunction
(E) cognitive dissonance

57. Piaget proposed that children develop knowledge by

(A) constructing reality out of their own experiences
(B) participating in traditional learning environments
(C) responding to physiological changes
(D) modeling various cultural influences
(E) drawing on genetically predisposed knowledge

58. A longitudinal study would be useful in assessing which of the following?

(A) Age differences
(B) Gender differences
(C) Cultural environments
(D) Changes in behavior over time
(E) Sequential studies

59. Calvin's fear of dogs was so great that he could not even visit his friends who had dogs or who lived in a neighborhood that had a lot of dogs. Once he sought help, he worked to overcome this fear first by witnessing his counselor playing with a dog and then, after a while, by actually touching and petting a dog himself. The method used to help Calvin overcome his fears is known as

(A) countertransference
(B) peer-counselor alliance
(C) rational-emotive therapy
(D) flooding
(E) systematic desensitization

60. Maurice is a drug-and-alcohol counselor who subscribes to Humanist principles. As such, he tries very hard not to judge his clients based on the stories they tell him about their addictions. He is carrying out the practice of

(A) transference
(B) systematic desensitization
(C) unconditional positive regard
(D) aversive therapy
(E) escape training

61. The manual of clinical syndromes published by the American Psychiatric Association that is used for descriptive diagnosis is commonly called the

(A) *ANOVA*
(B) *DSM-5*
(C) *APA Desk Reference*
(D) *Diagnosis of Disorders Digest*
(E) *Clinicians Reference Manual III*

GO ON TO THE NEXT PAGE.

62. Which of the following samples would be considered most representative of male college students?

    (A) A group of thirty fraternity brothers from Penn State
    (B) A random sample taken between classes in the business wing of various universities
    (C) Sixty male members of each class from Princeton, Yale, Harvard, Dartmouth, and Columbia
    (D) Twenty male members of each class from a cross-section of colleges and universities
    (E) One-thousand male college graduates from across the country

63. The myelin sheath that covers the axons of most neurons serves to do which of the following?

    (A) Increase the number of messages a dendrite can receive
    (B) Increase the speed with which messages can be transmitted
    (C) Maintain the amount of neurotransmitter needed to create an action potential
    (D) Decrease the amount of information a dendrite can convey in one firing
    (E) Decrease the amount of time it takes for an axon to fire across the synaptic cleft

Questions 64–65 refer to the situation described below.

The book *A Clockwork Orange* portrays a violent individual being forced to watch violent films while simultaneously being induced by medication to vomit as a means of "curing" him of his violent tendencies. During this "treatment," the music of Beethoven is played in the background. As a result, the violent individual becomes ill not only when he views physical violence, but also whenever he hears Beethoven.

64. In this experiment, Beethoven's music is the

    (A) conditioned response
    (B) unconditioned response
    (C) conditioned stimulus
    (D) unconditioned stimulus
    (E) neutral stimulus

65. In this experiment, the individual's illness in response to the medication is the

    (A) conditioned response
    (B) unconditioned response
    (C) conditioned stimulus
    (D) unconditioned stimulus
    (E) neutral stimulus

66. Which of the following questions best frames the nature-nurture controversy?

    (A) To what degree is human behavior a result of free will versus determinism?
    (B) To what degree do external conditioning stimuli override individual loci of focus in regard to human behavior?
    (C) To what degree does the human capacity to nurture its young parallel other species in nature?
    (D) To what degree do unconscious motives versus potential consequences shape human behavior?
    (E) To what degree do inborn biological processes versus environmental events determine human behavior?

GO ON TO THE NEXT PAGE.

67. During an action potential, what occurs inside a neuron is _____; what occurs between neurons is _____.

    (A) electrical; electrical
    (B) electrical; chemical
    (C) chemical; chemical
    (D) chemical; electrical
    (E) synaptic; polarized

68. Asia has just seen a brief video entitled "Twelve Steps to a Better You" that she found on YouTube. She is now talking to her friend Joyce and trying to relay the steps. She is doing well in recounting the first few and the last few, but she finds herself unsure about elements of steps 5 to 8. This is an example of

    (A) motivated forgetting
    (B) proactive interference
    (C) retroactive interference
    (D) serial position effect
    (E) source monitoring error

69. Myron has been depressed recently and he schedules an appointment with Dr. Smith, a psychiatrist. After meeting with Myron, Dr. Smith concludes that the major reason that Myron is depressed is that he categorizes events as "catastrophic" or "wonderful," more often "catastrophic," with no in-between. Dr. Smith is relying on which psychological perspective to make this determination?

    (A) Psychoanalytic
    (B) Behaviorist
    (C) Cognitive
    (D) Humanist
    (E) Evolutionary

70. Amanda's parents are taking her to a haunted house for Halloween for the first time. If the house is truly scary, this should have the most noticeable effect on which part of Amanda's brain?

    (A) Amygdala
    (B) Pineal gland
    (C) Hippocampus
    (D) Cerebellum
    (E) Corpus callosum

71. Stephen hypothesizes that the more time that children spend on digital devices, the less time they spend in imaginative play. His researchers interview many children about their habits and their play, and they calculate weekly averages for time spent on devices and time spent in imaginative play. In comparing these two variables, which correlation coefficient provides the most support for Stephen's hypothesis?

    (A) 0.85
    (B) 0.30
    (C) 0
    (D) −0.27
    (E) −0.66

72. Kathy was driving during an ice storm and she went into a skid. As her car was spinning around, she immediately felt both fear and her heart pounding. These sensations are consistent with which theory of emotion?

    (A) James-Lange
    (B) Cannon-Bard
    (C) Schachter two-factor
    (D) Optimal arousal
    (E) Facial feedback hypothesis

73. The instrument that has traditionally been used in sleep research to assess activity in the brain is called the

    (A) signal detection device (SDD)
    (B) computerized axial tomography (CAT)
    (C) magnetic resonance imaging (MRI)
    (D) positron emission tomography (PET)
    (E) electroencephalograph (EEG)

74. Curtis stares at an image of a yellow star for a full minute. When he moves his gaze to a blank piece of white paper, he is likely to see an afterimage that is

    (A) green
    (B) yellow
    (C) red
    (D) blue
    (E) black

GO ON TO THE NEXT PAGE.

75. The obsessive fear of being in places or situations from which escape might be difficult is known as

    (A) claustrophobia
    (B) arachnophobia
    (C) social phobia
    (D) agoraphobia
    (E) paranoia

76. When a person experiences a discrepancy between an attitude and a behavior, the person experiences

    (A) cognitive dissonance
    (B) dissociation
    (C) behavioral dysfunction
    (D) metacognition
    (E) countertransference

77. People who have previously not gotten along are often able to put aside their differences in the face of a mutual crisis. Their need to work together is often referred to as a(n)

    (A) communal goal
    (B) superordinate goal
    (C) subordinate goal
    (D) alliance formation
    (E) truce agreement

78. Which of the following accomplishments accurately reflects why Wilhelm Wundt is sometimes referred to as the "father of psychology?"

    (A) He founded the first psychological laboratory in the late nineteenth century.
    (B) He developed psychoanalytical theory through his work in clinical environments.
    (C) He conducted experiments throughout the nineteenth century that led to the belief that all behavior is learned.
    (D) His research demonstrated that psychology should be free from all philosophical questions.
    (E) He created a standard of measurement in the late nineteenth century that later came to be known as inferential statistics.

79. Although they disagreed with his personal infidelities, many Americans supported President Bill Clinton's position and policy decisions during his term in office. This dichotomy of opinion demonstrates a split in

    (A) external locus of control
    (B) internal validity
    (C) self-representation
    (D) attitudinal coherence
    (E) approval ratings

80. Sanja hears a sound that she recognizes as the front door being shut. In order for her to detect the sound and process it so that she knows what it is, Sanja's ear funnels the sound waves to the inner ear in order to stimulate the cilia of the inner ear. This is a critical step in the process of

    (A) auditory transduction
    (B) olfactory perception
    (C) sensory interaction
    (D) decibel cognition
    (E) kinesthetic transference

81. Which of the following most accurately explains why a pool with water temperature of 82 degrees may feel cool to a person who has been sunbathing, yet warm to a person who has been inside in the air conditioning?

    (A) Sensory restriction
    (B) Perceptual constancy
    (C) Relative clarity
    (D) Absolute threshold
    (E) Sensory adaptation

82. According to the Gestalt theory of perception, being able to identify a three-sided object as being a triangle, even though it is partially blocked from view is an example of

    (A) proximity
    (B) similarity
    (C) closure
    (D) continuity
    (E) connectedness

GO ON TO THE NEXT PAGE.

83. Psychoactive substances are drugs that alter consciousness by

    (A) inducing the secretion of excitatory hormones into the bloodstream
    (B) imitating the behaviors of various pheromones
    (C) facilitating or inhibiting neural transmission at the synapse
    (D) increasing an individual's hypnotic susceptibility
    (E) flooding post-synaptic receptors with subliminal commands

84. A child is frightened by the sudden barking of a neighbor's dog. Once her mother picks her up, the child begins to calm down as which of the following biological processes occurs?

    (A) The parasympathetic nervous system resumes control and reverses the sympathetic responses.
    (B) The sympathetic nervous system resumes control and reverses the parasympathetic responses.
    (C) The autonomic nervous system resumes control and reverses the peripheral responses.
    (D) The peripheral nervous system resumes control and reverses the autonomic responses.
    (E) The endocrine system resumes control and reverses the responses brought on by neurotransmitters.

85. On the parietal lobe, the somatosensory strip allots space to different body parts, for purposes of evaluating incoming sensory information, based on

    (A) size
    (B) likelihood of injury
    (C) evolutionary development
    (D) sensitivity
    (E) distance from the central nervous system

86. Which of the following is an example of a result of operant conditioning?

    (A) Milo starts at the sound of a buzzer because it sounds very similar to the alarm clock that wakes him every morning.
    (B) Paula is promoted to vice president of her company and vows to not lose touch with her employees.
    (C) Rebecca cancels her credit card to avoid paying the annual fee but plans to reinstate it in the new year.
    (D) Ashmed speaks louder than usual when he talks to his mother on the phone because she is hard of hearing.
    (E) Pika avoids eating red meat after she hears several horror stories about mad cow disease.

87. Which of the following best states why the study of twins is significant to the field of behavioral genetics?

    (A) If a psychological attribute is genetically influenced, then fraternal twins are more likely to share this attribute than are identical twins or other siblings.
    (B) If a psychological attribute is genetically influenced, then siblings reared together are more likely to share it than are identical or fraternal twins who are reared apart.
    (C) The degree of relatedness in MZ twins can be determined through studying the behavioral genetics of related DZ twins.
    (D) If a psychological attribute is genetically influenced, then identical twins are more likely to share this attribute than are fraternal twins and other siblings.
    (E) Phenotypic variances in twins are more obvious than in other siblings because twins have a 1.0 degree of relatedness.

88. Detection of a just noticeable difference (JND) depends on the

    (A) presence of a "no stimulus" control and the sensitivity of the signal-detection equipment
    (B) initial determination of the absolute threshold and the variation of the difference threshold
    (C) frequency of the existing stimulus and the presence of one or more sensory modalities
    (D) establishment of a 50 percent "hit" rate and a long enough series of trials
    (E) intensity of the new stimulus and that of the stimulus already present

GO ON TO THE NEXT PAGE.

89. Lizette and her family watch the sunset over the ocean. While walking home in the increasing darkness, Lizette notices that she can no longer distinguish the colors of objects. Which of the following best explains why Lizette cannot see color in dim light?

    (A) Rods, which are specialized for color vision, require more light to be activated, whereas cones, which produce images in black, white, and gray, allow for vision in dim light.
    (B) Cones, which are specialized for color vision, require more light to be activated, whereas rods, which produce images in black, white, and gray, allow for vision in dim light.
    (C) Cones, which are specialized for black and white vision, require a small amount of light to be activated, whereas rods, which produce images in color, require greater amounts of light for vision.
    (D) The receptive fields in the retina respond to the loss of light through light adaptation, the process of rapidly adjusting to a diminution of light.
    (E) In order to perceive aspects of color such as hue, brightness, and saturation, rods require a great deal of light, while cones can perceive images in black, white, and gray with little light.

90. The "cocktail party effect" refers to

    (A) the impact of alcohol on the dopamine reward system
    (B) altered perceptual constancies
    (C) multitasking by trying to listen to several conversations at once
    (D) selective attention in trying to focus on one of several conversations
    (E) a loosening of social inhibitions

91. Jay suffers from periods of amnesia and frequent loss of a sense of personal identity. It is likely that Jay has a(n)

    (A) schizophrenic disorder
    (B) associative disorder
    (C) antisocial personality disorder
    (D) retrograde amnesia disorder
    (E) dissociative disorder

92. Which of the following correctly categorizes the components of Ivan Pavlov's research on conditioning?

    (A) The dogs (subjects) were presented with food (CS) while also being presented with the sights and sounds of the presenter (UCS). After a time, the dogs salivated in response to the presenter (UCR).
    (B) The dogs (subjects) were presented with food (UCR) while also being presented with the sights and sounds of the presenter (CR). After a time, the dogs salivated in response to the presenter (CS).
    (C) The dogs (subjects) were presented with food (UCS) while also being presented with the sights and sounds of the presenter (CS). After a time, the dogs salivated in response to the presenter (CR).
    (D) The dogs (subjects) were presented with food (CR) while also being presented with the sights and sounds of the presenter (UCR). After a time, the dogs salivated in response to the presenter (UCS).
    (E) The dogs (subjects) were presented with food (neutral stimulus) while also being presented with the sights and sounds of the presenter (UCS). After a time, the dogs salivated in response to the presenter (CR).

93. In Pavlov's conditioning of dogs, the point at which the dogs salivated at the sound of the tone without the food being present is referred to as

    (A) an unconditioned stimulus
    (B) acquisition
    (C) discrimination
    (D) generalization
    (E) spontaneous recovery

94. In developmental research, studying the same subjects over time is known as

    (A) cross-sectional research
    (B) cross-cultural research
    (C) in-cohort sequential research
    (D) longitudinal research
    (E) correlational research

GO ON TO THE NEXT PAGE.

95. The goal of projective personality tests, such as the Rorschach and Thematic Apperception Test (TAT), is to

(A) gain insight into potential biochemical abnormalities
(B) uncover unconscious thoughts and feelings
(C) assess basic personality traits
(D) assess cultural influences on personality
(E) predict how personality is suited to particular occupations

96. Which of the following accurately summarizes a depressed person's view according to Aaron Beck's negative triad theory?

(A) Depressed individuals cope with the three primary stresses—change, death, and monetary instability—through withdrawal.
(B) Depressed individuals believe that when they are in a group, at least three individuals will view them negatively.
(C) Depressed individuals hold a negative view of themselves, the world, and their futures.
(D) Depressed individuals view the world in three stages—separation anxiety, development of an external locus of control, and failure to achieve.
(E) Depressed individuals tend to form friendships with other depressed individuals, usually in groups of three.

97. Which of the following is an example of imprinting?

(A) A mother eagle will fly under her young while they are learning to fly in case they begin to fall.
(B) A newborn gosling will "attach" to the first moving object it sees, usually its mother.
(C) An infant who is left by its primary caregivers for significant periods of time develops an indifference to their presence.
(D) A mother cat teaches her kittens how to clean themselves.
(E) A premature infant grows rapidly in part as a result of constantly being held by a primary caregiver.

98. Each of the following is a step taken by a therapist who is employing systematic desensitization EXCEPT

(A) helping the client experience the desired state of relaxation through hypnosis
(B) teaching the client to relax through techniques such as deep breathing
(C) constructing a hierarchy of feared images
(D) instructing the client to picture each fearful image while maintaining a relaxed state
(E) encouraging the client to confront her fears in real life

99. Max was typically out of control whenever he attended preschool. Teachers tried time-outs and other punishments to no avail. His parents and the school decided to work with Max by giving him a sticker each time he behaved for a full hour. Once he accumulated ten stickers, he could present them to his parents who would give him a reward. The method the school and parents chose to employ is referred to as

(A) negative reinforcement
(B) a token economy
(C) a point value system
(D) negative punishment
(E) classical conditioning

100. Which of the following best states a conclusion of Stanley Milgram's study of obedience?

(A) When faced with a difficult decision, people are more likely to follow the opinions of the crowd than to diverge from those opinions.
(B) When challenged to commit a crime, people will most often refuse if they are not coerced, but will agree if an authority figure coerces them.
(C) When asked to inflict pain on others, people are likely to inflict mild amounts of pain without remorse.
(D) When asked to participate in a study, people are more likely to agree if they are offered some sort of compensation.
(E) When an authority figure is present, people are more likely to obey orders than to question the wisdom of the orders.

END OF SECTION I

IF YOU FINISH BEFORE TIME IS CALLED, YOU MAY CHECK YOUR WORK ON THIS SECTION. DO NOT GO ON TO SECTION II UNTIL YOU ARE TOLD TO DO SO.

PSYCHOLOGY
Section II
Time—50 minutes

Percent of total grade—$33\frac{1}{3}$

Directions: You have 50 minutes to answer BOTH of the following questions. It is not enough to answer a question by merely listing facts. You should present a cogent argument based on your critical analysis of the question posed using appropriate psychological terminology.

1. Jack, a three-year-old boy, has been throwing many tantrums lately and has been ignoring his parents' directions. Jack's parents are growing increasingly frustrated by his oppositional behavior. They decide to consult a developmental expert to ask for advice in dealing with their child. The developmental expert suggests that they consider the following factors in understanding Jack's behavior:

   - Egocentrism
   - Preconventional morality
   - Erikson's stage of initiative vs. guilt
   - Observational learning

   A. Define and provide an example of the application of each of the concepts listed above to explain Jack's behavior.

   B. Explain how Jack's parents should integrate the knowledge of his developmental stage in their plan to deal with his tantrum behavior.

2. Sharlene runs a company that markets nutritional supplements. She has read articles about the importance of a nutritional lunch for high school students' performance in their classes after lunch. She also knows about criticisms of the nutritional value of the school lunches available in local high schools. She wants to market her products to the local school system. To that end, she sets up, with the School Board's permission, the following experiment:
   Half of the students on each lunch shift will be provided the nutritional supplements; the other half will not. After lunch, evaluators hired by Sharlene's company will sit in classrooms and rate students' on-task behavior on a one-to-ten scale. These ratings will then be matched with the records of which students received the supplements.
   Answer the following questions about Sharlene's study:

   - Why is this an experiment and not a correlational study?
   - What is the independent variable?
   - What is the operational definition of the dependent variable?

   Explain how the following concepts could affect the validity of Sharlene's study:

   - Random assignment
   - Double-blind procedure

   What is a possible ethical concern with Sharlene's study?

   What is a possible confounding variable for this study?

STOP

END OF EXAM

Practice Test 2:
Answers and
Explanations

ANSWER KEY

1. D	26. E	51. C	76. A
2. D	27. E	52. C	77. B
3. D	28. A	53. C	78. A
4. A	29. A	54. B	79. D
5. C	30. C	55. E	80. A
6. E	31. C	56. A	81. E
7. B	32. A	57. A	82. C
8. B	33. B	58. D	83. C
9. D	34. E	59. E	84. A
10. D	35. E	60. C	85. D
11. A	36. E	61. B	86. D
12. E	37. C	62. D	87. D
13. B	38. D	63. B	88. E
14. A	39. D	64. C	89. B
15. C	40. A	65. B	90. D
16. C	41. C	66. E	91. E
17. B	42. A	67. B	92. C
18. A	43. B	68. D	93. B
19. D	44. C	69. C	94. D
20. D	45. E	70. A	95. B
21. B	46. E	71. E	96. C
22. C	47. C	72. B	97. B
23. A	48. D	73. E	98. A
24. B	49. D	74. D	99. B
25. D	50. B	75. D	100. E

MULTIPLE-CHOICE SECTION: ANSWERS AND EXPLANATIONS

1. **D** *Understand the Question/Key Words:* Circle *toxic* and *taste*. *Predict the Answer:* Bitter or nasty. Toxic substances won't be (B), sweet, or (E), bland, and probably not (C), salty. Choice (D), bitter, is the strongest choice.

2. **D** *Understand the Question/Key Words*: Circle *Freud* and *perspectives*. *Predict the Answer*: Psychoanalytic. If you missed this one, you'd better hit the books.

3. **D** *Understand the Question/Key Words*: An automatic reaction to something is called a… *Predict the Answer*: Reflex. Rephrasing the question makes the answer much more obvious. Now use POE to quickly scan the answers. Watch out for (C), aversive stimulus, and (E), drive.

4. **A** *Understand the Question/Key Words*: These things make up your personality. They are known as personality… *Predict the Answer*: Traits. If you are unsure, use POE. As in (A), are emotional, cognitive, and behavioral tendencies *traits* that make up personality? Sounds good. Keep it, and check the others. As in (B), are emotional, cognitive, and behavioral tendencies *moods* that make up personality? No. Cross it off. As in (C), are emotional, cognitive, and behavioral tendencies *temperaments* that make up personality? If you are unsure, leave it, although temperaments are more like moods. As in (D), are emotional, cognitive, and behavioral tendencies *tenets* that make up personality? No, beliefs don't make up personality. Finally, as in (E), are emotional, cognitive, and behavioral tendencies *personalities* that make up personality? No. Choice (A) is the best answer.

5. **C** *Understand the Question/Key Words*: Psychology came from what origin? *Predict the Answer*: Philosophy. If you aren't sure, use POE to get rid of choices that wouldn't make sense. You need something that is concerned with thought processes and relationships and is older than psychology. Cross off (A), biochemistry, (B), physics, and (E), statistics, because none of these answers are concerned with thought processes. Watch out for (D), cross-cultural anthropology.

6. **E** *Understand the Question/Key Words*: She plays peek-a-boo, which means what, developmentally? *Predict the Answer*: She knows that the fact that she cannot see her mother does not mean her mother is gone. In other words, she has developed object permanence. If you don't remember the term, use POE. Would a sense of (A), playing versus learning, mean she knows her mother is not gone? No. Cross it off. Would a sense of (B), transitivity, mean she knows her mother is not gone? No, it is something to do with transience or changing. Would a sense of (C), metacognition, mean she knows her mother is not gone? She is too young for this level of complex thought. Would a sense of (D), attachment anxiety, mean she knows her mother is not gone? No, it would mean the opposite. Would a sense of (E), object permanence, mean she knows her mother is not gone? Bingo.

7. **B** *Understand the Question/Key Words*: Psychologists who study a few subjects in great depth are using… *Predict the Answer*: A case study. Choice (A), an experiment, shows cause and effect relationships. Choice (C), naturalistic observation, is often used by anthropologists to study people and animals in their natural environment. Choice (D), correlational research, is used to study the relationship between or among variables. Choice (E), longitudinal research, is used by developmental psychologists to assess change over time.

8. **B**   *Understand the Question/Key Words*: Circle *definition of learning*. *Predict the Answer*: A change in behavior based on experience. Use POE to get rid of (A) because of the word "temporarily" and (C) and (E) because they use extreme language (sole, not). Learning involves a permanent change, not a mere association, so the answer is (B).

9. **D**   *Understand the Question/Key Words*: If you don't sleep for two days, you may begin to experience… *Predict the Answer*: Hallucinations. If you are unsure, use POE. Sleepless doesn't mean without food or water so get rid of (A), hunger, and (B), thirst. Choice (E) is also way off base.

10. **D**   *Understand the Question/Key Words*: When you struggle between what you want to do and what you ought to do, you are experiencing… *Predict the Answer*: cognitive dissonance. Watch out for (B), which is a trap answer. The general adaptation syndrome concerns chronic stress, and the word "tension" in the question may trick you into thinking about stress. None of the other answer choices come close to cognitive dissonance.

11. **A**   *Understand the Question/Key Words*: Circle *endorphins*. What do they do? *Predict the Answer*: Make you feel good. Now use POE to find an answer that is close to yours. If you don't remember what endorphins do, POE will get rid of (D) and (E) because of the extreme language.

12. **E**   *Understand the Question/Key Words*: Nell doesn't want to get in trouble like her brother did, so she won't throw her stuffed animal into the toilet. What is this called? *Predict the Answer*: Nell is learning by watching her brother's experience (vicariously through her brother). This is called vicarious conditioning. If you are unsure, use POE. Would (A), prepared conditioning, mean learning from watching her brother's experience? No, this is not a psychological concept. Cross it off. Would (B), tutelage, mean learning from watching her brother's experience? No. Would (C), scheduled reinforcement, mean learning from watching her brother's experience? No, that is not taking place here. Would (D), shaping, mean learning from watching her brother's experience? Again, shaping is more direct. Would (E), vicarious learning, mean learning from watching her brother's experience? Yup.

13. **B**   *Understand the Question/Key Words*: *Jeopardy!* requires which type of intelligence? *Predict the Answer*: Crystallized intelligence—knowledge of facts. If you are unsure, use POE. Does (A), IQ, mean knowledge of facts and trivia? No, it is a score on a very specific test. Don't confuse IQ with intelligence. Does (B), crystallized intelligence, mean knowledge of facts and trivia? It sounds good. Keep it, and check the others. Does (C), fluid intelligence, mean knowledge of facts and trivia? No, it involves thinking and problem-solving skills. Does (D), general intelligence, mean knowledge of facts and trivia? It might. Keep it. Does (E), multiple intelligence, mean knowledge of facts and trivia? No, it involves a theory of various intelligences. Choice (B), crystallized intelligence, is more clearly associated with factual knowledge than (D), general intelligence.

14. **A**   *Understand the Question/Key Words*: Circle *true of memory recall*. *Predict the Answer*: Not sure what they want, so evaluate each answer based on what you know of memory. Choice (A) sounds logical and is also true—people recall information that is in keeping with their personal schemas. Choice (B) is wrong because working memory is irrelevant to recall. Is (C) true? No, so cross it off. Same goes for (E). (D) doesn't sound true either. It must be (A).

15. **C** *Understand the Question/Key Words*: What do objects that absorb light look like? *Predict the Answer*: Dark. Dark objects absorb light while bright objects reflect light. Beware of (A), black. The question does not say "objects that absorb all color."

16. **C** *Understand the Question/Key Words:* Chantal is trying to push her unwanted negative qualities onto her mother so that the qualities are less threatening. This is called… *Predict the Answer*: Projection. Use POE to get rid of (A), repression, because that would mean that Chantal was trying to push these unwanted feelings back into her unconscious mind. Choice (B), regression, would mean that she was trying to revert back to an earlier stage of psychosexual development. Choice (D), displacement, would imply that she was taking out her frustrations with her mother on a more socially acceptable target. Choice (E), denial, would mean that Chantal was failing to accept that something unwanted or frightening was happening to her.

17. **B** *Understand the Question/Key Words*: Circle *humanistic perspective. Predict the Answer*: Humanists believe that people can control their behavior and that they strive to reach their full potential. Use POE to find an answer that agrees with this statement. Choice (A) is the biological perspective, (C) is the behaviorist perspective, (D) is the psychodynamic perspective, and (E) is the cognitive perspective.

18. **A** *Understand the Question/Key Words*: Circle *visual*. Which lobe is involved in vision? *Predict the Answer*: Occipital lobe. If you don't know, use POE to get rid of (D), frontal (you probably know that the frontal lobe is used for a variety of more-complex tasks), and (E), cerebral, because this isn't a lobe of the brain.

19. **D** *Understand the Question/Key Words*: When are mean, median, and mode equal to the same number? *Predict the Answer*: In a normal distribution. If you don't remember, use POE. Choices (A) and (C) represent distributions where scores are overwhelmingly low or high, respectively. Choice (B), asymmetrical, is a generic term for a skewed distribution. Choice (E), abnormal, is not generally a term used to describe distributions.

20. **D** *Understand the Question/Key Words*: When a six-month-old gets upset when Mom leaves, it's called… *Predict the Answer*: Separation anxiety. Watch out for (A), attachment anxiety, and (B), reactive attachment disorder. Choices (C), object permanence, and (E), detachment adaptation, would require a different response from the child.

21. **B** *Understand the Question/Key Words*: Circle *B. F. Skinner. Predict the Answer*: Skinner = behaviorism. If you missed this question, hit the books.

22. **C** *Understand the Question/Key Words*: She is using a survey to try to correlate guilt with other emotions. This kind of study is called… *Predict the Answer*: Correlational study. If you don't remember the term, use POE. Would (A), a demographic study, try to correlate two or more emotions? No. Would (B), an observational study, try to correlate two or more emotions? No, and it wouldn't involve a survey. Would (C), a correlational study, try to correlate two or more emotions? Sounds good. Would (D), an experimental study, try to correlate two or more emotions? Maybe, but not by using a survey. Would (E), a statistical study, try to correlate two or more emotions? Use of statistics usually comes after the study. The answer is (C).

23. **A** *Understand the Question/Key Words*: Which term is used to describe many psychotic disorders? *Predict the Answer*: Schizophrenia. If you are unsure, use POE to get rid of (C), dissociative disorder, and (D), depression, because they are specific disorders and (E) because it is a made-up term.

24. **B** *Understand the Question/Key Words*: Circle *firing of a neuron*. *Predict the Answer*: All or nothing. Use POE to get rid of answers that don't make sense. Get rid of (A) because firing does not occur gradually, (C) because this is also a false statement, and (E) because a neuron cannot fire "harder." Choice (D) is also a false statement.

25. **D** *Understand the Question/Key Words*: The fact that Xavier wants to hang out with some new friends is called a(n)... *Predict the Answer*: Affiliation need. Choices (A), fraternization need, (B), assimilation need, and (E), loneliness need, are not true psychological terms, and (C) is too strong.

26. **E** *Understand the Question/Key Words*: Learning the meaning of something in order to increase your ability to memorize it is called... *Predict the Answer*: Semantic memory. If you are unsure of the exact term, POE should get rid of (C) and (D) because applying meaning is not simply rehearsing.

27. **E** *Understand the Question/Key Words*: Circle *outer ear*. *Predict the Answer*: Collect and magnify sound. Even if you are not sure, don't give the outer ear too much credit. Get rid of (A), (B), and (D).

28. **A** *Understand the Question/Key Words*: What kind of variable is eating breakfast in this study? *Predict the Answer*: Eating breakfast is an either/or thing, so it is a categorical variable. Even if you are not sure, POE can get rid of (C), dependent variable, because it is not being observed and measured, (D), independent variable, because it is not being manipulated, and (E), conditioned variable, because it is not conditioned.

29. **A** *Understand the Question/Key Words*: Circle *left hemisphere*. *Predict the Answer*: Language functions. Even if you don't remember, use POE. Choices (B), logic, and (C), analytical reasoning, are the same, so neither can be right. Choices (D), mathematical reasoning, and (E), spatial reasoning, are two right-hemisphere functions, so (A), language, is your best guess.

30. **C** *Understand the Question/Key Words*: Molding behavior by first praising all attempts and later only praising improved attempts is called... *Predict the Answer*: Shaping. If you don't remember the term, use POE. Could (A), negative reinforcement, mean to first praise all attempts and then only praise improvements? No. Cross it off. Could (B), negative punishment, mean to first praise all attempts and then only praise improvements? No. Could (C), shaping, mean to first praise all attempts and then only praise improvements? Sure. Keep it, and check the others. Could (D), chaining, mean to first praise all attempts and then only praise improvements? No, chaining is linking together skills someone already has. Could (E), discriminating, mean to first praise all attempts and then only praise improvements? No. The answer must be (C).

31. **C** *Understand the Question/Key Words*: When a client takes out on her counselor the feelings she has for her parents, it's called... *Predict the Answer*: Transference. If you don't remember the term, use POE. Could (A), suppression, mean to take out on the counselor feelings you have for your parents? No, it would involve keeping the feelings in. Could (B), conflicting motives, mean to

take out on the counselor feelings you have for your parents? It has the right tone but is still too weak. Cross it off. Could (C), transference, mean to take out on the counselor feelings you have for your parents? Yes. Could (D), countertransference, mean to take out on the counselor feelings you have for your parents? No, that's when the counselor puts stuff on the client. Choice (E), reaction formation, would mean that she was taking on the opposite opinion of what she really feels.

32. **A** *Understand the Question/Key Words*: Circle the last phrase. What is it called when you remember something you were not consciously trying to remember? *Predict the Answer*: Tip-of-the-tongue phenomenon. If you don't remember the term, you know what to do: POE. Could (A), tip-of-the-tongue phenomenon, mean to remember something you were not consciously trying to remember? Yes. Quickly check the others. Could (B), chunking, mean to remember something you were not consciously trying to remember? No, it is a learning technique. Could (C), deductive reasoning, mean to remember something you were not consciously trying to remember? No. Could (D), inductive reasoning, mean to remember something you were not consciously trying to remember? Nope. Could (E), parallelism, mean to remember something you were not consciously trying to remember? No. Your answer must be (A).

33. **B** *Understand the Question/Key Words*: Circle *hypnosis* and *diminish*. *Predict the Answer*: Chronic pain. If you don't remember this, use common-sense POE to get rid of (A), antisocial personality disorder, (D), kinesthetic abilities, and (E), Alzheimer's disease.

34. **E** *Understand the Question/Key Words*: Why do mnemonic devices work? *Predict the Answer*: They link information to stuff you already know. POE should get rid of (A) because stuff you already know is in your LTM, not your STM and (D) because it is impractical and unrealistic. Don't be thrown by the technical language of (B). Choice (E) is the closest to your answer.

35. **E** *Understand the Question/Key Words*: What's it called when you wake up horribly scared by a bad dream? *Predict the Answer*: A nightmare. POE will help you get rid of (A), hallucination, (B), phobia, and (C), narcoleptic event. You might be fooled by (D), night terror, but generally night terrors occur in a deeper sleep state than the REM sleep state that is typical of dreams, so they do not produce vividly memorable experiences.

36. **E** *Understand the Question/Key Words*: What is the term used to describe when prejudices are acted upon? *Predict the Answer*: Discrimination. Your clue is "behavioral component." Choices (A), bias, (B), conditioning, and (C), catharsis, are not directly related to the question. Choice (D), passive aggression, is way off base, so (E), discrimination, is the best answer.

37. **C** *Understand the Question/Key Words*: What happens when there is a break in the twenty-first chromosome pair? *Predict the Answer*: Down syndrome. Choice (C) says this.

38. **D** *Understand the Question/Key Words*: Circle *punishment* and *EXCEPT*. *Predict the Answer*: Remember that punishment is something that is intended to make an undesirable response less likely (whether it works or not). Does (A) intend this? Yes, so it is an example of punishment. Cross this off as you need something that isn't. Does (B) intend this? Yes, so cross it off. How about (C)? Yes again, so eliminate it. Choice (E) also attempts to lessen an undesirable response on the part of the puppy. Choice (D), refusing to return the boss's call after not getting the expected raise, is not intended

to lessen an undesirable behavior on the part of the boss, if one could even define what that undesirable behavior was (not giving a raise is not an undesirable response, but a lack of a desired response). Your answer is (D).

39. **D** *Understand the Question/Key Words*: Jung's theory of all humans sharing a collective set of ideas, feelings, and symbols is called... *Predict the Answer*: Jung's theory of collective unconscious. Even if you don't remember the term, POE will help. Choice (A), cultural subconscious, is made up, (C), heritability coefficients, refers to something completely different, and (E), integrated intelligence, is made up. Choice (B), general awareness, is weak. The answer must be (D).

40. **A** *Understand the Question/Key Words*: What is active sleeping and dreaming called? *Predict the Answer*: REM sleep. All the other choices are deeper stages of sleep.

41. **C** *Understand the Question/Key Words*: Circle *placement of words and phrases in a sentence*. *Predict the Answer*: Syntax. If you don't remember, use POE to get rid of at least (D) and (E). Choice (B) is too broad.

42. **A** *Understand the Question/Key Words*: Animals won't put together the conditioned stimulus and the unconditioned stimulus if... *Predict the Answer*: They occur too far apart. Find the choice that is closest to yours—(A), the delay between the CS and UCS is too long, is the best answer.

43. **B** *Understand the Question/Key Words*: Circle *secondary drives* and *EXCEPT*. *Predict the Answer*: Four of the choices are secondary drives. Choice (B), sex, is a primary drive.

44. **C** When one's behavior and one's thinking are not in alignment, there are two ways one can bring them into alignment. An obvious way, but also often a hard way, is to change one's behavior to fit one's thinking. The fact that many New Year's resolutions are quickly abandoned shows how difficult it can be to change one's behavior to fit one's ideas. The other way to minimize this conflict between behavior and thought is to change one's thought process to justify the bad behavior. The name of this feeling of conflict is "cognitive dissonance." The other concepts are either irrelevant or made-up.

45. **E** *Understand the Question/Key Words*: Dysfunction in what part of the brain would cause staggering and slurred speech? *Predict the Answer*: The cerebellum. If you don't remember, you can probably use POE to get rid of (B), thalamus, (C), sensorimotor cortex, and (D), amygdala.

46. **E** *Understand the Question/Key Words*: Turkey made her sick. Why would chicken also make her queasy? *Predict the Answer*: Turkey and chicken are similar—stimulus generalization. If you don't remember the term, use POE. Choices (B), latent learning, and (C), prepared learning, are obviously out. Does (A), response generalization, mean associating similar stimuli? Be careful—it says response generalization. Does (D), unconditioned stimulus response, mean associating similar stimuli? Again, this is talking about a response. The answer must be (E), stimulus generalization.

47. **C** *Understand the Question/Key Words*: Circle *perception*. *Predict the Answer*: The process by which the brain organizes and interprets sensations. Use POE. Choice (A) is the definition of sensation, (B) doesn't go far enough because perception is more than initial processing, and (D) refers to sensory adaptation. Choice (E) takes it too far.

48. **D** *Understand the Question/Key Words*: What happens in order for you to perceive an increase in sound? *Predict the Answer*: More neurons fire more frequently. If you are unsure, use POE. Would (A), neurons firing more intensely, make you perceive an increase in sound? Can neurons fire more intensely? No, so cross this answer off. Choice (B) is way out of the ballpark. Would (C), changing frequency of sound waves, make you perceive an increase in sound? This phenomenon would be responsible for the sound seeming lower in pitch or higher in pitch, but not for it seeming louder (and it still being a pitch that is perceptible to the human ear). Would (D), more neurons firing more frequently, make you perceive an increase in sound? Yes. Choice (E) is way out because the "what" pathway is related to vision.

49. **D** *Understand the Question/Key Words*: What allows us to tell the difference between two similar stimuli? *Predict the Answer*: The difference threshold or just noticeable difference (JND). This may seem tricky because all of the other choices are also related to thresholds. Choice (A), subliminal perception, suggests that stimuli below the threshold can still unconsciously influence behavior. Choice (B), absolute threshold, refers to the ability to detect a stimulus 50 percent of the time. Choice (C), signal detection theory, refers to the ability to lower a threshold based on experience or expectation. Choice (E), Weber's law, refers to the need for stimuli to vary by a constant proportion in order for us to detect differences among stimuli.

50. **B** *Understand the Question/Key Words*: Jerome is a student at the Peddie School, and all students at the Peddie School study Latin. *Predict the Answer*: Jerome takes Latin. This is the only thing you definitely know.

51. **C** *Understand the Question/Key Words*: She is confident and self-directed. Therefore she has… *Predict the Answer*: An internal locus of control. If you don't remember the term, use POE. Would a confident, self-directed person have a manic coping strategy, as in (A)? No, that strategy would be dysfunctional. Cross this answer off. Would a confident, self-directed person have a discriminative expectancy, as in (B)? This term doesn't make sense. Cross it off. Would a confident, self-directed person have an internal locus of control, as in (C)? Hopefully this answer jogs your memory. Even if you aren't sure, the term sounds possible, so keep it and check the others. Would a confident, self-directed person have an external locus of control, as in (D)? No, that would involve looking to others for your own direction or self-worth. This answer is the opposite of what you want. Would a confident, self-directed person have generalized expectancy, as in (E)? No. (C) is it.

52. **C** *Understand the Question/Key Words*: How do we refer to an emotional release that reduces aggressive tendencies? *Predict the Answer*: The catharsis hypothesis. Choice (A), James-Lange theory of emotion, is a theory that posits that physiological arousal precedes emotional experience. Choice (B), counterconditioning, is a behavioral term. Choice (D), transference, is a term used in psychoanalysis. Choice (E), the two-factor theory, discusses the physiological arousal and cognitive evaluation that precede the experience of emotion.

53. **C** *Understand the Question/Key Words*: Circle *constant state that permits cells to live and function*. The body is in a state of… *Predict the Answer*: Homeostasis. This is a term you need to know. Even if you don't remember the exact term, you should be able to get rid of (B), set point, (D), kinesthesia, and (E), affect regulation. Watch out for (A), perceptual constancy—it is a trap answer, since "constancy" might remind you of the word "constant" in the question stem.

54. **B**   *Understand the Question/Key Words*: Circle *periods of special sensitivity*. The times in which one is primed for learning are called… *Predict the Answer*: Critical periods. If you are unsure of the term, review Chapter 13.

55. **E**   *Understand the Question/Key Words*: What causes people to act differently in a crowd than they would individually? *Predict the Answer*: Diffusion of responsibility. Use POE to rule out the other choices. Choice (A), social loafing, refers to people's tendency to exert less effort in a group than they would individually. Close, but not right. Choices (B), prejudice, (C), conformity, and (D), obedience, all increase when more people are present.

56. **A**   *Understand the Question/Key Words*: She leaves a bad thing and goes to the same bad thing. *Predict the Answer*: Freud's theory of psychoanalytic conflict. If you don't remember the name of the theory, use POE. Could leaving a bad thing for the same bad thing be an example of (A), psychodynamic conflict? It's definitely a conflict, and most likely one taking place in the unconscious. Keep this and check the others. Could leaving a bad thing for the same bad thing be an example of (B), opposing motives? She is not experiencing opposing motives—she is going to the same bad thing. Cross this answer off. Could leaving a bad thing for the same bad thing be an example of (C), id, ego, and superego? Not really. Could leaving a bad thing for the same bad thing be an example of (D), behavioral dysfunction? Her behavior is dysfunctional, but this was not a theory of Freud's. Choice (E) is a concept from social psychology, not Freudian theory.

57. **A**   *Understand the Question/Key Words*: Circle *Piaget*. How do children develop knowledge? *Predict the Answer*: From their own experiences. Use POE to find the answer closest to yours. Choice (B) is out, as is (C) and (E). Don't get drawn in by (D).

58. **D**   *Understand the Question/Key Words*: Which needs to be studied over a long period of time? *Predict the Answer*: Anything that is related to changes over time. Use POE to find an answer that is close to yours. Be careful on (A)—age differences could be measured by studying groups of people at different ages, not necessarily the same people at different ages. Look for an answer that is more clear. Choice (D), changes in behavior over time, is the closest to yours.

59. **E**   *Understand the Question/Key Words*: He slowly got over his fear by gradual exposure and eventual participation. This is called… *Predict the Answer*: Systematic desensitization. If you don't remember the term, use POE. Could (A), countertransference, mean gradual exposure and participation? No. Could (B), peer-counselor alliance, mean gradual exposure and participation? No, so cross it off. Could (C), rational-emotive therapy, mean gradual exposure and participation? Sounds possible. Keep it, and check the rest. Could (D), flooding, mean gradual exposure and participation? It doesn't sound very gradual. Cross it off. Could (E), systematic desensitization, mean gradual exposure and participation? Yes. This refers to a process of gradual exposure to a fear stimulus.

60. **C**   This is a basic precept of humanistic practice. Choice (A) is involved in psychoanalytic practice. Choices (B), (D), and (E) are involved with behaviorist practice.

61. **B** *Understand the Question/Key Words*: What's the APA diagnostic manual called? *Predict the Answer*: *DSM-5*. Use POE to get rid of (A), ANOVA, which is a measure of statistics; (C), APA Desk Reference; (D), Diagnosis of Disorders Digest; and (E), Clinicians Reference Manual III, because they are made-up titles.

62. **D** *Understand the Question/Key Words*: Circle *samples* and *male college students*. *Predict the Answer*: Find a group that represents males from a wide variety of colleges. Use POE. Choices (A) and (C) would not represent all college males, nor would (B) because the sampling is done in the business wing. Be careful of (E)—college graduates—some of whom graduated a half-century ago—do not represent college students.

63. **B** *Understand the Question/Key Words*: What does the myelin sheath do? *Predict the Answer*: Covers the axons to speed transmission of messages. If you remember that myelination is not complete in children, which contributes to their lack of coordination, use that information to infer that myelination improves some aspect of neural communication. Eliminate (D) and (E). Cross off (A) because dendrites don't receive messages. Choice (C) is also false.

64. **C** *Understand the Question/Key Words*: Circle *Beethoven's music*, and then identify what role it plays in the scenario. *Predict the Answer*: Conditioned stimulus. At the least, you should be able to use POE for (A), conditioned response, and (B), unconditioned response, because the music is a stimulus, not a response.

65. **B** *Understand the Question/Key Words*: Circle *illness in response to the medication*. What is that in the scenario? *Predict the Answer*: An unconditioned response. At the least, you know that the illness is a response so eliminate (C), conditioned stimulus, (D), unconditioned stimulus, and (E), neutral stimulus. Is it conditioned? No, because the medicine is inducing the illness.

66. **E** *Understand the Question/Key Words*: Circle *nature-nurture controversy*, and then jot down your understanding of the nature-nurture controversy. *Predict the Answer*: To what degree is behavior shaped by nature/genetics over nurture/environment? Use POE to find the answer that is closest to yours. Get rid of (A) and (B). Choice (C) is silly; it just throws in the terms *nurture* and *nature*. Choice (D) is comparing psychodynamic and behaviorist perspectives.

67. **B** When a resting potential becomes an action potential, this is a change in electrical charge inside the neuron. When the action potential reaches the axon terminal, a chemical (neurotransmitter) is emitted across the synaptic gap to the next neuron in the network.

68. **D** When a list being processed to short-term, or working, memory exceeds "Miller's Magic Number," seven plus or minus two, people have a tendency to remember items at the beginning or end of the list better than items in the middle. Choice (D) is the correct answer.

69. **C** The cognitive explanation for depression involves people engaging in selective perception, "all-or-nothing" thinking, and "catastrophizing." The psychoanalytic approach would emphasize childhood traumas and repressed memories. The behaviorist approach would emphasize how depressive tendencies could be reinforced by the person's environment. The humanist approach would emphasize obstacles preventing someone from achieving a coherent "self." The evolutionary approach would not apply.

70. **A** Choice (B) is involved in regulating sleep cycles. Choice (C) is involved with memory. Choice (D) is involved with coordinated muscular movements. Choice (E) allows communication between the right and left hemispheres of the brain. Choice (A) has been found to be involved in negative emotions, such as fear and anger.

71. **E** This is a strong inverse relationship. Choice (A) would apply to a strong direct relationship. Choices (B), (C), and (D) represent relatively weak correlations.

72. **B** She experienced physiological arousal and the emotion simultaneously, which is consistent with Cannon Bard. In James Lange, the arousal would precede and cause the emotion. In Schachter, the arousal would come first and the emotion would be determined by cognitive labeling of the arousal. Neither (D) nor (E) applies here.

73. **E** *Understand the Question/Key Words*: What instrument, traditionally used in sleep research, assesses brain activity? *Predict the Answer*: EEG. Choice (A), signal detection device, has nothing to do with brain activity detection. Choices (B), CAT, and (C), MRI, are used to locate brain lesions. Choice (D), PET, is a very recent technology, so it is not the one that has been traditionally used.

74. **D** *Understand the Question/Key Words*: Circle *afterimage*. He is looking at something yellow. His afterimage will be… *Predict the Answer*: Blue. Even if you don't remember afterimages, you should remember the pairs of colors red-green and yellow-blue. If you don't, you will likely remember that red and green go together (red-green color blindness is a common thing). Eliminate (A), green, and (C), red. Also, eliminate (B), yellow—this is too hard a question for the afterimage to be the same color. You can also guess that the opposite color image of black is white, so (D), blue, is your best guess.

75. **D** *Understand the Question/Key Words*: The fear of being in situations that are hard to escape from is called… *Predict the Answer*: Agoraphobia. Watch out for (A), claustrophobia, because it is a trap answer. This question doesn't say anything about small places. Common sense should also get rid of (E), paranoia.

76. **A** *Understand the Question/Key Words*: Circle *discrepancy between an attitude and a behavior*. If someone thinks one thing but does something else, s/he may experience… *Predict the Answer*: Cognitive dissonance—mental conflict. If you don't remember the term, use POE. Could (A), cognitive dissonance, mean mental conflict? Sure, that sounds right. Keep it, and check the others. Could (B), dissociation, mean mental conflict? No, cross it off. Could (C), behavioral dysfunction, mean mental conflict? No, it's about behavior. Cross it off. Could (D), metacognition, mean mental conflict? No, there is nothing about conflict here. Could (E), countertransference, mean mental conflict? No. It must be (A).

77. **B** *Understand the Question/Key Words*: A crisis can cause people to forget their differences and work together. This is called a(n)… *Predict the Answer*: Superordinate goal—their need to work together overrides their personal differences. Even if you don't remember the term, use POE. Get rid of (C), subordinate goal, because it is subordinate. Choice (E), truce agreement, is silly, and (A), communal goal, is too weak.

78. **A**   *Understand the Question/Key Words*: Circle *Wilhelm Wundt* and *father of psychology*. *Predict the Answer*: He founded the first psych lab. Even if you don't remember Wilhelm, use the info in the question and your brain power to POE. Choice (B) is out because it describes Freud. Choice (C) is out because you know that Pavlov and Skinner are the big guys in behaviorism. Choice (D) is extreme (all philosophical questions). Of the remaining choices, (A) sounds more impressive.

79. **D**   *Understand the Question/Key Words*: People disagreed with him and yet support him. This demonstrates a split in... *Predict the Answer*: Attitudinal coherence. If you don't remember the term, you know that people think both good and bad stuff about the guy, so it is a split in homogeneous ideas. Choice (D), attitudinal coherence, is the closest to "homogeneous ideas."

80. **A**   *Understand the Question/Key Words*: The sound waves stimulate the cilia of the inner ear. This is called... *Predict the Answer*: Transduction. If you don't recognize this as the description of transduction, POE what you can. Olfaction and kinesthesia have nothing to do with hearing, so eliminate (B), olfactory perception, and (E), kinesthetic transference. Choice (D), decibel cognition, is made up, and (C), sensory interaction, is not the same as perception.

81. **E**   *Understand the Question/Key Words*: Why does the water feel cool at first but then eventually feel comfortable once you have been in it for a while? *Predict the Answer*: Sensory adaptation. The water temperature is the same, but your body adapts to the coolness of the water.

82. **C**   *Understand the Question/Key Words*: What does it take to identify or recognize something, even when the object is obstructed? *Predict the Answer*: Matching it against something retained in LTM in Gestalt theory is known as *closure*. The other choices are also Gestalt principles, but they do not fit what the question asked. Choice (A), proximity, refers to the nearness of objects. Choice (B), similarity, matches like items. Choices (D), continuity, and (E), connectedness, are too closely related.

83. **C**   *Understand the Question/Key Words*: How do psychoactive drugs work? *Predict the Answer*: Kind of like neurotransmitters. Choice (A) is out because of hormones, (B) is way out, and (D) and (E) are silly.

84. **A**   *Understand the Question/Key Words*: She begins to calm down as what system takes back over? *Predict the Answer*: Her emergency response systems are turned off, and her parasympathetic system takes over. Don't confuse (B) with (A). Central and peripheral are not the right systems, so (C) and (D) are out. Get rid of (E)—the endocrine system does not control neurotransmitters.

85. **D**   This is why a great deal of space is given to the lips and the fingertips relative to much larger body parts, such as the torso.

86. **D**   *Understand the Question/Key Words*: Circle *operant conditioning*. What does it mean? *Predict the Answer*: It has to do with "day-to-day operations" as opposed to classical conditioning. Use POE to eliminate (B) and (C) because they have nothing to do with conditioning. Choice (A) is an example of classical conditioning.

87. **D** *Understand the Question/Key Words*: Why are twins significant when studying the role of genetics in behavior? *Predict the Answer*: Because identical twins come from the same egg, so they are genetically identical. In (A), don't confuse fraternal with identical twins. Choice (B) is emphasizing environmental factors. Choice (C) doesn't make sense (MZ twins are identical twins, whereas DZ twins are fraternal twins). Choice (E) is the "confuse the test-taker" answer—a statement with a lot of jargon that doesn't say anything important but does confuse you. Because you used smart strategies, you won't get trapped.

88. **E** *Understand the Question/Key Words*: Noticing a change in a stimulus depends on what? *Predict the Answer*: How intense the new stimulus is as compared with that of the existing stimulus. Choices (A) and (D) try to confuse you with technology—get rid of them. Choice (C) is silly—if you are present, so are your sensory modalities. Choice (B) is a "confuse the test-taker" answer.

89. **B** *Understand the Question/Key Words*: Why can't she see color in dim light? *Predict the Answer*: Color transduction (cones) requires more light than does the transduction of black and white images (rods). If you know that cones are color and rods are black and white, you can get rid of (A), (C), and (E). You can tell (D) is wrong because of "rapidly adjusting" to light changes.

90. **D** This is the phenomenon of trying to home in on a conversation of particular interest. It is the opposite of (C). It is not related to the effects of alcohol, as anticipated in (A), (B), and (E).

91. **E** *Understand the Question/Key Words*: Amnesia and loss of personal identity are characteristic of what? *Predict the Answer*: Dissociative disorder. You can use POE to get rid of (A), schizophrenic disorder, due to your knowledge of disorders. Choice (B) is a trap. This behavior is not antisocial, so get rid of (C). Choice (D), retrograde amnesia, is also a trap. This refers to a loss of most or all memories before an accident, not occasional amnesias with a loss of personal identity. Choice (E) fits the description the best.

92. **C** *Understand the Question/Key Words*: Which correctly identifies Pavlov's research? *Predict the Answer*: Subject: *dogs*; UCS: *food*; CS: *sight/sound of presenter of food*. CR: *salivating in response to presenter*. Read each choice very carefully. This is not hard, but it is tricky and time-consuming. If pressed for time, skip it and come back.

93. **B** *Understand the Question/Key Words*: In classical conditioning, what is it called when the learner first reacts to the conditioned stimulus when the unconditioned stimulus is not present? *Predict the Answer*: It is called acquisition. Choice (A), an unconditioned stimulus, prompts a response; it is not a reaction to a prompt. Choice (C), discrimination, occurs when a learner responds only to the conditioned stimulus and nothing else. Choice (D), generalization, occurs when the learner responds to the conditioned stimulus and to objects that are similar to the CS. Choice (E), spontaneous recovery, occurs when a conditioned response suddenly reappears in the absence of additional conditioning.

94. **D** *Understand the Question/Key Words*: Circle *same subjects over time*. Which type of study minimizes the effect of differences among age groups by studying these groups over long periods of time? *Predict the Answer*: Longitudinal research. Choices (A), (B), and (C) offer a snapshot of a particular

group at a particular time. Choice (E), correlational research, is not relevant to the question being asked.

95. **B**   *Understand the Question/Key Words*: What is the purpose of a projective personality test? *Predict the Answer*: To gain insight into unconscious motives. Choice (A), gaining insight into biochemical abnormalities, would require medical intervention. Choice (C), assessing basic personality traits, refers to objective personality tests, such as the MMPI. Choices (D) and (E) examine specific traits, but they offer no causal explanations for why these traits occur.

96. **C**   *Understand the Question/Key Words*: How does a depressed person see the world according to the negative triad theory? *Predict the Answer*: A depressed person has a negative view of himself, the world, and the future. Use the information in the question and your brain power if you don't know the study. Choice (A) is too narrow in focus, and (B) and (E) are kind of silly (three people to form a triad).

97. **B**   *Understand the Question/Key Words*: Circle *imprinting*. What does it mean? *Predict the Answer*: An animal will attach to the first moving object it sees, presumably its mother. If you don't know imprinting, you can still guess the meaning and use POE. Get rid of (A) and (C) because they don't sound like imprinting. Choice (E) is more of an example of a physiological response to positive attachment.

98. **A**   *Understand the Question/Key Words*: Circle *systematic desensitization* and *EXCEPT*. Four of the choices will be a step in systematic desensitization—one will not. *Predict the Answer*: Systematic desensitization involves 1) learning to relax, 2) creating a hierarchy of images of one's fear, 3) picturing each fearful image while remaining relaxed, and 4) confronting one's fear in real life. Find these responses, and cross them off. The remaining choice will be the answer. Choice (A) mentions hypnosis, which seems out of the pattern with the rest of the choices.

99. **B**   *Understand the Question/Key Words*: They used behavior modification that involved small rewards that can be traded in for bigger rewards. This is known as… *Predict the Answer*: Token economy. You should know that it is not (D) and (E) even if you are not sure what it is. It is also different from negative reinforcement, plus that is too easy an answer for question 99, so get rid of (A). Choice (C) might look good, but unfortunately, it's not a psychological concept. Token economy is the correct name.

100. **E**   *Understand the Question/Key Words*: Circle *Milgram* and *obedience*. What was the study and what were the conclusions? *Predict the Answer*: It'll be a big help if you know the study. Even if you didn't recognize his name, try to recall the most famous study on obedience ever done. This study is the one in which people were asked to punish a learner who was in the next room by administering electric shocks, beginning with mild shocks and ending with life-threatening shocks. The entire field was astounded that two-thirds of the participants actually administered the full-strength shocks, especially if an authority figure was in the room. So what is a conclusion of this study? If you know only a little of this information, you can still use POE to eliminate (A), crowd mentality, and (B) because the participants did not refuse.

FREE-RESPONSE SECTION: ANSWERS AND EXPLANATIONS

1.   Essay number one is worth seven points. One to two points are awarded for explaining each term and giving a relevant example of each term in Part A. Two points are awarded for explaining how his parents should treat his tantrum behavior in Part B.

This is what our "student" chose to do for her essays. Use this as a sample of a decent essay.

Sample Essay

A.   Age is key to understanding issues related to development. Jack is a three-year-old boy who is frustrating his parents with his constant tantrums and misbehavior. To understand how best to handle Jack's unwanted behavior, his parents must understand his cognitive and social stages of development if they are to effectively deal with his unwanted behaviors.

According to cognitive theorist Jean Piaget, Jack is in the preoperational stage of cognitive development. During this stage of cognitive development, which lasts roughly from ages 2 to 6 years of age, children are egocentric. Egocentrism is different from self-centeredness, which is behavioral and not cognitive. Jack's parents try to reason with him when he misbehaves, but that is very ineffective because he doesn't understand what they are trying to say. Jack will continue to have tantrums until they find a better way to reach him, because he does not understand their point of view or their expectations.

Lawrence Kohlberg also studied cognitive development as it relates to moral development. As a three-year-old, Jack is most likely in the preconventional stage of moral development. Jack's morality is based on a system of rewards and punishments. He is not able to make moral decisions at his age based on what is best for his parents, his family, or his community. However, understanding this, his parents can modify his behavior by appealing to his desire to gain rewards and avoid punishments.

Jack's social stage of development is also crucial to understanding his tantrum behavior. According to Erik Erikson, a psychosocial theorist, Jack is in the initiative versus guilt stage. During this stage, children begin to exert their independence and they become more assertive and sometimes aggressive. Jack is trying to exert his autonomy and he may do this in a very assertive way, such as by having tantrums in response to his parent's rules.

Although cognitive and social development are important factors to consider in evaluating Jack's behavior, we must also strongly consider environmental factors such as observational learning. Observational learning, or learning by imitation, may have a profound impact on Jack's behavior. For example, if Jack's parents model aggressive or assertive behaviors, Jack will learn to imitate these behaviors as he is in an impressionable stage in his development.

B.   Now that Jack's parents fully understand his developmental processes and the influence of observational learning on his behavior, they can successfully eliminate his negative behaviors. For example, when Jack has a tantrum, they would be best advised to ignore his behaviors rather than to call attention to them. Trying to reason with him in the past had been unsuccessful due to his egocentrism. They should also set clear and consistent rules for him so that he can explore his autonomy while acting appropriately. They must also be mindful of their own behaviors and not get angry when frustrated because Jack will imitate their behaviors. The most important thing that Jack's parents must consider is that they must be consistent and they must keep in mind that his behaviors are typical of his stage of development and are not necessarily inappropriate.

2.   Essay number two is worth seven points. Points are given based on a student's ability to touch on certain theories and reference specific AP Psychology phenomena. Each essay is unique, but here is our run-down of what a student should definitely address in his or her Free Response Essay for this question:

- This is an experiment because Sharlene is manipulating a variable and because there is both an experimental group and a control group.

- The independent variable is whether or not students receive the supplements.

- The operational definition of the dependent variable is the rating of "on-task behavior" given by the evaluators.

- The experiment will not be valid unless students are randomly assigned to the experimental group and the control group. This will limit the possibility of having a biased sample in either group.

- Sharlene and the evaluators should not know which students received the supplements and which did not because this could affect the ratings given. When the experimenters do not know who is in the experimental group, this is "double blind."

- There are several ethical concerns that would earn a point here. Students (and their parents) did not provide an informed consent for participation in the study. Students' participation was not voluntary. There is no indication that there will be confidentiality for the results. There is no indication that students will be debriefed on the results. There is no indication that efforts have been made to minimize potential harm to participants; for example, how will it be determined if a student has an allergy to one of the supplements?

- One confounding variable is expectation: the control group is not receiving a placebo, whereas the experimental group knows it is receiving something that is supposed to be helpful. This could cause the experimental group to perform better.

HOW TO SCORE PRACTICE TEST 2

Section I: Multiple-Choice

_____ × 1.0000 = _____
Number Correct   Weighted
(out of 100)   Section I Score
                                   (Do not round)

Section II: Free-Response

Question 1: _____ × 2.5000 = _____
                (out of 7)   (Do not round)

Question 2: _____ × 3.1250 = _____
                (out of 7)   (Do not round)

AP Score Conversion Chart Psychology

Composite Score Range	AP Score
107–150	5
90–106	4
73–89	3
56–72	2
0–55	1

Sum = _____
        Weighted
        Section II Score
        (Do not round)

Composite Score

_____ + _____ = _____
Weighted   Weighted   Composite Score
Section I Score   Section II Score   (Round to nearest
                                          whole number)

The Princeton Review®

Completely darken bubbles with a No. 2 pencil. If you make a mistake, be sure to erase mark completely. Erase all stray marks.

1. YOUR NAME: _____
(Print)   Last   First   M.I.

SIGNATURE: _____ **DATE:** ____ / ____ / ____

HOME ADDRESS: _____
(Print)
                    Number and Street

_____ **E-MAIL:** _____
City   State   Zip

PHONE NO.: _____ **SCHOOL:** _____ **CLASS OF:** _____
(Print)

IMPORTANT: Please fill in these boxes exactly as shown on the back cover of your test book.

OpScan /NSIGHT™ forms by Pearson NCS EM-255325-1:654321
Printed in U.S.A.

©TPR Education IP Holdings, LLC

5. YOUR NAME

First 4 letters of last name				FIRST INIT	MID INIT
Ⓐ	Ⓐ	Ⓐ	Ⓐ	Ⓐ	Ⓐ
Ⓑ	Ⓑ	Ⓑ	Ⓑ	Ⓑ	Ⓑ
Ⓒ	Ⓒ	Ⓒ	Ⓒ	Ⓒ	Ⓒ
Ⓓ	Ⓓ	Ⓓ	Ⓓ	Ⓓ	Ⓓ
Ⓔ	Ⓔ	Ⓔ	Ⓔ	Ⓔ	Ⓔ
Ⓕ	Ⓕ	Ⓕ	Ⓕ	Ⓕ	Ⓕ
Ⓖ	Ⓖ	Ⓖ	Ⓖ	Ⓖ	Ⓖ
Ⓗ	Ⓗ	Ⓗ	Ⓗ	Ⓗ	Ⓗ
Ⓘ	Ⓘ	Ⓘ	Ⓘ	Ⓘ	Ⓘ
Ⓙ	Ⓙ	Ⓙ	Ⓙ	Ⓙ	Ⓙ
Ⓚ	Ⓚ	Ⓚ	Ⓚ	Ⓚ	Ⓚ
Ⓛ	Ⓛ	Ⓛ	Ⓛ	Ⓛ	Ⓛ
Ⓜ	Ⓜ	Ⓜ	Ⓜ	Ⓜ	Ⓜ
Ⓝ	Ⓝ	Ⓝ	Ⓝ	Ⓝ	Ⓝ
Ⓞ	Ⓞ	Ⓞ	Ⓞ	Ⓞ	Ⓞ
Ⓟ	Ⓟ	Ⓟ	Ⓟ	Ⓟ	Ⓟ
Ⓠ	Ⓠ	Ⓠ	Ⓠ	Ⓠ	Ⓠ
Ⓡ	Ⓡ	Ⓡ	Ⓡ	Ⓡ	Ⓡ
Ⓢ	Ⓢ	Ⓢ	Ⓢ	Ⓢ	Ⓢ
Ⓣ	Ⓣ	Ⓣ	Ⓣ	Ⓣ	Ⓣ
Ⓤ	Ⓤ	Ⓤ	Ⓤ	Ⓤ	Ⓤ
Ⓥ	Ⓥ	Ⓥ	Ⓥ	Ⓥ	Ⓥ
Ⓦ	Ⓦ	Ⓦ	Ⓦ	Ⓦ	Ⓦ
Ⓧ	Ⓧ	Ⓧ	Ⓧ	Ⓧ	Ⓧ
Ⓨ	Ⓨ	Ⓨ	Ⓨ	Ⓨ	Ⓨ
Ⓩ	Ⓩ	Ⓩ	Ⓩ	Ⓩ	Ⓩ

2. TEST FORM

_____

6. DATE OF BIRTH

MONTH	DAY		YEAR	
◯ JAN				
◯ FEB				
◯ MAR	⓪	⓪	⓪	⓪
◯ APR	①	①	①	①
◯ MAY	②	②	②	②
◯ JUN	③	③	③	③
◯ JUL		④	④	④
◯ AUG		⑤	⑤	⑤
◯ SEP		⑥	⑥	⑥
◯ OCT		⑦	⑦	⑦
◯ NOV		⑧	⑧	⑧
◯ DEC		⑨	⑨	⑨

3. TEST CODE

⓪	⓪	⓪	⓪
①	①	①	①
②	②	②	②
③	③	③	③
④	④	④	④
⑤	⑤	⑤	⑤
⑥	⑥	⑥	⑥
⑦	⑦	⑦	⑦
⑧	⑧	⑧	⑧
⑨	⑨	⑨	⑨

4. PHONE NUMBER

⓪	⓪	⓪	⓪	⓪	⓪	⓪
①	①	①	①	①	①	①
②	②	②	②	②	②	②
③	③	③	③	③	③	③
④	④	④	④	④	④	④
⑤	⑤	⑤	⑤	⑤	⑤	⑤
⑥	⑥	⑥	⑥	⑥	⑥	⑥
⑦	⑦	⑦	⑦	⑦	⑦	⑦
⑧	⑧	⑧	⑧	⑧	⑧	⑧
⑨	⑨	⑨	⑨	⑨	⑨	⑨

7. SEX

◯ MALE
◯ FEMALE

8. OTHER

1 Ⓐ Ⓑ Ⓒ Ⓓ Ⓔ
2 Ⓐ Ⓑ Ⓒ Ⓓ Ⓔ
3 Ⓐ Ⓑ Ⓒ Ⓓ Ⓔ

Begin with number 1 for each new section of the test. Leave blank any extra answer spaces.

SECTION 1

1 Ⓐ Ⓑ Ⓒ Ⓓ Ⓔ   26 Ⓐ Ⓑ Ⓒ Ⓓ Ⓔ   51 Ⓐ Ⓑ Ⓒ Ⓓ Ⓔ   76 Ⓐ Ⓑ Ⓒ Ⓓ Ⓔ
2 Ⓐ Ⓑ Ⓒ Ⓓ Ⓔ   27 Ⓐ Ⓑ Ⓒ Ⓓ Ⓔ   52 Ⓐ Ⓑ Ⓒ Ⓓ Ⓔ   77 Ⓐ Ⓑ Ⓒ Ⓓ Ⓔ
3 Ⓐ Ⓑ Ⓒ Ⓓ Ⓔ   28 Ⓐ Ⓑ Ⓒ Ⓓ Ⓔ   53 Ⓐ Ⓑ Ⓒ Ⓓ Ⓔ   78 Ⓐ Ⓑ Ⓒ Ⓓ Ⓔ
4 Ⓐ Ⓑ Ⓒ Ⓓ Ⓔ   29 Ⓐ Ⓑ Ⓒ Ⓓ Ⓔ   54 Ⓐ Ⓑ Ⓒ Ⓓ Ⓔ   79 Ⓐ Ⓑ Ⓒ Ⓓ Ⓔ
5 Ⓐ Ⓑ Ⓒ Ⓓ Ⓔ   30 Ⓐ Ⓑ Ⓒ Ⓓ Ⓔ   55 Ⓐ Ⓑ Ⓒ Ⓓ Ⓔ   80 Ⓐ Ⓑ Ⓒ Ⓓ Ⓔ
6 Ⓐ Ⓑ Ⓒ Ⓓ Ⓔ   31 Ⓐ Ⓑ Ⓒ Ⓓ Ⓔ   56 Ⓐ Ⓑ Ⓒ Ⓓ Ⓔ   81 Ⓐ Ⓑ Ⓒ Ⓓ Ⓔ
7 Ⓐ Ⓑ Ⓒ Ⓓ Ⓔ   32 Ⓐ Ⓑ Ⓒ Ⓓ Ⓔ   57 Ⓐ Ⓑ Ⓒ Ⓓ Ⓔ   82 Ⓐ Ⓑ Ⓒ Ⓓ Ⓔ
8 Ⓐ Ⓑ Ⓒ Ⓓ Ⓔ   33 Ⓐ Ⓑ Ⓒ Ⓓ Ⓔ   58 Ⓐ Ⓑ Ⓒ Ⓓ Ⓔ   83 Ⓐ Ⓑ Ⓒ Ⓓ Ⓔ
9 Ⓐ Ⓑ Ⓒ Ⓓ Ⓔ   34 Ⓐ Ⓑ Ⓒ Ⓓ Ⓔ   59 Ⓐ Ⓑ Ⓒ Ⓓ Ⓔ   84 Ⓐ Ⓑ Ⓒ Ⓓ Ⓔ
10 Ⓐ Ⓑ Ⓒ Ⓓ Ⓔ   35 Ⓐ Ⓑ Ⓒ Ⓓ Ⓔ   60 Ⓐ Ⓑ Ⓒ Ⓓ Ⓔ   85 Ⓐ Ⓑ Ⓒ Ⓓ Ⓔ
11 Ⓐ Ⓑ Ⓒ Ⓓ Ⓔ   36 Ⓐ Ⓑ Ⓒ Ⓓ Ⓔ   61 Ⓐ Ⓑ Ⓒ Ⓓ Ⓔ   86 Ⓐ Ⓑ Ⓒ Ⓓ Ⓔ
12 Ⓐ Ⓑ Ⓒ Ⓓ Ⓔ   37 Ⓐ Ⓑ Ⓒ Ⓓ Ⓔ   62 Ⓐ Ⓑ Ⓒ Ⓓ Ⓔ   87 Ⓐ Ⓑ Ⓒ Ⓓ Ⓔ
13 Ⓐ Ⓑ Ⓒ Ⓓ Ⓔ   38 Ⓐ Ⓑ Ⓒ Ⓓ Ⓔ   63 Ⓐ Ⓑ Ⓒ Ⓓ Ⓔ   88 Ⓐ Ⓑ Ⓒ Ⓓ Ⓔ
14 Ⓐ Ⓑ Ⓒ Ⓓ Ⓔ   39 Ⓐ Ⓑ Ⓒ Ⓓ Ⓔ   64 Ⓐ Ⓑ Ⓒ Ⓓ Ⓔ   89 Ⓐ Ⓑ Ⓒ Ⓓ Ⓔ
15 Ⓐ Ⓑ Ⓒ Ⓓ Ⓔ   40 Ⓐ Ⓑ Ⓒ Ⓓ Ⓔ   65 Ⓐ Ⓑ Ⓒ Ⓓ Ⓔ   90 Ⓐ Ⓑ Ⓒ Ⓓ Ⓔ
16 Ⓐ Ⓑ Ⓒ Ⓓ Ⓔ   41 Ⓐ Ⓑ Ⓒ Ⓓ Ⓔ   66 Ⓐ Ⓑ Ⓒ Ⓓ Ⓔ   91 Ⓐ Ⓑ Ⓒ Ⓓ Ⓔ
17 Ⓐ Ⓑ Ⓒ Ⓓ Ⓔ   42 Ⓐ Ⓑ Ⓒ Ⓓ Ⓔ   67 Ⓐ Ⓑ Ⓒ Ⓓ Ⓔ   92 Ⓐ Ⓑ Ⓒ Ⓓ Ⓔ
18 Ⓐ Ⓑ Ⓒ Ⓓ Ⓔ   43 Ⓐ Ⓑ Ⓒ Ⓓ Ⓔ   68 Ⓐ Ⓑ Ⓒ Ⓓ Ⓔ   93 Ⓐ Ⓑ Ⓒ Ⓓ Ⓔ
19 Ⓐ Ⓑ Ⓒ Ⓓ Ⓔ   44 Ⓐ Ⓑ Ⓒ Ⓓ Ⓔ   69 Ⓐ Ⓑ Ⓒ Ⓓ Ⓔ   94 Ⓐ Ⓑ Ⓒ Ⓓ Ⓔ
20 Ⓐ Ⓑ Ⓒ Ⓓ Ⓔ   45 Ⓐ Ⓑ Ⓒ Ⓓ Ⓔ   70 Ⓐ Ⓑ Ⓒ Ⓓ Ⓔ   95 Ⓐ Ⓑ Ⓒ Ⓓ Ⓔ
21 Ⓐ Ⓑ Ⓒ Ⓓ Ⓔ   46 Ⓐ Ⓑ Ⓒ Ⓓ Ⓔ   71 Ⓐ Ⓑ Ⓒ Ⓓ Ⓔ   96 Ⓐ Ⓑ Ⓒ Ⓓ Ⓔ
22 Ⓐ Ⓑ Ⓒ Ⓓ Ⓔ   47 Ⓐ Ⓑ Ⓒ Ⓓ Ⓔ   72 Ⓐ Ⓑ Ⓒ Ⓓ Ⓔ   97 Ⓐ Ⓑ Ⓒ Ⓓ Ⓔ
23 Ⓐ Ⓑ Ⓒ Ⓓ Ⓔ   48 Ⓐ Ⓑ Ⓒ Ⓓ Ⓔ   73 Ⓐ Ⓑ Ⓒ Ⓓ Ⓔ   98 Ⓐ Ⓑ Ⓒ Ⓓ Ⓔ
24 Ⓐ Ⓑ Ⓒ Ⓓ Ⓔ   49 Ⓐ Ⓑ Ⓒ Ⓓ Ⓔ   74 Ⓐ Ⓑ Ⓒ Ⓓ Ⓔ   99 Ⓐ Ⓑ Ⓒ Ⓓ Ⓔ
25 Ⓐ Ⓑ Ⓒ Ⓓ Ⓔ   50 Ⓐ Ⓑ Ⓒ Ⓓ Ⓔ   75 Ⓐ Ⓑ Ⓒ Ⓓ Ⓔ   100 Ⓐ Ⓑ Ⓒ Ⓓ Ⓔ

YOUR NAME: (Print) _____ Last _____ First _____ M.I.

SIGNATURE: _____ **DATE:** ___ / ___ / ___

HOME ADDRESS: _____
(Print)   Number and Street

_____ _____ _____   **E-MAIL:** _____
City   State   Zip

PHONE NO.: _____   **SCHOOL:** _____   **CLASS OF:** _____
(Print)

IMPORTANT: Please fill in these boxes exactly as shown on the back cover of your test book.

OpScan *i*NSIGHT™ forms by Pearson NCS EM-255325-1:654321
Printed in U.S.A.

©TPR Education IP Holdings, LLC

5. YOUR NAME

First 4 letters of last name | FIRST INIT | MID INIT

Ⓐ Ⓐ Ⓐ Ⓐ Ⓐ Ⓐ
Ⓑ Ⓑ Ⓑ Ⓑ Ⓑ Ⓑ
Ⓒ Ⓒ Ⓒ Ⓒ Ⓒ Ⓒ
Ⓓ Ⓓ Ⓓ Ⓓ Ⓓ Ⓓ
Ⓔ Ⓔ Ⓔ Ⓔ Ⓔ Ⓔ
Ⓕ Ⓕ Ⓕ Ⓕ Ⓕ Ⓕ
Ⓖ Ⓖ Ⓖ Ⓖ Ⓖ Ⓖ
Ⓗ Ⓗ Ⓗ Ⓗ Ⓗ Ⓗ
Ⓘ Ⓘ Ⓘ Ⓘ Ⓘ Ⓘ
Ⓙ Ⓙ Ⓙ Ⓙ Ⓙ Ⓙ
Ⓚ Ⓚ Ⓚ Ⓚ Ⓚ Ⓚ
Ⓛ Ⓛ Ⓛ Ⓛ Ⓛ Ⓛ
Ⓜ Ⓜ Ⓜ Ⓜ Ⓜ Ⓜ
Ⓝ Ⓝ Ⓝ Ⓝ Ⓝ Ⓝ
Ⓞ Ⓞ Ⓞ Ⓞ Ⓞ Ⓞ
Ⓟ Ⓟ Ⓟ Ⓟ Ⓟ Ⓟ
Ⓠ Ⓠ Ⓠ Ⓠ Ⓠ Ⓠ
Ⓡ Ⓡ Ⓡ Ⓡ Ⓡ Ⓡ
Ⓢ Ⓢ Ⓢ Ⓢ Ⓢ Ⓢ
Ⓣ Ⓣ Ⓣ Ⓣ Ⓣ Ⓣ
Ⓤ Ⓤ Ⓤ Ⓤ Ⓤ Ⓤ
Ⓥ Ⓥ Ⓥ Ⓥ Ⓥ Ⓥ
Ⓦ Ⓦ Ⓦ Ⓦ Ⓦ Ⓦ
Ⓧ Ⓧ Ⓧ Ⓧ Ⓧ Ⓧ
Ⓨ Ⓨ Ⓨ Ⓨ Ⓨ Ⓨ
Ⓩ Ⓩ Ⓩ Ⓩ Ⓩ Ⓩ

2. TEST FORM

_____

6. DATE OF BIRTH

MONTH	DAY		YEAR	
○ JAN				
○ FEB				
○ MAR	⓪	⓪	⓪	⓪
○ APR	①	①	①	①
○ MAY	②	②	②	②
○ JUN	③	③	③	③
○ JUL		④	④	④
○ AUG		⑤	⑤	⑤
○ SEP		⑥	⑥	⑥
○ OCT		⑦	⑦	⑦
○ NOV		⑧	⑧	⑧
○ DEC		⑨	⑨	⑨

3. TEST CODE   **4. PHONE NUMBER**

⓪ ⓪ ⓪ ⓪ ⓪   ⓪ ⓪ ⓪ ⓪ ⓪ ⓪ ⓪
① ① ① ① ①   ① ① ① ① ① ① ①
② ② ② ② ②   ② ② ② ② ② ② ②
③ ③ ③ ③ ③   ③ ③ ③ ③ ③ ③ ③
④ ④ ④ ④ ④   ④ ④ ④ ④ ④ ④ ④
⑤ ⑤ ⑤ ⑤ ⑤   ⑤ ⑤ ⑤ ⑤ ⑤ ⑤ ⑤
⑥ ⑥ ⑥ ⑥ ⑥   ⑥ ⑥ ⑥ ⑥ ⑥ ⑥ ⑥
⑦ ⑦ ⑦ ⑦ ⑦   ⑦ ⑦ ⑦ ⑦ ⑦ ⑦ ⑦
⑧ ⑧ ⑧ ⑧ ⑧   ⑧ ⑧ ⑧ ⑧ ⑧ ⑧ ⑧
⑨ ⑨ ⑨ ⑨ ⑨   ⑨ ⑨ ⑨ ⑨ ⑨ ⑨ ⑨

7. SEX
○ MALE
○ FEMALE

8. OTHER
1 Ⓐ Ⓑ Ⓒ Ⓓ Ⓔ
2 Ⓐ Ⓑ Ⓒ Ⓓ Ⓔ
3 Ⓐ Ⓑ Ⓒ Ⓓ Ⓔ

Begin with number 1 for each new section of the test. Leave blank any extra answer spaces.

SECTION 1

1 Ⓐ Ⓑ Ⓒ Ⓓ Ⓔ   26 Ⓐ Ⓑ Ⓒ Ⓓ Ⓔ   51 Ⓐ Ⓑ Ⓒ Ⓓ Ⓔ   76 Ⓐ Ⓑ Ⓒ Ⓓ Ⓔ
2 Ⓐ Ⓑ Ⓒ Ⓓ Ⓔ   27 Ⓐ Ⓑ Ⓒ Ⓓ Ⓔ   52 Ⓐ Ⓑ Ⓒ Ⓓ Ⓔ   77 Ⓐ Ⓑ Ⓒ Ⓓ Ⓔ
3 Ⓐ Ⓑ Ⓒ Ⓓ Ⓔ   28 Ⓐ Ⓑ Ⓒ Ⓓ Ⓔ   53 Ⓐ Ⓑ Ⓒ Ⓓ Ⓔ   78 Ⓐ Ⓑ Ⓒ Ⓓ Ⓔ
4 Ⓐ Ⓑ Ⓒ Ⓓ Ⓔ   29 Ⓐ Ⓑ Ⓒ Ⓓ Ⓔ   54 Ⓐ Ⓑ Ⓒ Ⓓ Ⓔ   79 Ⓐ Ⓑ Ⓒ Ⓓ Ⓔ
5 Ⓐ Ⓑ Ⓒ Ⓓ Ⓔ   30 Ⓐ Ⓑ Ⓒ Ⓓ Ⓔ   55 Ⓐ Ⓑ Ⓒ Ⓓ Ⓔ   80 Ⓐ Ⓑ Ⓒ Ⓓ Ⓔ
6 Ⓐ Ⓑ Ⓒ Ⓓ Ⓔ   31 Ⓐ Ⓑ Ⓒ Ⓓ Ⓔ   56 Ⓐ Ⓑ Ⓒ Ⓓ Ⓔ   81 Ⓐ Ⓑ Ⓒ Ⓓ Ⓔ
7 Ⓐ Ⓑ Ⓒ Ⓓ Ⓔ   32 Ⓐ Ⓑ Ⓒ Ⓓ Ⓔ   57 Ⓐ Ⓑ Ⓒ Ⓓ Ⓔ   82 Ⓐ Ⓑ Ⓒ Ⓓ Ⓔ
8 Ⓐ Ⓑ Ⓒ Ⓓ Ⓔ   33 Ⓐ Ⓑ Ⓒ Ⓓ Ⓔ   58 Ⓐ Ⓑ Ⓒ Ⓓ Ⓔ   83 Ⓐ Ⓑ Ⓒ Ⓓ Ⓔ
9 Ⓐ Ⓑ Ⓒ Ⓓ Ⓔ   34 Ⓐ Ⓑ Ⓒ Ⓓ Ⓔ   59 Ⓐ Ⓑ Ⓒ Ⓓ Ⓔ   84 Ⓐ Ⓑ Ⓒ Ⓓ Ⓔ
10 Ⓐ Ⓑ Ⓒ Ⓓ Ⓔ   35 Ⓐ Ⓑ Ⓒ Ⓓ Ⓔ   60 Ⓐ Ⓑ Ⓒ Ⓓ Ⓔ   85 Ⓐ Ⓑ Ⓒ Ⓓ Ⓔ
11 Ⓐ Ⓑ Ⓒ Ⓓ Ⓔ   36 Ⓐ Ⓑ Ⓒ Ⓓ Ⓔ   61 Ⓐ Ⓑ Ⓒ Ⓓ Ⓔ   86 Ⓐ Ⓑ Ⓒ Ⓓ Ⓔ
12 Ⓐ Ⓑ Ⓒ Ⓓ Ⓔ   37 Ⓐ Ⓑ Ⓒ Ⓓ Ⓔ   62 Ⓐ Ⓑ Ⓒ Ⓓ Ⓔ   87 Ⓐ Ⓑ Ⓒ Ⓓ Ⓔ
13 Ⓐ Ⓑ Ⓒ Ⓓ Ⓔ   38 Ⓐ Ⓑ Ⓒ Ⓓ Ⓔ   63 Ⓐ Ⓑ Ⓒ Ⓓ Ⓔ   88 Ⓐ Ⓑ Ⓒ Ⓓ Ⓔ
14 Ⓐ Ⓑ Ⓒ Ⓓ Ⓔ   39 Ⓐ Ⓑ Ⓒ Ⓓ Ⓔ   64 Ⓐ Ⓑ Ⓒ Ⓓ Ⓔ   89 Ⓐ Ⓑ Ⓒ Ⓓ Ⓔ
15 Ⓐ Ⓑ Ⓒ Ⓓ Ⓔ   40 Ⓐ Ⓑ Ⓒ Ⓓ Ⓔ   65 Ⓐ Ⓑ Ⓒ Ⓓ Ⓔ   90 Ⓐ Ⓑ Ⓒ Ⓓ Ⓔ
16 Ⓐ Ⓑ Ⓒ Ⓓ Ⓔ   41 Ⓐ Ⓑ Ⓒ Ⓓ Ⓔ   66 Ⓐ Ⓑ Ⓒ Ⓓ Ⓔ   91 Ⓐ Ⓑ Ⓒ Ⓓ Ⓔ
17 Ⓐ Ⓑ Ⓒ Ⓓ Ⓔ   42 Ⓐ Ⓑ Ⓒ Ⓓ Ⓔ   67 Ⓐ Ⓑ Ⓒ Ⓓ Ⓔ   92 Ⓐ Ⓑ Ⓒ Ⓓ Ⓔ
18 Ⓐ Ⓑ Ⓒ Ⓓ Ⓔ   43 Ⓐ Ⓑ Ⓒ Ⓓ Ⓔ   68 Ⓐ Ⓑ Ⓒ Ⓓ Ⓔ   93 Ⓐ Ⓑ Ⓒ Ⓓ Ⓔ
19 Ⓐ Ⓑ Ⓒ Ⓓ Ⓔ   44 Ⓐ Ⓑ Ⓒ Ⓓ Ⓔ   69 Ⓐ Ⓑ Ⓒ Ⓓ Ⓔ   94 Ⓐ Ⓑ Ⓒ Ⓓ Ⓔ
20 Ⓐ Ⓑ Ⓒ Ⓓ Ⓔ   45 Ⓐ Ⓑ Ⓒ Ⓓ Ⓔ   70 Ⓐ Ⓑ Ⓒ Ⓓ Ⓔ   95 Ⓐ Ⓑ Ⓒ Ⓓ Ⓔ
21 Ⓐ Ⓑ Ⓒ Ⓓ Ⓔ   46 Ⓐ Ⓑ Ⓒ Ⓓ Ⓔ   71 Ⓐ Ⓑ Ⓒ Ⓓ Ⓔ   96 Ⓐ Ⓑ Ⓒ Ⓓ Ⓔ
22 Ⓐ Ⓑ Ⓒ Ⓓ Ⓔ   47 Ⓐ Ⓑ Ⓒ Ⓓ Ⓔ   72 Ⓐ Ⓑ Ⓒ Ⓓ Ⓔ   97 Ⓐ Ⓑ Ⓒ Ⓓ Ⓔ
23 Ⓐ Ⓑ Ⓒ Ⓓ Ⓔ   48 Ⓐ Ⓑ Ⓒ Ⓓ Ⓔ   73 Ⓐ Ⓑ Ⓒ Ⓓ Ⓔ   98 Ⓐ Ⓑ Ⓒ Ⓓ Ⓔ
24 Ⓐ Ⓑ Ⓒ Ⓓ Ⓔ   49 Ⓐ Ⓑ Ⓒ Ⓓ Ⓔ   74 Ⓐ Ⓑ Ⓒ Ⓓ Ⓔ   99 Ⓐ Ⓑ Ⓒ Ⓓ Ⓔ
25 Ⓐ Ⓑ Ⓒ Ⓓ Ⓔ   50 Ⓐ Ⓑ Ⓒ Ⓓ Ⓔ   75 Ⓐ Ⓑ Ⓒ Ⓓ Ⓔ   100 Ⓐ Ⓑ Ⓒ Ⓓ Ⓔ

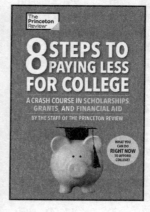